PENGUIN REFERENCE BOOKS

# A DICTIONARY OF BIOLOGY

M. ABERCROMBIE took a degree in zoology at Oxford, and then began research work at Cambridge. Later he taught in the Zoology Department, Birmingham University. He was Professor of Embryology and then Professor of Zoology at University College, London, and is now Director of the Strangeways Research Laboratory, Cambridge. He is a Fellow of the Royal Society.

C. J. HICKMAN is Professor of Plant Sciences at the University of Western Ontario, London, Canada. His chief interests are in the study of fungi and plant diseases. He took a degree in Botany at the University of Birmingham and, after working on plant diseases in the Advisory Service of the Ministry of Agriculture and Fisheries, and as a Research Officer at the Agricultural Research Council, he returned to the University of Birmingham as Lecturer and later Reader. He moved to Western Ontario in 1960.

M. L. JOHNSON (Mrs Abercrombie) taught zoology at Birmingham University for some years, and researched on respiration of invertebrates and on nerve degeneration. Results of other investigations have been summarized in *The Anatomy of Judgment* and *Perceptual and Visuo-Motor Disorders in Cerebral Palsy*. She was formerly Reader in Architectural Education at the Bartlett School of Architecture, University College, London.

# A DICTIONARY OF
# Biology

—

M. ABERCROMBIE, C. J. HICKMAN,

AND M. L. JOHNSON

—

**SIXTH EDITION**

PENGUIN BOOKS

Penguin Books Ltd, Harmondsworth, Middlesex, England
Penguin Books Inc., 7110 Ambassador Road, Baltimore, Maryland 21207, U.S.A.
Penguin Books Australia Ltd, Ringwood, Victoria, Australia
Penguin Books Canada Ltd, 41 Steelcase Road West, Markham, Ontario, Canada
Penguin Books (N.Z.) Ltd, 182–190 Wairau Road, Auckland 10, New Zealand

—

First published 1951
Reprinted 1951
Second edition 1954
Reprinted 1955
Third edition 1957
Reprinted 1958, 1959, 1960
Fourth edition 1961
Reprinted 1961, 1962, 1963, 1964, 1965
Fifth edition 1966
Reprinted 1968, 1969, 1970, 1971, 1972
Sixth edition 1973
Reprinted 1973, 1974, 1975, 1976

—

Copyright © M. Abercrombie, C. J. Hickman,
and M. L. Johnson, 1951, 1954, 1957, 1961, 1966, 1973

—

Made and printed in Great Britain
by Hunt Barnard Printing Ltd, Aylesbury
Set in Monotype Baskerville

# AUTHORS' NOTE

APART from the million or more named organisms, with which this dictionary is not concerned, there are tens of thousands of other biological terms, from which we have attempted to select some three thousand of the commoner ones. The choice of terms is difficult, and so too is the choice of information to be presented under each heading. We should be glad to have comments about these points, and about inaccuracies of fact, from users of the dictionary.

Our grateful thanks go to our friends and colleagues whose criticisms and suggestions have greatly assisted us in the preparation and revision of the dictionary.

M. A.<br>
C. J. H.<br>
M. L. J.

# USING THE DICTIONARY

MANY unfamiliar terms, especially the rarer ones, are defined with the help of other technical terms, perhaps equally unfamiliar. This is unfortunately necessary to keep the dictionary within bounds, and may often require that several terms have to be followed up before reaching an entirely intelligible definition. Every biological term used in a definition is, we hope, itself defined elsewhere in the dictionary; except that some semi-technical terms, which can be found in any English dictionary, are omitted. Terms that are not strictly biological will usually be found in the *Dictionary of Science* (Penguin Reference Book).

The letters (q.v.) after a word that occurs in a definition indicate that the entry under this word adds important information to the subject under discussion. The letters Cf. are intended to point out a contrasting term.

(Bot.) or (Zool.) before a definition means that what follows applies only to plants or to animals respectively. It is not used where the limitation is obvious.

(Adj.) means that the term defined is an adjective, when this is not clear from the definition.

# A

ABAXIAL (Dorsal). (Of a leaf surface), facing away from the stem. Cf. *Adaxial*.

ABDOMEN. In vertebrates: region of the body containing the viscera other than heart and lungs (i.e. intestine, liver, kidneys, etc.); in mammals, but not in other vertebrates, bounded anteriorly by diaphragm. In arthropods: posterior group of segments similar to each other.

ABDUCENS NERVE. Sixth cranial nerve of vertebrates. Almost entirely motor, supplying external rectus eye-muscle. See *Eye-muscles*. A ventral root.

ABIOGENESIS. Spontaneous generation (q.v.).

ABSCISIC ACID (ABSCISIN, DORMIN). Growth-inhibiting plant hormone (a sesquiterpene). Present in a variety of plant organs – leaves, buds, fruits, seeds and tubers. Promotes senescence and abscission of leaves, induces dormancy in buds and seeds. Antagonizes influences of growth promoting hormones. Believed to act by inhibiting nucleic acid and protein synthesis.

ABSCISSION LAYER. Layer at base of leaf-stalk in woody dicotyledons and gymnosperms, in which the parenchyma cells become separated from one another through dissolution of the middle lamella before leaf-fall.

ABYSSAL. Inhabiting deep water (roughly below 1,000 metres).

ACANTHODII. Group of fossil fish, the earliest known Gnathostomes, mainly Devonian, 350 to 400 million years ago, but lasted from Silurian to Permian. Bony skeleton. Spines at front margin of fins, and a row of spines between pectoral and pelvic fins. Heterocercal tail.

ACARINA (ACARIDA). Order of Arachnida including mites and ticks; some are important parasites, e.g. *Sarcoptes* causing scabies, cattle tick carrying redwater fever.

ACCESSORY NERVE. Eleventh cranial nerve of tetrapod vertebrates. Really a branch of the vagus, clearly separate only in mammals.

ACCLIMATION, ACCLIMATIZATION. Slow change in the physiology of an organism, as a result of its exposure to a changed environment (e.g. a lowered temperature), which improves its ability to adjust to the new conditions.

ACCOMMODATION. Changing the focus of the eye. In man and a few other mammals occurs by changing curvature of lens; at rest, lens is focused for distant objects; it is focused for near objects by becoming more convex with the contraction of the ciliary muscles in ciliary body (q.v.) (see Fig. 3, p. 107). Few mammals can accommodate. Most birds and reptiles accommodate by changing curvature of the lens; in fish and amphibians, lens is moved backwards and forwards in relation to retina (as in focusing a camera).

ACELLULAR. (Of an organism), not divided into separate cells. Many organisms consisting of one cell are quite complex in structure and in function and, in contrast to the term unicellular, 'acellular' emphasizes the biological equivalence of such organisms to the whole of a multicellular organism rather than to one of its cells.

ACETABULUM. Cup-like hollow on each side of hip girdle into which head of femur (thigh bone) fits, forming hip joint, in tetrapod vertebrates.

ACETYLCHOLINE (ACh). Substance secreted at the ends of many nerve fibres (cholinergic fibres) when nerve impulses arrive there. Where such a nerve fibre ends at a synapse, e.g. in sympathetic and parasympathetic ganglia, ACh is the agent which stimulates the contiguous nerve cell and hence in effect 'passes the impulse on'; and similarly where the fibre connects with an effector, e.g. at the nerve-muscle junction. After secretion ACh is very rapidly destroyed by the enzyme cholinesterase, being broken down into acetate and choline. It is the acetyl ester of choline (q.v.).

ACHENE. Dry, one-seeded fruit formed from a single carpel, with no special method of opening to liberate the seed; may be smooth-walled, e.g. buttercup; feathery, e.g. traveller's joy; spiny, e.g. corn buttercup; or winged (*samara*), e.g. sycamore.

ACHLAMYDEOUS. (Of flowers), lacking petals and sepals, e.g. willow.

ACID DYES. Dyes consisting of an acidic organic grouping of atoms (anion) which is the actively staining part, combined with a metal. Stain particularly cytoplasm and collagen. Cf. *Basic dyes*.

ACOELOMATE. Having no coelom (e.g. the phyla Coelenterata, Platyhelminthes, Nemertea, Nematoda).

ACOUSTIC. Concerned with hearing. *A. nerve*, Auditory nerve (q.v.).

ACQUIRED CHARACTERISTICS, INHERITANCE OF. Transmission to offspring of variations, which appeared in the parents as responses to environmental influences. E.g. exposure to sunlight causes darkening of the skin of white human beings, compared to others less exposed: an acquired characteristic. If this acquired characteristic were inherited, offspring of the darker parents would then tend, even if only very slightly, to be darker than offspring of the lighter parents, when both groups of offspring are reared in equal sunlight. The view that such inheritance occurs is commonly known as Lamarckism (q.v.) or Neo-Lamarckism. It is not widely thought that such inheritance is of importance in organisms reproducing sexually. When an acquired variation occurs, the gametes are not usually affected in such a way as to reproduce these variations in the offspring. It has however been shown that natural selection (q.v.) may change successive generations of a population so that a characteristic at first acquired only in response to the environment may come to develop independently of the environmental stimulus (*genetic assimilation*). Organisms reproducing asexually may, of course, hand on to their offspring part of the body complete with its acquired characteristics.

ACRANIA (CEPHALOCHORDATA). Sub-phylum of Chordata containing only species of amphioxus, all marine. Unlike Vertebrata they have no brain, skull, or cartilaginous or bony skeleton; but they have typical chordate dorsal tubular nerve-cord with double nerve roots, notochord, gill-slits, muscle blocks (myotomes); and they have an unexpected feature, found in no other chordate though in many invertebrates – nephridia as excretory organs. They may be closely related to early ancestors of fish and other vertebrate groups. A very early fossil probably belonging to the group has been discovered (*Jaymoytius* from the Silurian).

ACRASIALES. Cellular or communal slime moulds. Group (Order) characterized by aggregation, but not coalescence, of amoebae to form a *pseudoplasmodium*. Form spores in minute inconspicuous fructifications (*sporocarps*). Affinity uncertain. See *Myxomycophyta*.

ACROPETAL. (Bot.). Development of organs in succession towards apex, the oldest at base, youngest at tip, e.g. leaves on a shoot. Also used in reference to direction of transport of substances within a plant, i.e. towards the apex. Cf. *Basipetal*.

ACROSOME. Part of head of animal sperm, usually forming a cap over the nucleus. It contains enzymes concerned in fusion with the egg during fertilization.

ACTH (CORTICOTROPIN). Adreno-cortico-tropic hormone, a polypeptide secreted by anterior lobe of pituitary, controlling secretory activity of adrenal cortex, particularly the secretion of glucocorticoids. Its own rate of secretion is controlled by a polypeptide hormone liberated from the hypothalamus.

ACTIN. Protein that, in conjunction with myosin (q.v.), provides the structural framework of the contractile mechanism in muscles, and probably in other cells. The actin molecule normally occurs in filament form (F-actin) made up of a string of globular units (G-actin).

ACTINOMORPHIC. (Of flowers), regular; capable of bisection vertically in two or more planes into similar halves, e.g. buttercup. Also known as *radially symmetrical*, a term used to describe animals having a similar organization, e.g. jelly-fish. Cf. *Zygomorphic*.

ACTINOMYCETE. Member of order of gram-positive bacteria (Actinomycotales) with cells arranged in hypha-like filaments. Mostly saprophytes, some parasites. Source of streptomycin.

ACTINOMYCIN. Antibiotic that combines with DNA, thus preventing transcription.

ACTINOPTERYGII. A class of fish (or often regarded as a sub-class of the class Osteichthyes); includes all common fish except sharks and skates. Characterized by bony skeleton; absence of a central skeletal axis in paired fins, their skeletal support being like the ribs of a fan; no opening of nostrils into mouth; air-bladder.

Ganoid scales (q.v.) in primitive species. Cf. *Chondrichthyes, Cross-opterygii* and *Dipnoi*, the other three classes of living fish. Appear first in Devonian (350 to 400 million years ago); originally fresh-water, but later colonized the sea.

ACTINOZOA (ANTHOZOA). Sea-anemones, corals, sea-pens, etc. Class of Coelenterata (of subphylum Cnidaria). No medusa stage; polyp more complexly organized than that of other Coelenterata; possessing an intucking of ectoderm into coelenteron (stomo-daeum); and vertical partitions in coelenteron (mesenteries). See *Alcyonaria.* Cf. *Hydrozoa, Scyphozoa.*

ACTION POTENTIAL. Of a nerve impulse; a localized change of electrical potential between the inside and outside of a nerve fibre, which marks the position of an impulse as it travels along the fibre. In the absence of an impulse the inside is electrically negative to the outside (the resting potential); and during the passage of an impulse past any point on the fibre it changes momentarily to positive. This wave of potential change is the most easily detectable and measurable aspect of an impulse. A similar action potential occurs in a muscle fibre when it is stimulated.

ACTION SPECTRUM. Wavelengths ($\lambda$) that are active in promoting or inhibiting a particular reaction, e.g. action spectra for photo-synthesis show maximum absorption and activity in blue and red parts of visible spectrum.

ACTIVATED SLUDGE. Material consisting largely of bacteria and protozoa, used in, and produced by, one method of sewage dis-posal. Sewage is mixed with some activated sludge and agitated with air; organisms of the sludge multiply and purify the sewage, and when it is allowed to settle they separate out as a greatly increased amount of activated sludge. Part of this is added to new sewage and part disposed of.

ACTIVE CENTRE (SITE). The part of an enzyme molecule that combines with the substrate. A relatively small number of the atoms of the enzyme molecule are involved.

ACTIVE TRANSPORT. Transfer of substance from region where its concentration is low to where it is high, especially through a membrane; accomplished by means of expenditure of energy from metabolism. Probably all cells can do this.

ACTOMYOSIN. Complex of two proteins, actin (q.v.) and myosin (q.v.), forming a major constituent of muscle.

ACUSTICO-LATERALIS SYSTEM. Lateral line system (q.v.).

ADAPTATION. (1) Evolutionary. Any characteristic of living organ-isms which, in the environment they inhabit, improves their chan-ces of survival and ultimately of leaving descendants, in comparison with the chances of similar organisms without the characteristic; natural selection therefore tends to establish adaptations in a popu-lation. An adaptation to a particular feature of the environment means a characteristic which is an adaptation because it reduces destruction by that particular feature. An adaptation to a particular *activity* of an organism (e.g. to flying) means simply a characteristic which makes possible or improves performance of that activity without necessarily being measured in terms of survival, though usually that is implied. (2) Physiological. Change in an organism as a result of exposure to certain environmental conditions which makes it react more effectively to these conditions. (3) Sensory. Change in excitability of a sense-organ as a result of continuous stimulation such that a more intense stimulus becomes necessary to produce the same response. E.g. contact of an object with the skin at once excites the touch receptors; but if contact is simply maintained the touch receptors quickly cease to respond, though they will respond again to a more intense stimulus. Different receptors differ much in the extent of their adaptation.

ADAPTIVE (INDUCIBLE) ENZYME. Enzyme formed by an organism in appreciable amounts only in response to the presence of its substrate or a similar substance. Bacteria especially are known to adjust their enzyme make-up in this way. Cf. *Constitutive Enzyme*.

ADAPTIVE RADIATION. Evolution, from a primitive type of organism of several divergent forms adapted to distinct modes of life. E.g. at beginning of Tertiary the basal stock of placental mammals radiated into many forms adapted to running, flying, swimming, burrowing, etc.

ADAXIAL. (Of a leaf surface), facing the stem. Cf. *Abaxial*.

ADENOHYPOPHYSIS. See *Pituitary Body*

ADENOSINE TRIPHOSPHATE. ATP (q.v.).

ADH. Anti-diuretic hormone (q.v.).

ADIPOSE TISSUE. Fatty tissue. Connective tissue, the cells of which contain large globules of fat.

ADP (ADENOSINE DIPHOSPHATE). Co-enzyme, associated in energy transfer in living organisms with ATP (q.v.).

ADRENAL (SUPRARENAL) GLAND. An organ of hormone secretion in vertebrates. There is a single pair, one near each kidney, in man and other mammals; but there are multiple adrenals in many other vertebrates. In all tetrapods each gland has two components, distinct in function but closely fused together. (*a*) Medulla, the inner part of the gland in mammals, embryologically derived from nervous tissue (neural crest), secreting adrenaline and noradrenaline. Its activity is controlled by the sympathetic nervous system. Medullary tissue seems to have largely an emergency function, secreting its hormones when the animal is driven to fight or flee; it is not essential for a quiet life. (*b*) Cortex, the outer part of the gland in mammals, embryologically derived from the lining of the coelom. It secretes various steroid hormones, which fall into three classes, though there is some overlapping of function: sex hormones, especially androgens, in both sexes of mammals; glucocorticoids, including cortisone and hydrocortisone, which promote carbohydrate formation from fat and protein, and have other effects; and mineralocorticoids, especially aldosterone, which control the salt and water balance of the body. Cortical hormone (especially glucocorticoid) secretion is controlled by a pituitary hormone (see *ACTH*). The adrenal cortex is indispensable for life. Medullary (=chromaffin) tissue and cortical (=interrenal) tissue are variously arranged within the adrenal of non-mammalian vertebrates; in many fish they are separated into distinct organs.

ADRENALINE (ADRENIN, EPINEPHRINE). Hormone secreted, together with closely related noradrenaline, by the medulla of the adrenal gland (q.v.). Both substances are also secreted at many nerve endings of sympathetic nervous system, and this accounts for similarity of the action of adrenal medullary hormone to the effects of massive stimulation of sympathetic system (increased work of heart, blood pressure and blood-sugar; dilation of blood-vessels of muscles, heart and brain, and contraction of those of skin and viscera; widening of pupil; erection of hair, etc.). The relative amounts of adrenaline and noradrenaline secreted vary between different species of vertebrate. The two hormones have similar but not identical action. Both occur in some invertebrates. Adrenaline is amino-hydroxyphenyl-propionic acid.

ADRENERGIC. Of a motor nerve fibre, secreting at its end adrenaline and noradrenaline when nerve-impulse arrives there. These substances stimulate the effector innervated by the nerve fibre. Many vertebrate sympathetic motor nerve fibres are adrenergic. Cf. *Cholinergic*.

ADVENTITIOUS. Arising in abnormal position; of roots, developing from part of plant other than roots, e.g. from stem or leaf cutting; of buds, developing from part of plant other than in axil of leaf, e.g. from root.

AERENCHYMA. Tissue of thin-walled cells with large, air-filled intercellular spaces, found in roots and stems of some aquatic and marsh plants.

AEROBIC RESPIRATION. Respiration (q.v.) in presence of free (i.e. gaseous or dissolved) oxygen. Cf. *Anaerobic respiration*.

AESTIVATION. (1) (Bot.). The arrangement of the parts in a flower-bud. (2) (Zool.). Dormancy during summer or dry season; it occurs e.g., in lung-fish (Dipnoi). See *Hibernation*.

AFFERENT. Leading towards, e.g. of arteries leading to vertebrate gills; or of nerve-fibres conducting impulses towards central nervous system (sensory fibres). Cf. *Efferent*.

AFTER-RIPENING. Refers to dormancy (see *Dormant*) exhibited by certain seeds, e.g. hawthorn, apple, which, although embryo is apparently fully developed, will not germinate immediately seed is formed. Embryo will not grow even when removed from seed coat and provided with favourable conditions but has to undergo certain chemical and physical changes before it is capable of growth.

Possibly associated with delay in production of required growth promoting hormones or with gradual breakdown of growth inhibitors.

AGAMOSPERMY. All types of apomixis (q.v.) in which embryos and seeds are formed by asexual means; excludes vegetative reproduction.

AGAR. Mucilage (mixture of polysaccharides, some sulphated) obtained from certain seaweeds; forms a gel with water, melting at a higher temperature than it solidifies at; is used to solidify culture media on which micro-organisms are grown.

AGGLUTINATION. Sticking together, e.g. of bacteria (one of the effects of antibodies); or of red blood corpuscles (as when blood of incompatible blood groups is mixed).

AGNATHA. Class of vertebrates (sometimes made a sub-phylum, the other vertebrate classes then being grouped as the sub-phylum Gnathostomata). Represented now by very few species (order Cyclostomata, i.e. the lampreys and hagfishes). Aquatic, fish-like in many respects, but without jaws, and the two pairs of fins or legs characterizing nearly all other vertebrates are absent (though there may be one pair). The earliest fossil vertebrates known belong to this group; these are the Heterostraci, which lived in the Silurian (possibly Ordovician) 400 to 450 million years ago.

AGONISTIC BEHAVIOUR. Aggressive behaviour towards another member of the same species, involving threat or fighting.

AIR-BLADDER. Swim-bladder (q.v.) or lung (q.v.) of fish.

AIR-SACS. Of birds: thin-walled, air-filled extensions of the lungs, lying in abdomen and thorax, and extending even into some of the bones. Of some insects: thin-walled diverticula of tracheae. In both, important in respiration.

ALBINISM. Failure of development of skin pigments. In mammals, including man, commonly due to an autosomal recessive gene.

ALBUMEN. Egg-white of birds and some reptiles. A solution of glycoprotein in water, between the ovum (the yolk) and the shell membranes. Secreted by the oviduct. It is eventually absorbed by the embryo.

ALCYONARIA. Soft corals, sea pens, etc.; an order of Coelenterates, class Actinozoa. Have eight tentacles and eight mesenteries; unlike the ordinary corals and the anemones which commonly have many.

ALDOSTERONE. See *Adrenal gland.*

ALEURONE GRAINS. Granules of protein occurring in storage regions of plants; common in seeds.

ALEUROPLAST (ALEURONE-PLAST). Colourless plastid (leucoplast) storing protein; found in many seeds, e.g. brazil nuts.

ALGAE. Simple, photosynthetic plants with unicellular organs of reproduction. Plant body (thallus, q.v.) unicellular; or multicellular, filamentous or flattened, ribbon-like, with relatively complex internal organization in higher forms but non-vascular.

Aquatic plants, marine or freshwater, or plants of damp situations, e.g. damp walls, tree trunks, in soil.

Algae has been abandoned as a formal taxon in recent classifications, component groups being now considered as sufficiently distinctive to merit recognition as divisions. These are based on structure, pigments, chemical nature of cell wall, flagella, assimilatory products; and comprise Bacillariophyta, Charophyta, Chlorophyta, Chrysophyta, Cryptophyta, Cyanophyta, Euglenophyta, Phaeophyta, Pyrrophyta, Rhodophyta, Xanthophyta.

ALIMENTARY (ENTERIC) CANAL. The gut; a tube concerned with digestion and absorption of food. In some animals it has one opening only (Coelenterates, flatworms), but in most it has an opening (mouth) into which food is taken and another (anus) from which unassimilated material is ejected.

ALKALOIDS. Group of nitrogen-containing, basic organic compounds present in plants of a few families of Dicotyledons, e.g. Solanaceae, Papaveraceae; possibly end-products of nitrogen metabolism. Of great importance because of their poisonous and medicinal properties, e.g. atropine, cocaine, morphine, nicotine, quinine, strychnine.

ALLANTOIS. Sac-like outgrowth of ventral side of hinder part of gut present in embryos of amniote vertebrates; represents a large and precocious development of urinary bladder. Allantois grows during development so that it extends right outside the embryo proper, to lie in wall of yolk-sac of birds and reptiles, or under chorion of mammals. It is always covered with connective tissue containing a rich network of blood-vessels, communicating with embryonic circulation. In reptiles and birds, respiration takes place via these blood-vessels, which lie immediately under outer layer of yolk-sac which itself is pressed close against inside of shell; excretory products are stored in allantoic cavity (see *Uricotelic*); and the greater part of allantois is left behind in the shell at hatching. In placental mammals the allantoic blood-vessels supply blood to placenta (q.v.) serving not only for respiration but for nutrition and excretion; cavity may be large and accumulate urine, but is often very small; most of allantois and its blood-vessels are detached from embryo at birth. See Fig. 8, p. 225.

ALLELES (ALLELOMORPHS). Two or more genes (q.v.) are said to be alleles (of each other), allelic or allelomorphic (to each other) when they (1) occupy the same relative position (locus) on homologous chromosomes, and, when in the same cell, undergo pairing during meiosis (q.v.); (2) produce different effects on the same set of developmental processes; and (3) can mutate one to another. Several genes allelomorphic to each other are called an allelomorphic series; not more than two members of a series can simultaneously be present in a normal diploid cell.

ALLOGAMY. (Bot.). Cross fertilization.

ALLOGENEIC (ALLOGENIC). With a different set of genes. Cf. *Isogeneic, Syngeneic.*

ALLOGRAFT. Graft from a donor with a genetic constitution different from that of the host.

ALLOPATRIC. (Of geographical relationship of different species or sub-species), not occurring together, i.e. having different areas of distribution. Cf. *Sympatric.*

ALLOPOLYPLOID. A polyploid (q.v.) organism to which two different species have each contributed one or more sets of chromosomes. Cultivated wheats are probably allopolyploids. See *Allotetraploid.* Cf. *Autopolyploid.*

ALL-OR-NONE LAW. Statement about certain irritable tissues, that they have in standardized conditions only two possible reactions to stimuli of whatever intensity; either no response, or response of one invariable strength. Applies to nerve-cells; and, with qualification that rapidly *repeated* stimuli cause stronger contraction, to muscle-fibres.

ALLOSTERIC. Of a protein molecule, carrying (at least) two separate chemical groups combining specifically with other molecules, combination at one group influencing combination at the other. E.g. an enzyme (q.v.) may have one group ('active site') which reacts with substrate in the usual way; and another group which reacts with a specific inhibitor substance which stops the enzyme activity. See *End-product inhibition.*

ALLOTETRAPLOID (AMPHIDIPLOID). Allopolyploid (q.v.) which arises when an ordinary hybrid between two different species, containing a set of chromosomes from each parent, doubles its chromosome number. An ordinary hybrid is usually sterile because its chromosomes cannot pair during meiosis. But if it becomes an allotetraploid it solves this difficulty because each chromosome then has a homologue with which it can pair. An entirely new species is thus immediately created. Tobacco probably originated in this way. Since interspecific hybridization and successful polyploidy (q.v.) is rarer in animals than in plants, allotetraploidy is known at present only in plants. Artificial preparation of allotetraploids has great scope in the production of new agricultural and horticultural varieties. Doubling of the chromosome number can be achieved in several ways, particularly by colchicine (q.v.).

ALS. Anti-lymphocytic serum. Serum containing antibodies to lymphocytes.

ALTERNATION OF GENERATIONS. In life cycle (q.v.), alternation of a generation having sexual reproduction with a generation having asexual reproduction. The sexually and asexually reproducing forms are often very different from each other. Occurs among animals in, e.g. hydroids, jelly fish, tapeworms; in these both generations are diploid. In plants seen most clearly in, e.g., ferns where the two generations are independent. The fern plant is a diploid *sporophyte* and reproduces asexually by formation of haploid spores following meiosis. Germination of the spores initiates the *gametophyte* generation, a small prothallus (q.v.), which reproduces sexually. Male and female gametes fuse together to form a zygote which develops into a new fern plant.

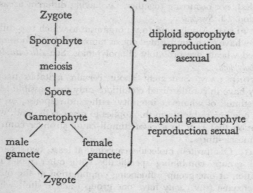

Great differences exist between the plant groups with respect to the relative prominence and degree of independence shown by gametophyte and sporophyte generations. In many members of the Thallophyta, spores are not produced by the diploid generation, which cannot therefore be termed 'sporophyte'. Nevertheless, one can recognize, as in all sexually reproducing plants, an alternation between haploid and diploid phases in the life history. The mycelium of many Phycomycete and Ascomycete fungi is haploid and commonly gives rise to asexually produced haploid spores as well as to gametes. The diploid phase is confined to the zygote, meiosis occurring with the first division of the zygote nucleus. Other members of these groups are diploid in the vegetative condition, while in the Basidiomycetes the mycelium consists of dikaryon (q.v.) cells, a condition usually considered equivalent to the diploid condition. The haploid phase, initiated by the basidiospore, is brought to an end early in the life cycle by union of two basidiospores, or anastomosis of hyphae produced by them, to form a dikaryon. Amongst algae, various conditions exist, e.g. dominant gametophyte with diploid phase confined to the zygote; dominant diploid plant bearing dependent gametophyte; distinct gametophyte and true sporophyte plants. In mosses and liverworts the dominant generation, the moss or liverwort plant, is the gametophyte; the sporophyte, the capsule, is small, nutritionally dependent on the gametophyte. In flowering plants, there are separate male and female gametophytes reduced to microscopic proportions. The male gametophyte is shed as the pollen grain;

the female gametophyte, the embryo sac, is retained on the sporophyte in the ovule. The sporophyte generation is the plant itself (herb, shrub, tree).

ALVEOLUS. (1) Minute air-filled sac in vertebrate lung, thin-walled and surrounded by blood-vessels. There are large numbers of alveoli in each lung, and it is through their surfaces that the respiratory exchange of oxygen and carbon dioxide occurs. In most vertebrates they connect with the mouth by a system of ramifying air-tubes (bronchi and bronchioles). (2) Expanded sac of secretory cells which forms internal termination of each duct in many glands (e.g. mammary glands). (3) Cavity in jaw-bone into which a tooth fits.

AMETABOLA. Apterygota (q.v.).

AMINO ACID. Organic compound containing both basic amino ($NH_2$) and acidic carobxyl (COOH) groups. Fundamental constituents of living matter because some hundreds or thousands of amino acid molecules are combined to make each protein molecule. There are twenty different amino-acids commonly found in proteins (q.v.), and there are a few other rare ones. Essential formula of naturally occurring ones ($\alpha$-amino-acids) is R-CH($NH_2$)-COOH, where R is a variable grouping of atoms (fundamentally a carbon chain or ring), an amino group always being attached to the carbon atom next to the carboxyl group. Amino acids are synthesized by autotrophic organisms such as most green plants. Certain ('essential') amino acids must, like vitamins (q.v.), be obtained from the environment by heterotrophic organisms. There are eight such for man (valine, leucine, phenylalanine, tryptophan, lysine, isoleucine, methionine, threonine), and almost the same list is known for a ciliate, an insect, a bird, and the rat. Other ('non-essential') amino acids are not required from the environment, since the organism can synthesize them, though in some cases only from essential ones.

AMITOSIS. Uncommon process of division of nucleus by simple constriction into two halves, without formation of a spindle, dissolution of nuclear membrane, or appearance of chromosomes, all of which occur in mitosis (q.v.). Formation of daughter nuclei with identical sets of chromosomes, as after mitosis, almost certainly does not result. Whether duplication of chromosomes occurs and the diploid number of chromosomes is approximately maintained in nuclei originating by amitosis is uncertain. Occurs, e.g. in endosperm tissue of flowering plants, macronucleus of Ciliophora (which is highly polyploid).

AMMOCOETE. Larva of Lamprey (a cyclostome). See *Endostyle*,

AMMONITE. Member of a group of extinct cephalopod molluscs, related to the living pearly nautilus, with chambered shell. Abundant in the Mesozoic.

AMNION. The embryo of amniote vertebrates (reptiles, birds, mam-

mals) develops in a fluid-filled sac. The wall of this sac has two
layers of epithelium with mesoderm and coelomic space between,
formed usually by folds of extraembryonic ectoderm and mesoderm which grow up around, and eventually roof over, the embryo. The inner epithelium of the wall is the amnion, though the
term is also applied to the whole sac. The outer epithelium is
usually called the chorion. Amniotic fluid within the sac provides a
fluid environment for the embryo, necessary for animals reproducing on land. In mammals the fluid probably cushions embryo
against distortion by maternal organs pressing on it. See Fig. 8,
p. 225.

AMNIOTE. Any reptile, bird, or mammal. The *Amniota* form a grouping of vertebrate classes contrasted with the Anamniota. Consists
of the essentially land-living vertebrate classes whose embryos have
an amnion and allantois (Reptilia, Aves, Mammalia).

AMOEBA. Genus of rhizopod Protozoa. Single-celled animals of
irregular and constantly changing shape and semi-fluid consistency, moving and feeding by projection of temporary processes
(pseudopodia) from their surfaces. Sometimes erroneously regarded as the most primitive animals and ancestral to others.

AMOEBOCYTE. Cell capable of active amoeboid movement found in
blood and other body fluids of invertebrates. Often phagocytic.

AMOEBOID. Moving by pseudopodia (q.v.).

AMPHIBIA. A class of vertebrates. Represented now by three orders:
frogs, toads (Anura); newts, salamanders (Urodela); tropical burrowing worm-like Apoda. In the course of evolution they were the
first vertebrates to inhabit the land (late Devonian, about 370
million years ago), being descended immediately from fish (Choanichthyes). The early Amphibia were immediate ancestors of the
reptiles which themselves gave rise to mammals and birds.
Amphibia differ from fish in having the four pentadactyl (q.v.)
legs typical of tetrapods, hip girdle jointed to the vertebral column
at the sacrum, and an ear-drum connected to the inner ear by a
rod of bone (columella auris), which crosses the middle-ear. They
differ from reptiles in that fertilization is not accomplished by
coition, and the eggs are unprotected by a shell and embryonic
membranes. Consequently most Amphibia have to become temporarily aquatic for the purpose of reproduction. Fossil Amphibia
are distinguished from fossil reptiles by, e.g. having a single vertebra concerned in the sacrum, instead of two. Modern Amphibia
have diverged far from those which were ancestral to Reptilia,
losing much of their bony skeleton.

AMPHICRIBRAL BUNDLE. See *Vascular Bundle*.

AMPHIDIPLOID. Allotetraploid (q.v.).

AMPHIMIXIS. True sexual reproduction (q.v.) as opposed to
*Apomixis* (q.v.).

AMPHINEURA. A small class of Mollusca, including the chitons;

marine, mostly living on rock surfaces, with very reduced head and primitive nervous system.

AMPHIOXUS. Primitive chordate animal of genus *Branchiostoma* or *Asymmetron*, up to two inches long, found in localized areas of shallow seas in many parts of the world. See *Acrania*.

AMPHIPODA. Order of Crustacea, including freshwater shrimps.

AMPHIVASAL BUNDLE. See *Vascular Bundle*.

AMYLASES (DIASTASES). Group of enzymes which split starch or glycogen variously to dextrin, maltose, glucose. Widely distributed in plants and animals, e.g. in malt, pancreatic juice and in micro-organisms.

AMYLOPLAST. Colourless plastid (*leucoplast*) storing starch; found, e.g. in cotyledons, endosperm and in storage organs such as potato tubers. See *Starch*.

ANABOLISM. Synthesis by living things of complex molecules from simpler ones. See *Catabolism, Metabolism*.

ANAEROBIC. Living in absence of free oxygen (gaseous or dissolved). *Anaerobic respiration*: liberation of energy by breakdown of substances not involving consumption of oxygen. See *Respiration, Fermentation*. Cf. *Aerobic*.

ANALOGOUS. An organ of one species is said to be analogous to an organ of another when both organs have the same function (q.v.) and when they are not homologous (q.v.); e.g. tendrils of pea and vine, or eyes of squid and vertebrates, are analogous. Possession of analogous organs does not imply a close evolutionary relationship of the organisms bearing them. It merely indicates adaptation to similar conditions.

ANAMNIOTA. Grouping of vertebrate classes sometimes used in classification in contrast to Amniota (q.v.). Consists of Agnatha, fishes, and Amphibia.

ANANDROUS. (Of flowers) lacking stamens.

ANAPHASE. Stage of mitosis (q.v.) or meiosis (q.v.) when daughter chromosomes are separating towards poles of spindle.

ANATROPOUS. (of ovule) inverted through 180°, micropyle pointing towards placenta. Cf. *Orthotropous, Campylotropous*.

ANDRODIOECIOUS. Having male and hermaphrodite flowers on separate plants.

ANDROECIUM. Collective name for the stamens of a flower (q.v.).

ANDROGEN. General name for any substance with male sex hormone activity in vertebrates, i.e. responsible for development and maintenance of many male sexual characteristics. Androgens are tested by the large growth of comb of castrated cock which they produce. Natural androgens in vertebrates are steroids, produced mainly by testis, to small extent by ovary and adrenal cortex. See *Testosterone, Oestrogen*.

ANDROMONOECIOUS. Having male and hermaphrodite flowers on the same plant.

ANEMOPHILY. Pollination by wind. Cf. *Entomophily*.

ANEUPLOID. Having more or less than an integral multiple of the haploid number of chromosomes; therefore genetically unbalanced. Cf. *Euploid*. See *Monosomic, Trisomic, Nullisomic*.

ANGIOSPERMAE. Flowering plants; sub-division of Spermatophyta. Distinguished from other sub-division, Gymnospermae, by having the ovules borne within a closed cavity, the *ovary*, formed by the megasporophyll; after fertilization the ovary becomes a *fruit*, enclosing one or more seeds. Micro- and mega-sporophylls (stamens and carpels) borne in flowers. Gametophyte generations very reduced. Female gametophyte develops entirely within wall of megaspore which at maturity is a large cell containing eight nuclei, the embryo sac (q.v.). Male gametophyte, initiated by pollen grain (microspore), consists of two non-motile male gametes and a tube cell, within pollen tube. Xylem characteristically has vessels. Includes two classes, Monocotyledoneae and Dicotyledoneae, distinguished by the number of seed leaves (cotyledons) in the embryo, one in the former, two in the latter class.

ANGSTROM (Å). See *Micrometre*.

ANIMAL POLE. (Zool.). Point on surface of egg nearest to its nucleus, marking one end of the graded distribution of substances which occurs in most eggs. The other end, at opposite side of egg, is the *vegetal pole*. The *animal-vegetal* axis between the two poles passes through the nucleus. Quantity of yolk, when present, is usually graded along the axis, and is least at animal, most at vegetal pole.

ANISOGAMY. Condition in which gametes are unlike; may be (1) restricted to condition in which they differ in size, but are similar in form (excluding therefore oogamy, q.v.); or may be (2) include oogamy, and all other grades of difference. Cf. *Isogamy*.

ANNELIDA (ANNULATA). Ringed or segmented worms (bristle-worms, earthworms, leeches). Phylum of animals having well-marked metameric segmentation; coelom; blood system; nephridia; well-defined nervous system. They are thus more complexly organized than flatworms and roundworms. Includes classes Chaetopoda, Archiannelida, Hirudinea, Gephyrea.

ANNUAL. Plant that completes its life-cycle, from seed germination to seed production, followed by death, within a single season. Cf. *Biennial, Ephemeral, Perennial*.

ANNUAL RING. Annual increment of secondary wood (xylem) in stems and roots of woody plants of temperate climates. Because of the sharp contrast in size between small wood elements formed in the late summer and large elements formed in spring the limits of successive annual rings appear in a cross section of stem as a series of concentric lines.

ANNULAR THICKENING. Internal thickening of wall of a xylem vessel or tracheid, in form of rings at intervals along its length.

Occurs in cells of protoxylem and, whilst providing mechanical support, permits longitudinal stretching as neighbouring cells grow.

ANNULATA. Annelida (q.v.).

ANNULUS. (1) Ring of tissue surrounding the stalk (stipe) of fruit bodies of certain basidiomycete fungi, e.g. mushroom; (2) Line of cells concerned in the opening of moss capsules and fern sporangia to liberate spores.

ANOPLURA. Sucking lice. Order of small exopterygote insects, parasitic on mammals, whose blood they suck. Include human louse, important as the carrier of typhus. Cf. *Mallophaga*.

ANOXIA. Deficiency of oxygen in the tissues.

ANTAGONISM. (1) Interference with, or inhibition of, growth of one kind of organism by another through the creation of unfavourable conditions, e.g. by exhaustion of food supply or by production of a specific antibiotic substance (e.g. penicillin). (2) Of drugs, hormones, etc., producing opposing effects (cf. *Synergism*). Includes *ion antagonism*, the prevention of effects of individual ions by other ions present. E.g. magnesium is an anaesthetic, calcium opposes this action. See also *Physiological saline*. (3) Of muscles, producing opposite movements so that contraction of one must be accompanied by relaxation of the other (and reflexes usually assure this).

ANTENNA. First appendage (paired) of head of Insecta and Myriapoda, second of Crustacea; usually much jointed, whip-like, mobile; function sensory (touch, smell, etc.) but in some Crustacea may be used for swimming or attachment.

ANTENNULE. First appendage (paired) of head of Crustacea, usually sensory.

ANTERIOR. (1) Of lateral flowers, that part farthest away from the main axis, i.e. facing the bract. See Fig. 4, p. 112. (2) Of animals situated at, or relatively nearer to, the front (head) end (usually the end directed forward when the animal is moving). In human anatomy, anterior side is however the front surface, which is equivalent to *ventral* side of other Mammals.

ANTERIOR ROOT. Of nerve, synonymous with ventral root (q.v.).

ANTHELMINTHICS. Drugs used to remove parasitic worms (helminths) from their hosts.

ANTHER. Terminal portion of a stamen (q.v.), containing pollen in *pollen sacs*.

ANTHERIDIUM. Male sex organ of algae, fungi, Bryophyta and Pteridophyta.

ANTHEROZOID. Synonymous with *Spermatozoid* (q.v.).

ANTHESIS. Flowering.

ANTHOCEROTAE. Hornworts, class of Bryophyta. Small group, widely distributed, especially in tropical and warm temperate regions, growing on moist soils. Plant is a thin, lobed, dorsiventral thallus, anchored by rhizoids. Chloroplasts unique outside algae in each containing a pyrenoid. Capsule cylindrical and, by means of an intercalary meristem near base, is able to continue growth and to produce spores, as long as gametophyte lives.

ANTHOCYANINS. Group of water soluble, flavonoid pigments (glycosides) occurring in solution in vacuoles in flowers, fruits, stems and leaves. Change colour depending on acidity of solution. Responsible for most red, purple and blue colours in plants, especially in flowers, contribute to autumn colouring of leaves and tint young shoots and buds in spring. Colours may be modified by other colourless or yellow flavonoids.

ANTHOZOA. Actinozoa (q.v.).

ANTHROPOID APES. The most nearly related to man of all living animals: gibbons, orang, chimpanzee, gorilla. They are Catarrhine Primates, forming the family Pongidae, all inhabiting Old World.

ANTHROPOIDEA (PITHECOIDEA). Sub-order of the order Primates. Includes monkeys, anthropoid apes, and man. Divided into two groups, Platyrrhini and Catarrhini. Large eyes, facing forwards: strong tendency to use hands for manipulation; relatively large brain.

ANTIAUXINS. Chemicals which can prevent the action of auxins (q.v.) in plants, e.g. 2, 6-dichlorophenoxyacetic acid; 2, 3, 5-triodobenzoic acid.

ANTIBIOTIC. Substance produced by living organisms which diffuses into its surroundings and is toxic there to individuals belonging to other species. Antibiotics have been obtained from many micro-organisms that inhabit the soil and may be an important factor in the competition amongst micro-organisms that is a characteristic of their life in this environment. The phenomenon of antibiosis has been successfully exploited in medicine, the first discovered antibiotic being penicillin, produced by several species of *Penicillium*, which is very toxic towards most gram-positive bacteria such as *Streptococcus pneumoniae* cause of pneumonia.

ANTIBODY. A protein produced in a vertebrate animal when a certain kind of substance (an antigen) which is normally foreign to its body fluids gains access to them; the antibody combines chemically with the antigen. Antibodies tend to be highly specific, in that they combine only with antigens of a particular kind. Antigens are large molecules, mostly proteins or carbohydrates; and the specificity of their reaction is due to the structure of certain small areas on the surface of these molecules. These active areas evoke antibodies carrying matching structures that in turn combine only with the specific active areas. Importance of antibody formation is as defence mechanism against invasion by parasites, particularly by bacteria and viruses. Antibodies at present seem to be peculiar to vertebrates. When parasites or their poisonous products enter the tissues the animal produces antibodies, which circulate dissolved in the body fluids. This antibody production is stimulated by antigens forming part of, or produced by, the parasites. A given parasite is likely to bear several antigens, some peculiar to its species or strain, and therefore to evoke several sorts of antibodies equally specific. In some cases different pathogens have the same antigen, so that immunity to one confers immunity to another, e.g. vaccinia and smallpox. The combination of antibody with antigen kills or immobilizes parasites, or makes them more susceptible to phagocytes (q.v.) or makes their poison innocuous. Antibodies are formed by a complex system involving lymphocytes, plasma cells and perhaps macrophages; and once produced they are found mainly in the blood, and may persist there long after disappearance of the antigen, conferring immunity to a new infection by the same sort of parasite. A new infection also induces a much more rapid production of the specific antibodies than the first infection; this is called a secondary response. Immunity to disease from vaccination or inoculation is due to antibodies. Antibodies cannot be formed until late in embryonic development. Substances quite unconnected with parasites can act as antigens when injected, e.g. almost any foreign protein, and the specificity of the reaction provides an extraordinarily sensitive test for different proteins. Grafting of foreign tissues also leads to the production of antibodies against their antigens.

ANTICLINAL. (Bot.). (Of planes of division of cells) situated approximately at right angles to outer surface of plant part. Cf. *Periclinal*.

ANTICOAGULANT. Substance which prevents the clotting of blood, e.g. heparin (q.v.). See *Saliva*.

ANTIDIURETIC HORMONE (ADH). Hormone secreted from posterior lobe of pituitary. A peptide, synthesized in hypothalamus. In mammals, stimulates water reabsorption by uriniferous tubule (q.v.), hence diminishes volume of urine, and deficiency causes diabetes insipidus.

ANTIGEN. Substance capable of stimulating formation of an antibody (q.v.).

ANTIGIBBERELLINS. Organic compounds varying widely in structure that cause plants to grow with short and thick stems or with appearance opposite to that obtained with gibberellin (q.v.). Gibberellin can reverse the action of most of these compounds. They are not necessarily chemically related to gibberellin. Of agricultural importance are such compounds as phosphon, and maleic hydrazide (used, e.g. to retard growth of grass, reducing frequency of cutting).

ANTIMETABOLITE. Chemical substance sufficiently like a given metabolite to take part in some of its reactions, but sufficiently unlike to fail to take part in others. Hence it can become involved in a metabolic system, but blocks it at some stage.

ANURA (SALIENTIA). Frogs and toads. An order of the class Amphibia. Long hind legs for jumping; no tail; soft skin important in respiration, with no scales.

ANUS. The opening of the alimentary canal to the exterior through which undigested remains of food, bacteria associated with them, and solid excretions are expelled. This is its only function, except in some aquatic animals which use hind-end of gut for respiration (e.g. some dragon-fly larvae). Present in most Metazoa but absent in all Platyhelminthes and Coelenterata. See *Cloaca*.

AORTA. In man and other mammals, the great artery which leaves the heart (from the left ventricle), and through which passes the arterial blood supply for the whole body (at about four litres per minute in man) to be distributed via the numerous arteries which branch off the aorta. See *Aorta, Dorsal*.

AORTA, DORSAL. Artery of vertebrates through which passes arterial blood to all the body, except the head and in some species the front limbs. Lies just below vertebral column, throughout most of the latter's length. In tetrapod vertebrates it is the continuation of the systemic arch (in mammals this arch, and sometimes the dorsal aorta too, is called the aorta). In fish it arises from the arteries drawing blood from the gills (efferent branchial arteries). In its course it gives off several large branches to viscera and limbs, and eventually in the tail becomes the caudal artery.

AORTA, VENTRAL. Large artery of fish and embryonic amniotes, which leads from ventricle of heart, and gives off branches to gills or aortic arches.

AORTIC ARCHES. Paired arteries (usually six) of vertebrate embryos, connecting ventral aorta with dorsal aorta by running up between gill slits or gill-pouches on each side, one in each visceral arch. In fish, develop into arteries carrying blood to and from gills. In tetrapods the two most anterior pairs (between mouth and the pouch equivalent to spiracle; and between latter and second pouch) disappear. Third pair forms proximal part of carotid arteries, fourth becomes systemic arch (on one side only, in birds and mammals), fifth disappears, and sixth forms part of pulmonary arteries.

APETALOUS. Lacking petals, e.g. wood anemone.

APHANIPTERA. Fleas. Order of endopterygote insects. Wingless; parasites of mammals and birds whose blood they suck; strong legs, good jumpers; larvae grub-like.

APHIS. Green flies, etc.; genus of hemipteran insects which suck plant juices. Some carry virus diseases and as such are of great economic importance.

APHYLLOUS. Leafless.

APICAL MERISTEM. Growing point (zone of cell division) at tip of root and stem in vascular plants, having its origin in a single cell (initial), e.g. Pteridophyta, or in a group of cells (initials), e.g. Spermatophyta. In the latter the apex of the growing point (*promeristem*) consists of actively dividing cells. Behind the promeristem division continues and differentiation begins, becoming progressively greater towards the mature tissues. One (older) concept of the organization of the growing point in flowering plants recognizes differentiation into three regions (*histogens*), *dermatogen*, a superficial layer of cells giving rise to the epidermis, *plerome*, a central core of tissue that gives rise to the vascular cylinder and pith, and *periblem*, tissue lying between dermatogen and plerome, that gives rise to cortex. It is now evident that the respective roles assigned to these histogens are by no means universal, nor is it always possible to distinguish between periblem and plerome, especially in the shoot apex. Now becoming widely accepted is the *Tunica-Corpus* concept, an interpretation of the shoot apex which recognizes two tissue zones in the promeristem, *tunica*, consisting of one or more peripheral layers, in which the planes of cell division are predominantly anticlinal, enclosing *corpus*, or central tissue of irregularly arranged cells in which the planes of cell division vary. No relation is implied between cells of these two regions and differentiated tissue behind apex as in histogen concept. Although epidermis arises from outermost tunica layer, underlying tissue may originate in tunica or in corpus, or in both, in different plant species.

In addition to providing for growth in length of main axis, apical meristem of stem is the site of origin of primordia of leaves and buds. In roots two types of apical meristem occur, one in which vascular cylinder, cortex and root cap can be traced to distinct layers of cells in the promeristem and a second type in which all tissues have a common origin in one group of promeristem cells. In contrast to that of stem, apical meristem of roots provides only for growth in length, lateral roots originating some distance from apex, and endogenously, from pericycle.

APLANOSPORE. Non-motile asexual spore found in certain algae and fungi; develop variously in different forms, e.g. singly from thallus cell, or in numbers within a sporangium.

APOCARPOUS. (of the gynoecium of flowering plants) having separate carpels, e.g. buttercup. See *Flower*.

APODA (GYMNOPHIONA). An order of Amphibia. Tropical, burrowing, limbless, wormlike. Unlike all other living Amphibia, have scales, buried in the skin.

APOGAMY. See *Apomixis*.

APOMICT. Plant produced by *Apomixis* (q.v.).

APOMIXIS. Reproduction which has superficial appearance of ordinary sexual cycle (amphimixis) but actually occurs without fertilization and/or meiosis. Usually taken to include *parthenogenesis* (q.v.); *apospory*, in some plants, where an ordinary diploid sporophyte cell substitutes for the spore, meiosis being omitted, so that the gametophyte is diploid; and *apogamy*, in Pteridophytes, in which a gametophyte cell gives rise directly to a sporophyte, the gametophyte being diploid. Has also been applied recently to include vegetative reproduction whenever the normal sexual processes are not functioning or are greatly reduced in activity. See *Agamospermy*.

APOSEMATIC COLORATION. Warning Coloration (q.v.).

APOSPORY. See *Apomixis*.

APOTHECIUM. Cup or saucer-shaped fruit body of certain ascomycete fungi (Discomycetes or cup-fungi), and lichens, lined with a
hymenium of asci and paraphyses. Sessile or stalked, often brightly
coloured; varying from a few millimetres to more than forty centi-
metres across.

APPENDAGE. Any considerable projection from the body of an
animal. *Paired a*. One of a bilaterally symmetrical pair of appendages. Two such pairs (limbs or fins) occur in all gnathostome
vertebrates. There is frequently one pair per segment in arthropods (e.g. walking-legs, mouth-parts, antennae) and annelids.

APPENDIX, VERMIFORM. Small diverticulum of caecum (at junction of large and small intestines) of man, apes, and some other
mammals, containing much lymphoid tissue.

APPETITIVE BEHAVIOUR. Behaviour, e.g. locomotory activity,
variable according to circumstances, that increases the chances of
an animal satisfying some need, e.g. for food. The satisfaction of the
need is achieved, when a suitable stimulus is 'found', by a more
stereotyped *consummatory act*, e.g. eating, which ends the appetitive
behaviour.

APPOSITION. (Bot.). Growth in thickness of cell walls by successive
deposition of material, layer upon layer. Cf. *Intussusception*.

APTERYGOTA (AMETABOLA). Sub-class of wingless insects, including orders Thysanura (bristle-tails, silver-fish), Collembola
(spring-tails), and Protura. It is believed that they are primitively
wingless as distinct from other wingless insects, e.g. fleas, which
are derived from winged ancestors. Cf. *Pterygota*.

AQUEOUS HUMOUR. Fluid which fills space between cornea and
vitreous humour of the vertebrate eye. The iris and lens lie in it.
Much like cerebrospinal fluid in composition. It is continuously
secreted (by the ciliary body, q.v.) and absorbed. See Fig. 3,
p. 107.

ARACHNIDA. Class of Arthropoda containing scorpions, spiders,
ticks, mites, harvest-men, king crabs. Most living members are
terrestrial, breathing air, but king-crabs are aquatic. No antennae; first pair of appendages used for grasping; second may be
grasping, sensory, or locomotory; remaining four pairs locomotory.

ARCHAEOPTERYX AND ARCHAEORNIS. Earliest known fossil
birds (Jurassic, 140–170 million years ago), with teeth, claws on
three-fingered hands, long tail containing numerous vertebrae; in
many respects extremely like a reptile but with feathers (which are
well preserved in the fossils).

ARCHEGONIATAE. Members of Cryptogamia (q.v.) in which female
sex organ is an archegonium (q.v.), i.e. Bryophyta and Pteridophyta.

ARCHEGONIUM. Female sex organ of liverworts, mosses, ferns, and related plants, and most gymnosperms; multicellular, consisting of a neck, composed of one or more tiers of cells, and a swollen base (venter), containing the egg-cell.

ARCHENTERON. Cavity within early embryo (at gastrula stage) of many animals, communicating with exterior by blastopore (q.v.). Formed by invagination of mesoderm and endoderm cells during gastrulation. Ultimately becomes gut cavity.

ARCHESPORIUM. Cells or cell from which spores are ultimately derived, e.g. in developing pollen sac, fern sporangium.

ARCHIANNELIDA. Class of Annelida consisting of a few genera of small marine worms of simplified structure, possibly derived from Polychaeta.

ARCHICHLAMYDEAE. Sub-class of Angiospermae in which the individual members of the corolla are entirely separate from each other or the perianth is incomplete. Cf. *Sympetalae*.

ARCTOGEA. Zoogeographical region amalgamating Palaearctic, Nearctic, Ethiopian and Oriental; as distinct from Neogea and Notogea, which have very distinctive faunas.

ARIL. Brightly coloured, succulent investment of the seed in a few plants, e.g. yew, developed from stalk or base of ovule.

ARISTA. Awn (q.v.).

AROUSAL. A state of general responsiveness in an animal, induced by sensory stimulation or internal processes, which is the result of the activity of a particular part of the brain in mammals, the *reticular formation*.

ARTEFACT. Something which does not occur in the undisturbed living cell or organism, but was produced in it during investigation, or during its preparation for investigation (especially during fixation and dehydration).

ARTERIOLE. Small artery of vertebrates, less than $\frac{1}{2}$ mm. diameter. Smooth muscle of wall well developed, and under control of autonomic nervous system. Acts as a kind of stopcock regulating blood flow through capillaries (which are continuations of the arterioles).

ARTERY. Blood vessel carrying blood from the heart towards the tissues. In vertebrates arteries have thick walls, containing elastic and collagen fibres and smooth muscle, to withstand the high blood pressure near the heart. They are lined with smooth flat cells (endothelium), like other blood vessels. Arterial system starts with one or few arteries at heart, which by repeated branching as they proceed away from the heart give rise to an increasing number of ever smaller arteries, until the branches become arterioles (q.v.).

ARTHROPODA. The largest phylum in the animal kingdom in number of species, including crabs, insects, spiders, centipedes, etc. Hard jointed exoskeleton; paired jointed legs; coelom small; no nephridia; no cilia (present in Onychophora). Contains classes

Trilobita, Crustacea, Myriapoda, Arachnida, Insecta. See also *Onychophora*.

ARTICULATE WITH. Be attached by means of a movable joint to: e.g. the arm articulates with the shoulder girdle.

ARTIFICIAL INSEMINATION. Artificial injection of semen into female. Much used in animal breeding, since sperm of animal with desirable hereditary qualities can be transported over long distances and used to inseminate numerous females, under conditions optimum for fertility.

ARTIFICIAL PARTHENOGENESIS. Artificial activation of development of an egg (that is not normally parthenogenetic) without contact with sperm. This can be done in many animals (including rabbits) by treating eggs in various ways, e.g. cooling; pricking with a needle; treating with acid. In a small proportion of instances the activated egg can develop into an adult. *See Parthenogenesis.*

ARTIODACTYLA. Even-toed ungulates. Order of mammals containing pigs, hippopotami, camels, and ruminants (deer, giraffes, sheep, goats, antelopes, oxen). Walk on their toes, on which there are hooves, and are characterized by fact that weight-bearing axis of the foot lies between third and fourth toe. The number of toes may be four (pigs, hippopotami) or more usually two, the typical 'cloven hoof'. One of the two great groups of hoofed mammals (ungulates), the other being the Perissodactyla. See also *Ruminant*.

ASCIDIAN. Sea-squirt; a member of the Urochordata.

ASCOCARP. General term for fruit body (cleistocarp, apothecium, or perithecium) of an ascomycete fungus.

ASCOMYCETES. A group of fungi (see *Mycophyta*).

ASCORBIC ACID (VITAMIN C). Vitamin known to be required by man and other primates and by guinea pigs, a bird and a bat, but synthesized by other animals studied. Water soluble. Deficiency causes scurvy, preventing collagen-formation (e.g. in healing wounds). Widely present in organisms.

ASCOSPORE. See *Ascus*.

ASCUS. In Ascomycete fungi, cell (spherical, cylindrical or club-shaped) in which fusion of haploid nuclei occurs during sexual reproduction, followed by meiosis and formation of, usually, eight haploid ascospores.

ASEXUAL REPRODUCTION. Reproduction without gametes (excludes parthenogenesis). In plants consists of either spore-formation or vegetative reproduction (q.v.). In Metazoa spore-formation does not occur; asexual reproduction is by fission (q.v.) or gemmation (q.v.).

ASSIMILATION. Absorption and building up of simple food-stuffs, or products of digestion of food-stuffs, into complex constituents of the organism.

ASSOCIATION. (Of plants), climax plant community dominated by particular species and named according to them, e.g. deciduous forest association, heath association. This, the original conception of the meaning of association, is not now universally held; e.g. Swedish and continental workers apply the term to very small natural units of vegetation.

ASSORTATIVE MATING (A. BREEDING). Sexual reproduction in which the pairing of male and female is not at random, but involves a tendency for males of a particular kind to breed with females of a particular kind: e.g. the two parents of each pair may tend to be more alike than is to be expected by chance.

ASTER. A system of striations in the cytoplasm, radiating from the centriole, and consisting of microtubules (q.v.); often conspicuous during cleavage of the egg, or during fusion of nuclei at fertilization; also probably present in many other animal cells during their division. Absent in higher plants.

ASTEROIDEA. Starfishes. Class of Echinodermata. Star-shaped, arms not sharply marked off from central part of body.

ATAVISM. Recurrence in descendants of a character which had been possessed by an ancestor, after an interval of several or many generations. Not a current scientific term.

ATLAS. First vertebra of tetrapods, modified for joint with skull. In amniotes, which have freer head movement, it is modified further than in Amphibia; it consists of a simple bony ring, and there is a peg (odontoid process) on the next vertebra (axis) which projects forwards into the ring (through which spinal cord also runs). This peg represents part of the atlas (its centrum), which has become detached and fused to the axis. Nodding the head takes place at skull-atlas joint; rotating head at atlas-axis joint.

ATP (ADENOSINE TRIPHOSPHATE). A nucleotide coenzyme that takes part in many chemical reactions in all organisms. It provides a common source of energy for a range of different cellular activities. One of the phosphate groupings of ATP is readily transferred to other substances by enzyme action, simultaneously transferring a considerable amount of energy. This transfer of phosphate from ATP seems to be the main mechanism by which organisms make energy available for chemical synthesis, muscular contraction, osmotic work, etc. ATP is formed from adenosine diphosphate (ADP) by utilization of light energy in photosynthesis and by means of the energy derived from catabolic processes; the energy of both is thus made available for various kinds of work through ATP. See *Phosphagen*.

ATPASE. Enzyme that hydrolyses ATP (q.v.) with release of one phosphate group.

ATRIUM. Chamber, closed except for a small pore, surrounding gill-slits of Amphioxus and Urochordata. Also synonym of Auricle (q.v.)

ATROPHY. Diminution in size of an organ, or in amount of a tissue or constituent of a tissue.

ATTACHMENT CONSTRICTION. Spindle attachment (q.v.).

**ATTENUATION.** (Of pathogenic micro-organisms) loss of virulence.

**AUDITORY (OTIC) CAPSULE.** Part of skull of vertebrates enclosing auditory organ.

**AUDITORY NERVE (ACOUSTIC NERVE).** Eighth cranial nerve of vertebrates, innervating inner ear. A dorsal root, embryologically a sensory branch of seventh cranial nerve.

**AUDITORY ORGAN.** Sense-organ for detecting sound. In vertebrates the auditory organ (see *Ear, inner*) also detects position in relation to gravity, and acceleration.

**AURICLE (ATRIUM).** One of the chambers of the heart; receives blood from veins and passes it to ventricle (q.v.). Has muscular walls, but is not as powerful a pumping organ as the ventricle. A fish has a single auricle, but in land-living (tetrapod) vertebrates, which breathe mainly or entirely by lungs, there are two auricles, one receiving oxygenated blood from lungs, other deoxygenated from the rest of the body. Most Mollusca have two auricles, one receiving blood from each side of the body. (Bot.) Small ear- or claw-like appendages occurring one on each side at the base of leaf-blades in certain plants.

**AUSTRALIAN (NOTOGEA).** Zoogeographical region consisting mainly of Australia and New Guinea (see *Wallace's line*).

**AUSTRALOPITHECINE.** Member of a group of fossil primates from Africa. Distinctly human in some features, especially of limbs and teeth, but ape-like in others, especially of skull. Walked upright. Early Pleistocene.

**AUTECOLOGY.** Ecology of individual species as opposed to communities (*synecology*).

**AUTOCATALYTIC.** Catalysing its own production; so that the more that is produced, the more catalyst there is for further production.

**AUTOCHTHONOUS.** Of soil micro-organisms, metabolic activity and population more or less stable, unaffected by addition of organic matter. Cf. *Zymogenous*. Use less readily assimilated compounds, either those remaining after decay of organic matter by zymogenous organisms or compounds unused by them.

**AUTOECIOUS.** Of rust fungi (order Uredinales of Basidiomycetes), having the different spore forms of the life-cycle all produced on one host species, e.g. mint rust. Cf. *Heteroecious*.

**AUTOGAMY.** A curious sexual process found in some Protozoa and in some Diatoms in which the nucleus of an individual divides into two parts which reunite. Term also used for self-fertilization in plants.

**AUTOGRAFT.** Graft originating from the individual which receives it. Cf. *Homograft, Heterograft, Isograft*.

**AUTO-IMMUNITY.** A diseased state in which the mechanisms of immunity (q.v.) to an antigen are brought to bear by an animal on some constituent of its own tissues.

**AUTOLYSIS.** Self-dissolution that tissues undergo after death of their cells, due to action of their own enzymes. See *Lysosome*.

AUTONOMIC. (Of plant movements) arising as a result of internal stimuli, e.g. nutation (q.v.). Alternatively described as autogenic or spontaneous. Cf. *Paratonic*.

AUTONOMIC NERVOUS SYSTEM. (1) Of vertebrates, motor nerve supply to smooth muscles (e.g. in gut, blood-vessels, etc.) and glands. A characteristic feature is that it does not involve single nerve fibres running all the way from central nervous system to effector (as with supply to striped muscles); but the nerve fibres (*preganglionic*) which leave C.N.S. stop short of effectors, and form synapses with a second group of nerve cells whose nerve-fibres (*postganglionic*), which are mainly unmyelinated, then continue to effectors. The cell-bodies of the postganglionic fibres, and the synapses, occur in ganglia or in the organ where the effectors are. The system is subdivided into *sympathetic* (or *orthosympathetic*) system, and *parasympathetic* system. In mammals and birds (other vertebrates are less well known) preganglionic fibres of sympathetic system leave the spinal cord (in thoracic and lumbar region) through ventral roots, and go to chains of *sympathetic ganglia*, one on each side just ventral to vertebral column, where they meet postganglionic nerve-cells, or pass through the paired ganglia and meet them in another, median, row of ganglia (e.g. the solar plexus). From all these ganglia postganglionic fibres go to effectors. Preganglionic fibres of parasympathetic system on the other hand leave C.N.S. (a) through cranial nerves, especially vagus, (b) through ventral roots of hind end of spinal cord (sacral region), and the postganglionic cell-bodies are scattered amongst the effectors or are in ganglia very close to the effectors. The sympathetic system is the larger of the two; it alone supplies skin and limbs. Many internal organs receive nerve-fibres from both systems, and in such cases they may act antagonistically; e.g. smooth musculature of gut is stimulated to peristalsis by parasympathetic supply (mostly from vagus), inhibited by sympathetic supply. Parasympathetic and preganglionic sympathetic fibres are cholinergic; postganglionic sympathetic fibres often adrenergic, sometimes (e.g. those to sweat glands) cholinergic. Much of the co-ordination of activities of the autonomic system occurs in spinal cord, medulla, and hypothalamus. (2) The motor system as described under (1), together with the sensory fibres from internal receptors which are concerned in reflex activities of this motor system.

AUTOPOLYPLOID. Polyploid (q.v.) in which all the chromosomes come from the same species. Cf. *Allopolyploid*.

AUTORADIOGRAPH. Photographic picture of the localization of radio-active substance in tissues, obtained by laying photographic emulsion in the dark on a thin preparation (usually a section) of the tissue and developing the image that is produced by the radio-activity. Commonly used in tracer work.

AUTOSOME. Chromosome which is not a sex-chromosome.

AUTOSTYLIC JAW-SUSPENSION. Attachment of primitive upper
jaw (palatoquadrate) of vertebrates direct to neurocranium (see
*Hyostylic Jaw-Suspension*). Occurs in the earliest known fishes with
jaws (Acanthodii) which were probably succeeded by hyostylic
descendants. Autostyly was then reacquired independently by
Holocephali (q.v.) and by Dipnoi and tetrapods; in these, the
palatoquadrate actually fuses with the brain-case.

AUTOTOMY. Self-amputation of part of the body, e.g. lizard can
break off tail when it is seized by a predator, muscular action snap-
ping a vertebra. Lost part is usually regenerated.

AUTOTROPHIC. (Of an organism) independent of outside sources of
organic substances for provision of its own organic constituents,
which it can manufacture from inorganic material. An autotrophic
organism may be phototrophic (q.v.) or chemotrophic (q.v.) as
regards its supply of energy. Most chlorophyll-containing plants
are autotrophic, manufacturing organic materials from water,
carbon-dioxide, nitrates, and other salts with sunlight as the phototrophic source of energy (see *Chlorophyll*). A few bacteria are autotrophic, using inorganic materials, and chemotrophic, using energy
produced by inorganic oxidations, e.g. of hydrogen sulphide by
sulphur bacteria or of hydrogen by hydrogen bacteria. All other
organisms, which are *heterotrophic*, depend ultimately on the synthetic activities of autotrophic organisms. See *Metabolite*.

AUXINS. Group of plant hormones, produced by regions of active
cell divison and enlargement, e.g. growing tips of stems and roots,
that regulate many aspects of plant growth. Promote growth by
increasing rate of cell elongation, including curvature responses of
organs to stimuli of geotropism (q.v.) and phototropism (q.v.), and
by cell division, e.g. initiation of cambium activity in association
with cytokinins (q.v.), adventitious root formation in cuttings;
cause dominance of certain parts of plant over others, e.g. inhibition
of lateral bud development by apical bud; involved in flower
initiation, sex determination, fruit growth; delay leaf fall and fruit
drop. Actively transported in polar (basipetal) manner in young
tissues.

Auxins occurring naturally in plants include indole-3-acetic acid
(IAA) and indole-3-acetonitrile (IAN). IAA has been isolated from
such diverse sources as corn endosperm, fungi, bacteria, human
saliva and, the richest natural source, human urine. In addition to
naturally occurring auxins many substances with plant growth
regulation effects, the so-called synthetic auxins, have been made
in the laboratory. Some of these are now used on a very large scale
for regulating some growth processes of agriculturally and horticulturally important plants, e.g. inhibition of sprouting of potato
tubers, thus lengthening period for which they can be stored,
prevention of fruit drop in orchards, synchronous flowering (and
thus fruiting) in pineapple, parthenocarpic fruit production, e.g. in

tomato, avoiding disadvantage of poor pollination. At increased though still relatively low concentration auxins inhibit growth and death may result. Some of the synthetic auxins have differential toxicity towards different plants (toxicity of 2, 4-dichlorophenoxy-acetic acid to dicotyledonous and non-toxicity to monocotyledonous plants is best example) and this has been exploited very successfully in the control of weeds in cereal crops and lawns. See *Hormone*.

AUXOTROPH. Strain of a micro-organism (alga, bacterium or fungus) which requires growth factors not needed by wild type (q.v.) or by prototrophs (q.v.).

AVES. The birds, a class of vertebrates. Characterized by feathers, warm blood, wings developed from fore-limbs. Apart from some fossil forms (e.g. *Archaeopteryx*) birds form a highly uniform class. Descended from reptiles related to dinosaurs and crocodiles; and still have many reptilian features.

AWN (ARISTA). Stiff, bristle-like appendage occurring frequently on the flowering glumes of grasses and cereals.

AXENIC. (Of a culture of an organism) having no other kind of organism present; a pure culture.

AXIL. (Of a leaf) angle between its upper side and the stem on which it is borne; normal position for lateral buds.

AXIS. (Embryonic axis) The complex elongated structure comprising nervous system, notochord and somites in a vertebrate embryo. (Axis vertebra) Second vertebra of amniote, modified for supporting the head. See *Atlas*.

AXIS CYLINDER. Axon (q.v.).

AXOLOTL. Aquatic larval stage of an American salamander (genus *Ambystoma*, Order Urodela) which is remarkable in that it does not metamorphose, but breeds while keeping its larval form (the phenomenon of neoteny, q.v.). Such breeding axolotls occur only in some districts; in others, *Ambystoma* metamorphoses and breeds as normal adult form.

AXON. The long process of a nerve cell, normally conducting impulses *away from* the nerve cell-body (cf. *Dendrite*). Often covered by myelin. See *Nerve-Fibre*.

# B

BACILLARIOPHYTA. Diatoms. Division of algae. Microscopic, unicellular plants, occurring singly or grouped into colonies. In addition to chlorophylls a and c, chloroplasts contain α-, β-, ε-carotene and xanthophylls including fucoxanthin. Cell wall of pectic materials impregnated with silica, finely sculptured; composed of two halves, one of which overlaps the other. Asexual reproduction by cell division, sexual reproduction isogamous or anisogamous. Abundant in marine and freshwater plankton and benthos. With dinoflagellates (Pyrrophyta, q.v.) and a few other algae provide basis for all life in sea. Past deposition of countless numbers of the silicified cell walls has formed the deposits known as siliceous or diatomaceous earths, and oil reserves of diatoms of past ages have contributed to the petroleum supplies of today.

BACILLUS. Genus of spore-producing bacteria. Also used generally for rod-shaped bacteria.

BACKBONE. Vertebral column (q.v.).

BACKCROSS. Cross of a hybrid with one of its parents.

BACTERIA (SCHIZOMYCOPHYTA). Group (Division) of unicellular or multicellular, microscopic, procaryotic (q.v.) organisms, lacking chlorophyll (a few have *bacteriochlorophyll*). Have usually been classified with plants rather than with animals but are distinct from both. A third kingdom, Protista (q.v.) is sometimes constituted for bacteria and all other organisms of simple biological organization. In shape rod-like, more or less spiral, filamentous, occasionally forming a mycelium, or, in some forms, spherical, varying in breadth mostly from 0.5 to 2.0 micrometres; non-motile or motile by one or more flagella. Multiplication is by simple fission; other forms of asexual reproduction, by formation of aerially dispersed spores, flagellated swarmers, occur in some bacteria. Sexual reproduction has also been demonstrated in certain forms. Ubiquitous, occurring in large numbers in favourable habitats, e.g. a gram of soil may contain from a few thousand to several hundred million bacteria; a cubic centimetre of sour milk, many millions. Most bacteria are saprophytes or parasites. A few are autotrophic (q.v.), either obtaining energy by oxidation processes or from light in the presence of bacteriochlorophyll. The activities of bacteria are of great importance. In the soil they are concerned in the decay of plant and animal tissues, making available food materials for higher plants, and certain bacteria are of particular significance in this respect in making available nitrogenous compounds. See *Nitrogen Cycle*. Others are sources of antibiotics, e.g. *Streptomyces griseus*, source of streptomycin. Bacteria also play an important

part in the disposal of sewage. As agents of plant disease, bacteria
are not so important as fungi, but they cause many serious diseases
in animal and man, e.g. tuberculosis, diphtheria, typhoid, pneumonia.

BACTERICIDAL. Lethal to bacteria. Cf. *Bacteriostatic*.

BACTERIOCHLOROPHYLL. See *Chlorophyll*.

BACTERIOLOGY. Study of bacteria.

BACTERIOPHAGE (PHAGE). A virus (q.v.) that parasitizes bacteria.
Consists of polyhedral head, 500 to 1000 Angstrom units across,
containing genetic material, DNA (or occasionally RNA), enclosed by a wall of protein which is prolonged into a hollow tail.
Initiates infection by attaching itself by tail to wall of bacterial cell.
Through enzyme action wall is perforated and bacteriophage
DNA passes through into bacterial cell whose synthetic machinery
it organizes to make more bacteriophage DNA, and more bacteriophages. These are released by lysis of host cell.
Studies of bacteriophage and their genetic recombination in bacteria have been very fruitful in adding to knowledge of genes and
gene action. See *Lysogeny, Transduction*.

BACTERIOSTATIC. Inhibiting growth of bacteria but not killing
them. Cf. *Bactericidal*.

BALANOGLOSSUS. Genus of worm-like burrowing animals belonging
to the Hemichordata (q.v.), with vertebrate affinities.

BALEEN. Whalebone. Transverse plates of keratin, derived from
epidermis, hanging from the upper jaw on each side of the mouth
of the toothless whalebone whales (rorquals and right whales).
Frayed inner edges form a filter, retaining the small animals on
which the whale feeds.

BARBS. Of feathers. The filaments, in a row at each side of the longitudinal axis, which together make the expanded part (vane) of a
feather. See *Barbules*.

BARBULES. Of feathers. Minute filaments in a row at each side of
a barb. Those of one side bear hooks, those of the other a groove.
Barbules of adjacent barbs hook together and link barbs into a
firm vane. Down-feathers and ostrich feathers have no interlocking
mechanism, so their barbs are free.

BARK. Protective, corky tissue of dead cells, present on the outside of
older stems and roots of woody plants, e.g. tree trunks, produced by
activity of cork cambium. Bark may consist of cork only, or, when
other layers of cork are formed at succesively deeper levels, it may
consist of alternating layers of cork and dead cortex or phloem
tissue (when it is known as *rhytidome*). Popularly regarded as every-
thing outside the wood.

BARR BODY. Sex chromatin (q.v.).

BASAL BODY. See *Centriole*.

BASAL LAMINA. Thin layer of collogen-like protein, secreted by
epithelial and some other cells, visible by electron microscopy

close to the cell surface on the basal side of epithelia, about 500–1000 Angstrom units thick.

BASEMENT MEMBRANE. Delicate intercellular membrane, visible in light microscope, which underlies most animal epithelia. Besides the basal lamina, consists of mucopolysaccharide and very fine (reticulin) fibres.

BASE PAIRING. Two strands of nucleic acid, RNA or DNA, can associate laterally by bonds between specific pairs of the bases contained in their nucleotides. Adenine in one strand will link (by hydrogen bonding) to thymine (in DNA) or uracil (in RNA) in the other; and guanine to cytosine. DNA usually consists of two associated complementary strands (coiled together into a helix) the arrangement of their nucleotides permitting such base pairing throughout.

BASE RATIO. In DNA, the amount of adenine (A) and thymine (T) (which are paired, see *Base pairing*) equals the amount of guanine (G) and cytosine (C) (also paired). But the ratio of the amount of A plus T to that of G plus C, which is the base ratio, varies widely.

BASIC DYES. Dyes consisting of a basic organic grouping of atoms (cation) which is the actively staining part, combined with an acid, usually inorganic. Stain particularly nucleic acids, and therefore nuclei. Cf. *Acid dyes*.

BASIDIOMYCETES. A group of fungi (see *Mycophyta*).

BASIDIUM. In Basidiomycete fungi, cell in which fusion of haploid nuclei occurs during sexual reproduction, followed by meiosis and formation of, usually, four haploid *basidiospores*. Club-shaped or cylindrical cell, or divided into four cells, spores borne externally on minute stalks (sterigmata).

BASIPETAL. (Bot.). (Of organs), development in succession towards the base, oldest at the apex, youngest at base. Also used in reference to direction of transport of substances within a plant, i.e. away from apex. Cf. *Acropetal*.

BASOPHILIC. Staining strongly with basic dye. Especially character-istic of nucleic acids, and hence of nucleus (during the mitosis of which, basophily is localized in chromosomes) and of cytoplasm when actively synthesizing proteins.

BATRACHIA. Amphibia (q.v.).

BENNETTITALES. Order of extinct Gymnospermae (q.v.) that flourished during the Mesozoic (q.v.). Resembled cycads (Cyca-dales) somewhat in external appearance and anatomy of stem and leaf. Differed from them in possessing cones containing both micro- and mega-sporophylls and in form of these sporophylls.

BENTHOS. Those animals and plants living on the bottom of sea or lake (crawling or burrowing there; or may be attached, e.g. seaweeds and sessile animals), from high water mark down to the deepest levels. The benthos is divided into littoral organisms (down to 200 metres deep) and deep water organisms. See *Pelagic*, *Nekton*, *Plankton*.

BERRY. Many-seeded succulent fruit in which wall (*pericarp*) consists of outer skin (*epicarp*), comparatively thick fleshy *mesocarp* and inner membranous *endocarp*, e.g. gooseberry, currant, tomato. Cf. *Drupe*.

BICOLLATERAL BUNDLE. See *Vascular Bundle*.

BIENNIAL. Plant that requires two years to complete its life-cycle, from seed germination to seed production and death. During the first season biennials, e.g. carrot, cabbage, store up food which is used in the second season when they produce flowers and seed. Cf. *Annual*, *Ephemeral*, *Perennial*.

BILATERAL CLEAVAGE. Cleavage (q.v.) which produces a bilaterally symmetrical arrangement of blastomeres lacking the peculiar arrangement and oblique divisions of spiral cleavage (q.v.). Occurs in Echinodermata, Chordata, etc.

BILATERALLY SYMMETRICAL. Capable of being halved in one, and only one, plane in such a way that the two halves are approximately mirror-images of each other. Usually this plane lies antero-posteriorly and dorso-ventrally, thus separating similar right and left halves. Almost all freely moving animals are bilaterally symmetrical, e.g. all vertebrates, arthropods, and worm-shaped animals. Similar condition in flowers, e.g. snapdragon, is often called *zygomorphy*. See *Radially Symmetrical*.

BILE. Secretion of liver of vertebrates, passed through bile-duct to duodenum. Important in digestion of fats, which, through action of bile-salts, are converted into minute droplets (emulsified). Contains also pigments which are waste-products of haemoglobin destruction.

BILE DUCT. Duct from liver to duodenum of vertebrates. Conveys bile. See *Gall-Bladder*.

BILE SALTS. Sodium salts of taurocholic and glycocholic acids (bile acids, see *Steroids*), secreted in bile. Strongly lower surface tension, emulsifying fat. Responsible for bitter taste of bile.

BILHARZIA. Schistosoma (q.v.).

BINOCULAR VISION. Type of vision occurring in primates and many other vertebrates, especially active predators, in which eye-balls can be so directed that image of an object falls on both retinas. Extent to which eyes must be converged to bring the images on to a special part of each retina (see *Fovea*) may be one of the mechanisms of distance judgement. Stereoscopic vision (perception of shape in depth) depends on two slightly different images being received, because the two eyes look from different angles.

BINOMIAL NOMENCLATURE. The present method of naming species of animals and plants scientifically. When a new organism is discovered a description of it is published, often in Latin, and it is given a name, always in Latin. The name is in two parts (binomial); one part (the specific epithet or trivial name) peculiar to the new species; the other part (the generic name) designating the genus (q.v.) to which it belongs, and therefore applied in the same way to other closely related species, if there are any, but to no other genus. The generic name is written first with a capital letter, the specific second, usually with a small letter, e.g. *Canis familiaris* (the dog) is one species, *Canis lupus* (the wolf) is another of the same genus. Such scientific names are usually written in italics. Strictly the name (sometimes abbreviated) of the author responsible for naming and describing the species should follow, e.g. *Canis lupus* Linn. (the author here being Linnaeus). When subsequent to the original description the species has been transferred to a different genus, the original author's name is put into brackets. It is usual for one specimen to be designated as the 'type' of a given species; in any later splitting of the species the original specific epithet must continue with the type and those specimens like it (see *Type Specimen*). These and other rules form part of the International Rules of Nomenclature, with separate rules for Botany and Zoology. Naming is supervised by an international committee. The binomial system was introduced by the early herbalists, and was first systematically applied by Linnaeus in the middle of the eighteenth century. The names used by Linnaeus in the *Species Plantarum* (1753) and in the tenth edition of his *Systema Naturae* (1758) are the basis of the system for plants and animals respectively, apart from a few groups with which he did not deal, for which other classical descriptive works serve. Species not included in these are given the epithet first applied to them. If such an epithet is later found not to have been the first given to the species, it must, according to the rules of priority, be replaced by the earlier one, which leads to some instability of nomenclature. Provision is however made in special cases for waiving the rules. Where sub-species or varieties have been defined, a trinomial system is commonly used, the third name indicating the sub-species or variety, e.g. *Troglodytes troglodytes troglodytes*, the British wren.

BIO-ASSAY. Quantitative estimation of biologically active substances by the amount of their actions in standardized conditions on living organisms or parts of organisms, e.g. androgen estimation on capon's comb.

BIOCHEMISTRY. Study of chemical substances and chemical processes of living things.

BIOGENESIS, PRINCIPLE OF. The biological rule that a living thing can originate only from a parent or parents on the whole similar to itself. It denies both spontaneous generation (q.v.) and such fanciful notions current 300 years ago as the origin of geese from barnacles. If allowance is made for alternation of generations, complex life cycles, extreme sexual dimorphism, castes, and hybridization, it is true; though it may possibly need further qualification in the case of the simpler viruses, which it has been suggested may arise from normal constituents of cells.

BIOLOGIC SPECIALIZATION. See *Physiologic Specialization*.

BIOLOGICAL CONTROL. Artificial control of pests and parasites by use of other organisms, e.g. of mosquitoes by fishes or by insectivorous plants which feed on the larvae; or of prickly pear in Australia by parasitic insects.

BIOLOGY. Study of living things.

BIOLUMINESCENCE. Production of light by living organisms, e.g. fireflies, numerous marine animals, many bacteria and fungi. The light is due to an enzyme-catalysed chemical reaction which produces very little heat. It is of various colours. In animals may be under nervous control. See *Phosphorescence*.

BIOMASS. The weight of all the organisms forming a given population or trophic level, or inhabiting a given region.

BIOME. Major regional ecological community of plants and animals extending over large natural areas, e.g. tropical rain forest, coral reef. The plants of land biomes comprise the *formations* (q.v.) of plant ecologists.

BIOMETRY. Application of mathematics to the study of living things; particularly statistical study of resemblances and differences between groups of related organisms.

BIONOMICS. (Zool.) Study of the relation of an organism or population of organisms to its environment, animate and inanimate.

BIOPHYSICS. Application of physics to the study of living things.

BIOPOIESIS. Generation of living from non-living material.

BIOSPHERE. That part of the earth and its atmosphere which is inhabited by living things.

BIOSYSTEMATICS. Aspect of systematics (q.v.) concerned with variation and evolution of species. More or less equivalent to experimental taxonomy.

BIOTIC FACTORS. Environmental influences that arise from activities of living organisms, as distinct from e.g. climatic factors.

BIOTYPE. (1) Naturally occurring group of individuals having the same genetic composition. (2) Physiologic race, see *Physiologic specialization*.

BIRAMOUS APPENDAGE. Forked appendage of Crustacea. The two branches may be similar, e.g. abdominal appendages of crayfish, or dissimilar.

BISEXUAL. Hermaphrodite (q.v.).

BIURET REACTION. Biochemical test used for proteins in solution. Employs copper sulphate in alkaline solution, which gives purple colour with proteins and with a few other substances.

BIVALENT. Two homologous chromosomes while they are pairing during meiosis (q.v.).

BIVALVE. Animal with a shell in two parts hinged together, e.g.

lamellibranch Mollusca (mussels, etc.), Brachiopoda (lamp shells).

BLADDER. See *Gall Bladder, Swim Bladder, Urinary Bladder.*

BLADDERWORM. Cysticercus (q.v.).

BLASTEMA. (Zool.). Mass of undifferentiated cells which later develops into an organ. One of the two main ways by which an animal regenerates a lost part is by initial formation of a blastema (e.g. limb or tail of newt, head of flatworm); the other way being by remodelling of remaining tissue (morphallaxis).

BLASTOCOELE. Cavity which appears within the mass of cells formed towards end of period of cleavage of the egg of many animals. See *Blastula.*

BLASTOCYST. Stage in mammalian development resulting from cleavage, which is roughly the equivalent of a blastula. A thin-walled hollow sphere (trophoblast) with at one side a knob or sheet of cells destined to become the embryo proper.

BLASTODERM. Superficial sheet of cells formed as result of cleavage (q.v.) of a yolky egg. In a yolky vertebrate egg (such as hen's egg) the blastoderm is a flat disc of cells at one pole of the yolk. In an insect's egg it is a layer of cells which completely surrounds the internal mass of yolk.

BLASTOMERE. (Zool.). One of the cells formed from the fertilized egg during cleavage.

BLASTOPORE. (Zool.). Transitory opening on surface of embryo in gastrula stage, by which the internal cavity (archenteron) communicates with the exterior; produced by invagination (q.v.), of superficial cells in the course of movements of gastrulation (q.v.), to form endoderm and mesoderm. In many animals the blastopore becomes the anus; in others it closes up at the end of gastrulation, and the anus later breaks through at the same place or nearby. In some animals gastrulation movements carry endoderm and mesoderm cells inwards at a particular place without forming an open pore (e.g. in a primitive streak, q.v.); the place of inward migration may then be called a virtual blastopore. See *Organizer.*

BLASTULA. Stage of embryonic development of animals, at or near the end of period of cleavage, and immediately preceding gastrulation movements. Usually (in those animals with complete cleavage) consists of a hollow ball of cells.

BLEPHAROPLAST. See *Centriole.*

BLIND SPOT. Place where optic nerve enters retina of vertebrate eye; devoid of rods and cones and hence blind. See Fig. 3, p. 107.

BLOOD. A fluid of animals contained in vessels or spaces with endo-thelial walls, circulated by muscular action of vessels or specialized parts of them (hearts), usually containing respiratory pigments, and carrying oxygen, food-materials, excretions, etc., through the body. Present in Nemertea, Annelida, Arthropoda, Mollusca, Brachiopoda, Phoronidea, Chordata.

BLOOD CLOTTING (B. COAGULATION). Conversion of liquid

blood to jelly, occurring when blood-vessels are injured. Prevents escape of blood. In vertebrates, a soluble blood-protein (fibrinogen) is converted to tangle of insoluble threads (fibrin) by an enzyme (thrombin). Thrombin is formed from a blood-protein (prothrombin) by an activator (thrombokinase) liberated from injured tissues or from blood platelets (q.v.); removal of free calcium from blood (as by adding oxalate or citrate) inhibits thrombin formation. In some Arthropoda clotting is by projection of thread-like processes from blood-corpuscles.

BLOOD CORPUSCLE. Cell which circulates in blood. Particularly abundant in vertebrates. See *Red Blood Cell, White Blood Cell*.

BLOOD FILM. Thin smear of blood, made on a slide, fixed, dried, and stained. Used for examination of corpuscles and detection of blood parasites.

BLOOD-GROUP. Group of people bearing the same antigens on their red blood cells. There are four main groups, whose blood cannot be mixed without clumping of their red blood cells; they are A, B, AB and O. Clumping (agglutination) occurs when blood from any two different groups is mixed, owing to a reaction between substances (agglutinogens) on red blood cells, and other substances (agglutinins) in plasma. Group A has agglutinogen A on its cells and agglutin anti-B (which reacts with agglutinogen B) in its plasma. Group B has agglutinogen B and agglutinin anti-A (which reacts with agglutinogen A). Group AB has both agglutinogens but neither agglutinin. Group O has neither agglutinogen but both agglutinins. Possession of agglutinins is not due to acquired immunity; every individual has the agglutinins which react with the agglutinogens he has not got. The four groups are due to different combinations of three multiple allelomorphs, g, $I^A$, $I^B$; g is recessive to the other two, which show no dominance to each other. Homozygous g is group O, homozygous $I^A$ or heterozygous $I^A$g are group A; homozygous $I^B$ or heterozygous $I^B$g are group B; heterozygous $I^A I^B$ is AB. Proportions of the four groups within population are very different in different parts of the world. From point of view of blood transfusion, introduction of corpuscles containing agglutinogen for which recipient has agglutinin must be avoided. The converse is not so important. Members of the population differ in other antigens carried on red blood cells (e.g. M and N antigens, forming M, MN, and N types); but since agglutinins for these are not normally present in plasma, they have not the same significance in transfusion, though immunity to them may be acquired by repeated transfusion. See *Rh factor*. Similar blood groups occur in other Primates.

BLOOD PLASMA. Blood from which all blood corpuscles have been removed, e.g. by centrifuging. A clear almost colourless fluid in vertebrates which clots as easily as whole blood. See *Plasma Proteins*.

BLOOD PLATELETS. Minute bodies, probably fragments of cells, in mammalian blood. Roughly 250,000 per cu. mm. of human blood. For function, see *Blood Clotting*. In other vertebrates represented by small spindle-shaped nucleated cells, *thrombocytes*.

BLOOD PRESSURE. Usually refers to pressure of blood in main arteries, which in 'normal' human beings fluctuates roughly between 120 and 80 mm. of mercury according to stage of heart beat (maximum at systole, minimum at diastole). Pressures throughout the whole circulation diminish from arteries next to heart round to veins next to heart; in mammals reaching atmospheric or less in large veins.

BLOOD SERUM. Fluid expressed from clotted blood or from clotted blood plasma. Roughly, plasma deprived of clotting constituents.

BLOOD-SUGAR. Glucose dissolved in blood. In vertebrates supplied to blood by liver (where it is stored as glycogen) and removed therefrom by all body cells for use as food. In mammals maintained at a fairly constant level (80–180 mg. per 100 ml. blood in man), chiefly controlled by hormones (insulin and glucagon from pancreas adrenalin and glucocorticoids from adrenal gland). If level is too low (hypoglycaemia) the cells are starved, and this rapidly damages brain-cells; if too high (hyperglycaemia as in diabetes mellitus) glucose is excreted by kidney.

BLOOD-VESSEL. Tube through which blood flows. See *Artery, Arteriole, Capillary, Venule, Vein*.

BLUBBER. Thick layer of fatty tissue below dermis of skin, insulating against heat-loss, in aquatic mammals (whales, dugongs). See *Cetacea, Sirenia*.

BODY CAVITY. Internal cavity of most triploblastic animals (absent in Platyhelminthes, Nemertea) in which many organs are suspended, allowing their mutual displacement, which is especially important for the gut. Varies much in size in different groups. Bounded externally by *body wall*. Contains fluid. May develop embryologically in several ways, e.g. from coelom (earthworm, vertebrate), from blood system (Arthropoda) or as intercellular spaces (Nematoda). *Primary body cavity*, the haemocoel (q.v.). *Secondary body cavity*, the coelom (q.v.).

BONE. Skeletal substance peculiar to vertebrates. Consists of cells distributed in a matrix consisting largely of collagen fibres together with a complex salt (bone salt) mainly of calcium and phosphate. Bone salt, 60 per cent by weight of bone, is responsible for hardness; collagen for tensile strength. The cells are connected by fine channels which permeate the matrix. Larger channels contain blood-vessels and nerves.

BONY FISH. Osteichthyes (q.v.).

BOTANY. Study of plants.

BOWMAN'S CAPSULE. Part of Malpighian corpuscle of vertebrate kidney. Small sac ($\frac{1}{8}$ to $\frac{1}{16}$ mm. diameter in man); inward projection of its wall contains tuft of capillaries (glomerulus, q.v.); from it leads uriniferous tubule (q.v.).

BRACHIAL. (Adj.). Of the arm. *B. plexus.* Interconnections formed in shoulder region between the spinal nerves supplying the fore-limb (arm) of tetrapods (fifth to ninth spinal nerves in man).

BRACHIOPODA (LAMP SHELLS). Phylum of animals with a two-valved shell, superficially resembling, but not closely related to, Lamellibranchs. During adult life fixed by a stalk or by one shell; feed by currents made by ciliated epithelium. Group is now small in numbers of indviduals and of species, but was larger in Palaeozoic and Mesozoic times.

BRACT. Small leaf with relatively undeveloped blade, in axil of which arises a flower or a branch of an inflorescence.

BRACTEOLE. Small bract.

BRAIN. Anterior part of central nervous system, present in almost all bilaterally symmetrical animals, enlarged in connection with aggregation of sense organs in head region. To a varying degree co-ordinates reactions of whole body.

BRAIN STEM. Vertebrate brain excluding cerebral hemispheres and cerebellum.

BRANCHIAL. (Adj.). Of the gills.

BRANCHIAL ARCH. Visceral arch (q.v.) lying between adjacent gill-slits of fish, i.e. the third and following visceral arches in most fish.

BRANCHIOPODA. Sub-class of Crustacea; aquatic; appendages uniform and usually flattened; abdomen without appendages; includes fairy shrimps, brine shrimps, water-fleas.

BRONCHIOLE. Small (less than 1 mm. diameter) air-conducting tube of tetrapod lung, arising as branch of a bronchus, terminating in alveoli. Smooth muscle abundant in walls, controlling size of lumen; the cartilage and mucus glands found in the bronchi are absent.

BRONCHUS. Large air-tube of tetrapod lung. Each lung has one large bronchus, connecting it to trachea; within the lung the bronchus branches into smaller and smaller bronchi, and finally into bronchioles. Have cartilage plates, smooth muscle, and mucus-secreting gland-cells in wall; and lining-cells bear cilia beating towards mouth, which remove dust, etc.

BRUSH BORDER. See *Microvilli.*

BRYOPHYTA. Division of plant kingdom comprising Hepaticae (liverworts), Musci (mosses), Anthocerotae (hornworts). A small group of plants with wide distribution. Habitats various, e.g. wet banks, on soil, rock surfaces; some are epiphytes (q.v.), others aquatic. Small plants, flat, prostrate, or with a central stem up to a foot in length bearing leaves. Lacking vascular tissue. Attached to substratum by rhizoids. Reproducing sexually by fusion of male and female gametes produced in multicellular sex organs: antheridia, liberating male gametes motile by flagella, and archegonia, containing a single egg. Sexual reproduction is followed by development of a capsule, containing spores, which give rise, directly or indirectly, to new plants. Bryophyta show a well-marked alternation of generations (q.v.). The plant itself is the gametophyte generation, and the capsule is the sporophyte generation, nutritionally dependent on the gametophyte.

BRYOZOA. Polyzoa (q.v.).

BUCCAL. (Adj.). Of the mouth. *B. cavity*. Mouth cavity lined by derivative of ectoderm. *B. membrane*. Embryonic membrane closing off the mouth, formed by ectoderm of buccal cavity externally, endoderm of pharynx internally.

BUD. Compact, undeveloped shoot, consisting of a short stem bearing crowded, overlapping, immature leaves.

BUDDING. (1) (Bot.). Form of grafting in which grafted part is a bud; (2) (Bot.). Asexual reproduction in which a new cell is formed as an outgrowth of a parent cell, e.g. yeast. Cf. *Fission*; (3) (Zool.). Gemmation (q.v.).

BUFFERED. Resisting changes in pH (q.v.) when acid or alkali is added. A property of many biological fluids, and of seawater.

BULB. Organ of vegetative reproduction; modified shoot consisting of a very much shortened stem enclosed by fleshy, scale-like leaves, e.g. tulip, or leaf-bases, e.g. onion. Cf. *Corm*.

BULBIL. Small bulb.

BULLA. See *Ear, Middle*.

# C

CADUCOUS. (Bot.). Not persistent. Of sepals, falling off as flower opens, e.g. poppy; of stipules, falling off as leaves unfold, e.g. lime.

CAECUM. A blindly-ending branch of gut or other hollow organ. In amniote vertebrates and small fish there may be one or two caeca at the junction of small and large intestines; very large and important in digestion in some mammals, e.g. rabbit; vestigial in man.

CAINOZOIC. Cenozoic (q.v.).

CALCICOLE. (Of plants) growing best on calcareous soils.

CALCIFUGE. (Of plants) growing best on acid soils.

CALCITONIN (THYROCALCITONIN). Vertebrate hormone secreted by parafollicular cells of mammalian thyroid, or from separate gland (developed from gill pouches) in other vertebrates. Controls blood level of calcium, opposing the action of the parathyroid (q.v.) by reducing release of calcium from bone.

CALLOSE. Carbohydrate deposited on the sieve-plates of sieve-tubes (q.v.), bringing their activity to an end, either permanently or seasonally.

CALLUS. (Bot.). Superficial tissue developing in woody plants in response to wounding, usually by activity of cambium, protecting the injured surface. (Zool.). Material, at first containing collagen and cartilage, and later becoming bone tissue, which makes initial union of a broken bone.

CALORIE (=KILOCALORIE). (Written with capital C.) Amount of heat required to raise 1 kg of water from 15° to 16° C. One thousand times larger than the ordinary caloric of physics. Used as measure of energy turn-over in animals. E.g. daily energy output (as heat, work, and energy content of excretions) of an active man is on the average equivalent to about 3000 Calories, and food yielding that amount of heat when burned must be provided to maintain this output.

CALYPTRA. Hood-like covering of the capsule of mosses and liverworts, developed from archegonial wall.

CALYPTROGEN. Layer of actively dividing cells formed over apex of growing part of roots in many plants, e.g. grasses; gives rise to root-cap (q.v.).

CALYX. Outermost part of a flower, consisting usually of green, leaf-like members known as *sepals* that in the bud stage enclose and protect the other flower parts. See *Flower*.

CAMBIUM. A meristem (q.v.). Layer of actively dividing cells lying between xylem and phloem; forms additional xylem and phloem elements in the process known as *secondary thickening* (q.v.). The cambium of a vascular bundle is *fascicular* cambium; that formed from cells of parenchyma between vascular bundles and linking up with fascicular cambium to form a complete ring is *interfascicular* cambium. See *Cork*.

CAMBRIAN. Geological period (q.v.); lasted approximately from 570 till 500 million years ago.

CAMPYLOTROPOUS. (Of ovule), curved over so that funicle appears to be attached to the side, between chalaza and micropyle. Cf. *Anatropous, Orthotropous*.

CANADA BALSAM. Gum commonly used, dissolved in xylene, for making permanent microscopical preparations. The object is placed in a thin layer of balsam solution between cover-slip and slide. The balsam dries hard, and because its refractive index is like that of proteins and other constituents of biological objects, it makes them very transparent.

CANINE TOOTH. 'Dog' or 'eye' tooth of mammals. Usually conical and pointed, one on each side of upper and lower jaws, between incisors and premolars. Missing or reduced in many rodents and ungulates. Sometimes enlarged to tusks (wild boar, sabre-toothed tiger).

CAPILLARY, BLOOD. Minute tube (very roughly 5–20 micrometres internal diameter; a given capillary can dilate or constrict) conveying blood, which it receives from a small artery (arteriole in vertebrates) and gives up to small vein; with a wall consisting of a single layer of flattened cells (endothelium), supported by some fine connective tissue fibres. In vertebrates, capillaries in very large numbers permeate almost all the tissues. The main exchange of substances between blood and tissues occurs through capillary walls, which are permeable to small molecules (such as oxygen, glucose, amino-acids, which pass from blood to tissues; carbon dioxide which passes from tissues to blood). Walls are also freely permeable to water and salts. The reason why the water of the blood does not leak away through capillaries is that the large molecules of the blood, especially plasma proteins, are retained by capillary walls and hold back water by osmosis. In Arthropoda and Mollusca capillaries are physiologically largely replaced by haemocoel.

CAPILLITIUM. (1) Tubular protoplasmic threads in fruit bodies of Myxomycetes (slime moulds), shown to assist discharge of spores in some species by their movements in response to changes in humidity. (2) Sterile hyphae in fruit bodies of certain fungi, e.g. puff-balls.

CAPITULUM. Kind of inflorescence (q.v.).

CAPSID (OF VIRUS). Coat of virus particle (virion). Protects enclosed nucleic acid. Is involved in penetration of host cell, aiding attachment to host cell membrane and, in some bacteriophages, providing mechanism for injection of virus nucleic acid into host cell. See *Virus*.

CAPSOMER. Sub-unit of coat of virus particle (virion). See *Virus*.

CAPSULE. (1) In flowering plants, dry dehiscent fruit developed from a compound ovary (q.v.); opening to liberate seeds in various ways, e.g. by longitudinal splitting from apex to base, the separated parts being known as *valves*, as in iris; by formation of pores near top of fruit, as in snapdragon; or in the *pyxidium*, by detachment of a lid following equatorial dehiscence as in scarlet pimpernel. (2) In liverworts and mosses, organ within which spores are formed. (3) In some kinds of bacteria, gelatinous envelope surrounding the cell wall. (4) (Zool.) Connective tissue investment of an organ, providing mechanical support.

CARAPACE. (1) Shield of exoskeleton covering part of the body (several segments) of some Arthropoda, e.g. crabs. (2) Dorsal part of 'shell' of Chelonia, consisting of plates beneath the skin fused with ribs of vertebral column.

CARBOHYDRATE. Compound of general formula $C_x(H_2O)_y$; e.g. sugars, starch, cellulose. Carbohydrates play an essential part in metabolism of all organisms. They are not present in nearly such large amounts in animals as in plants, in which cellulose is a principal structural component, and starch the principal stored food.

CARBON CYCLE. World-wide circulation of carbon atoms brought about mainly by living things. Essentially, carbon from carbon dioxide is built into complex organic compounds by plants during photosynthesis. These compounds are then broken down again to carbon dioxide during respiration and by decay produced by bacteria and fungi after death; or the plants are eaten by herbivorous animals which in turn may be eaten by carnivores (see *Foodchain*) and the carbon compounds are sooner or later broken down to carbon dioxide by respiration or death and decay of the animals.

CARBONIFEROUS. Geological period (q.v.); lasted approximately from 345 till 280 million years ago.

CARCINOGEN. Producer of cancer, e.g. certain hydrocarbons which produce local cancer when injected into, or painted repeatedly on, susceptible animals.

CARDIAC. Concerning the heart. *C. cycle*, succession of muscular contractions, and movements of heart valves, which make up activity of heart from one beat to next. *C. end of stomach*, region of stomach joined to oesophagus. *C. muscle*, special kind of muscle, arranged in a meshwork of muscle fibres with cross-striations, which gives motive power to heart. Undergoes automatic rhythmical contractions.

CARDINAL VEINS. Main longitudinal veins, one on each side, returning blood from most of the body to ducti Cuvieri (q.v.) and thence to heart, in fish and embryos of tetrapods. *Anterior cardinals* (jugulars) are in front of ducti Cuvieri, *posterior cardinals* are behind. See *Vena cava inferior*.

CARINA. Keel (q.v.).

CARINATES. Living birds other than ratites. Most of them are capable of flight, with well-developed wings, barbules on feathers, and keel (carina) on sternum for attachment of wing muscles. The term is not now commonly used in classification of birds.

CARNASSIAL TOOTH. Molar or premolar, modified for shearing flesh. In many Carnivora (e.g. dog, cat), lower first molar and upper last premolar.

CARNIVORA. Order of placental mammals containing flesh-eating forms (cats, wolves, bears, seals). Most members of the order (but not seals) have well-developed incisor and canine teeth and usually a pair of carnassial teeth on each side. Possess claws, often retractile.

CARNIVORE. Flesh-eater. Cf. *Herbivore, Omnivore.* In narrower sense, member of order Carnivora.

CAROTENE. Carotenoid (q.v.) plant pigment.

CAROTENOIDS. Group of yellow, orange and red plant pigments located in chloroplasts and in plastids in other plant parts where chlorophyll is absent, e.g. carrot roots, many flowers; and in photosynthetic lamellae of blue-green algae and some bacteria. Also occur in some fungi. Increase in concentration in many ripening fruits, e.g. tomato. Not essential to, but assist in, photosynthesis by absorbing light and passing energy on to chlorophyll. Protect cells from photochemical damage in several bacteria, including both photosynthetic and non-photosynthetic species. Long chain compounds (tetraterpenes). Include carotenes ($\alpha$, $\beta$-, etc.) and xanthophylls (lutein, flavoxanthin, fucoxanthin, zeaxthanthin, etc.). Carotene of food is changed to vitamin A in vertebrate liver.

CAROTID ARTERY. Main artery supplying blood from heart to head of vertebrates. One on each side. See *Aortic Arches.*

CAROTID BODY. Vascular structure close to carotid sinus (q.v.) containing sensory nerve endings responding to oxygen and carbon dioxide content of blood, producing reflex changes in respiration.

CAROTID SINUS. Small swelling in carotid artery containing sensory nerve endings responding to blood pressure, producing reflex adjustments of circulation.

CARPAL BONES. Bones of the proximal part of the foot of the forelimb (roughly of the wrist) in tetrapods. Compact group of primitively 10–12 bones; reduced to eight in man. Articulate on proximal side with radius and ulna, on distal side with metacarpals. See Fig. 7, p. 213.

CARPEL. Female reproductive organ of flowering plants, a megasporophyll; consisting of ovary containing ovules (q.v.) which become seeds after fertilization, and stigma (q.v.) a receptive surface for pollen grains, often borne at the apex of a stalk, the style. See *Flower.*

CARPOGONIUM. Female sex organ of red algae. Consists of swollen basal portion containing the egg and an elongated terminal projection (trichogyne) which receives the male gamete.

CARPOSPORE. Spore produced after sexual reproduction in red algae; borne at end of outgrowth of fertilized carpogonium. See *Cystocarp*.

CARPUS. Region of fore-leg of tetrapod vertebrates containing carpal bones (q.v.); roughly the wrist.

CARTILAGE. Skeletal tissue of vertebrates consisting of rounded cells scattered in a resilient polysaccharide-containing matrix, with numerous collagen fibres. Devoid of blood-vessels in adult. A carti-lage-like substance occurs in Cephalopoda (squids, octopuses), where it supports the brain.

CARTILAGE-BONE (REPLACING BONE). A bone which replaces embryonic cartilage, e.g. limb bones; hip girdle; vertebral column; parts of skull such as auditory capsule. Cf. *Dermal bone*.

CARUNCLE. Warty outgrowth seen on seeds of a few flowering plants, e.g. castor oil, obscuring micropyle (q.v.).

CARYOPSIS. Fruit of grasses. An achene (q.v.) with ovary wall (pericarp) united with seed coat (testa).

CASPARIAN STRIP. Area impervious to water in form of a strip running completely round radial and transverse walls of cells of endodermis (q.v.), resulting from impregnation of primary wall with substances giving reaction for suberin and lignin, respectively; may be as wide as wall itself, or narrow, thread-like. Thought to ensure that movement of water and solutes across endodermis is completely subject to regulatory activity of living protoplasm of its cells.

CASTE. Of social insects, a type of structurally and functionally specialized individual. E.g. among hive bees there are three castes, queens (fertile females), workers (females, usually sterile), drones (males). Among ants there may be several different kinds of workers (all sterile females). In termites the distinction between castes is not related to sex (as it is in the bees and ants), e.g. 'soldiers' may be sterile males or females. See *Poly-morphism*.

CATABOLISM (KATABOLISM). Breaking down by living things of complex organic molecules, with liberation of energy. See *Meta-bolism, Anabolism*.

CATALASE. Enzyme which breaks down the poisonous substance hydrogen peroxide, formed during plant and animal metabolism, to water and oxygen. Its prosthetic group (q.v.), containing iron, is the same as that of haemoglobin.

CATARRHINE. Old world anthropoid. Characterized by narrow nasal septum and by menstrual cycle, e.g. baboon, chimpanzee, man. Cf. *Platyrrhine*.

CATECHOLAMINE. The biologically important catecholamines are adrenaline (q.v.) and noradrenaline (q.v.) and the substances from which these are synthesized.

CATERPILLAR. Larva of certain insects (e.g. butterflies); soft-bodied, with three pairs of jointed legs on thorax, and short unjointed prolegs on abdomen.

CATHEPSIN. Intracellular proteolytic enzyme, normally situated in lysosomes (q.v.).

CATKIN. Kind of inflorescence (q.v.).

CAUDAD. Towards the tail.

CAUDAL. Concerning the tail.

CAULIFLORY. Production of flowering shoots on older, thickened, leafless branches or main trunk. Common among Angiosperm trees of lower stories of canopy in tropical forests, e.g. cocoa.

CAULINE. Belonging to the stem or arising from it.

CELL. (Zool.). Discrete mass of protoplasm, bounded by a plasma membrane. (Bot.). As in Zoology, but including also the surrounding cell wall (usually of cellulose or chitin). Sometimes used for cell-wall only.

Most animals and plants can conveniently be considered as made up of two components, though of course these form an integrated system in the normal organism: (a) the protoplasm, in which are situated the systems of enzymes (q.v.) responsible for controlling the chemical reactions (metabolism, q.v.) characteristic of living things, and the nucleic acid systems responsible for synthesis of the enzymes and of themselves; (b) a component, made by the protoplasm, devoid of these enzyme systems, largely composed of fibrous materials which provide mechnical support for the protoplasm, e.g. cellulose in plants, collagen in animals.

The protoplasmic component of the larger plants or animals is not usually a continuous mass; it consists of numerous discrete units. Each unit is microscopically small (a man contains something like a million million of them; (each is bounded by an extremely thin membrane (see *Plasma-membrane*) which allows some substances to pass through but not others, and so partially isolates the inside of each unit from its surroundings; and usually each contains one nucleus (q.v.), sometimes more than one, very rarely none. The shapes of such units are very various, and they may often have some special function highly developed, e.g. power of contraction in muscle; of photosynthesis in green plants. But all of them have the common features of metabolism (q.v.). Every unit originates from a pre-existing unit, usually by division into two, involving mitosis (q.v.) or some similar process which distributes the nuclear material (DNA) between the two products (but see also *Fertilization*).

Each of these units in an animal is called a cell. Each in a plant is usually called a protoplast, every protoplast being consistently surrounded, with peculiar intimacy, by a wall commonly of cellulose (which a zoologist would regard as intercellular material). The protoplast and its cell-wall are together known as the cell in botany. Historically the first use of the word cell was for the plant

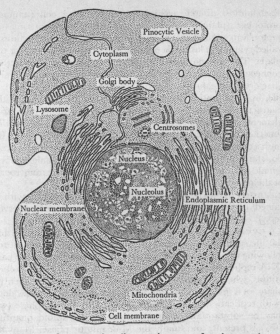

*Fig. 1. Diagram of a section of a cell as seen by means of an electron microscope.
The whole might measure 20 micrometres wide. The nucleus, in its nuclear membrane, is the large round body in the centre, containing two darker nucleoli. In
the cytoplasm, which makes up the rest of the cell, are various bodies: mitochondria (just above the label, and elsewhere); endoplasmic reticulum (consisting of parallel membranes); centrosomes (to left of the label, one cut
transversely, the other longitudinally); lysosomes (one below the label);
Golgi body (parallel membranes below the label); pinocytic vesicle, with one
just forming by an inpushing of the cell membrane.* (Reproduced by kind
permission from the *Scientific American* of September 1961.)

cell-wall and the space it enclosed: and even when the space contains no protoplast, the word is still applied in this way. Since
there is rarely a parallel in animals to the plant cell-wall, divergent
usages have unfortunately developed.

Although a cell or protoplast has been characterized above as a
discrete unit bounded by a membrane, there are cases where, while
the elements are almost entirely separated from each other by
their membranes, they are in places continuous (by intercellular
bridges or plasmodesmata, q.v.), in plants constituting a *symplasm*.

Each almost discrete element is still called a cell (animal) or protoplast (plant). There exist also large continuous masses of protoplasm with many nuclei, which are regarded as units and called syncytia, plasmodia or coenocytes rather than cells or protoplasts. There is no agreed demarcation between a collection of connected cells and a syncytium, etc. Many microscopic organisms (bacteria, algae, fungi, protozoa) consist of a single cell throughout life, in plants and bacteria complete with cell-wall, each with the characteristics (listed above) of a plant or animal protoplasmic element, though naturally without specialization of particular function, since all functions must be fulfilled by the one cell. Every multicellular animal or plant which reproduces sexually, as most do, starts as a single cell (formed by fusion of a male cell with a female cell), which by continuous doubling forms the numerous cells of the adult.

CELL-BODY (PERIKARYON). The mass of cytoplasm with contained nucleus, from which arise the branches of a nerve-cell (q.v.).

CELL CYCLE. The cycle of changes concerned with replication during the life span of a cell, from the mitosis that gives it origin to the following mitosis that divides it into daughter cells. On the basis of DNA replication the cycle is divided into the $G_1$ phase, following mitosis, when the diploid quantity of DNA is present; then the S phase, of a few hours, during which the quantity of DNA doubles (with replication of the chromosomes); then the $G_2$ phase (which may be substantially omitted) when the tetraploid quantity of DNA is present; and finally the M or mitotic phase. Many other biochemical events are correlated with the DNA cycle. The total duration of the cell cycle is rarely less than 10 hours; it may be much longer, and becomes indefinitely long when cells cease all division, such cells usually becoming arrested in $G_1$ (or $G_0$ as it is sometimes called in these circumstances).

CELL-DIVISION. Division of cell, both cytoplasm and nucleus, into two. The nucleus usually divides by mitosis (q.v.), occasionally by amitosis (q.v.). The cytoplasm divides by constriction in animals; by formation of a middle lamella across its equator in plants.

CELL-LINEAGE. Developmental history in terms of descent by cell division of later cells from earlier cells. The cell-lineage of an organ traces the succession of cells, from the zygote onwards, which culminates in the group of cells constituting that organ.

CELL-MEMBRANE. Plasma-membrane (q.v.).

CELL PLATE. (Bot.). Plate of differentially staining material which appears at telophase in the phragmoplast (q.v.) across the equatorial plane of the spindle. Believed to be forerunner of middle lamella (q.v.). See Cell-wall.

CELL-THEORY. Theory, initiated by Schleiden and Schwann, 1838–9, that all animals and plants are made up of cells (q.v.) and their products, and that growth and reproduction are fundamentally due to division of cells.

CELLULOSE. Fundamental constituent of cell wall in higher plants, many algae and some fungi. Occurs also in Urochordata. Long chain polysaccharide made up of β-glucose units. In primary cell wall long chain cellulose molecules are aligned in parallel and bonded together in groups of up to 200 to form crystalline *micelles*. Micelles and unoriented cellulose molecules form a loose network with pectin filling the interstices. This organization allows for wall extension in cell growth and more cellulose is laid down between existing micelles. In secondary wall micelles associate to form long strands, *microfibrils*, separated by non-cellulose material, and laid down in successive layers, in different directions, conferring rigidity on wall. Fibrous nature of cellulose is responsible for its use in textile industries (cotton, linen, artificial silk). See *Cell-wall*.

CELL-WALL. Limiting layer of plant cells, formed by, and closely investing, the protoplasm; comparatively rigid and giving mechanical support to plant tissue. In living cells traversed by extremely fine cytoplasmic threads, the plasmodesmata, which form delicate protoplasmic connections between adjacent cells. The walls of newly formed cells are at first very thin but as the cells assume their permanent character the walls thicken. In formation of new cells pectic material is laid down in the cell plate across equatorial plane of division spindle to form the *middle lamella*, intercellular material that cements together adjacent cells. Each new cell lays down a *primary wall* consisting of cellulose, hemicelluloses and pectic substances. When cell has reached full size it may remain with primary wall only, e.g. some forms of parenchyma. In other cells a *secondary wall* is laid down inside primary wall. During deposition of these layers certain small areas remain virtually unthickened forming pits. Pits of adjacent walls usually coincide so that in these areas the protoplasts are separated only by the pit membrane consisting of the middle lamella and a very thin layer of primary wall on each side of it. Through pit membranes pass the majority of plasmodesmata (q.v.). Some cell walls undergo further modification, e.g. cuticularization of epidermal cells and suberization of cork cells, rendering them impermeable to water; lignification of fibres, vessels, tracheids, conferring on them increased strength and rigidity. See *Cellulose*.

CEMENT. Bone-like substance which makes a thin covering to root of vertebrate tooth (i.e. below gum level) and in some mammals (e.g. ungulates) covers parts of enamel of crown.

CENOZOIC (CAINOZOIC). See *Geological Periods and Epochs*. The present era, the age of mammals; extends from about 65 million years ago.

CENTRAL DOGMA. See *Code, genetics*.

CENTRAL NERVOUS SYSTEM (C.N.S.). A mass of nervous tissue

which co-ordinates the activities of an animal. In vertebrates the C.N.S. is the brain and spinal cord, which together are basically a single hollow tube with very thick walls, enclosed within skull and backbone. In most invertebrates the C.N.S. consists of a few solid cords of nervous tissue, often associated with larger masses called *ganglia* (q.v.). In some invertebrates however (Coelenterata, Echinodermata) the place of a C.N.S. in providing co-ordination is taken by a diffuse *nerve-net* (q.v.).

The C.N.S. is in a position to co-ordinate the activities of an animal with each other and with the environment because almost all the messages (impulses, q.v.) sent from the sense-organs travel straight into the C.N.S., and almost all impulses received by the muscles, glands, etc., come out from the C.N.S. The C.N.S. contains many fairly direct nervous pathways between certain sense-organs and certain muscles or glands (see *Reflex*) which ensure that some stimuli are followed rapidly by their appropriate standardized responses. But there is also great opportunity in the C.N.S. for co-ordination of a variety of stimuli by interaction between nerve cells, because of the large number of junctions (synapses) between nerve cells which occur there. In vertebrates for instance, the great majority of synapses occurs in the C.N.S. The C.N.S., however, is not to be regarded simply as a means of reconciling and co-ordinating the immediate activities of the sense-organs; it has an activity of its own independent of the stimuli of the moment, most obvious in the influence of past experience on present performance. The rest of the nervous system, other than the C.N.S., is the peripheral nervous system. See *Nervous System*, *Nerve-cell*.

CENTRE (NERVE). Region of central nervous system with a restricted special function, e.g. respiratory centre in medulla of vertebrates which controls respiratory movements. The term is physiological (cf *Nucleus of Brain*).

CENTRIOLE. Minute rod-shaped body, 300–500 nm long and 150 nm diameter, present in many resting cells, just outside the nuclear membrane. Cylindrical, containing nine short, parallel, peripheral fibrils, each fibril consisting of one to three sub-fibrils. Doubles during or after mitosis, and at the beginning of the next mitosis the two centrioles move apart and form the poles of the spindle, and the centres of the asters when present. Absent in higher plants. Similar structures, known variously as *basal bodies*, *kinetoplasts*, *kinetosomes*, *blepharoplasts*, are connected to axial filaments of flagella (q.v.) and cilia, e.g. in sperm, zoospores.

CENTROMERE. Spindle-attachment (q.v.).

CENTROSOME. Region of differentiated cytoplasm containing centriole.

CENTRUM. Massive part of each vertebra, lying ventral to spinal cord. Replaces embryonic notochord. Each centrum is firmly but flexibly attached to adjacent centra by collagen fibres.

CEPHALIC INDEX. Measure of shape of human head: breadth as percentage of length (back to front).

CEPHALOCHORDATA. Acrania (q.v.).

CEPHALOPODA (SIPHONOPODA). Class of Mollusca including octopus, squids, cuttle-fish. Head well developed, with crown of mobile tentacles; eyes large and complex; nervous system highly centralized.

CERCARIA. One of the larval forms of flukes (Trematoda); produced asexually by redia larvae (q.v.) while these are parasitic in snails. Cercariae are infective to a new host to which they gain access either in food (sheep liver-fluke) or by penetrating skin (*Schistosoma*). This new host may be the definitive one, in which the cercariae become sexually mature flukes; or in some species it may be a second intermediate host, where they live for some time before being swallowed by definitive host and becoming sexually mature.

CERCI. Paired appendages, often sensory, at hind end of abdomen of many insects. 'Forceps' of earwigs are modified cerci.

CEREAL. Flowering plant of the family Gramineae whose seeds are used as food, e.g. wheat, oats, barley, rye, maize, rice, sorghum.

CEREBELLUM. Outgrowth of anterior end of dorsal surface of hind-brain of vertebrates, varying from a mere transverse commissure in cyclostomes to a conspicuous part of the brain in birds and mammals (with a cortex of grey matter in mammals). Particularly concerned in co-ordination of complex muscular movements.

CEREBRAL CORTEX. Layer of grey matter (q.v.) rich in synapses, superficial to white matter, present in cerebral hemispheres of amniotes, and some anamniotes, but really extensive only in mammals (neopallium, q.v.).

CEREBRAL HEMISPHERES. Paired outpushings of front end of fore-brain of vertebrates. In early vertebrates mainly concerned with sense of smell; but in amniotes general co-ordinating functions become predominant; and in mammals hemispheres are largest part of brain, with a much folded cortex by which much of animal's activities are controlled.

CEREBROSPINAL. (Adj.). Of the brain and spinal cord of vertebrates.

CEREBROSPINAL FLUID (C.S.F.). Fluid which fills the cavity inside vertebrate brain and spinal cord, and the pia-arachnoid (q.v.) space outside them, the inside and outside communicating by holes in the roof of the hind-brain. Secreted continuously by choroid plexuses (q.v.) and reabsorbed by veins of surface of brain. It is a solution of the small molecules of the blood (salt, glucose, etc.; though not in the same concentration as in the blood) almost devoid of protein and containing very few cells. About 100 ml. is present in man.

CERUMEN. Ear wax. Secretion of skin glands (perhaps modified sweat glands) of external ear passage in mammals.

CERVICAL. (Adj.). Of the neck, or of the cervix of the uterus. *C. vertebrae* have reduced or absent ribs; they are concerned in movement of head. Mammals (even giraffes) are peculiar in having seven, whatever the length of their neck, with the exception of the manatee (*Manatus*, order Sirenia, 6) and two kinds of sloth (*Bradypus*, 9 or 10, and *Choloepus*, 6, both order Xenarthra).

CERVIX (C. UTERI). Cylindrical posterior part of the uterus of mammals, which leads into the vagina. Contains numerous glands supplying mucus to vagina.

CESTODA. Tapeworms (q.v.). Class of Platyhelminthes. Parasites; with cuticle; without gut. Complicated life cycle.

CETACEA. Whales, porpoises, dolphins. An order of placental Mammals. They are completely aquatic, and have many special features connected with this mode of life, such as layer of fat (blubber) in the skin; no hind limbs and only traces of pelvic girdle; fore-limbs paddle-like; tail-fin transverse (unlike fishes); often a dorsal fin.

CHAETA. Bristle, made largely of chitin, characteristic of chaetopod Annelida (bristleworms, earthworms) in which they occur in groups projecting from the skin, segmentally arranged. In some cases assist locomotion, e.g. earthworm. Term may also be applied to bristles of other animals, e.g. of Brachiopoda. See *Seta.*

CHAETOGNATHA. Arrow-worms. Small phylum of marine animals of doubtful affinities. Includes *Sagitta*, abundant in plankton.

CHAETOPODA. A class of Annelida including bristleworms (order Polychaeta) and earthworms (order Oligochaeta). Well-segmented; coelom spacious; chaetae present.

CHALAZA. (Bot.). Basal region of Angiosperm ovule where stalk (funicle) is attached. (Zool.). Of a bird's egg. Twisted strand of fibrous albumen; two are attached to the vitelline membrane, at opposite poles of the yolk, lying in the long axis of the egg; they stabilize the position of the yolk and early embryo in the albumen.

CHAMAEOPHYTES. Class of Raunkiaer's Life Forms (q.v.).

CHAROPHYTA Stoneworts (from characteristic incrustation with calcium carbonate). Division of algae Occur in ponds. Possess chlorophylls a and b and store reserve food as starch. Thallus multicellular, filamentous, anchored to bottom by rhizoids and bearing lateral branches in whorls. Wall of cellulose. Exceptional in possessing multicellular sex organs, antheridia and oogonia.

CHELA. A pincer. e.g. of lobster.

CHELONIA. Tortoises and turtles. Order of reptiles with body enclosed in plates of bone usually covered by epidermal horny plates (tortoiseshell). Shoulder and pelvic girdles unique in being inside the ribs. No teeth.

CHEMOAUTOTROPHIC (CHEMOSYNTHETIC). Obtaining energy from a simple inorganic reaction, the nature of which varies according to species, e.g. oxidation of hydrogen sulphide to sulphur by *Thiobacillus*. Several kinds of autotrophic bacteria are chemoauto-trophic.

CHEMORECEPTOR. Sensory receptor which detects and differentiates substances according to their chemical structure, by contact with their molecules, e.g. smell, taste.

CHEMOSYNTHETIC. Chemoautotrophic (q.v.).

CHEMOTAXIS. Taxis (q.v.) in which stimulus has the form of a gradient of chemical concentration, e.g. movement of polymorph leucocytes in response to substances diffusing from bacteria; or of fern spermatozoids to archegonia in response to malic acid diffusing from archegonial necks.

CHEMOTROPHIC. Of organisms, obtaining energy by chemical reactions independent of light. The reactions may be based on inorganic substances (this is chemoautotrophic) or organic substances obtained from the environment. Cf. *Autotrophic, Heterotrophic, Phototrophic*.

CHEMOTROPISM. (1) (Bot.). Tropism (q.v.) in which stimulus has the form of a gradient of chemical concentration, e.g. downward growth of pollen tubes into stigma due to presence of sugars. (2) (Zool.). Sometimes used synonymously with chemotaxis (q.v.).

CHIASMA (plural CHIASMATA). (1). Connections between chromatids of homologous chromosomes, visible during meiosis (q.v.), where the interchange involved in crossing-over (q.v.) has occurred. See *Meiosis*. Fig. 6B, page 181. (2). See *Optic Chiasma*.

CHILOPODA. Centipedes. Order (or class) of Arthropoda. See *Myriapoda*.

CHIMAERA (CHIMERA). (1) Organism whose tissues are of two or more genetically different kinds. Can occur as a result of mutation or abnormal distribution of chromosomes, affecting one cell and all its descendants, during development; or as a result of natural or artificial grafting of two different plants or animals, whose cells become associated, producing mixing of characters: such a plant is often called a *graft hybrid*. See *Mosaic*. (2) Generic name of a fish 'King of the Herrings' (Holocephali).

CHIROPTERA. Bats. Order of placental mammals. Characterized by membranous wing spread between arms, legs, and sometimes tail, and supported by greatly elongated fingers.

CHITIN. Nitrogen-containing polysaccharide (q.v.) with long fibrous molecules, forming material of considerable mechanical strength and resistance to chemicals. Present in covering layer (cuticle, q.v.) of insects. Similar substance is found in cell walls of many fungi.

CHLAMYDOSPORE. Thick-walled fungus spore capable of surviving conditions unfavourable to growth of the fungus as a whole; asexually produced from a cell or portion of a hypha.

CHLORENCHYMA. Parenchymatous tissue containing chloroplasts (q.v.).

CHLOROCRUORIN. Respiratory pigment (green, fluorescing red) in blood of certain Polychaeta. A protein containing iron; closely related to haemoglobin.

CHLOROPHYLL. Green pigment found in all algae and higher plants (with exception of a few saprophytes and parasites); located in chloroplasts (q.v.) except in blue-green algae (Cyanophyta) where it is borne on numerous photosynthetic membranes scattered in cytoplasm at cell periphery. Magnesium porphyrin compounds chemically related to prosthetic groups of haemoglobin and cytochrome. Responsible for light capture in *photosynthesis* (q.v.) and is site of first stage of transformation of light energy to chemical energy. Several chlorophylls exist, with minor differences in chemical structure; chlorophyll a is the only one common to all organisms that possess chlorophyll (the only one in blue-green algae) and is believed to be specifically required. In a few photo-synthetic bacteria other kinds of chlorophyll, *bacteriochlorophylls*, occur.

CHLOROPHYTA. Green algae. Division of algae. Possess chlorophylls a and b, α- and β-carotene, xanthophylls, and store reserve food as starch. Cellulose cell wall. Largest group of algae, very diverse. Primitive forms microscopic, unicellular, motile by flagella, or non-motile; occurring singly or grouped into colonies. Higher forms multicellular with filamentous or flattened thallus. Asexual reproduction by cell division, fragmentation of thallus or by zoo-spores. Sexual reproduction isogamous or anisogamous, both gametes, or only male gamete, motile. Widely distributed, aquatic, both in fresh and salt water, or terrestrial in damp places, e.g. soil, shaded walls, tree trunks, etc.

CHLOROPLAST. Plastid containing chlorophyll; occurring (one to many) in cells of algae (excepting blue-green algae) and higher plants. Site of photosynthesis (q.v.). In higher plants usually disc shaped, arranged in single layer in cytoplasm; changing shape and position in cell in relation to light intensity; in algae variously shaped, cup-shaped, spiral, stellate, or in form of a network, one to several per cell, often accompanied by pyrenoids (q.v.). Develop from pro-plastids; and in some algae, bryophytes, lycopods, multiply by division. Consist of a double membrane enclosing a homogenous *stroma* in which are embedded a number of *grana*, each consisting of a series of membrane-bounded, flattened, disc-shaped vesicles forming lamellae known as *thylakoids*, closely arranged like coins in a pile. The membranes of the thylakoids bear the photosynthetic pigments. Grana are linked with each other by similar lamellae lying parallel one with another but farther apart than those of the grana and lacking chlorophyll. Reactions involved in absorption of light energy and its conversion to chemical energy go on in grana. Subsequent utilization of chemical energy in reduction of carbon dioxide to form carbohydrates occurs in stroma.

In algae grana do not occur and the thylakoids traverse the stroma of the chloroplast as a whole, roughly parallel to each other. Chloroplasts do not occur in blue-green algae or photosynthetic bacteria, thylakoids lying free in the cytoplasm: many per cell, varying in arrangement and shape in different forms – vesicular, tubular, lamellate or irregular.

CHLOROSIS. Disease of green plants characterized by yellow (chlorotic) condition of parts that are normally green; caused by conditions preventing chlorophyll formation, e.g. lack of light.

CHOANAE (INTERNAL NARES). Of vertebrates. Internal openings of nasal cavity (q.v.) into mouth. Present, as are also external nares opening on to face, in group Choanata; remaining vertebrate classes have only external nares. Situated near front of roof of mouth, except in those choanates with a false palate (see *Pálate*) in which they are at the back.

CHOANATA. Grouping of vertebrate classes sometimes used in classification. Includes Choanichthyes, Amphibia, Reptilia, Aves (birds), and Mammalia. These are more closely related to each other than to the other vertebrate classes. Having axial skeleton in their paired limbs, and nostrils opening into the mouth (choanae) as well as on to face.

CHOANICHTHYES. Sometimes regarded as a class of fish containing Crossopterygii and Dipnoi. Characterized by bony skeleton; paired fins with a central skeletal axis; nostrils opening both on to face and into mouth (but not in coelacanths); cosmoid scales (q.v.) or derivatives of them. Cf. *Actinopterygii* and *Chondrichthyes*, the other two classes of living fish.

CHOANOCYTE (COLLAR-CELL). Peculiar kind of cell with a flagellum surrounded by a thin protoplasmic sheath or collar, found only in sponges and a small group of Flagellata (Choanoflagellata).

CHOLESTEROL. A sterol found in all animals studied, but not in higher plants or most bacteria. An important constituent of animal cell membranes. A vitamin for insects, not for vertebrates.

CHOLINE. An organic base, a vitamin for cockroaches, and probably for some mammals which do not synthesize all they require. Choline is a constituent of certain important fats (lecithin, q.v.) and of acetylcholine (q.v.). Formula: $HO.C_2H_4.N(CH_3)_3.OH$.

CHOLINERGIC. Of a nerve fibre, secreting acetylcholine (q.v.) at its end when nerve impulses arrive there. In vertebrates, motor fibres to striped muscle, parasympathetic fibres to smooth muscle, and fibres connecting C.N.S. to sympathetic ganglia are all cholinergic. Cholinergic nerve fibres probably occur in Arthropods and other invertebrates. Cf. *Adrenergic*.

CHOLINESTERASE. Enzyme which splits and hence inactivates acetylcholine (q.v.).

CHONDRICHTHYES. Cartilaginous fish. Class of vertebrates containing the Selachii (sharks, dogfish, skates, rays), Holocephali (chimaeras), and some fossil groups. Characterized by absence of true bone (although the cartilaginous skeleton is often calcified); complicated copulatory organs ('claspers') formed from pelvic fins of males; denticles (q.v.); no air bladder. (Cf. *Actinopterygii* and *Choanichthyes*, the other two classes of living fish.) Almost exclusively marine, and unlike the other fish classes, have been so throughout their known fossil history, though ancestors probably lived in freshwater. First appear in late Devonian. See *Elasmobranchii*.

CHONDRIOSOMES. Mitochondria (q.v.).

CHONDROCRANIUM. The part of skull first formed in embryo of vertebrates, as cartilaginous investment of part of brain and inner ear. In most vertebrates some or all of this cartilage is later replaced by bones, and the skull completed by membrane bones external to chondrocranium.

CHORDA-MESODERM. Mesoderm and notochord of vertebrate embryo. In early stages of development, before differentiation, these tissues often form a continuous mass or layer of similar cells, and they are closely related in physiology of development also, e.g. see *Organizer*; consequently it is convenient for some purposes to group them together.

CHORDATA. Phylum of animals with notochord (q.v.), hollow dorsal nerve cord, and gill slits. Includes subphyla Vertebrata (Craniata) and Protochordata.

CHORIO-ALLANTOIC GRAFTING. Grafting living pieces of tissue on the outer surface of chorion, in region where allantois is fused with chorion, of a young living chick embryo. After the shell is sealed, chick continues development and blood-vessels of allantois invade graft and maintain it.

CHORION. (Zool.). Embryonic membrane of amniote vertebrate, consisting of outer ectodermal epithelium with layer of mesoderm beneath. In Sauropsida, the more superficial of the two layers which enclose the amniotic cavity. See *Amnion*. In mammals, the superficial layer enclosing all the embryonic structures (equivalent therefore to sauropsid chorion plus outer layer of yolk-sac); its outer epithelium is trophoblast (q.v.); forms placenta (q.v.). See Fig. 8, p. 225. (2) Non-cellular membrane secreted around ovum by cells of ovary, e.g. the superficial envelope or 'shell' of an insect egg.

CHOROID. Layer, in vertebrate eye, immediately outside retina, containing blood-vessels and pigment. See Fig. 3, p. 107.

CHOROID PLEXUS (CHORIOID PLEXUS). Numerous projections, into cavity (ventricle) of brain, of the non-nervous epithelium which constitutes its roof in some regions, enclosing tufts of blood-vessels. Secretes cerebrospinal fluid. One plexus occurs in roof of each of the four ventricles in man.

CHROMAFFIN TISSUE OR CELL. Producer of adrenaline or noradrenaline (in adrenal medulla and also widely distributed in

vertebrate body). Stains with chromates. *C. granule*, vesicle in c.
cell, containing adrenaline or noradrenaline; discharges into blood
vessel when the cell is stimulated to secrete.

CHROMATID. One of the two strands, which result from duplication
of a chromosome at S phase, visible during prophase and metaphase of mitosis or meiosis. They separate at anaphase and are then
known as daughter-chromosomes.

CHROMATIN. Nucleo-protein of chromosomes, which stains strongly
with basic dyes.

CHROMATOPHORE. (1) (Bot.). Chromoplast (q.v.). (2) Zool.). Cell
with pigment as granules in its cytoplasm. In many vertebrates
(e.g. chamaeleon, frog) and Crustacea, rapidly changing dis-
position (concentration or dispersion) of the pigment granules
within the cell, alters colour of animal. (3) In procaryotic organisms (bacteria and blue-green algae), membrane-bounded vesicles
(thylakoids) bearing photosynthetic pigments.

CHROMOCENTRE. Granule of condensed chromatin (heterochromatin) numbers of which are found scattered within most interphase nuclei.

CHROMOMERES. Darkly staining granules found in constant arrangement along prophase chromosomes during meiosis. Chromomeres
in corresponding positions on homologous chromosomes pair during
meiosis in many organisms. Probably mark positions where chromosome thread is more tightly coiled than in other regions.

CHROMOPLAST (CHROMATOPHORE). Pigmented plastid (q.v.) of
plant cells. May be red, orange, or yellow, e.g. tomato fruits, carrot
roots, containing carotenoid pigments; or green (chloroplasts),
containing chlorophyll. Former are common in fruits and flowers,
and develop from leucoplasts or chloroplasts; chloroplasts are responsible for the green colour of plants. In algae variously coloured
owing to presence with chlorophyll of other pigments, xanthophyll,
carotene, fucoxanthin, phycoerythrin, phycocyanin.

CHROMOSOME. Thread-shaped body, consisting largely of DNA and
protein, numbers of which occur in the nucleus of every animal or
plant cell. Bacteria and viruses have structures of similar function,
but consisting of DNA (or in some viruses RNA) only. They occur
in pairs, usually several different pairs per nucleus, in somatic cells
of animals and higher plants (but see *Endomitosis*). The two members of each pair are identical in appearance and are said to be *homologous* (to each other). Homologous chromosomes associate in a
characteristic way (pairing, q.v.) during meiosis. Chromosomes of
different pairs are often visibly different from each other in e.g. size,
shape. There are one to over 100 pairs per nucleus according to
species (man has twenty-three, *Drosophila melanogaster* four pairs)
and most cells of most individuals of a given species have a set of
similar chromosomes which is characteristic of that species.
Gametes, and cells of the gametophyte (q.v.) of plants, have only

one member of each pair in their nuclei. Chromosomes are usually
visible only during mitosis or meiosis, when they contract in length,
finally becoming short thick rods (a few micrometres long), probably by coiling up into a spiral. Fine threads have however been
seen in the living resting nucleus which are probably the extended
chromosomes. Chromosomes stain strongly with basic dyes (they
are *basophilic*) during mitosis and meiosis.

Chromosomes are elaborately differentiated in structure along their
length. This differentiation consists of a series of different genes
(q.v.) in single file, presumably along a linear strand of DNA;
a spindle-attachment at some point in their length; and regions of
heterochromatin (q.v.). The arrangement of these elements is
practically the same in all homologous chromosomes. In some
species the arrangement of many of the genes (i.e. of the loci) has
been discovered (see *Chromosome Map*); it can be correlated with
visible markings on the giant salivary gland chromosomes (q.v.).
A short time before every nuclear division (mitosis, q.v.) each
chromosome doubles and the two duplicates separate to the two
daughter nuclei at mitosis. Essentially, this involves the replication
(q.v.) of the DNA. For the behaviour of chromosomes during
gamete formation, of great importance to genetics, see *Meiosis*, Fig.
6B, p. 181.

See *Sex Chromosome, Autosome, Salivary Gland Chromosome, Lampbrush
Chromosome*.

CHROMOSOME MAP. Plan showing positions of the genes on a
chromosome. For eucaryotes, it can be constructed from data of
crossing-over (q.v.), the frequency of crossing-over between the
genes taken in pairs indicating their linear order, i.e. *relative*
positions; the distances on such a map are given in units of cross-
over value. This provides a *linkage map*. Or it can be constructed
by observations of localized aberrations of a chromosome (especially salivary) which produce phenotypes known to be
associated with presence or absence of particular genes. The results
of the two methods agree. Various methods of chromosome map-
ping are used for procaryotes; for bacteria, especially by the inter-
ruption at various times of the linear transfer of a chromosome
between two cells during mating.

CHRYSALIS. Pupa (q.v.).

CHRYSOLAMINARIN (LEUCOSIN). Polysaccharide reserve food
material found in algae belonging to divisions Chrysophyta and
Xanthophyta.

CHRYSOPHYTA. Golden brown algae. Division of algae. Golden
brown in colour due to abundance of carotenoid pigments, including $\alpha$, $\beta$-carotene, fucoxanthin and other xanthophylls present
with chlorophyll a. Reserve foods stored as oils and as polysaccharide chrysolaminarin (=leucosin). Many lack cell wall. Where
present wall composed of pectic substances, with cellulose in some

forms; may also bear superficial scales (calcified or silicified in some species). Flagella one or two, variable in type and length. Highly diverse group of microscopic marine and fresh water algae, unicellular, colonial, filamentous, amoeboid, many planktonic, with interesting links to the other simple organisms, protozoa, fungi.

CILIARY BODY. Thickened circular rim of choroid of vertebrate eye, at border of cornea, containing *ciliary muscles* which produce accommodation (q.v.). It secretes aqueous humour (q.v.). To it the lens is attached; and from it the iris springs. See Fig. 3, p. 107.

CILIARY FEEDING. Feeding by filtering minute organisms from a current of water drawn through or towards the animal by cilia, as in amphioxus.

CILIATA. Group of ciliated unicellular organisms. See *Ciliophora*. Includes *Paramecium*.

CILIATED EPITHELIUM. (Zool.). Sheet of cells, each cell with several cilia on exposed surface. The cilia beat in co-ordinated rhythm. A common method of moving fluids in animal body, e.g. in many microphagous animals (q.v.) or in respiratory passages of land vertebrates.

CILIOPHORA. Class of Protozoa, characterized by the possession of cilia and double nucleus (macro- and micro-nucleus). Some of the most complex single-celled organisms known belong to this group. Includes Ciliata, which are ciliated throughout life, and Suctoria, which are ciliated only in their immature form.

CILIUM (PL. CILIA). Fine cytoplasmic thread projecting, along with many others, from the surface of a cell. Cilia of a cell or of a whole epithelium lash with orderly beat in a constant direction. Each cilium moves the fluid surrounding it by lashing stiffly through it like an oar, and then bending on its recovery stroke so as to offer less resistance. Have same internal structure as flagellum (q.v.) from which they probably only differ in their relative shortness. Present in one group of Protozoa (Ciliophora) and all Metazoa except Arthropoda (though present in Onychophora) and Nematoda. In Metazoa commonly occur on *ciliated epithelia*. Cilia like those of animals occur only in few plants, e.g. Cycads; but the term is often used in botany synonymously with flagellum (q.v.).

CIRCADIAN RHYTHM (DIURNAL RHYTHM). Endogenous rhythmic changes that occur in an organism with a periodicity of approximately twenty-four hours when organism is isolated from daily rhythmical changes in its environment. These rhythms are widely demonstrable amongst plants and animals. Examples are leaf movements and growth in plants, sleep rhythms and running activity in animals. Such rhythms are considered to be a fundamental expression of the ability of plants and animals to measure time although the underlying biochemical and biophysical processes are largely unknown. Circadian rhythms are considered to be a basis of photoperiodism (q.v.): the two component phases of the circadian rhythm are postulated as skotophile ('dark loving') and photophile ('light loving').

CIRCULATORY SYSTEM. The system of blood vessels.

CIRCUMNUTATION. See *Nutation*.

CIRRIPEDIA. Barnacles. Sub-class of Crustacea; aquatic; sessile. Feed by drawing a current of water towards the mouth with their whip-like appendages; or parasitic.

CISTERNAE. Flattened sac-like vesicles of endoplasmic reticulum (q.v.) and Golgi apparatus (q.v.).

CIS-TRANS EFFECT. Two mutations at non-corresponding places somewhere in a given pair of homologous chromosomes (within the cells of a diploid organism) can be in either of two arrangements. (1) Both mutations may be on one chromosome of the pair, the homologous chromosome being normal (*cis* arrangement); or (2) each member of the pair carries one of the mutations (*trans* arrangement). Similarly, two types of heterokaryon are possible, the cis heterokaryon where both mutations are carried in the same nucleus, and the trans heterokaryon, where the two mutations are in different nuclei. If the two mutations are in functionally different parts of the given pair of chromosomes (i.e. in different *cistrons*), the cis and trans arrangements will not be phenotypically different; since a normal functional unit (cistron) would be present in one of the pair of homologous chromosomes, ensuring a normal gene product, say a particular enzyme: the mutations behave as classical recessives. In these circumstances, when the mutations are in the trans arrangement, *complementation* (q.v.) is said to occur between the two chromosomes, each supplying the deficiency of the other. The outcome is otherwise when the two mutations lie in different parts of a given pair of homologous functional units (cistrons). In the cis arrangement, one of the pair of functional units, and hence the organism, will be normal. But in the trans arrangement the functional unit concerned is defective in both chromosomes and there will be no normal gene product, no complementation. This difference of effect of the cis and trans arrangements is the *cis-trans effect*. It follows that a functional unit of a chromosome or cistron may be defined, and was originally defined, simply by means of breeding experiments, as a length of chromosome (or DNA) within which a cis-trans effect occurs, or within which complementation does not occur.

CISTRON. A gene defined functionally, i.e. a length of DNA producing the RNA that in turn produces a specific polypeptide chain that functions in the economy of the cell or organism. See *Cis-trans effect*.

CITRIC ACID CYCLE. Krebs Cycle (q.v.).

CLADISTIC. (Of similarity of plants) close, reflecting recent origin from common ancestor. A kind of *patristic* (q.v.) relationship.

CLADOCERA. Water-fleas. Order of Crustacea.

**CLADODE (PHYLLOCLADE).** Modified stem having appearance and function of a leaf, e.g. butcher's broom.

**CLASS.** One of the kinds of group used in classification of organisms, e.g. Mammalia; Dicotyledoneae. Consists of a number of similar orders (sometimes of only one order). Similar classes are grouped in a phylum (or more usually in Botany in a division). See *Classification*.

**CLASSIFICATION.** Organisms are classified scientifically in a hierarchical series of groups. The smallest group regularly used is the species (q.v.). Species which are more like each other than like other species are grouped together in a genus; similarly genera are grouped into families, families into orders, orders into classes, classes into phyla or divisions, and phyla or divisions into kingdoms, the highest taxonomic rank. Various sub-groups are also used as necessary. All groups of any one kind, e.g. all families, are supposed to have approximately the same 'weight', e.g. every family is supposed to differ from its related families belonging to the same order, by a roughly equal amount and the same degree of difference should be found in every order. Consequently a single peculiar family like that comprising genera of amphioxus cannot be put in an order along with any other family, and must form an order, and in this case a class and sub-phylum, by itself.

Usual form of classification, *natural* classification, is based on overall resemblances, as distinct from *artificial* classification based on one or few characters and used for special purposes, e.g. ease of identification. Since the more closely related by descent organisms are, the more features they have in common, natural system of classification may also reflect degrees of evolutionary relationship, i.e. it may also be *phylogenetic*. The system generally accepted is not a rigid one. Biologists differ among themselves on many points of classification, and the system is always subject to modification as more and more is learnt about organisms, and about their fossil history. At present the criteria used for classifying organisms are almost entirely structural; but as we learn more of biochemical and physiological differences, other criteria will no doubt be used in constructing the classificatory system.

**CLAVICLE.** Dermal bone of ventral side of shoulder-girdle of many vertebrates. Collar-bone of man. See Fig. 10, p. 265.

**CLEARING.** Part of usual process of preparation of tissues for microscopical examination. Consists in soaking tissue in substances such as benzene or xylene, after dehydration (q.v.). These substances bridge the gap, caused by mutual insolubility, between the alcohol used in dehydration and the substances usually used in the next stage of preparation, e.g. paraffin wax (see *Microtome*), or Canada balsam (q.v.), by being miscible with both. Incidentally the tissue becomes very transparent in most clearing agents.

**CLEAVAGE (SEGMENTATION).** Repeated subdivision of the zygote cytoplasm, accompanying corresponding nuclear mitosis, which follows fertilization. In animals often produces a mass of small cells, the blastula. Usually called segmentation in plants. See *Holoblastic, Meroblastic, Bilateral cleavage, Spiral cleavage*.

CLEIDOIC EGG. Egg of terrestrial animal enclosed within protective shell, which largely isolates it from its surroundings, permitting only respiration and some loss (occasionally gain) of water. See *Uricotelic*. E.g. egg of bird or insect. Contrasted with most marine eggs, which exchange water and salts fairly freely with their surroundings.

CLEISTOCARP. Completely closed fruit body of certain Ascomycete Fungi, e.g. powdery mildews, from which spores are liberated by decay or rupture of its wall.

CLEISTOGAMY. Fertilization within an unopened flower, e.g. violet.

CLIMAX. Community of organisms the composition of which is more or less stable, in equilibrium with existing natural environmental conditions, e.g. oak forest in lowland Britain. Cf. *Plagioclimax*.

CLINE. Continuous gradation of form differences in a population of a species, correlated with its geographical or ecological distribution.

CLISERE. Succession of climaxes (q.v.) in an area as a result of climatic changes.

CLITELLUM. Saddle-like region of some Annelida (earthworms, leeches). Prominent in sexually mature animals. Contains glands which secrete a mucus sheath around copulating animals thus binding them temporarily together, and a cocoon in which fertilization and development of eggs occur.

CLITORIS. Homologue of penis in female mammal.

CLOACA. Terminal part of gut of most vertebrates into which kidney and reproductive ducts open; in such cases there is only one posterior opening to the body, the cloacal aperture, instead of (as in most mammals) separate anus and urinogenital openings. Also terminal part of intestine in some invertebrates, e.g. sea cucumbers.

CLONE. The descendants produced vegetatively or by apomixis from a single plant; asexually or by parthenogenesis from a single animal; by division from a single cell. The members of a clone are of the same genetic constitution, except insofar as mutation occurs amongst them.

CLUB MOSS. See *Lycopodiales*.

CNIDARIA. Hydroids, jellyfish, sea-anemones, corals. Subphylum of Coelenterata. Have thread cells; body of a polyp or medusa; locomotion by muscular action, not cilia (cf. *Ctenophora*). Contains classes Hydrozoa, Scyphozoa, Actinozoa.

CNIDOBLAST. Thread cell (q.v.).

CNIDOCIL. Sensory hair of thread cell (q.v.).

C.N.S. Central nervous system (q.v.).

COBALAMINE (VITAMIN B$_{12}$). Cobalt-containing vitamin required by many organisms. Lack of it upsets cell division. In man, the haemopoietic principle necessary for red blood cell formation is produced from the vitamin by a substance secreted in the stomach.

COCCIDIOSIS. Disease of rabbits, fowls, etc., caused by certain Sporozoa parasitic in, e.g. intestine, liver.

COCCUS. Globular bacterium.

COCCYX. Tail vertebrae fused together. In man, consists of three to five vestigial vertebrae.

COCHLEA. That part of the inner ear concerned in the reception of sound with analysis of its pitch. A projection of the saccule. Found in crocodiles, birds, and mammals. In the latter coiled in a spiral.

COCOON. Protective covering of eggs, larvae, etc.; e.g. eggs of some annelids are fertilized and develop in a cocoon. See *Clitellum*. Larvae of many insects spin a cocoon in which pupae develop (cocoon of silkworm moth is source of silk).

CODE, GENETIC. In protein synthesis, the exact sequence of amino acids laid down in the protein is determined by the sequence of nucleotides (there being 4 different nucleotides) in the *Messenger RNA* (q.v.), which in turn depends on the sequence of nucleotides in DNA. The genetic code is the system of correspondence between nucleotide sequence and amino acid sequence. Each of the 20 amino acids is specified by a different arrangement, called a *codon*, of 3 adjacent nucleotides (triplet code). There are 64 possible arrangements of 3 nucleotides, and many amino acids are specified by more than one triplet. The translation of the code, which occurs only in the nucleic acid to protein direction (the 'central dogma' of molecular biology), is performed by *Transfer RNA* (q.v.).

CO-DOMINANT. See *Dominant*.

CODON. Sequence of three adjacent nucleotides, in Messenger RNA (q.v.) or in the corresponding DNA, that determines a particular amino acid. See *Code, genetic*.

COELACANTHINI. A large order of Crossopterygii, almost all fossil (from Devonian onwards) and fresh-water, but with living marine representatives off S. Africa (see *Latimeria*).

COELENTERATA. Phylum of animals containing hydroids, jellyfish, sea-anemones, corals, comb-jellies. All aquatic, most marine. Body built on a fairly simple plan; more or less radially symmetrical; of jelly-like consistency; gut (coelenteron) has one opening only; nervous system diffuse; no excretory system; no blood system. The body-wall is usually described as having only two layers of cells (diploblastic, q.v.); but while this statement is true of the delicate hydroids and of *Hydra* which is usually cited as a 'type' of the group, it needs qualification for jellyfish, sea-anemones, and comb-jellies. See *Mesogloea*. Phylum contains subphyla Cnidaria (classes Hydrozoa, Scyphozoa, Actinozoa) and Ctenophora.

COELENTERON. The single cavity within the body of a coelenterate. It serves as a gut, and in some groups eggs and sperm are discharged into it. Has a single opening.

COELOM. Main body cavity (q.v.) of many triploblastic animals, in which gut is suspended. Situated in the mesoderm, lined by epithelium (mesothelium). Contains fluid which, unlike blood, is not circulated by muscular walls (except in some leeches). Germ-cells mature in its walls or in a specialized part of it (the gonads); and when they are ripe they are often shed into the coelom, and are then usually transported to exterior by *coelomoducts* (e.g. oviducts of vertebrates). In many animals plays important part in collecting excretions which are removed from it by nephridia or coelomoducts. Coelom is spacious in Echinodermata, Vertebrata, polychaete and oligochaete Annelida (though not in Hirudinea) where it forms the perivisceral cavity. In Arthropoda and Mollusca it forms only the cavity of gonads and excretory organs, and not the perivisceral cavity, which is a haemocoel.

COELOMODUCT. Duct formed from lining of coelom (i.e. from mesoderm) connecting coelom with exterior; sometimes used for conveying products of gonads to exterior; sometimes excretory, e.g. kidneys of Mollusca.

COENOBIUM. Colony of algal cells, constant in number and arranged in a specific manner, coordinated and behaving as a unit, e.g. *Volvox*.

COENOCYTE. (Bot.). Multinucleate mass of protoplasm formed by division of nucleus but not of cytoplasm of an original cell with single nucleus, e.g. many fungi and some green algae. Cf. *Plasmodium*, *Syncytium*, *Cell*.

COENOSPECIES. Group of species related by the possibility, directly or indirectly, of forming fertile hybrids one with another.

COENZYME. Organic compound playing essential part in reaction catalysed by some enzyme or system of enzymes, without being consumed in the process. In systems of enzymes, which catalyse a chain of reactions, a coenzyme usually undergoes a chemical change under the influence of one of the enzymes, and is then reconstituted by a later enzyme in the chain. Many coenzymes are known, and the same one may function in reactions catalysed by different enzyme systems.

COLCHICINE. Drug (an alkaloid) which prevents mitosis proceeding beyond metaphase (by inhibiting spindle through disruption of microtubules). In actively dividing tissue of an organism treated with colchicine there is an accumulation of cells arrested in metaphase making easy the detection of proliferating regions. Reversion of colchicine-inhibited metaphase nuclei to the resting state results in polyploidy (q.v.) since the chromosomes have duplicated without the chromatids separating into daughter nuclei. This is a method of inducing polyploidy artificially, important in obtaining new agricultural and horticultural varieties. See *Allotetraploid*.

COLEOPTERA. Beetles. A very large order of endopterygote insects. Forewings horny, covering hind part of body; hind wings membranous, may be small or absent. Larvae may be active predators (campodeiform) or caterpillar-like (eruciform) or a grub (apodous). Some important agricultural pests belong to this order, e.g. bollweevil, wireworm.

COLEOPTILE. Protective sheath surrounding plumule (q.v.) in grass seedlings.

COLEORHIZA. Protective sheath surrounding radicle (q.v.) in grass seedlings.

COLLAGEN. Fibrous protein, which on boiling yields gelatin. Forms intercellular fibres ('white fibres' of vertebrate connective tissue). One of principal skeletal substances, binding cells and tissues together, probably throughout the Metazoa. Fibres made of collagen have a high tensile strength (exemplified by tendon) but unlike elastin fibres have little reversible extensibility. Identifiable by a peculiar amino acid, hydroxyproline, which hardly occurs elsewhere in animals. Superficial cuticle of some invertebrates, e.g. earthworm, is a protein like collagen. Leather is tanned, i.e. fixed, collagen of dermis. See *Fibroblast, Reticulin Fibres*.

COLLAR-CELL. Choanocyte (q.v.).

COLLATERAL BUNDLE. See *Vascular Bundle*.

COLLATERAL CIRCULATION. Alternative route(s) through blood vessels that blood can take to supply a given part of the body. If main route becomes blocked, an alternative route usually enlarges.

COLLEMBOLA. Springtails; order of small wingless insects (see *Apterygota*) which jump by sharply extending the abdominal appendages.

COLLENCHYMA. Tissue providing mechanical support to young, actively growing plant structures, stems, petioles, leaves; uncommon in roots. Consisting of living cells with walls strengthened by cellulose thickening, usually in the corners; still capable of extension. Commonly found in cortex of herbaceous stems and along veins of leaves. Cf. *Sclerenchyma*.

COLON. Large intestine of vertebrates, excluding the narrower terminal rectum. In amniotes and some Amphibia, but not in fish, clearly marked off from small intestine by valve, and probably largely concerned with absorption of water from faeces.

COLONIAL ANIMAL. Kind of animal which is organized as associations (colonies) of incompletely separate individuals. E.g. many Hydrozoa, Polyzoa.

COLOSTRUM. Maternal milk of mammal formed during the first few days after the birth. Particularly rich in proteins, including antibodies in some mammals, especially ungulates.

COLUMELLA. (1) Dome-shaped structure present in sporangia of many phycomycete fungi of the order Mucorales (pin moulds), produced by formation of convex septum cutting off sporangium from hypha bearing it. (2) Sterile central tissue of moss capsule.

COLUMELLA AURIS. Rod of bone or cartilage connecting ear-drum to inner ear, and transmitting sound, in reptiles, birds, and Anura. Homologous with hyomandibula of fishes, stapes of mammals.

COMMENSAL. (Of members of different species) living in close association, e.g. in same burrow, shell, or house, without much mutual influence, i.e. not symbiotic.

COMMISSURE. (1) Transverse cord of nerve-fibres uniting members of each pair of ganglia in double nerve-cord of Arthropoda and Annelida. (2) *Circum-oesophageal commissure*, nerve cord connecting ganglia in head above oesophagus with those below it, in e.g. Arthropoda and Annelida. (3) Bundle of nerve-fibres connecting right and left sides of brain or spinal cord in vertebrates. (4) Nervous cords uniting ganglia of Molluscs.

COMMON. (Of a vascular bundle), passing through stem and leaf. Cf. *Cauline*.

COMMUNITY. Ecological term for any naturally occurring group of different organisms inhabiting a common environment, interacting with each other especially through food relationships, and relatively independent of other groups. Communities may be of varying sizes, and larger ones may contain smaller ones. See *Association, Consociation, Society*.

COMPANION CELLS. Small cells, characterized by dense cytoplasm and prominent nucleus, lying side by side with sieve-tube cells in phloem of flowering plants and arising with them by longitudinal division of common parent cells.

COMPENSATION POINT. In darkness green plants respire, taking up oxygen and giving off carbon dioxide. In weak light photosynthesis begins as well, removing carbon dioxide and releasing oxygen. With increase in light intensity rate of photosynthesis increases until a point, the *compensation point*, is reached at which rates of photosynthesis and respiration are equal and there is neither absorption nor evolution of either carbon dioxide or oxygen. With further increase in light intensity carbon dioxide is absorbed and oxygen is given off. The compensation point has also been defined in terms of carbon dioxide concentration. The $CO_2$ *compensation point* is the concentration of carbon dioxide in the surrounding atmosphere at which rates of carbon dioxide intake and evolution in photosynthesis and respiration respectively, are equal. It differs in different plant species.

COMPENSATORY HYPERTROPHY. Increase in size of residual part of a tissue or organ, some of which has been removed or put out of action, e.g. when one kidney is removed other enlarges. See *Hypertrophy, Regeneration*.

COMPETENCE. Of embryonic tissues; ability to react to a stimulus which causes development in a particular direction. Before determination (q.v.) tissues are usually competent to develop in a number of different directions. When tissues become determined, they lose their competence.

COMPETITIVE INHIBITION. Where two processes compete for some material which both use, inhibition of one process by diversion of available supplies of the material to the other. Particularly used of competing enzyme systems.

COMPLEMENT. A group of substances, normally present in the blood of vertebrates, which takes an essential part in the lethal action (lysis) of antibody (q.v.) on bacteria and other cells. Activity is rapidly destroyed by heat. Complement often disappears from serum in which an antigen-antibody reaction has occurred: this 'complement-fixation' can be used to test for presence of an antigen or an antibody, and is basis of Wasserman test for syphilis.

COMPLEMENTAL MALES. Males which live attached to females, and are usually small and more or less degenerate, except for reproductive organs; found in e.g. certain Crustacea, angler-fish.

COMPLEMENTATION. (1) *Inter-cistron* complementation. The effect of two homologous chromosomes, each mutant and defective but in different cistrons, which when together in a diploid organism or in a heterokaryon, supply each other's deficiencies and give a phenotype which is very similar to, or identical with, normal (wild type). (2) *Intra-cistron* (or inter-allele) complementation. Interaction in a diploid organism or in a heterokaryon of two alleles of the same cistron to give a phenotype closer to, but not identical with normal (wild type) than either could give alone. See *Cis-trans effect*.

CONCENTRIC BUNDLE. See *Vascular Bundle*.

CONCEPTACLE. Cavity containing sex organs, occurring in groups on terminal parts of branches of thallus in some brown algae, e.g. bladder wrack.

CONDITIONED REFLEX. A reflex (q.v.) modified by experience, the original sensory component (i.e. the stimulus, sense organ, and sensory nerve path involved in it) being replaced by a different sensory component, the motor component (i.e. the response) remaining unchanged. E.g. food placed in a dog's mouth evokes reflex flow of saliva. If the introduction of food is accompanied by ringing a bell, and this is repeated several times, the bell alone eventually becomes able to evoke the salivation; though the effect is temporary unless reinforced from time to time by administering both food and bell. The original salivation reflex, which is inborn, i.e. does not depend on the experience of the animal, is the *unconditioned reflex*; it is not lost as a result of the experiment. The induced response to the bell alone is a conditioned reflex.

CONDUCTION. Passage of a physiological disturbance through a cell or tissue as a result of stimulation at one point, e.g. conduction of nerve impulse. See *Impulse*.

CONDYLE. Ellipsoid knob of bone, which fits into a corresponding socket of another bone, the condyle and its socket forming a joint allowing movement in one or two planes but no rotation; e.g. condyle at each side of lower jaw, where it articulates with skull;

occipital condyles on skull of tetrapods, fitting into atlas vertebra.

CONE. (Bot.). (*Strobilus*). Reproductive structure consisting of a number of sporophylls (q.v.) more or less compactly grouped on a central axis, e.g. cone of pine tree. (Zool.) Kind of light-sensitive nerve-cell present in retina of most vertebrates (though usually not in those which live in dim light). The cone-shaped outer segment of the cell, which is the light-sensitive part, consists largely of a stack of flat and parallel unit membranes (q.v.) at right angles to the cell length; it develops embryologically from a cilium and retains its characteristic 9+2 pattern of fibrils (see *Flagellum*). There are about 6 million cones in the retina of a primate. Concerned in colour discrimination, and in the most acute discrimination of detail. See *Fovea, Rod.*

CONIDIOPHORE. See *Conidium*.

CONIDIUM. Asexual spore of certain fungi cut off externally at apex of specialized hypha (conidiophore).

CONIFERALES. Order of Gymnospermae including extinct forms and nearly all living gymnosperms, pine, spruce, cedar, yew, larch, etc.; characteristic of temperate regions, majority tall, evergreen, forest trees. Usually monoecious with distinct male and female cones. Microsporophylls borne directly on cone axis; female cones compound, ovules borne on ovuliferous scales in the axils of bracts arising from the cone axis.

CONJUGATION. (1) Union of gametes, free-swimming or not, especially in isogamy (q.v.). (2) Union between two cells in certain bacteria (*Escherichia* and related genera) allowing passage of genetic material from one, the donor cell, to the other, the recipient cell. One important difference from sexual reproduction in other organisms is that usually only part of genetic material is transferred from the donor cell. (3) Process by which sexual reproduction is effected in most Ciliata. In the simplest cases two individuals partially fuse; macronuclei disintegrate and micronuclei undergo changes, including meiosis, resulting in production of two gamete nuclei from each; one gamete nucleus from each organism passes into the other organism and there fuses with the stationary gamete nucleus, so that a zygote nucleus results in each individual. The organisms then separate, the zygote nycleus undergoes further divisions and ultimately gives rise to a micronucleus and macronucleus. (4) Also used more loosely as synonymous with syngamy.

CONJUNCTIVA. The layer of mucus-secreting epidermis, with underlying connective tissue, covering the white of the eye and lining the eyelids in vertebrates.

CONNECTIVE TISSUE. Vertebrate tissue consisting of *connective tissue fibres* usually mainly of collagen (q.v.), but with varying amounts of elastin and reticulin; scattered cells (fibroblasts and macrophages); blood and lymph vessels; tissue fluid in spaces; and an amorphous polysaccharide-containing matrix. Supporting or

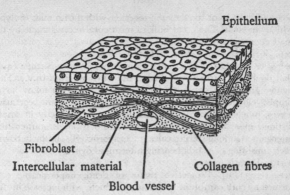

*Fig. 2. Diagram of a piece of connective tissue covered with epithelium*

packing in function. Many modifications occur. See *Adipose Tissue, Fascia*. See Fig. 2.

CONSOCIATION. (Of plants), climax unit of natural vegetation dominated by *one* particular species; e.g. beechwood, dominated by the common beech tree. Cf. *Association*.

CONSTITUTIVE ENZYME. Enzyme whose synthesis, unlike that of an adaptive enzyme (q.v.) does not have to be induced by the presence of the substrate or similar substance.

CONSUMMATORY ACT. See *Appetitive behaviour*.

CONTACT INSECTICIDE. Poison which kills insects without their eating it, by e.g. penetrating body surface or blocking spiracles.

CONTOUR FEATHERS. Feathers with barbules (q.v.), forming smooth surface of bird.

CONTRACTILE VACUOLE. Of Protista, particularly in many fresh water species, and of fresh water sponges, a membrane-surrounded vacuole which periodically expands, filling with water, and then suddenly contracts, expelling its contents to exterior of cell. It probably removes the water which continually enters the cell by osmosis from the environment or with food.

CONVERGENCE. Evolution such as to produce an increasing similarity in some characteristic(s) between groups of organisms which were initially different.

COPEPODA. Sub-class of Crustacea; some minute marine species occur in the plankton in such numbers as to be important for fishes.

CORACOID. Bone of shoulder-girdle of vertebrates, on ventral side. Meets scapula at glenoid cavity. A cartilage-bone. Reduced to small process of scapula in mammals (except monotremes). See Fig. 10, p. 265.

CORAL. Calcareous skeleton or fused skeletons of various Coelenterates and Polyzoa or the skeleton together with the animals (polyps) which secrete it. The great bulk of most coral reefs is made by the madreporarians (Actinozoa).

CORD. See *Spinal Cord*. *Umbilical Cord*.

CORDAITALES. Order of extinct, palaeozoic Gymnospermae (q.v.) that flourished particularly during the Carboniferous (q.v.). Tall, slender trees with dense crown of branches bearing many large, simple, elongated leaves. Sporophylls distinct from vegetative leaves, much reduced in size and arranged compactly in small, distinct, male and female cones. Microsporophylls stamen-like, interspersed among sterile scales; megasporophylls similarly borne, each consisting of a stalk bearing a terminal ovule.

CORIUM. Dermis (q.v.).

CORK (PHELLEM). Protective tissue of dead, impermeable cells formed by cork cambium (phellogen), which, with increase in diameter of young stems and roots, replaces the epidermis. Developed abundantly on the trunk of certain trees, e.g. cork oak, from which it is periodically stripped for commercial use.

CORM. (Bot.). Organ of vegetative reproduction; swollen stem base containing food material and bearing buds in the axils of scale-like remains of leaves of previous season's growth, e.g. crocus, gladiolus. Cf. *Bulb*.

CORMOPHYTES. Plants possessing stem, leaf and root, i.e. ferns and related plants (Pteridophyta) and seed plants (Spermatophyta).

CORNEA. The transparent epithelium and connective tissue at front surface of the eye of vertebrates, overlying iris and lens. Mainly responsible in land vertebrates for the refraction which results in focusing an image on retina.

CORNIFICATION. Conversion of cells into keratin, e.g. in epidermis.

COROLLA. Usually conspicuous, often coloured part of a flower, within the calyx, consisting of a group of petals. See *Flower*.

CORONARY VESSELS. Arteries and veins of vertebrates carrying blood supply of heart muscle.

CORPORA ALLATA. Small glandular organs in the head of insects. Produce a 'juvenile' hormone which ensures that the larva maintains larval characteristics after moulting, rather than changing into an adult.

CORPUS LUTEUM. Temporary organ of internal secretion, of the hormone progesterone (q.v.). Formed in mammals in interior of a ruptured Graafian follicle after ovulation, by ingrowth of follicle wall, which becomes yellow secretory *luteal tissue* (corpus luteum means 'yellow body'). Formation occurs as a result of action of luteinizing hormone (q.v.) and its secretory activity requires presence of lactogenic hormone (q.v.) of pituitary. If ovulation does not result in fertilization, then corpus luteum soon degenerates (see *Oestrous Cycle*). If fertilization occurs, corpus luteum persists and continues secreting during part or all of pregnancy. Bodies similar to corpus luteum occur in viviparous vertebrates other than mammals.

CORRELATION (in development). Co-ordination of growth of one part of a plant with that of other part(s), e.g. apical dominance, inhibition by shoot apex of growth of lateral buds.

CORTEX. An outer layer or rind. (1) Of plants, parenchyma tissue surrounding the vascular cylinder in stems and roots and bounded on the outside by the epidermis (q.v.). See *Stele*. (2) *Adrenal c.*, see *Adrenal gland*. (3) Of *brain*, see *Cerebral Cortex*. (4) Of *cell*, see *Ectoplasm*.

CORTICOSTEROIDS (CORTICOIDS). Various steroids produced in cortex of adrenal gland (q.v.); some are hormones.

CORTICOTROPIN. ACTH (q.v.).

CORTISONE. One of the hormones produced by the cortex of the adrenal gland (q.v.), predominantly a glucocorticoid, 17-hydroxy-11-dehydrocorticosterone. Has the usual complex effects of cortical hormones, and notably produces a diminution of local inflammation and healing responses.

CORYMB. Kind of inflorescence (q.v.).

COSMOID SCALE. Scale typical of primitive Choanichthyes. Three layers; outer like a layer of fused teeth (denticles), consisting of dentine with pulp cavities and thin superficial covering of modified, enamel-like dentine (ganoine); middle of loose, vascular bone; inner layer of bone in compact laminated sheets. Scale grows thicker by adding to inner layer only (cf. *Ganoid scale*).

COSTAL. Concerned with rib.

COTYLEDON. Leaf, forming part of embryo (q.v.) of seeds; much simpler in structure than later formed leaves and usually lacking chlorophyll. Monocotyledons have one, dicotyledons two cotyledons in each seed. In gymnosperms the number varies. Cotyledons play an important part in the early stages of seedling development. In some seeds, e.g. peas, beans, they are storage organs from which the seedling draws food; in other seeds, e.g. grasses, food stored in another part of the seed, the endosperm (q.v.), is absorbed by the cotyledons and passed on to the seedling. In addition, the cotyledons of many plants later appear above ground, develop chlorophyll, and synthesize food material by photosynthesis (q.v.).

C.O.V. Cross-over value (q.v.).

COVERSLIP. Extremely thin (about ⅛ mm.) piece of glass used to cover specimens (sections, whole mounts, etc.), which have been prepared on a slide for microscopical examination.

COXA. Basal segment of insect leg.

CRANIAL NERVE. Peripheral nerve emerging from brain of vertebrate, i.e. originating within the skull; as distinct from spinal nerve, which emerges from spinal cord. Dorsal and ventral roots (see *Nerve Root*) of several segments exist amongst these nerves, but (unlike those of spinal cord) remain separate. Each root is numbered and named as a separate nerve, but the numbering bears little relation to segmentation of head. Olfactory and optic nerves are not equivalent to either dorsal or ventral roots. There are ten cranial nerves on each side in living anamniotes, eleven or twelve in amniotes and fossil amphibians. Include nerves supplying eyes, ears, nose, jaw muscles, skin of face, etc. See *Olfactory, Optic, Oculo-motor, Trochlear, Trigeminal, Abducens, Facial, Auditory, Glossopharyn-geal, Vagus, Accessory, Hypoglossal nerves.*

CRANIATA. Vertebrata (q.v.).

CRANIUM. Skull (of vertebrates). See *Neurocranium, Splanchnocranium.*

CRETACEOUS. Geological period (q.v.) lasting approximately from 135 till 65 million years ago.

CRINOIDEA. Feather stars, sea-lilies. Class of Echinodermata. Have long, branched, feathery arms. Usually sedentary and stalked, but the only British form (*Antedon*) is free as adult, sedentary as larva. Long and important fossil history, from Cambrian onwards.

CRISTA. See *Mitochondria.*

CRITICAL GROUP. Group of related organisms in which, though variations exist, it is difficult to detect and define units suitable for taxonomic recognition.

CROCODILIA. Alligators and crocodiles. An order of Reptilia, with internal openings of the nose far back in the mouth owing to the presence of a long bony false palate (q.v.) (as in mammals).

CROP. In vertebrates, expanded part of oesophagus in which food is stored, e.g. in pigeon; in invertebrates, an expanded part of gut near head end in which food may be stored or digested.

CROPMILK (PIGEON'S MILK). Secretion consisting of crop epithe-lium of male and female pigeon on which nestlings are fed. Like mammalian milk, production is strongly influenced by hormone prolactin (q.v.).

CROSS. Act or product of cross-fertilization.

CROSS-FERTILIZATION. Fusion of male and female gametes derived from different individuals of the same species. Cf. *Self-Fertilization.*

CROSSING-OVER. Failure of linkage (q.v.) between genes of the same linkage-group, due to mutual exchange, between chromatids of homologous chromosomes, of parts containing corresponding loci. Takes place during pairing of chromosomes at meiosis, and in some organisms, e.g. *Drosophila*, certain fungi, has also been shown to occur at mitosis. Points on the chromosomes where crossing over has just occurred are visible during meiosis (q.v.), and are known as chiasmata. See Fig. 6B, p. 181.

CROSSOPTERYGII. Sub-class of Osteichthyes or of Choanichthyes. Almost all freshwater. Bony skeleton; paired fins with a central skeletal axis; cosmoid scales (q.v.) or derivatives of them. Many fossil forms, which include ancestors of land vertebrates, but only one known living genus (*Latimeria* q.v.). Differ from Dipnoi in having normal conical teeth. First appeared in Devonian (about 400 million years ago), and their known fossil record ceases 70 million years ago.

CROSS-OVER VALUE (C.O.V.). Frequency of crossing over between two genes in different parts of the same chromosome, expressed as percentage of gametes in which one of the two genes has been exchanged for an allele from the homologous chromosome. See *Chromosome map*.

CROSS-POLLINATION. Transference of pollen from stamens of a flower to stigma of a flower of another plant of the same species. Cf. *Self-pollination*.

CRUSTACEA. Class of Arthropoda, including shrimps, crabs, water-fleas, etc. Mostly aquatic; two pairs of antennae; one pair of mandibles; other limbs biramous. See *Cirripedia, Cladocera, Copepoda, Amphipoda, Isopoda, Decapoda*.

CRYOPHYTES. Plants growing on ice and snow; micro-plants, largely consisting of algae but including also some mosses, fungi, and bacteria. Algal forms may be so abundant as to colour substratum, e.g. 'red snow' due to presence of species of *Chlamydomonas*.

CRYPTIC COLORATION. Coloration of animals which conceals by resemblance to surroundings.

CRYPTOGAMIA. Name given by early systematic botanists to a group of plants consisting of Thallophyta, Bryophyta, and Pteridophyta; so called because the organs of reproduction in these plants are not prominent as they are in conifers and flowering plants (Phanerogamia).

CRYPTOPHYTA. Division of algae. Small group of unicellular, mainly motile algae with two slightly unequal flagella emerging from a sub-apical pit (gullet). Cells dorsi-ventrally compressed, majority naked with firm cell membrane, others with cellulose wall. Reproduction by cell division. Variously pigmented. Possess chlorophylls a and c, carotenoids α-, ε- carotene, xanthophylls; and, in some genera, phycobilin pigments distinct from those of Cyanophyta (q.v.) and Rhodophyta (q.v.). Food reserve is starch or starch-like. A few heterotrophs occur, saprophytic or ingesting food particles. Occur in marine and fresh water.

CRYPTORCHID. With testes not descended from abdominal cavity into scrotum.

CRYPTOZOIC (Of animals). Inhabiting crevices, e.g. under stones, leaves.

C.S.F. Cerebrospinal fluid (q.v.).

CTENOPHORA. Comb-jellies, sea-gooseberries, Venus' girdle, etc. Sub-phylum of Coelenterata (sometimes considered distinct phylum). Without thread cells; body neither polyp nor medusa; move by cilia fused in rows forming 'combs' or 'ctenes'; no vegetative reproduction; no sedentary phase. Cf. *Cnidaria*.

CUSP. Projection on biting-surface of mammalian molar tooth.

CUTICLE. Superficial non-cellular layer covering animal or plant; secreted by epidermis. In *higher plants* forms a continuous layer over aerial parts broken only by stomata and lenticels; protects against mechanical injury, but chief function is preventing excessive water-loss. See *Cutin*. In *Metazoa* it is present in most invertebrates, mainly made of collagen-like protein, or of chitin. In Arthropoda it is firm enough to act as skeleton and is composed of chitin and protein, hardened by lime-salts in Crustacea. In insects, it has a very thin, fairly waterproof, covering of wax which prevents excessive water-loss. In vertebrates, stratum corneum (q.v.), which is cellular, is occasionally called cuticle.

CUTICULARIZATION. Process of cuticle formation.

CUTIN. Complex mixture of oxidation and condensation products of fatty acids of which plant cuticle (q.v.) is composed.

CUTINIZATION. Impregnation of plant cell wall with cutin.

CUTIS. Skin; in vertebrates composed of epidermis and dermis.

CUTTING. Artificially detached part of plant used as a means of vegetative propagation.

CUVIERIAN DUCT. Ductus Cuvieri (q.v.).

CYANOPHYTA (MYXOPHYTA). Blue-green algae. Division comprising primitive algae with procaryotic (q.v.) cell structure. In addition to chlorophyll a, possess β-carotene, xanthophylls and phycocyanin (blue) and phycoerythrin (red) pigments. Due to different proportions of pigments species differ in colour – black, purple, red, yellow, green, blue. Reserve foods are a form of starch (amylopectin), and protein. Cell wall contains cellulose and pectin (often forming a gelatinous sheath).

Microscopic, unicellular or forming colonies; or multicellular, filamentous. Asexual reproduction by cell division, non-motile spores, or fragmentation. Flagella entirely absent, but some filamentous forms exhibit gliding movement. Thought to be without sexual reproduction but recent demonstration of genetic recombination in one species indicates existence of some form of sexuality. Related to bacteria in procaryotic cell organization but thought to represent distinct evolutionary line.

Widely distributed wherever water occurs. Marine and in freshwater, often planktonic; in hot springs, cold arctic water; in soil, on damp mud; some are symbionts (q.v.), e.g. with fungi in lichens. Some blue-green algae produce animal toxins, others fix atmospheric nitrogen and play an important part in maintaining soil fertility, e.g. in rice paddies.

CYCADALES. Order of Gymnospermae with fossil (Mesozoic), and a few living, representatives. Most primitive living seed plants. Indigenous to tropical and sub-tropical zones; living to a great age, up to 1000 years. Stem unbranched, tuberous or columnar, up to 20 metres in height, bearing a crown of fern-like leaves. Dioecious. Microsporophylls distinct from vegetative leaves, arranged in a compact cone. Megasporophylls leaf-like structures, loosely grouped, or highly modified, grouped in a compact cone. Male gametes motile by cilia.

CYCADOFILICALES (PTERIDOSPERMAE). Order of extinct, palaeozoic Gymnospermae (q.v.) that flourished particularly during the Carboniferous (q.v.). Of great phylogenetic interest. Reproducing by seeds but possessing fern-like leaves and internal anatomy combining fern-like vascular system with development of secondary wood. Micro- and megasporophylls little different from ordinary vegetative fronds, not arranged in cones.

CYCLIC AMP. Form of adenosine monophosphate produced by the enzyme adenyl cyclase at the cell surface from ATP, and diffusing thence into the interior of the cell, where it activates various enzymes. The production of c-AMP is known to occur in a number of cells sensitive to particular hormones (e.g. adrenaline, glucagon, TSH; not the steroid hormones) when the hormone impinges on the cell; and it is an essential link in the chain of reactions set going by the hormone. c-AMP seems also to be concerned in the release of the neural transmitters adrenaline and noradrenaline, when an impulse arrives at an adrenergic ending.

CYCLOPIA. Having a single median eye; sometimes occurs in vertebrates through defective induction (q.v.) of eyes by head mesoderm during embryonic development.

CYCLOSIS. (Bot.). Circulation of protoplasm in cells.

CYCLOSTOMATA. (1) Order of class Agnatha. Consists of lampreys and hagfish, the only living representatives of Agnatha (see *Ostracodermi*). Eel-like aquatic animals, with jawless sucking mouth, single nostril, no bone or scales, and no paired fins. They attach themselves by their mouths to fish, whose flesh they rasp with horny tongue, sucking the blood. (2) Sub-order of Polyzoa.

CYME. Kind of inflorescence (q.v.).

CYPSELA. Characteristic fruit of the family Compositae (sunflower, daisy, etc.). Like an achene (and usually so described) but formed from an inferior ovary and thus sheathed with other floral tissues outside ovary wall. Strictly a pseudo-nut as it is formed from two carpels.

CYSTICERCOID. Larva of certain tapeworms, cysticercus-like but with small bladder.

CYSTICERCUS (BLADDER WORM). Larval form of some tapeworms, consisting of a scolex tucked into a large bladder (cf. *Cysticercoid, Plerocercoid*); occurs in intermediate host; grows into mature tapeworm if swallowed by definitive host. See *Onchosphere*.

CYSTOCARP. Structure developed after fertilization in red algae; consisting of filaments bearing terminal carpospores (q.v.), produced from the fertilized carpogonium, the whole being enveloped in some genera by filaments arising from neighbouring cells.

CYSTOLITH. Stalked body consisting of ingrowth of cell wall bearing deposit of calcium carbonate; found in epidermal cells of certain plants, e.g. stinging nettle.

CYTOCHROME. Mixture of similar substance (proteins, with an iron-containing prosthetic group allied to that of haemoglobin) concerned, mostly as coenzymes, in cell respiration; widely distributed in aerobic organisms. Wing muscles of insects are particularly rich in it. Its oxidation by molecular oxygen, and subsequent reduction by oxidizable substances in the cell (both processes under influence of enzymes), is main way in which atmospheric oxygen enters into metabolism of cell; about 90 per cent of oxygen consumption is mediated by cytochrome. The cytochromes have characteristic absorption spectra, which makes it possible to study their reactions in living cells and tissues.

CYTOGENETICS. Science which links the study of the visible appearance of the chromosomes with genetics.

CYTOKINESIS. In a dividing cell, division of cytoplasm as distinct from division of nucleus.

CYTOKININS (PHYTOKININS). Group of plant hormones recognized (and named) because of stimulatory effect on division of plant cells. Effect requires presence of auxin (q.v.). Chemically identified as purines; first one discovered, *kinetin*, was isolated from DNA preparations from yeast and from animal tissues. *Zeatin* occurs in sweet corn kernels. Substances with similar physiological action occur in some plant tissues (fruitlets, coconut milk and other liquid endosperms); also isolated from micro-organisms causing plant tumours, witches brooms and from the infected tissues themselves. Cytokinins influence other aspects of plant growth, e.g. promote cell enlargement and seed germination, stimulate bud formation, delay senescence, counteract apical dominance. Effects believed to be associated with increase in nucleic acid metabolism and protein synthesis. Question of transport in plants not yet resolved. See *Auxins, Hormone, Gibberellins*.

CYTOLOGY. Study of cells.

CYTOLYSIS. Dissolution of cells, particularly by destruction of their surface membranes.

CYTOPATHIC. Damaging to cells.

CYTOPLASM. All the protoplasm of a cell excluding the nucleus. It is usually a transparent slightly viscous fluid with inclusions of various sizes ranging from microscopically visible plastids and Golgi apparatus to invisible ribosomes. Differentiated externally as a plasma-membrane (q.v.). See Fig. 1, p. 51.

CYTOPLASMIC INHERITANCE. Non-mendelian (extra-chromosomal) inheritance by self-propagating cytoplasmic entities; as distinct from gene (q.v.) inheritance. See *Plasmagene, Plastogene*.

CYTOSOL. Biochemical term for the soluble part of the cytoplasm when all cell organelles and other particles have been removed by centrifugation.

CYTOTAXONOMY. (Bot.). Classification based on characters of somatic chromosomes (number, size, and shape).

CYTOTOXIC. Poisonous to cells.

# D

DARWINISM. Theory of evolution by natural selection (q.v.).

DAUGHTER CELLS (D.-NUCLEI). The two cells (or nuclei) resulting from division of a single cell, usually by mitosis.

DEAMINATION. Removal of amino ($NH_2$) group. In mammals occurs to many amino-acid molecules by action of deaminating enzymes in liver and kidney; the liberated ammonia being turned into urea by the liver, the carbon-containing residue probably providing energy by being oxidized.

DECAPODA. (1) Order of Arthropoda, class Crustacea, including crabs, lobsters, crayfish, shrimps. (2) Sub-order of Mollusca, class Cephalopoda; squids, cuttlefish, etc.

DECIDUA. Mucous membrane (endometrium) lining uterus in the thickened and modified form it acquires during pregnancy in many mammals (not in 'ungulates', see *Placenta*). Some or all of the decidua comes away with the placenta at birth.

DECIDUOUS. (Of plants) shedding leaves at a certain season, e.g. autumn. Cf. *Evergreen*.

DECIDUOUS TEETH. Milk teeth. First of the two sets of teeth which most mammals have; similar to the second (permanent) set which replaces it, except in having grinding teeth corresponding only to the premolars, not to the molars, of that set.

DEDIFFERENTIATION. See *Differentiation*.

DEFICIENCY DISEASE. Disease due to deficiency of some essential food substance, e.g. vitamin, mineral element, or essential amino acid.

DEGENERATION. Of an organ, loss of whole or part during life-cycle or in course of evolution. Of cells, death with accompanying changes. Of nerves, death and destruction of nerve fibres but not of their supporting cells. Evolutionary, loss of structure and function leading to a vestigial organ (q.v.).

DEGLUTITION. Swallowing, a complex reflex set off by stimulation of pharynx, involving contraction of muscles of mouth and pharynx, closing of the back of the nose by soft palate, raising of larynx against epiglottis, inhibition of breathing, peristalsis in oesophagus.

DEHISCENT. (Of fruits) opening to liberate the seeds, e.g. pea, viola, poppy.

DEHYDRATION. (In preparation of tissues for microscopical examination) the elimination of water, usually by soaking in successively stronger concentrations of ethyl alcohol. An essential preliminary to embedding (q.v.), or placing in Canada balsam (q.v.), both of these substances being quite immiscible with water. See *Clearing*, *Microtome*.

DEHYDROGENASE. Enzyme which catalyses oxidation of substrate by removing hydrogen from it. The hydrogen may combine with molecular oxygen (see *Oxidase*) or with another substance. Most oxidizing enzymes are dehydrogenases.

DEME. Basic unit in terminology of categories in experimental taxonomy (q.v.). Any group of individuals of a specified taxon of plants possessing clearly definable genetical, cytological, or other characteristics, e.g. *gamodeme*, group of individuals which are capable of interbreeding.

DEMOGRAPHY. Study of human populations.

DENATURATION. Structural change produced in soluble (globular) proteins by mild heat or various chemicals, rendering them less soluble than in their original ('native') condition, involving an unfolding of the peptide chains. Of DNA (q.v.), separation of the two strands, as by heating.

DENDRITES. Branching cytoplasmic projections of a nerve cell (q.v.) which have synapses with, and receive impulses from, axons of other nerve cells.

DENDROGRAM. Tree-like diagram indicating degrees of resemblance amongst members of a group of organisms.

DENITRIFYING BACTERIA. Soil bacteria which in absence of oxygen break down nitrates and nitrites with evolution of free nitrogen. See *Nitrogen Cycle*.

DENSITY-DEPENDENT FACTOR. Factor, controlling growth of population (usually of organisms), which itself depends on the existing density of population; usually the higher the density the more strongly the factor limits growth, thereby providing self-regulation of the population.

DENTAL FORMULA. Formula indicating, for a given species of mammal, the number of each kind of its teeth. The number in the upper jaw of one side is written above that in the lower jaw of one side; and the categories are given in the order: incisors, canines, premolars, molars. The formula of the primitive mammal is i$\frac{3}{3}$. c$\frac{1}{1}$. p$\frac{4}{4}$. m$\frac{3}{3}$. The human formula is i$\frac{2}{2}$. c$\frac{1}{1}$. p$\frac{2}{2}$. m$\frac{3}{3}$.

DENTARY. The only bone of the lower jaw of mammals, one on each side; one of several lower jaw bones in other vertebrates. A dermal bone.

DENTICLES (PLACOID SCALES). Tooth-like scales present in many fish. They completely cover body of elasmobranchs. Composed of dentine, with pulp-cavity. Teeth are probably modified denticles.

DENTINE. Main constituent of teeth. Like bone in structure, but contains no cells, though cell-processes penetrate it from cells in pulp cavity of tooth. Formed from mesoderm or neural crest of embryo. Ivory is dentine.

DEOXYRIBONUCLEIC (DESOXYRIBOSENUCLEIC) ACID. DNA (q.v.).

DEPENDENT DIFFERENTIATION. Of an embryonic tissue, differentiation which is dependent on a stimulus coming from some other tissue. See *Competence, Induction, Organizer, Self-Differentiation.*

DERMAL BONE (MEMBRANE BONE). Bone arising near surface of embryo (though it may later sink deeper) from concentration of mesenchyme cells, with no cartilage precursor (see *Cartilage Bone*). Occurs in skull and shoulder-girdle of most vertebrates, e.g. roofing bones of skull; dentary; clavicle. In some very early vertebrates it formed extensive superficial armour, e.g. Ostracodermi.

DERMAPTERA. Small order of exopterygote insects, including earwigs, with fan-like hind wings folding under short stiff forewings.

DERMATOGEN. See *Apical Meristem.*

DERMIS (CORIUM). Innermost of the two layers of the skin of vertebrates, the outer being the epidermis (q.v.). Much thicker than epidermis. Consists of connective tissue, with abundant collagen fibres mainly parallel to surface; scattered cells; blood and lymph vessels; sensory nerves. Sweat-glands and hair-follicles project down from epidermis into dermis. Responsible for tensile strength of skin. May contain scales or bone.

DERMOPTERA. 'Flying lemurs', though it would be more appropriate to call them gliding insectivores. Small order of mammals with hairy membrane stretching along side of body, between wrist, ankle, and tip of tail.

DETERMINANT. (Antigenic.) The part of an antigen molecule that actually forms a specific bond with a corresponding antibody molecule. (Genetic.) A factor that transmits inheritance, either a gene (q.v.) or a plasmagene (q.v.).

DETERMINED. Term applied to embryonic tissues, meaning that in all conditions in which they can develop at all, they will form only one particular sort of adult tissue or organ, i.e. their fate is fixed. See *Competence, Presumptive.*

DETRITUS. Organic debris from decomposing plants and animals.

DEUTOPLASM. Yolk.

DEVONIAN. Geological period (q.v.); lasted approximately from 395 till 345 million years ago.

DEXTRIN. Polysaccharide carbohydrate formed as an intermediate product in hydrolysis of starch to glucose; a short chain of, generally, six to twelve glucose units (glucose residues).

DEXTROSE. Glucose (q.v.).

DIADELPHOUS. (Of stamens) united by their filaments to form two groups, or having one solitary and the others united, e.g. pea. Cf. *Monadelphous, Polyadelphous.*

DIAGEOTROPISM. Orientation of plant part by growth curvature in response to stimulus of gravity so that its axis is at right-angles to direction of gravitational force, i.e. horizontal; exhibited by rhizomes of many plants. See *Geotropism, Plagiogeotropism.*

DIAKINESIS. Final stage in prophase of first division of meiosis (q.v.), following diplotene. Chromosomes move to periphery of nucleus, close to the nuclear membrane. They become short and thick as a result of a further process of coiling and contraction that begins in an earlier stage (pachytene) and the number of chiasmata decreases (see Terminalization). Nucleoli disappear. Diakinesis ends with disappearance of nuclear membrane and appearance of division spindle.

DIALYSIS. Method of separating small molecules, e.g. salts, from colloids, e.g. proteins, in mixed solution, by putting mixture in bag made of a membrane, e.g. collodion, permeable to small but not to large molecules, with excess water outside the bag into which small molecules diffuse.

DIAPAUSE. Of some species of insects, period of suspended development or growth, accompanied by greatly decreased metabolism. Often correlated with seasons, e.g. it may be hibernation (q.v.).

DIAPHRAGM. Sheet of tissue, part muscle, part tendon, covered by serous membrane, separating cavities of thorax (occupied by lungs and heart) from cavity of abdomen (occupied by intestine, liver, etc.). Present only in mammals. Diaphragm is arched up into thorax at rest and its flattening is a very important part of mechanism of inspiration of breath in most mammals.

DIAPHYSIS. Shaft of a long limb-bone, or central portion of a vertebra, in mammals. See *Epiphysis*.

DIASTASE. Amylase (q.v.).

DIASTOLE. Phase of heart-beat when heart muscle relaxes, and heart refills with blood from veins; or of contractile vacuole (q.v.) when it refills with fluid. Cf. *Systole*.

DIATOMS. Bacillariophyceae (q.v.).

DICHASIUM. Kind of inflorescence (q.v.).

DICHLAMYDEOUS (DIPLOCHLAMYDEOUS). (Of flowers), having perianth segments in two whorls.

DICHOGAMY. Condition in which male and female parts of a flower mature at different times, ensuring that self-pollination does not occur. See *Protandrous, Protogynous*, Cf. *Homogamy*.

DICHOTOMOUS. Dividing into two equal branches.

DICOTYLEDONEAE. Larger of the two classes into which flowering plants (Angiospermae) are divided; distinguished from the smaller class, *Monocotyledoneae*, by presence of two seed leaves (cotyledons) in the embryo and by other structural features, e.g. net-veined leaves; stem vascular tissue in form of a ring of open bundles; flower parts in fours or fives or in multiples of these numbers. Includes many forest trees, oak, elm, beech, etc.; fruit trees, food plants, e.g. potatoes, beans, cabbage; and ornamentals, e.g. rose, clematis, snapdragon.

DICTYOSOME. Unit of Golgi apparatus (q.v.) several of which occur as discrete bodies in cells of invertebrates and of plants. At telophase in division of plant cells dictyosomes become grouped in equatorial position around periphery of division spindle and form small vesicles which fuse to form cell plate (q.v.). See *Golgi apparatus*.

DICTYOSTELE. Amphiphloic siphonostele (q.v.) that is broken up by crowded leaf gaps into a network of distinct vascular strands (meristeles), each surrounded by an endodermis. Present in stems of certain ferns.

DIDELPHIA. Marsupialia (q.v.).

DIDYNAMOUS. (Of stamens), four in number in two pairs, those of one pair longer than those of the other, e.g. foxglove.

DIFFERENTIATION. Process of change in cells, tissues or organs during development (embryonic, regenerative or other) resulting in the appearance, where they were previously lacking, of the structures and functions that characterize the kinds of cells, tissues or organs in different parts of an adult, or of the organism at some other relatively stable phase of its life history. Before the process the cells, etc. are termed *undifferentiated*; after it they are *differentiated*. Change in the reverse direction is dedifferentiation.

DIFFUSION PRESSURE DEFICIT (DPD). Net capacity of plant cell to absorb water; can be expressed by the equation

$$DPD = (P_1 - P_0) - T$$

where $P_1$ is osmotic pressure of vacuole solution, $P_0$ that of solution outside cell and T the turgor pressure.

DIGESTION. Breakdown of complex foodstuffs by enzymes to simpler compounds which can be incorporated into metabolism. In many animals it is *extracellular*, i.e. enzymes are secreted into gut cavity, in which digestion takes place, e.g. vertebrates, arthropods; in others it is wholly or partly *intracellular*, the cell of the gut phagocytosing solid food particles, e.g. coelenterates, lamellibranchs.

DIGIT. Finger or toe or pentadactyl limb (q.v.). Contains phalanges. See Fig. 7, p. 213.

DIGITIGRADE. Walking on toes, not on whole foot; i.e. on ventral surface of digits only, e.g. cat, dog. Cf. *Plantigrade, Unguligrade*.

DIKARYON (DICARYON) (of fungus hypha or mycelium) composed of cells containing two haploid nuclei which undergo simultaneous division during formation of each new cell. Forms a third phase (*dikaryophase*) interposed between haploid and diploid phases. Occurs in Ascomycetes where it is usually short and in Basidiomycetes where it is relatively long. Nuclei may be genetically identical, or different. Cf. *Monokaryon*.

DIMORPHISM. Existing in two forms, e.g. submerged and aerial leaves of water crowfoot; male and female individuals in animals.

DINOSAUR. Fossil reptile belonging to one of the two orders Saurischia and Ornithischia, into which the old order Dinosauria is now split.

DIOECIOUS. Unisexual, the male and female sexual reproductive organs borne on different individuals. Cf. *Monoecious, Herma-phrodite.*

DIPLANETISM. (1) Occurrence of two zoospore (q.v.) stages, whether morphologically distinct or identical, separated by encystment. (2) Applied only to former condition. Characteristic of asexual reproduction of some Phycomycete fungi.

DIPLOBLASTIC. Having the body made of two cellular layers only (ectoderm and endoderm). The Coelenterata are diploblastic, and all other Metazoa are triploblastic. In small simple Coelenterata such as *Hydra* the diploblastic condition is clear, but it is obscured (see *Mesogloea*) in large jelly-fish and sea-anemones. In diploblastic animals, however, unlike triploblastic, no *organs* develop from the middle layer, but only from the ectoderm and endoderm.

DIPLOID. (Of a nucleus) having the chromosomes in pairs, the mem-bers of each pair being homologous (q.v.), so that twice the haploid number is present. Characteristic of almost all animal cells except the gametes; of the zygotes of many green algae and of many fungi, which undergo meiosis so that later stages are haploid; and of the sporophyte of other algae, Bryophyta and vascular plants. See *Alternation of Generations, Meiosis, Dikaryon.*

DIPLONT. Diploid stage of an organism, ending with meiosis. Cf. *Haplont.*

DIPLOPODA. Millipedes. Order or class of Arthropoda; see *Myria-poda.*

DIPLOTENE. Stage in prophase of first division of meiosis (q.v.), following pachytene, in which pairs of chromatids derived from homologous chromosomes begin to separate from each other except at certain points of connection (chiasmata) where interchange occurs between chromatid segments (crossing -over).

DIPNOI (DIPNEUSTI). Lung-fish. A sub-class of Osteichthyes or of Choanichthyes. Fresh-water. Fairly common fossils, but only three living genera, all tropical: *Protopterus* (African), *Lepidosiren* (South American), *Epiceratodus* (Australian). Bony skeleton; paired fins with a central skeletal axis; nostrils opening both on to face and into mouth; cosmoid scales (q.v.) or derivatives of them. Differ from Crossopterygii in their peculiar tooth plates, used to crush shells of small molluscs on which they feed. Have functional lungs, like Polypterus and many early fossil fish of other groups. First appear in Devonian (about 400 million years ago).

DIPTERA. Flies. Large order of endopterygote insects. Only one pair of wings, hind pair reduced to pegs (halteres, q.v.). Larva cater-pillar-like or grub-like. Adults have mouth parts highly specialized, e.g. for sucking nectar of flowers, or blood. Some blood-suckers are of great medical and economical importance because they transmit certain diseases, e.g. mosquitoes, tse-tse flies.

DISACCHARIDE. A sugar, a compound of two monosaccharides (q.v.). The biologically important disaccharides have 12 carbon atoms (formed from two hexoses), e.g. sucrose, maltose, lactose.

DISPLACEMENT ACTIVITY. When two incompatible forms of behaviour of an animal are simultaneously stimulated, the animal may perform an apparently unconnected and irrelevant action, a displacement activity. E.g. when stimuli tending to produce both approach and flight are received together, a rat may instead turn to grooming itself.

DISTANCE RECEPTOR. Exteroceptor (q.v.) responding to stimuli (e.g. light, sound) which allows orientation of the animal to source of the stimuli.

DISTAL. Situated away from; especially from place of attachment. In a limb, away from the body; in a blood-vessel, away from the heart; in a nerve, away from the central nervous system. Cf. *Proximal.*

DIURESIS. Increased output of urine by kidney. E.g. occurs after drinking much water.

DIURNAL RHYTHM. Circadian rhythm (q.v.).

DIVERTICULUM. (Zool.). Blind-ending tubular or sac-like outpushing from a cavity.

DIVISION. Major group used in classifying plants. See *Phylum.*

DIZYGOTIC TWINS (FRATERNAL TWINS). Twins developed as result of simultaneous fertilization of two separate ova. Such twins are genetically no more alike than siblings (q.v.). Cf. *Monozygotic twins.*

DNA. Deoxyribonucleic acid, a compound consisting of a large number of nucleotides attached together in single file to form a long strand. Usually two such strands are linked together parallel to each other by base pairing (q.v.), and coiled into a helix. They may be separated ('melted' or 'denatured' DNA) by heat. Each nucleotide contains the sugar deoxyribose, and one of 4 different bases, 2 pyrimidine (thymine and cytosine) and 2 purine (adenine and guanine). It is now clear that DNA is the material of inheritance (see *Gene*) of almost all living things. It has the necessary great variety of structure, produced by different arrangements of the four different nucleotides. It passes on its structure to copies of itself, probably made by separating the two strands and forming a new matching strand, by base pairing with individual nucleotides, for each of the old strands (semi-conservative replication). Its structure is also translated into the structure of protein molecules when these are synthesized, by an elaborate mechanism involving RNA (see *Messenger RNA*). It is found mainly in the chromosomes of plants and animals and in the bacteria and viruses exclusively in corresponding structures.

DOMINANT. (1) (Genetics). A gene which produces the same character when it is present in single dose along with a specified allele (heterozygous), as it does in double dose (homozygous), is said to be dominant to that allele. The allele which is ineffective in the heterozygote is said to be *recessive* to that dominant. When a gene is called dominant without qualification it is usually implied that it is dominant to the normally occurring ('wild-type') allele(s). A dominance-recessiveness relation is common between two genes (the gene most frequently present at a given locus in a wild population is usually dominant to its alleles), but it is not universal. (2) (Plant Ecology). Of a plant species, the most characteristic species in a particular plant community, to a large extent governing the type and abundance of other species in the community, e.g. beech trees in a beechwood. When more than one dominant species occurs in a particular plant community, they are called *Codominants*. (3) (Animal behaviour). Of a member of a group of animals, able habitually to win aggressive encounters with certain other members of the group.

DONOR. An individual from whom tissue is taken to transfer to another, e.g. in grafting; blood transfusion.

DOPA. Dihydroxy phenylalanine, an intermediate substance in the production of adrenaline and noradrenaline, and also of melanin.

DORMANT. In a resting condition; alive, but with relatively inactive metabolism. Dormancy may involve the whole organism as in higher plants and animals, or be confined to reproductive bodies, e.g. resting spores, sclerotia of fungi, spores of bacteria, and in animals, resting eggs, statoblasts. Dormancy involves cessation of growth. In higher plants it may simply be due to unfavourable conditions, e.g. low temperature, lack of moisture, ending as soon as the limiting conditions are removed. Many seeds, e.g. pea, wheat, though capable of germination immediately after harvesting, are thus dormant in the seedsman's hands. On the other hand a dormant period is a part of an annual rhythm for most plants. Often this type of dormancy has survival value, corresponding with unfavourable conditions, e.g. winter dormancy in deciduous trees, but such a relationship is not universal. After vegetative growth and flowering in spring, many bulbs, e.g. snowdrop, daffodil, have a dormant period coinciding with conditions favourable to the growth of other plants and dormancy frequently occurs amongst plants in moist, tropical climates. Dormancy of seeds in conditions otherwise favourable to germination, is seen in many plants, e.g. hawthorn, *Daphne mezereum*, and noxious weed wild oats. It is associated, in different plants, with incomplete development of the embryo, impermeable nature of the seed coat limiting entry of water, oxygen, presence of inhibitors, lack of growth stimulators. Dormancy of some deciduous trees is regulated by photoperiod (possibly through activity of a hormone, *abscisic acid* (q.v.)). Germination of some seeds is also regulated by photoperiod. See also *Hibernation, Aestivation, Diapause*.

DORMIN. Abscisic acid (q.v.).

DORSAL. (Zool.). Situated at, or relatively nearer to, the back, i.e.

the side of the animal which (if not in the animal, at least in the group to which the animal belongs) is normally directed upwards with reference to gravity. In human beings, it is directed backwards. Opposite of ventral. *D. aorta*, see *Aorta, Dorsal*. (Bot.). Also used of leaves, synonymous with Abaxial (q.v.).

DORSAL LIP. Of blastopore (q.v.). Part of rim of blastopore corresponding to future dorsal side, in Amphibian embryo. See *Organizer*.

DORSAL ROOT (POSTERIOR R., SENSORY R.). Nerve-root (q.v.) of vertebrates containing the sensory fibres.

DORSIVENTRAL LEAVES. Showing differences in structure between upper and lower sides. Characteristic of the more or less horizontal leaves of dicotyledons, e.g. sycamore. Below the upper epidermis, lying regularly side by side and with their long axes at right-angles to it, are one or more layers of elongated cells forming the palisade mesophyll. Between this and the lower epidermis is the spongy mesophyll, consisting of irregularly shaped cells with large intercellular spaces. Cf. *Isobilateral*.

DOUBLE FERTILIZATION. In Angiosperms union of one male nucleus with egg nucleus to form zygote and of the other with primary endosperm nucleus to form endosperm nucleus. See *Embryo sac*.

DOUBLE RECESSIVE. Individual which is homozygous for a particular recessive gene. To test whether an individual showing character of a dominant gene is homozygous or heterozygous, it is crossed to corresponding double recessive (constituting a *test-cross*); if homozygous, all offspring show dominant phenotype; if heterozygous, half show dominant and half recessive phenotypes.

DOWN-FEATHER. See *Barbules*.

DPN. NAD (q.v.).

DRIVE. In animal behaviour, the state of activity and responsiveness to stimuli concerned with the satisfaction of some need; e.g. hunger drive.

DROSOPHILA. Fruit-fly or banana-fly. Genus of the order Diptera. Experiments on *Drosophila melanogaster* by T. H. Morgan and his school established the foundations of modern genetics in relation to chromosomes; and it has been widely used in genetical research ever since. See *Salivary Gland Chromosome*.

DRUPE. Succulent fruit in which wall (*pericarp*) consists of outer skin (*epicarp*), thick fleshy *mesocarp* and hard, stony *endocarp* enclosing a single seed. Commonly called stone-fruit, e.g. plum, cherry. Cf. *Berry*. In some plants, e.g. coconut, mesocarp is very fibrous. Pericarp here consists of tough, leathery epicarp, very thick fibrous mesocarp and hard endocarp enclosing seed and forming with it the 'nut' we buy.

DUCTLESS GLAND. Endocrine gland (q.v.).

DUCTUS CUVIERI (CUVIERIAN DUCT). Main vein of fish (and of tetrapod embryo) returning blood from cardinal veins (in body-wall) to heart (under gut) in a fold of coelomic lining which forms the posterior wall of pericardial cavity. There is one on each side. Becomes vena cava superior (q.v.) in adult tetrapods.

DUODENUM. First part of small intestine of vertebrates. Leads out of stomach (junction being guarded by pyloric sphincter). Receives bile and pancreatic ducts. A region of active digestion.

DURA MATER. Firm connective tissue covering brain and spinal cord of vertebrates, containing blood-vessels. See *Meninges*, *Pia-arachnoid*.

# E

EAR, INNER (MEMBRANOUS LABYRINTH). The sense-organ of
vertebrates which detects position with respect to gravity; acceleration; and sound. Lies in wall of skull (in auditory capsule) connected by auditory nerve to brain. Consists of two connected sacs
containing otoliths (q.v.). From one (utricle) arise semicircular
canals (q.v.). From other (saccule) arises organ of hearing, which is
developed as the cochlea (q.v.) in some tetrapods. Whole inner
ear is filled with a fluid (endolymph) and separated from surrounding skull wall by another fluid (perilymph).

EAR, MIDDLE (TYMPANIC CAVITY). Cavity between ear-drum
and auditory capsule, present in tetrapod vertebrates (not Urodela,
Apoda, Snakes). Derived from a gill pouch (spiracle). Communicates with mouth by eustachian tube and is filled with air. Crossed
by ear ossicles. Encased in bony projection of skull (bulla) in most
mammals.

EAR OSSICLE. Bone in middle ear, connecting ear-drum to inner ear,
in tetrapod vertebrates. Transmits vibrations of ear-drum caused
by aerial sound waves to the fluid of the inner ear. A single ossicle,
columella auris (q.v.), representing hyomandibula of fishes,
is present in ear of reptiles, birds, and many amphibians. Three
ossicles, malleus, incus, and stapes, of interesting evolutionary history, are present in mammalian ear. Stapes represents columella.
Malleus represents a bone of lower jaw (articular) which in other
vertebrates articulates with quadrate bone of upper jaw forming
jaw-joint; but a new kind of joint in mammals (between dentary
and squamosal) frees articular; and it also frees quadrate, which
becomes incus. The three ossicles of mammals form a lever system,
diminishing amplitude of sound waves and increasing force on inner
ear.

EAR, OUTER OR EXTERNAL. Part of ear of tetrapod external to
ear-drum. Absent in Amphibia and some reptiles, where ear-drum
(if present) is at skin surface. In other tetrapods, ear-drum is at inner
end of short tube (*external auditory meatus*); this, in mammals, with
the flap of skin and cartilage (pinna) at outer opening of meatus,
makes up outer ear.

ECAD. (Bot.). A habitat form, showing characteristics imposed by
habitat conditions and non-heritable.

ECDYSIS. Moulting. In arthropoda, periodic shedding of cuticle
(q.v.). In insects inner part of old cuticle is absorbed, the rest is
split at line of weakness, and the insect draws itself out, clothed in
a preformed soft new cuticle. By swallowing air the insect quickly
increases its bulk and the new cuticle finally hardens a size larger
than the old. The lining of all but the finest tracheae (q.v.) is shed

with the old cuticle. Ecdysis in insects is initiated by a hormone (ecdysone); it does not usually occur in adult insects. In reptiles, periodic shedding of outer layer of epidermis occurs in all, except crocodiles.

ECDYSONE. Steroid hormone, secreted from the prothoracic glands of insects, initiating ecdysis (q.v.).

ECESIS. Germination and establishment of colonizing plants.

ECHIDNA. Spiny anteater, a very primitive monotreme mammal of New Guinea and Australia.

ECHINODERMATA. Phylum of animals containing sea-urchins, sea-cucumbers, starfish, brittle-stars, feather-stars, and sea-lilies. Marine; more or less radially symmetrical (with usually five axes of symmetry); calcareous skeletal plates in the skin; tube feet; coelom well developed, consisting of several intricate spaces, one of which is the water vascular system; larva (when present) more or less bilaterally symmetrical with coelom in three segments. Their mode of development shows them to be related to the same stock that gave rise to vertebrates. Includes classes Asteroidea, Ophiuroidea, Echinoidea, Holothuroidea, Crinoidea. Palaeozoic rocks contain remains of several other groups of echinoderms now extinct; they were mostly sedentary forms. It seems that modern free-living echinoderms were derived from radially symmetrical sedentary forms.

ECHINOIDEA. Sea-urchins, heart-urchins, cake-urchins; class of Echinodermata; more or less globular in shape; spiny; skeletal plates in skin joined to form firm skeleton.

ECHOLOCATION. Determination of position of objects by detecting the reflection from them of sounds (usually high-pitched) produced by the animal. Many mammals use it, e.g. bats, porpoises.

ECOLOGY. Study of the relations of animals and plants, particularly of animal and plant communities, to their surroundings, animate and inanimate.

ECOSPECIES. Group of plants comprising one or more ecotypes (q.v.) within a coenospecies (q.v.) whose members can reproduce amongst themselves without loss of fertility in offspring. Approximates to conventional 'species'.

ECOSYSTEM. A community of organisms, interacting with one another, plus the environment in which they live and with which they also interact; e.g. a pond, a forest. A system consisting of *producers*, autotrophic organisms (mainly green plants), *consumers*, heterotrophic organisms (animals) and *decomposers*, heterotrophic organisms (chiefly bacteria and fungi) latter breaking down dead organisms, absorbing nutrients for growth and releasing nutrients to environment for use by producers; all of these activities being influenced by physical conditions of environment. See *Food-chain*.

ECOTYPE. Group of plants within a species adapted genetically to a particular habitat but able to cross freely with other ecotypes of the same species.

ECTOBLAST (EPIBLAST). See *Ectoderm*.

ECTODERM (ECTOBLAST, EPIBLAST). Superficial germ-layer of animal embryo, developing mainly into epidermis, nervous tissue, and nephridia (when present). Term is usually applied to the germ-layer while it is still a distinctly demarcated region of the embryo, after gastrulation but before differentiation into the derived tissues; and all the tissues at later stages derived from the embryonic layer may be called ectodermal. See *Germ-layer, Endoderm, Mesoderm*.

ECTOPARASITE. Organism living parasitically on the outside of another organism. E.g. flea. Cf. *Endoparasite*.

ECTOPLASM. (Bot.). (*Ectoplast*) Synonymous with external plasma membrane (q.v.). (Zool.). (*Cell cortex*). Outer layer of cytoplasm, which differs from inner cytoplasm (endoplasm) in many cells, though the two regions grade into each other. Unlike endoplasm, ectoplasm is usually semi-solid (a fibrous gel, in which case it may be called *plasmagel*) and often contains relatively few granules, e.g. in many ova and Protozoa. In planktonic Protozoa it may be highly vacuolated. Ectoplasm has important role in many forms of cell movement, including cell-division and amoeboid movement; but active as it is this is not the kind of ectoplasm which undertakes table-turning.

ECTOPROCTA. Sea-mats: group of small colonial aquatic animals sometimes regarded as a class of Polyzoa (q.v.), sometimes as a separate phylum.

ECTOTROPHIC. (Of mycorrhizas) with the mycelium of the fungus forming an external covering to the root, e.g. in pine trees. Cf. *Endotrophic*. See *Mycorrhiza*.

EDAPHIC FACTORS. Environmental conditions that are determined by the physical, chemical, and biological characteristics of the soil.

EDEMA. Oedema (q.v.).

EDENTATA. Three orders of placental mammals, with teeth reduced or absent, which used to be grouped together as one order. Sloths, armadillos, American anteaters (Xenarthra); aard-vaark (Tubulidentata); scaly anteaters (Pholidota).

E.E.G. (ELECTROENCEPHALOGRAM). Record of the rhythmical waves of change in electrical potential occurring in vertebrate brain, mainly cerebral cortex, which can be detected through intact skull. Patterns in man can be correlated with various physiological and pathological states such as epilepsy.

EELWORMS. Nematodes; applied only to plant-parasitic and free-living forms.

EFFECTOR. Organ or cell by which an animal acts. Main effectors are muscles, glands, cilia, chromatophores, thread-cells.

EFFERENT. Leading away from. E.g. of arteries leading from verte-

brate gills, or of arteriole from glomerulus; or of nerve fibres conducting impulses from central nervous system (motor fibres). Cf.
*Afferent.*

EGG MEMBRANES. Protective membranes surrounding the eggs of
animals, especially well-developed in those of terrestrial species.
Classified according to mode of origin: (1) Those secreted by ovum
itself, vitelline membrane, q.v.; (2) Those secreted by cells in the
ovary, e.g. chorion, q.v., of insect eggs; (3) Those secreted
by oviduct, e.g. white and shell of bird's egg, jelly of frog's
spawn.

ELAIOPLAST. Colourless plastid (leucoplast) storing oil; common in
liverworts and monocotyledons. Term is also applied to chloroplasts
of many brown algae in which reserve storage product is oil.

ELASMOBRANCHII. Often synonymous with Chondrichthyes (q.v.).
Sometimes made a sub-class of Chondrichthyes, including all
members of this class except Holocephali.

ELASTIN. A fibrous protein in the form of highly extensible and
elastic fibres ('yellow fibres') found sparsely scattered in vertebrate
connective tissue; numerous in some places, e.g. in lungs, walls of
large arteries.

ELATER. (1) Elongated cell with wall reinforced internally by one or
more spiral bands of thickening, numbers of which occur among
spores in capsules of liverworts; assist in discharge of spores by their
movements in response to changes in humidity. (2) Appendage
of spores of horsetails; formed from outermost wall layer, coiling
and uncoiling as air is dry or moist, possibly assisting in spore
dispersal.

ELECTROENCEPHALOGRAM. E.E.G. (q.v.).

ELECTRON MICROSCOPE. See *Microscope.*

ELECTRON MICROGRAPH. Photograph taken with electron microscope.

ELYTRON (plural ELYTRA). Modified front wing of beetles (Coleoptera). Thick and tough, at rest it protects the thin hind-wing
folded beneath it.

E.M. Electron microscope; or electron micrograph.

EMASCULATION. Removal of stamens from hermaphrodite flowers
before they have liberated pollen, as a preliminary to artificial
hybridization.

EMBEDDING. See *Microtome.*

EMBRYO. (Bot.). Young plant developed after sexual or parthenogenetic reproduction from an ovum. In seed plants the embryo is
contained in the seed and consists of an axis bearing at its apex the
apical meristem of the future shoot, or a young bud (plumule) in
some species, at the other end the root (radicle); and one or more
seed leaves (cotyledons). (Zool.). Animal in process of development
from fertilized (or parthenogenetically activated) ovum. The
embryo is contained in egg-membranes (q.v.), or, in viviparous

species, in maternal body; and termination of embryonic period is usually taken to be hatching from membranes, or birth.

EMBRYO SAC. Large oval cell in nucellus of ovule of flowering plants in which fertilization of egg and development of embryo occurs; female gametophyte containing a number of nuclei derived by division of megaspore (q.v.) nucleus. Number and arrangement of these differs in different forms but most commonly there is, at micropylar end, the *egg-apparatus*, consisting of egg nucleus and two others, *synergidae*; at opposite end three nuclei which become separated by cell walls forming *antipodal* cells, probably aiding in nourishment of young embryo; in centre, two *polar* nuclei which fuse to form *primary endosperm nucleus*. At fertilization one male nucleus fuses with egg nucleus forming a zygote which develops into embryo; second male nucleus fuses with primary endosperm nucleus to form *endosperm* nucleus, which divides to form endosperm.

EMBRYOLOGY. Study of development of embryos.

EMBRYONIC MEMBRANE. Extraembryonic membrane (q.v.).

EMBRYOPHYTA. Older classification group (sub-kingdom) including all plants possessing multicellular sex organs and an embryo (develops within archegonium in mosses, liverworts, ferns and related plants, and within embryo sac in seed plants). Named *Metaphyta* in more recent classification system.

ENAMEL. Hard covering of exposed part (crown) of teeth. Occurs also on denticles. Formed by epithelium of mouth, unlike dentine (q.v.). Consists mainly of crystals of a calcium phosphate-carbonate salt, with very little (3-5 per cent) organic substance.

ENATION. Outgrowth produced by local hyperplasia (q.v.) on leaf as a result of virus infection.

ENCYSTED. Surrounded by a cyst or shell.

ENDEMIC. Confined to a given region, e.g. an island or country. (Of pest or disease-producing parasites), continuously occurring in a particular area.

ENDERGONIC. (Of a chemical reaction), requiring energy, as in synthesis by green plants of organic compounds from water and carbon dioxide by means of energy absorbed from sunlight. Cf. *Exergonic*.

ENDOBLAST (ENTOBLAST, HYPOBLAST). See *Endoderm*.

ENDOCRINE (DUCTLESS) GLAND. (Zool.). Gland producing hormones (q.v.).

ENDOCRINOLOGY. Study of hormones, their production, nature, and effects.

ENDOCYTOSIS. Collective name for pinocytosis (q.v.) and phagocytosis (q.v.).

ENDODERM (ENTODERM, ENDOBLAST, ENTOBLAST, HYPOBLAST). Germ-layer of animal embryo, composed, like mesoderm, of cells which have moved from surface of embryo into its interior during gastrulation; developing into greater part of lining of gut with its associated glands, etc. Term is usually applied to the germ-layer while it is still a demarcated region of the embryo, after gastrulation but before differentiation into derived tissues; and all tissues at later stages derived from the embryonic layer may be called endodermal. See *Germ-Layer, Ectoderm, Mesoderm.*

ENDODERMIS. Innermost layer of cortex, surrounding the stele. Characteristic of all roots, and of stems of pteridophytes and some dicotyledons. Consists of closely fitting cells with distinctive wall modifications. Most characteristic is band of wall material, *Casparian strip,* impervious to water, in radial and transverse walls. With age, especially in monocotyledons, cells (except *passage cells*) may become further modified by deposition of layer of suberin over entire inner surface of wall followed, particularly on inner tangential wall, by layer of cellulose, sometimes lignified. Important physiologically in control of transfer of water and solutes between cortex and vascular cylinder, since these must pass through proto-plasts of endodermal cells. See *Casparian strip, Passage cell.*

ENDOGAMY. Inbreeding (q.v.).

ENDOLYMPH. See *Ear, inner.*

ENDOMETRIUM. Glandular mucous membrane (q.v.) lining uterus of mammals. Undergoes cyclical growth and regression or destruction during sexual maturity. See *Oestrous Cycle, Placenta.*

ENDOMITOSIS. Doubling of chromosomes without division of nucleus, producing polyploidy (q.v.). Doubling may be repeated many times in a single nucleus. Occurs particularly in insects, where different adult tissues have characteristic degrees of polyploidy, and in some vertebrate and plant tissues.

ENDOPARASITE. Organism living parasitically within another. E.g. tapeworm, many fungi. Cf. *Ectoparasite.*

ENDOPLASM. (Bot.). (*Endoplast*) Cytoplasm internal to plasma membrane. (Zool.). Internal cytoplasm of many cells, e.g. ova, Protozoa, which differs from ectoplasm (q.v.), usually in greater fluidity (in which case it may be called *plasmasol*) and in presence of many granules and organelles.

ENDOPLASMIC RETICULUM (ERGASTOPLASM). Complex mesh-work of tubular channels, often expanded into slit-like cavities (*cisternae*) together with more or less flattened vesicles, all bounded by unit membranes, occuring in the cytoplasm of many eucaryote cells; usually only visible by electron microscopy. The membranes are sometimes seen to connect with nuclear membrane and Golgi apparatus, and occasionally with invaginations of plasma membrane at cell surface. Particularly well-developed in actively growing cells, and frequently covered, on the outside of the vesicles or paired membranes, with small bodies (ribosomes) concerned in protein synthesis (without ribosomes the membrane is termed *smooth-surfaced,* with ribosomes *rough-surfaced*). Theory is that membranes may function, like plasma membrane, in regulating exchange of materials passing through them, and that channels may form a system conveying materials within the cell.

ENDOPROCTA. Small group of sedentary aquatic animals sometimes regarded as a class of Polyzoa (q.v.), sometimes as a separate phylum.

ENDOPTERYGOTA (HOLOMETABOLA). Sub-class of insects in which larva differs strongly from adult and gives rise to it by a process of drastic change (metamorphosis), e.g. butterflies; as distinct from the Exopterygota in which the adult form develops more gradually.

END-ORGAN. Structure connected to the C.N.S. by a fibre of the peripheral nervous system; either a receptor (q.v.) composed of one or several cells, or a motor end-plate (q.v.).

ENDOSKELETON. Skeleton lying inside the body, e.g. the bony skeleton of vertebrates. Cf. *Exoskeleton*. Arthropods, e.g. insects, although characterized by an exoskeleton may have an endoskeleton too; this is formed by folds of epidermis extending into the body and there secreting hardened cuticle.

ENDOSPERM. Nutritive tissue surrounding and nourishing the embryo in seed plants. (1) In flowering plants (Angiospermae) formed in embryo sac (q.v.) by division of endosperm nucleus after fertilization. In some seeds (*non-endospermic* or *exalbuminous*), endosperm is entirely absorbed by embryo by the time the seed is fully developed, e.g. pea and bean seeds; in other seeds (*endospermic* or *albuminous*), part of the endosperm remains and is not absorbed until the seed germinates, e.g. wheat, castor oil. (2) Also applied to tissue of female gametophyte in conifers and related plants (Gymnospermae) which is formed by cell division within embryo sac before fertilization, outer layers persisting in seed. Cf. *Perisperm*.

ENDOSTYLE. Structure concerned in ciliary feeding, present in Urochordata, Acrania, and ammocoete larva of lamprey. Consists of a ciliated and glandular groove or pocket in ventral wall of pharynx. Produces threads of mucus to which food particles adhere and which are passed round pharynx and backwards into gullet by ciliary action. Thyroid of adult lamprey develops from duct of endostyle of ammocoete larva. Thyroid of vertebrates is therefore considered to be homologous with endostyle.

ENDOTHELIUM. Single layer of smooth flattened cells lining heart, blood vessels, and lymph vessels, in vertebrates. See *Epithelium*.

ENDOTROPHIC. (Of mycorrhizas), with the mycelium of the fungus within cells of root cortex, e.g. in orchids. See *Mycorrhiza*. Cf. *Ectotrophic*.

END-PRODUCT INHIBITION (FEED-BACK INHIBITION). Where a pathway of successive enzymes leads to the formation of an important metabolite, the amount of the latter present may control the activity of the first enzyme in the pathway; the metabolite combines with and inhibits the enzyme. See *Allosteric, Enzyme*. Cf. *Repression*.

ENERGY FLOW. The movement of energy through the trophic levels of a food chain, starting with that absorbed (mostly from sunlight) by the autotrophic organisms, and reduced by respiration etc. at each level.

ENRICHMENT CULTURE. Microbiological technique allowing selection and isolation from a natural, mixed population of micro-organisms of those having growth characteristics desired by the investigator. Involves culturing on a medium the composition of which is adjusted so as selectively to encourage growth of organisms of desired type; e.g. a medium containing cellulose as sole carbon source and incubated at high temperatures, will promote growth of thermophilic cellulose decomposers from a mixture of micro-organisms (such as occur in a crumb of soil) seeded on to that medium. Encouragement of growth of physiologically and bio-chemically different sorts of micro-organisms can be achieved by altering various characteristics of medium, e.g. nutrient, pH, temperature, aeration. Used widely in bacteriology.

ENTERIC CANAL. Alimentary canal (q.v.).

ENTEROKINASE. Enzyme (peptidase) secreted by vertebrate small intestine which converts trypsinogen to trypsin (q.v.).

ENTEROPNEUSTA. Hemichordata (q.v.).

ENTOMOGENOUS. (Of fungi), parasitic on insects.

ENTOMOLOGY. Study of insects.

ENTOMOPHILY. Pollination by insects. Cf. *Anemophily*.

ENVIRONMENT. Collective term for the conditions in which an organism lives, e.g. temperature, light, water, other organisms. Cf. *Internal environment*.

ENZYME. A protein which is a catalyst (i.e. a substance which in minute amounts promotes chemical change without itself being used up in the reaction), by virtue of its power of increasing the reactivity of a specific substance or specific substances (called the *Substrate*). There are many different kinds, each kind directly promoting only a very limited range of chemical reactions.

Within all living things a large number of chemical reactions are always in progress. See *Metabolism*. Most of the reactions of meta-bolism would not occur perceptibly in the absence of enzymes, at the temperature and in the other conditions in which living things exist; and so metabolism is entirely dependent on enzymes. An enzyme produces its effect on the substrate by combining with it and activating it. so that the substrate undergoes further chemical change, at the same time losing its combination with the enzyme. (The substrate molecule being usually small in relation to the enzyme molecule, only a specific small part of the latter, the *active site*, takes part in the combination.) As the result of such a process, therefore, the enzyme is not consumed, but at the end of the process is free to deal with more substrate. Since the activation of the substrate is rapid, a very small amount of enzyme can produce a very great effect. One molecule of catalase can decompose 40,000 molecules of hydrogen peroxide per second at freezing point. Most enzymes are in fact present in relatively minute amounts.

Most enzymes activate only one kind of substrate each. Other enzymes are less highly specific, but even so each reacts only with chemically related substrates. There is correspondingly a large number of different enzymes, for all the different reactions of metabolism.

Each enzyme requires certain definite conditions for optimum performance, particularly as regards pH, the presence of specific accessory substances (co-enzymes, activators) and the absence of specific inhibiting substances.

Enzymes are unstable substances, and are easily destroyed or inactivated, e.g. by high temperature, or by a great range of chemical substances. Although they are not consumed by the reaction, enzymes slowly break down and have to be synthesized. Many of the micro-nutrients required by organisms probably go to regenerating certain enzymes and co-enzymes.

Enzymes are all produced within living cells and most of them do their work there, though they can often be extracted and can be studied outside the cell. Some enzymes (e.g. digestive enzymes of vertebrates) are normally secreted to the outside of cells. In metabolic processes of cells, and also in digestion, enzymes work very much as systems, the products of one reaction becoming the substrate of another.

The effective amount of any particular enzyme within a cell seems to be controlled in two main ways. (1) The synthesis of new enzyme molecules may be repressed or permitted through control of the activity of the gene ultimately responsible for their formation. *Enzyme induction* is the production of active enzyme, by removal of the repression of the relevant gene, when a metabolite, often a substrate for the enzyme, is administered to the cells (see Adaptive Enzyme). (2) The activity of already existing enzyme molecules may be inhibited, often by a product, not of the enzyme's own activity, but of the activity of another enzyme farther along the chain of enzymes which constitutes the enzyme system; thus providing an automatic self-limitation of the activity of the whole system. (See *End-product inhibition.*)

Closely similar enzymes, and enzyme systems, have been found in a wide variety of organisms, including plants, animals, and bacteria, and they account for the fundamental similarities of many aspects of their metabolism.

Several enzymes have been obtained pure and crystalline. Some of these are entirely protein (e.g. proteolytic enzymes); some are protein plus a prosthetic group (q.v.) (e.g. many concerned with

oxidation and reduction). Enzymes are usually named by attaching the suffix -*ase* to a root indicating the nature of the substrate
or of the reaction. See *Amylase, Dehydrogenase, Proteolytic Enzymes,
Adaptive Enzyme, Isoenzyme.*

EOCENE. Geological epoch (q.v.), subdivision of Tertiary, lasted
approximately from 54 till 38 million years ago.

EOSINOPHIL LEUCOCYTE. Polymorphonuclear leucocyte of vertebrates, containing granules staining in acid dyes such as eosin. In
human beings normally about 2-5 per cent of all leucocytes, but
become much increased in certain parasitic infections, and in
allergies.

EPHEMERAL. Plant with short life-cycle (seed germination to seed
production), having several generations in one year, e.g. groundsel.
Cf. *Annual, Biennial, Perennial.*

EPHEMEROPTERA. Mayflies. Order of exopterygote insects, with
aquatic nymphs which live a long time and may moult as many as
twenty-three times; but adults live only from a few minutes up to
a day and cannot eat or drink.

EPICOTYL. That portion of seedling stem above cotyledons.

EPIDEMIC. Large-scale temporary increase in prevalence of a disease
due to a parasite.

EPIDERMIS. Outermost layer of cells of a plant or animal. In plants
one cell-layer thick, covered in aerial parts by a non-cellular protective cuticle (q.v.). In vertebrates there is no non-cellular cuticle,
and epidermis is several cell-layers thick; outermost ones being
dead and horny (keratinized) in land-living vertebrates. See *Stratum
Corneum.* In invertebrates the epidermis is only one cell-layer
thick, and often secretes a cuticle.

EPIDIDYMIS. Long convoluted tube attached to testis of amniote
vertebrates. Receives into one end sperm from testis tubules, which
it stores and ripens. Other end leads into vas deferens and so
to exterior. Embryonically derived from mesonephros and its
duct.

EPIGAMIC CHARACTER. Character of an animal which is concerned in sexual reproduction; but other than the gonads and the
ducts with their associated glands which convey the gametes. E.g.
bird song.

EPIGEAL. (1) Of seed germination, seed leaves (cotyledons) appearing above ground, e.g. lettuce, tomato. Cf. *Hypogeal.* (2) Of animals,
inhabiting exposed surface of land, as distinct from undergound.

EPIGENESIS. Origin of entirely new structure during embryonic
development. Cf. *Preformation.*

EPIGLOTTIS. Flap of mucous membrane and cartilage in mammals
at base of tongue, on ventral wall of pharynx, against which glottis
is pushed and thus closed when swallowing.

EPIGYNOUS. See *Receptacle.*

EPINASTY. (Bot.). More rapid growth of upper side of an organ, e.g. in a leaf, resulting in downward curling of leaf-blade. Cf. *Hyponasty*.

EPINEPHRINE. Adrenaline (q.v.).

EPIPETALOUS. (Of stamens), borne on the petals, with stalks (filaments) more or less fused with petals and appearing to originate from them.

EPIPHYSIS. (1) Separately ossified end of growing bone, taking part in the joint; peculiar to mammalian limb-bone and vertebra. Epiphysis is separated from rest of the bone (diaphysis, q.v.) by a cartilage plate (epiphyseal cartilage); and growth in length of the whole bone occurs by encroachment into this plate of new bone from diaphysis side, and formation of new cartilage on epiphysis side. When growth is complete, epiphysis and diaphysis fuse. (2) A synonym for pineal body (q.v.).

EPIPHYTE. Plant attached to another plant, not growing parasitically upon it but merely using it for support, e.g. various lichens, mosses, and orchids, epiphytes on trees.

EPISOME. Discrete genetic elements that may become established in bacterial cell either in *autonomous* condition, replicating and being transferred independently of bacterial chromosome; or in *integrated* condition, attached to bacterial chromosome, participating with it in genetic recombination and transferred with it. Some episomes are viruses, others are not. Term was first applied to temperate bacteriophages (see *Lysogeny*) but other episomes without virus characteristics are now known, e.g. F (fertility or sex factor) in colon bacilli. Other genetic elements, *plasmids*, exist only in autonomous condition, incapable of integration with bacterial chromosome, e.g. a transferable factor (resistance transfer factor, RTF) conferring drug resistance on a variety of enteric bacteria.

EPISTASIS. Interaction between non-allelic genes in which presence of a certain (epistatic) allele at one locus prevents expression of an allele at a different locus. Analogous to dominance-recessiveness interaction between allelic genes. Cf. *Hypostasis*.

EPITHELIUM. (Zool.). Sheet or tube of firmly coherent cells, with minimal material between the cells. (The term is, however, often not applied to such sheets or tubes when they have been embryonically derived from mesoderm, e.g. lining of blood-vessels (endothelium) or of coelom (mesothelium).) Lines cavities and tubes and covers exposed surfaces of body; one surface of epithelium being therefore free, other resting usually on connective tissue. Its cells are frequently secretory, and secretory part of most glands is made of epithelium. Epithelia are classified according to height of cell (dimension at right angles to extension of sheet) relative to breadth, into *columnar*, *cubical*, and *squamous* (in order of diminishing relative height) and according to whether sheet is one cell thick (simple) or many (stratified). Examples of non-epithelial tissues are connective tissue, muscle, nervous tissue. See Fig. 2, p. 73. (Bot.).

Layer of cells lining schizogenously formed secretory canals and cavities, e.g. in resin canals of pine.

EPIZOITE. Non-parasitic sedentary animal living attached to another animal.

EQUATORIAL PLATE. Arrangement of chromosomes during metaphase of mitosis (q.v.) or meiosis (q.v.) when all lie approximately in one plane, at equator of spindle (q.v.).

EQUISETALES. Horsetails. Order of Pteridophyta with fossil record extending back to Palaeozoic. Attained their highest development in Carboniferous and included tree-like forms, e.g. *Calamites*. Now represented by single genus *Equisetum*. Perennial, herbaceous plants with rhizome sending up erect, grooved stems bearing at nodes whorls of rudimentary scale-leaves. Stem unbranched or bearing whorls of slender branches in axils of scale-leaves. Stem green, photosynthetic. Sporophylls compacted into distinct cones arising from cone axis at right angles and bearing several sporangia on under surface of terminal shield-shaped expansion. Homosporous, prothalli monoecious or dioecious depending on environmental conditions.

ERGASTOPLASM. Endoplasmic reticulum (q.v.).

ERGOT. (1) Disease of inflorescence of cereals and wild grasses caused by the ascomycete fungus *Claviceps purpurea*. (2) Dark spur-shaped sclerotium developing in place of a healthy grain in a diseased inflorescence. Ergots contain substances poisonous to man and animals. Some (ergotamine) are used in medicine.

ERYTHROBLAST. Cell of bone marrow, precursor of red blood corpuscle. Nucleated, undergoes mitosis, gradually develops haemoglobin.

ERYTHROCYTE. Red blood corpuscle (q.v.).

ERYTHROPOIETIN. Hormone that stimulates red blood cell production in response to reduced oxygen availability to the tissues; probably secreted by kidneys.

ESCAPE. Cultivated plant found growing as though wild.

ESOPHAGUS. See *Oesophagus*.

ESTERASE. One of the large group of different enzymes that hydrolyse various esters.

ESTROGEN, ESTROUS CYCLE. See *Oestrogen, Oestrous Cycle*.

ETAERIO. (Of fruits) an aggregation, e.g. of achenes, in buttercup; of drupes, in blackberry.

ETHIOPIAN. Zoogeographical region consisting of Africa south of the Sahara.

ETHOLOGY. Study of behaviour of an animal in its normal environment.

ETIOLATION. Phenomenon exhibited by green plants when grown in darkness. Such plants are pale yellow because of absence of chlorophyll, their stems are exceptionally long owing to abnormal lengthening of internodes, and their leaves reduced in size.

EUBACTERIA. Largest, most diverse group of bacteria. Most are unicellular, spherical, ovoid, cylindrical or helical in shape. Filamentous multicellular, and mycelial coenocytic forms also occur. Cell wall relatively thick and rigid, i.e. cell shape does not change (Cf. *Myxobacteria, Spirochaetes*). Includes non-motile forms and others motile by one or more flagella.

EUCARPIC. (Of fungi), mature thallus differentiated into distinct vegetative and reproductive portions. Cf. *Holocarpic.*

EUCARYOTIC (EUKARYOTIC). (Of cells or organisms). Having the nucleus separated from the cytoplasm by a nuclear membrane, and the genetic material borne on a number of chromosomes (q.v.) consisting of DNA and protein. Nuclear division is by mitosis. Cytoplasm contains membrane-bounded organelles most important of which for metabolism are mitochondria associated with respiration, and chloroplasts with photosynthesis. A flagellum (q.v.) or cilium, when present, contains eleven longitudinal strands, characteristically arranged. Eucaryotic cells are the unit of structure in all organisms except bacteria and blue-green algae. Cf. *Procaryotic.*

EUCHROMATIN. Chromosome material showing its maximum staining during metaphase (q.v.) and less dense staining in the interphase nucleus, when it is less condensed. Contains genes with major effects. Cf. *Heterochromatin.*

EUGENICS. Study of possibility of improving humanity by altering its genetic composition by encouraging breeding of those presumed to have desirable genes, and discouraging breeding of those presumed to have undesirable genes. It is rarely known who has which.

EUGLENOPHYTA. Division of algae. Possess chlorophylls a and b, β-carotene, xanthophylls, and store reserve food as polysaccharide *paramylum* and fat. Not completely autotrophic (q.v.), requiring vitamin $B_{12}$. Colourless, nonphotosynthetic forms occur; and change to this form can be induced but is irreversible. Unicellular, naked (without rigid cell wall), motile, one to three flagella per cell projecting from base of gullet at anterior end. Possess contractile vacuoles. Related to (link with) protozoa, and classified in class Flagellata by Zoologists. Asexual reproduction by cell division. Sexual reproduction rare, by copulation of individual cells. Mostly inhabiting fresh water, often abundant in water polluted by excretion.

EUPHOTIC ZONE. Zone near surface of sea (roughly upper 100 metres) into which sufficient light penetrates for active photosynthesis.

EUPLOID. Of a cell, having each of the different chromosomes of the set present in the same number; therefore with an exact multiple of the haploid chromosome number, e.g. diploid, polyploid. Cf. *Aneuploid.*

EURYHALINE. Able to tolerate wide variation of osmotic pressure of environment. Cf. *Stenohaline.*

EURYPTERIDA. An extinct (Palaeozoic) order of Arachnida, resembling scorpions in some features, but aquatic; some were very large (six feet long).

EURYTHERMOUS. Able to tolerate wide variations of temperature of environment. Cf. *Stenothermous.*

EUSPORANGIATE. (Of sporangia in vascular plants), arising from a group of parent cells and possessing a wall of two or more layers of cells. Spore production greater than in *leptosporangiate* (q.v.) type.

EUSTACHIAN TUBE. Tube connecting middle ear to pharynx in tetrapod vertebrates. Allows air pressure on inner side of ear-drum, i.e. in middle ear, to be equalized with that outside the animal, preventing distortion of ear-drum. See *Spiracle.*

EUTHERIA. Placentalia (q.v.).

EUTROPHIC. (Of lakes) highly productive in terms of organic matter formed, well supplied with nutrients. Cf. *Oligotrophic.*

EVERGREEN. Bearing leaves all the year round, e.g. laurel, pine. Cf. *Deciduous.*

EVOCATION. Induction in an embryonic tissue of a particular process of development, by a chemical substance (an *evocator*) diffusing from nearby tissue (or from an artificial implant). Best-known instance is evocation in vertebrates of neural development in ectoderm, as a result of diffusion of (an unknown) substance from under-lying chorda-mesoderm in gastrula stage. See *Organizer.*

EVOLUTION. Cumulative change in the characteristics of populations or organisms, occurring in the course of successive generations related by descent. The theory that evolution accounts for origin of all kinds of organisms now existing is opposed to the theory of special creation, i.e. that each kind of organism was created as such and is therefore not related by descent to any other. See *Natural Selection.*

EXCITABILITY. Irritability (q.v.).

EXCRETION. Getting rid of products of metabolism (either by storing them in insoluble form, or by removing them from body). In animals particularly applies to products of protein metabolism, organs mainly concerned being kidneys of vertebrates, Malpighian tubes of insects, and probably nephridia in many other invertebrates.

EXERGONIC. (Of a chemical reaction) yielding energy, as in oxidation of glucose to carbon dioxide and water during respiration. Cf. *Endergonic.*

EXODERMIS. Layer of closely fitting cortical cells with suberized walls, replacing the withered piliferous layer in older parts of roots.

EXOGAMY. Outbreeding. See *Inbreeding.*

EXOPTERYGOTA (HETEROMETABOLA, HEMIMETABOLA). Sub-class of insects in which adult form develops gradually by successive moults (cockroaches, mayflies, etc.) as distinct from the Endopterygota which have rapid metamorphosis.

EXOSKELETON. Skeleton covering the outside of the body, or situated in the skin. In Arthropoda the exoskeleton, e.g. cuticle (q.v.) of insects, or lime-impregnated cuticle of crabs, is superficial to the epidermis. Shell of many molluscs is a similar exoskeleton of lime-impregnated cuticle. In many vertebrates, e.g. scaly fish, tortoises, armadillo, the exoskeleton consists chiefly of bony plates beneath epidermis; in tortoise and armadillo these plates have a horny covering of keratin (q.v.) derived from epidermis. Cf. *Endoskeleton*.

EXPLANTATION. Tissue culture (q.v.).

EXPLORATORY BEHAVIOUR. Animal activity, not concerned with the direct satisfaction of a need (see Appetitive behaviour), which increases the information obtained by the animal about its surroundings.

EXPRESSIVITY. Intensity with which effect of a gene is realized in the phenotype. Influenced by genotype and environment to varying degrees. See *Penetrance*.

EXSICCATA (often abbreviated to EXSIC.). Dried, preserved plant material deposited in a herbarium.

EXTEROCEPTOR. Receptor (q.v.) which detects stimuli emanating from outside the animal, e.g. light, heat, sound. Cf. *Interoceptor*.

EXTRACELLULAR. (Zool.). Within an organism, but not within its constituent cells. Cf. *Intracellular*.

EXTRAEMBRYONIC. (Zool.). Derived from the zygote, but lying outside epidermis of embryo proper. *E. membranes* are those extraembryonic structures of vertebrates concerned in nutrition, respiration, and protection of embryo: yolk-sac, amnion, chorion, allantois.

EXTRORSE. (Of the dehiscence of an anther), away from centre of flower. Cf. *Introrse*.

EYE. Receptor organ for light. Some form of eye occurs very widely among animals, varying from the simple ocellus to the very complex organs of insects (see *Eye, Compound*), vertebrates (see Fig. 3) and cephalopod molluscs. Eyes of the two latter groups are extraordinarily similar, offering an interesting example of analogous (q.v.) organs. See parts labelled in Fig. 3, *Accommodation, Binocular Vision*.

EYE, COMPOUND. Eye of insects and Crustacea. Consists of a number of separate elements (ommatidia) each with light-sensitive cells and refractive system which can form an image; the ommatidia being separated from each other in varying degrees by pigment. According to the structure of the eye, and to the distribution of pigment between the ommatidia, the eye can form either *apposition* images, in which case each ommatidium will focus only rays almost parallel to its long axis, so that each forms an image of only

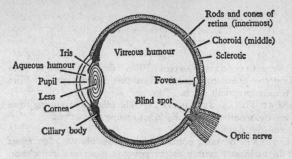

Rods and cones of
retina (innermost)

Choroid (middle)

Sclerotic

Iris · Vitreous humour

Aqueous humour

Pupil · Fovea

Lens · Blind spot

Cornea

Ciliary body · Optic nerve

*Fig 3. Section of mammalian eye through lens and optic nerve.*

a very small part of the visual field, an image of the whole resulting
from combination of these part images; or *superposition* images in
which the sense cells of an ommatidium may receive light from a
large part of the visual field so that the image received may overlap
those received by as many as thirty neighbouring ommatidia. The
superposition image thus gains in luminosity but loses in sharpness
compared with the apposition image. Diurnal insects have apposition eyes, nocturnal ones superposition, but there are many
intermediate grades; and in some cases one may change temporarily into the other by movement of pigment between the ommatidia
(dark adaptation).

EYE-MUSCLES. (a) *Extrinsic Eye-muscles.* Those outside eyeball. The
set of six muscles which move each eyeball, characteristic of all
vertebrates with functional eyes. Consists of anterior (i.e. near to
nose) pair of oblique muscles and four, more posterior (i.e. nearer
to ears), rectus muscles. Supplied by third, fourth, and sixth cranial
nerves. (See *Oculomotor, Trochlear, Abducens Nerves.*) (b) *Intrinsic
Eye-Muscles.* Those inside eyeball. See *Iris, Ciliary Body.*

EYE-SPOT. Light-sensitive organelle containing carotenoid pigment
found in many motile unicellular and colonial green algae and in
zoospores and gametes of non-motile forms; also called *stigma.*

# F

$F_1$ (FIRST FILIAL GENERATION). The offspring resulting from crossing the plants or animals of parental generation ($P_1$) from which an experiment starts.

$F_2$ (SECOND FILIAL GENERATION). The offspring resulting from crossing the members of the $F_1$ (q.v.) among themselves.

F FACTOR. See *Episome*.

FACIAL NERVE. Seventh cranial nerve of vertebrates. See *Hyoid Arch*. In mammals mainly motor, going to superficial muscles of face, and to salivary glands; also to taste-buds of front of tongue. A dorsal root (q.v.).

FACILITATION. Increase in the responsiveness of a nerve-cell or of an effector cell produced by summation (q.v.) of impinging impulses.

FACTOR (HEREDITARY). Gene (q.v.).

FAD. Flavin adenine dinucleotide. An oxidizing-reducing co-enzyme.

FAECES. Indigestible residue of food, together with residue of secretions, bacteria, etc., expelled from alimentary canal through anus.

FALLOPIAN TUBE (UTERINE TUBE). In female mammals, tube, with funnel-shaped opening just beside ovary, leading from peritoneal cavity to uterus. One on each side. By muscular and ciliary action it conducts eggs from ovary to uterus, and sperms from uterus to that place in upper part of tube where they fertilize descending eggs. Represents part of Müllerian duct of other vertebrates.

FAMILY. One of the kinds of group used in classifying organisms. Consists of a number of similar genera (sometimes of only one genus). Similar families are grouped in an order. In zoology, name of a family ends in – *idae*; in botany usually in – *ceae*. Families of flowering plants used to be called *natural orders*. See *Classification*.

FASCIA. Connective tissue; applied particularly to sheets thereof. E.g. *superficial fascia* of mammals, the loose connective tissue beneath dermis, containing fat in man and whale (blubber); *deep fascia*, tough sheets enclosing muscles and groups of muscles.

FASCIATION. Coalescing of stems, branches, etc., to form abnormally thick growths.

FASCICULAR (INTRAFASCICULAR) CAMBIUM. Cambium (q.v.) arising within a vascular bundle. Cf. *Interfascicular cambium*.

FAT. (1) Substance extractable from tissue by 'fat-solvent' (such as ether or hot alcohol) and containing a fatty acid. Lipide, Lipid, Lipin and Lipoid have all been used as synonyms for fat in this sense; but they have also been given more restricted meanings.

(2) In biochemical analysis 'fat' may refer simply to any substance extractable in fat solvent; and besides those containing fatty acids, would therefore comprise sterols (which however often occur chemically combined with fatty acids), steroids, carotene and, in plants, terpenes. (3) *True* (or *neutral*) *fat* is compound of glycerol and fatty acids.

FAT-BODY. (1) In many Amphibia and lizards, organ in abdomen containing fat as adipose tissue used up during hibernation. (2) In insects, diffuse tissue beneath skin, around gut, etc., storing fat, proteins, and sometimes glycogen and uric acid.

FATTY ACID. Organic aliphatic acid. Biological ones have usually straight chains and an even number of carbon atoms.

FAUNA. The animal population present in a certain place or at a certain epoch.

FEATHER FOLLICLE. Deep pit in epidermis surrounding base of feather. Wall of follicle at bottom of inpushing is continuous with base of feather.

FEED-BACK INHIBITION. See *End-product inhibition*.

FEMUR. Of tetrapod vertebrates, the thigh-bone. See Fig. 7, p. 213. Of insects, one of the segments (third from base) of the leg.

FERMENTATION. Decomposition of organic substances by organisms, especially bacteria and yeasts. E.g. decomposition of sugar forming ethyl alcohol and carbon dioxide by yeast in making of wine; or of ethyl alcohol forming acetic acid in making of vinegar. Not usually applied to decomposition of proteins, which is called putrefaction. Sometimes means anaerobic respiration.

FERN. See *Filicales*.

FERTILIZATION. The union of two special cells, the gametes (q.v.), the essential process of sexual reproduction. The resulting single cell is a zygote. Fertilization has two aspects: (a) fusion of two haploid nuclei which brings together in the zygote a selection of genes (q.v.) from two distinct individuals, i.e. the two parents, or from one individual in the case of self-fertilization; (b) initiation of development of a new individual. In parthenogenesis (q.v.) and pseudogamy (q.v.) aspect (b) occurs without aspect (a). *External fertilization*, union of gametes outside body of parents, as in many aquatic animals, e.g. Echinodermata. *Internal fertilization*, union of the gametes inside the female, as in most terrestrial animals (insects, tetrapods) and many aquatic animals of many different phyla. *Fertilization membrane*, tough membrane which appears at surface, or separates from surface, of many eggs when fertilized; in most cases it is the same as the vitelline membrane (q.v.).

FEULGEN METHOD. Staining method applied to histological sections, giving purple colour where there is deoxyribosenucleic acid (e.g. in chromosomes).

FIBRE. (Bot.). Element of sclerenchyma (q.v.); (Zool.). See *Collagen*, *Reticulin*, *Elastin*.

FIBRIN, FIBRINOGEN. See *Blood clotting.*

FIBROBLAST (FIBROCYTE). Kind of cell of irregular, branching shape, found distributed throughout vertebrate connective tissue. Function is apparently to form and maintain the extracellular collagen and mucopolysaccharide of this tissue. Similar shaped cell occurs in many invertebrates, possibly of same function.

FIBROUS ROOT. A fibrous root system consists of a tuft of adventitious roots of more or less equal diameter, arising from stem base or hypocotyl, and bearing smaller lateral roots, e.g. wheat, strawberry. Cf. *Tap root.*

FIBULA. The posterior of the two bones (other is tibia) in shank (below the knee) of hind-limb of tetrapod vertebrate. Lateral bone in lower leg of man. See Fig. 7, p. 213.

FILICALES. Ferns. Order of Pteridophyta including great majority of existing pteridophytes and a few extinct forms. Perennial plants with creeping or erect rhizome, or with erect aerial stem several metres in height, e.g. tropical tree ferns. Leaves characteristically large and conspicuous. Sporophylls like ordinary vegetative leaves, bearing sporangia on under surface, often in groups (sori), e.g. shield fern, or much modified, superficially unlike leaves, e.g. royal fern. Homosporous, prothalli bearing both antheridia and archegonia. Includes also a small group of aquatic, heterosporous ferns.

FIN. Of aquatic vertebrates: *Median f.* in mid-line of body, unpaired, either continuous, or as separate *dorsal, caudal* (which functions in propulsion of fish) or *ventral* fins. *Paired* fins are lateral: *pectoral* attached to shoulder-girdle, *pelvic* attached to pelvic girdle; these two pairs, homologues of tetrapod limbs though they do not contain comparable bones, occur in most fish but not in Agnatha; their usual function is control of direction of movement.

FIN-RAYS. Supports for fins; in most fish radiating skeletal rods, either cartilage, bone or collagen-like (elastoidin).

FISH. Pisces (q.v.).

FISSION. Reproduction by splitting into two equal parts (*binary fission*) or more than two equal parts (*multiple fission*). Binary fission occurs in many unicellular organisms, and some multicellular ones (e.g. corals); multiple fission occurs in the course of spore formation by Protozoa. Cf. *Budding.*

FITNESS. A measure of the response of a population of organisms to natural selection; based on the number of offspring contributed to the next generation in relation to the number of offspring required to maintain the particular population constant in size.

FIXATION. The first step in making permanent preparations of organisms or tissues for microscopic study; aims at killing cells, i.e. preventing subsequent change through metabolism or decay, with the least distortion of structure and in such a way that subsequent study is as easy as possible. Various chemicals are used as fixatives (e.g. formaldehyde, osmium tetroxide), often as mixtures. Almost all produce some artefacts, by aggregation of proteins or by dissolving structures.

FLAGELLATA (MASTIGOPHORA). Class of Protozoa characterized by possession of one or more flagella. Includes both plant- and animal-like forms and some with mixed characteristics. Opinions differ as to the position of some flagellated unicellular plants with chlorophyll and cellulose wall; some biologists include them in the Flagellata and some place them in the Algae. Different groups of Flagellata may be related to the various ancestors of the Metazoa, Parazoa, and Metaphyta, and it is possible that the other Protozoan groups were derived from flagellated forms.

FLAGELLUM. Fine long thread (about a quarter of a micrometre thick, and up to several hundred micrometres long) having lashing or undulating movement, projecting from a cell. Has an internal structure, shown by electron microscopy, consisting of an outer membrane continuous with plasma membrane and enclosing a matrix in which eleven fibrils (microtubules) are arranged longitudinally, a central pair of single fibrils being surrounded by nine double fibrils near the periphery. Anchored in cytoplasm on cylindrical body similar in structure to centriole (q.v.) known variously as *basal body, blepharoplast, kinetoplast, kinetosome*. Some flagella may bear exceedingly fine lateral projections (mastigonemes) along their length, or a delicate undulating membrane. Very widely distributed; characteristic of one group of unicellular organisms (Flagellata), present in most motile gametes, in zoospores, and in some metazoan cells, e.g. endodermal cells of *Hydra*. Usually only one or a few per cell, though occasionally, in some Protozoa, many. Motion of most flagella probably consists of waves which travel along them. Flagella are responsible for movement of those unicellular organisms and reproductive cells which bear them; and they move water through body of sponges. Flagella are also found in many bacteria, but are very much simpler in structure, consisting of a single fibril. See *Choanocyte*. Cf. *Cilium*.

FLAME CELL (SOLENOCYTE). Hollow cup-shaped cell with a bunch of cilia which work in the lumen. Flame cells are usually connected together by canals which ultimately open to the exterior of the animal. See *Nephridium*. Occur in several groups; Platyhelminthes, Nemertea, Rotifera, Annelida, larvae of Molluscs, amphioxus.

FLATWORMS. Platyhelminthes (q.v.).

FLORA. (1) Plant population of a particular area or epoch. (2) List of plant species (with descriptions) of a particular area arranged in families and genera, together with a key to aid identification.

FLORAL DIAGRAM. Diagram illustrating relative position and

number of parts in each of the sets of organs comprising a flower. See Fig. 4 below, and *Floral Formula.*

FLORAL FORMULA. An expression summarizing the information in a floral diagram (q.v.). The floral formula of buttercup, $K_5C_5A\infty$ $G\underline{\infty}$, indicates a flower with a calyx (K) of five free sepals, corolla (C) of five free petals, androecium (A) of an indefinite number of stamens and a gynoecium (G) of an indefinite number of free carpels. The line below the number of carpels indicates that the gynoecium is superior. The floral formula of the campanula, $K_5C_{(5)}A_5G(\overline{5})$, shows that the flower has five free sepals, five petals united ( ) to form a gamopetalous corolla, five stamens, and five carpels united ( ) to form a syncarpous gynoecium. The line above

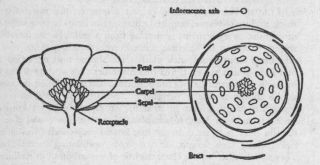

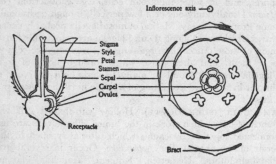

*Fig. 4. Diagrams illustrating flower structure; half-flower (median vertical (section) (left) and floral diagram (right). A. Buttercup; B. Campanula.*

the carpel number indicates that the gynoecium is inferior. See Fig. 4, above.

**FLORIGEN.** Hypothetical plant hormone suggested to explain transmission of flowering stimulus from leaf, where it is perceived, to growing point. See *Photoperiodism*.

**FLORISTICS.** Study of composition of vegetation in terms of the species (flora) present in it.

**FLOWER.** Specialized reproductive shoot, consisting of an axis (*receptacle*), on which are inserted four different sorts of organs. Outermost *sepals*, usually green, leaf-like, in the bud stage enclosing and protecting the other flower parts, and collectively known as the *calyx*. Within the sepals are the *petals*, usually conspicuous, brightly coloured parts, collectively known as the *corolla*. Calyx and corolla together constitute the *perianth*; they are not directly concerned in reproduction and are often referred to as *accessory* flower parts. Within the petals are the *stamens* (*microsporophylls*), each consisting of a filament (stalk) bearing an *anther*, in which *pollen grains* (*microspores*) are produced. In the centre of the flower is the *gynoecium*, comprising one or more *carpels* (*megasporophylls*), each consisting of an *ovary*, a terminal prolongation the *style*, bearing the *stigma*, receptive surface for pollen grains. The ovary contains a varying number of *ovules* which after fertilization develop into seeds. Stamens and carpels are together known as *essential* flower parts since they alone are concerned in reproduction. See Fig. 4, p. 112.

**FLUKE.** Parasitic flatworm (class Trematoda). Adults live in liver, gut, lung, or blood-vessel of a vertebrate, where they may cause serious disease (e.g. liver fluke; *Schistosoma*). Larvae (*miracidia*) which emerge from eggs passed out with excreta of host, parasitize snails, in which they reproduce asexually, giving rise to *rediae*, which ultimately produce *cercaria* (q.v.) larvae. These are immature flukes and are infective to another host, which may be the vertebrate in which the fluke becomes sexually mature, or in some cases another intermediate host.

**FLUORESCENT ANTIBODY TECHNIQUE.** Used for demonstrating the location of a particular antigen. Cells or tissues are treated with an antibody (specific to that antigen) which has been labelled by combining it with a substance that fluoresces in ultra-violet light. The antigen is located wherever fluorescence is observed.

**FMN.** Flavin mononucleotide. An oxidizing-reducing co-enzyme.

**FOETAL MEMBRANES.** Extraembryonic membranes (q.v.) of mammal.

**FOETUS.** Mammalian embryo after recognizable appearance of main features of fully developed animal; in man after about two months of gestation.

**FOLLICLE.** (Bot.). Dry fruit formed from a single carpel which splits open along a single line of dehiscence to liberate its seeds, e.g., larkspur, columbine. (Zool.). See *Ovarian Follicle, Graafian Follicle, Hair-Follicle*.

FOLLICLE-STIMULATING HORMONE (FSH). Gonadotropic hormone (q.v.) secreted by anterior lobe of pituitary in vertebrates. Stimulates growth of ovarian follicles and their oocytes in ovary, and formation of spermatozoa in testis.

FOLLICULAR PHASE. See *Oestrous Cycle*.

FONTANELLE. A gap in the skeletal covering of the brain, either in the chondrocranium, or between the dermal bones. The gap is covered only by skin and fascia. In human baby there is conspicuous parietal fontanelle on top of head between frontal and parietal bones.

FOOD-CHAIN. Chain of organisms, existing in any natural community, through which energy is transferred. Each link in the chain feeds on and obtains energy from the one preceding it and in turn is eaten by and provides energy for, the one following it. The number of links is usually three or four. At the beginning of the chain are green plants, and organisms whose food is obtained from green plants through the same number of links are described as belonging to the same *trophic* or *energy level*. Thus green plants occupy level one ($T_1$), the *producer* level. All other levels are *consumer* levels. $T_2$, herbivores, are primary consumers, $T_3$ and $T_4$, smaller and larger carnivores, respectively, are secondary consumers. At each trophic level much of the energy obtained is lost in respiration and thus fewer organisms can be supported at the succeeding one. Bacteria, fungi and some protozoa are consumers that operate in decomposition at all levels. All the food chains in a community make up the *food-cycle* or *food-web*.

FORAMEN. Opening. *F. magnum*, opening in back of vertebrate skull at articulation with vertebral column, through which spinal cord passes. *F. ovale*, of heart; opening between right and left auricles of embryonic mammal, allowing a large part of the oxygenated blood, which returns from the placenta through the vena cava inferior to the right auricle, to go straight to the left auricle, then to left ventricle and so through the aorta to the arteries of the body, instead of to the right ventricle and thence to pulmonary artery. Normally closes at birth.

FORAMINIFERA. Group of rhizopod Protozoa, mostly marine, which form shells usually of lime. Protrude, through pores in shell, many thread-like pseudopodia forming a network in which food is trapped. Some shells are microscopic, but others, colonial forms, may be 2 cm across. Foraminiferan shells form an important part of chalk, and of many deep-sea oozes (see *Globigerina Ooze*).

FORE-BRAIN (PROSENCEPHALON). Anterior of the three divisions marked out in the embryonic brain of vertebrates by constrictions. Gives rise during development to cerebral hemispheres, eyes, hypothalamus, etc.

FORM. (Bot.). Smallest of the groups used in classifying plants.

Category within species generally applied to members showing trivial variations from type, e.g. in colour of corolla. (Zool.). One of the kinds of a polymorphic species (see *Polymorphism*); a seasonal variant; or used as a neutral term in taxonomy when it is unclear as yet whether a species or sub-species or some minor grouping is the appropriate classification.

FORMATION. Climax community of plants extending over a very large natural area nature of which is determined by climate, e.g. tundra, tropical rain forest. Plant formations form the main natural vegetation types of the world.

FOSSIL. Remains of organism, or direct evidence of its presence, preserved in rocks. Generally hard parts only are preserved, usually partly or wholly replaced by minerals deposited from circulating water, as impressions or casts.

FOVEA. Shallow pit in retina of some vertebrates, which is place of greatest acuity of vision (Fig. 3, p.107). Contains no rods, but very numerous cones; and there are no blood-vessels, and no thick layer of nerve fibres, interposed between cones and incoming light, as in rest of retina. Occurs in diurnal birds and lizards, and in primates including man. An area of relatively acute vision, or *macula*, without a fovea, is found in many vertebrates (area containing yellow pigment surrounding fovea of man and some primates is *macula lutea*). In binocular vision the two eye-balls are orientated so that image of one object falls on both their foveae (or maculae); this object is 'looked at', i.e. it has predominant part in visual stimulation of the animal. Many vertebrates without binocular vision also similarly 'look at' objects with fovea or macula of one eye.

FRATERNAL TWINS. Dizygotic twins (q.v.).

FREE-MARTIN. Female member of unlike-sexed twins in cattle and occasionally in other ungulates. Sterile, and partially converted towards hermaphrodite condition by some influence (probably hormonal) of its twin brother, which reaches the free-martin because placental circulations fuse.

FRONTAL BONE. Dermal bone, a pair of which covers front part of brain in vertebrates (region of forehead in man). Air-spaces extend from nasal cavity into frontal bones of mammals (*frontal sinuses*).

FRUCTOSE (LAEVULOSE). A 6-carbon-atom sugar (hexose). Combined with glucose in sucrose. Widely distributed in plants.

FRUIT. Ripened ovary of the flower, enclosing seeds.

FRUSTULE. Diatom cell; wall consists of two halves or valves, the older (*epitheca*) fitting closely over the younger (*hypotheca*).

FSH. Follicle-Stimulating Hormone (q.v.).

FUCOXANTHIN. Carotenoid pigment present with chlorophyll in brown algae.

FUNCTION. The function of part of an organism is the way in which that part helps maintain the organism to which it belongs alive and able to reproduce; or sometimes it means simply the way it works, the processes going on in it. See *Adaptation* (Evolutionary).

FUNGI. Mycophyta (q.v.).

FUNGICIDE. Substance destructive to fungi.

FUNICLE. Stalk of ovule, attaching it to placenta (q.v.).

# G

$G_0$, $G_1$ and $G_2$ PHASES. See *Cell cycle*.

GALACTOSE. A hexose sugar; constituent of lactose, and commonly of plant polysaccharides (many gums, mucilages, and pectins) and of animal glycoproteins.

GALL-BLADDER. Small bladder in many vertebrates arising from bile duct (q.v.) near or in liver, storing bile between meals. Contractile walls empty bladder when there is food, especially fat, in intestine, probably activated to do so by hormones secreted by intestine wall.

GAMETANGIUM. (Bot.). Organ in which gametes are produced.

GAMETE (GERM-CELL). Reproductive cell whose nucleus and often cytoplasm fuses with that of another gamete (constituting fertilization), the resulting cell (zygote) developing into a new individual. Gametes are haploid. They are usually differentiated into female gamete (immobile, with massive cytoplasm, able to develop when stimulated, called the ovum) and male gamete (moves or is moved to female gamete, with little cytoplasm e.g. sperm of animals), one of each fusing to form the zygote. See *Heterogamy*, *Isogamy*, *Sperm*, *Ovum*, *Fertilization*. Some animal and plant species produce cells, which are also called gametes, of substantially the same kind as a female gamete of the same or related organism, but which develop into a new individual without fertilization (i.e. by parthenogenesis, q.v.); such gametes are usually diploid.

GAMETOCYTE. Cell which undergoes meiosis, forming gametes. See *Oocyte*; *Spermatocyte*.

GAMETOPHYTE. Phase of life cycle of plants which has haploid (q.v.) nuclei; during it the sex-cells are produced. It arises from a (haploid) spore produced by meiosis from a (diploid) sporophyte (q.v.). See *Alternation of Generations*.

GAMMA GLOBULINS. Class of serum proteins which contains many antibodies.

GAMOPETALOUS (SYMPETALOUS). (Of a flower), with united petals, e.g. primrose. Cf. *Polypetalous*.

GAMOSEPALOUS. (Of a flower), with united sepals, e.g. primrose. Cf. *Polysepalous*.

GANGLION. Small solid mass of nervous tissue containing numerous cell-bodies (q.v.). The central nervous system of many invertebrates consists largely of such ganglia, connected by nerve cords, very variously arranged but usually well-developed in the head (*cerebral ganglia*). In vertebrates the central nervous system has a different structure, but ganglia occur in the peripheral nervous system (see *Nerve-Root*) and autonomic nervous system. Some of the 'nuclei' of the brain are called ganglia.

GANOID. A primitive actinopterygian fish, e.g. Acipenser, Polypterus.

GANOID SCALE. Scale typical of primitive Actinopterygii. Same components as cosmoid scale (q.v.), but much thicker layer of superficial enamel-like substance (ganoine). Unlike cosmoid scale, grows in thickness by addition of layers of material all round, ganoine above as well as laminated bone below.

GASTRIC. (Adj.). Of the stomach.

GASTROPODA. Class of Mollusca, including snails, slugs, sea-hares. Marine, freshwater, and terrestrial. Head distinct, with eyes and tentacles; often a single (univalve) shell.

GASTRULA. Stage of embryonic development of an animal, succeeding blastula, when the gastrulation movements occur.

GASTRULATION. Embryological term for the complex of cell movements which occurs in almost all animals at the end of the cleavage period. See *Blastula*. The movements carry those cells whose descendants will form the future internal organs from their largely superficial position in the blastula to approximately their definitive positions inside the embryo. In many embryos, these presumptive internal organs undergo gastrulation in two main groups of cells, endoderm (future gut, etc.), and mesoderm (future muscle, blood, etc.). The ectoderm (future external layer, and also the future nervous system, which later becomes internal) is also rearranged during the gastrulation movements to approximately its definitive position. See *Blastopore*.

GEMMA. Organ of vegetative reproduction in mosses and liverworts; consisting of a small group of cells of varying shape and size that becomes detached from the parent and develops into a new plant; often formed in groups, in receptacles known as gemma-cups.

GEMMATION. Kind of asexual reproduction by formation of a group of cells (a gemma in plants) which develops into a new individual, or a new member of a colony of connected individuals. It may develop before or after it separates (completely or partially) from its parent. Occurs in many liverworts, mosses, coelenterates, ascidians. Commonly called *budding* in animals.

GEMMULE. Of sponges, a bud formed internally as a group of cells, which may become free by decay of parent and subsequently form a new individual. Freshwater sponges over-winter in this way.

GENE (HEREDITARY FACTOR). Unit of the material of inheritance. *The material of inheritance*. Much of the similarity between organisms related by descent is due to their possessing similar inherited material; i.e., a complex and diverse material that gives rise to accurate copies of itself; units of which are passed from parent to offspring; which is very stable in its properties; and which profoundly influences every aspect of the organism containing it. Each individual starts life with a set of this material received from its parent or parents. During subsequent growth (in a multicellular organism) or reproduction (when the organism is not multicellular) the material is duplicated repeatedly, with great exactness of copying (the process of *replication*); it influences the characteristics developed by the individual bearing it, so that similarity between related organisms results; and a set is handed on to each of the individual's progeny. One of the great biological discoveries of this century is that the material of inheritance is nucleic acid: a chain molecule, the links of which consist of four different nucleotides, and the complexity of which lies in the arrangement of the sequence of these nucleotides. In the majority of cases it is deoxyribonucleic acid (DNA) but in some viruses ribonucleic acid (RNA). In plants and animals the DNA is situated in the thread-like chromosomes of the nucleus (though it occurs also in some cytoplasmic structures) which contain much protein besides; in bacteria and viruses the chromosomes are simpler, consisting only of a long thread of DNA.

*The gene as a unit.* The DNA occasionally undergoes a localized change in its sequence of nucleotides, known as a *mutation*, the changed, mutant, form then being replicated and inherited instead of the original form of the DNA. Such mutant DNA then produces a difference in certain characters of the organisms that inherit it. The results of many different mutations can be found in any large population of individuals of a species. Some of these mutations will differ from each other in that each affects a different set of characters of the individual; and when, as is possible by various methods, the approximate positions (in the set of chromosomes) of the changes in DNA that constitute these different mutations is discovered, each is found to have its own characteristic place. Of the mutations found scattered amongst the individuals of a population there will however also be some that form pairs or larger groups, in that the members of a given pair or group affect the *same* set of characters, but differ from each other by affecting it in different ways; and within any one of these groups the mutations turn out to have altered the DNA in nearly or quite the same relative place in the chromosomes, the short length of chromosome within which they occur being a gene.

A *gene* is then a short length of a chromosome, influencing a particular set of characters in a particular way, the set of characters and the length of chromosome constituting a unit because the set of characters is affected as a whole by any mutation occurring anywhere within this length of DNA. (A gene thus defined as part of a chromosome which functions as a unit is often called a *cistron*.)

*Gene function.* How can there be such units of function within the DNA? Because each gene belonging to the large group of *structural genes* is responsible, during protein synthesis, for the exact sequence of amino-acids making up one specific kind of polypeptide chain (a protein molecule consists of one or more polypeptide chains). The set of characters influenced by one such gene is that set which is dependent, directly or indirectly, on the presence of its particular protein (most proteins, being enzymes, are likely to have widespread effects). The genes of another large group, the regulative genes, produce their effects by influencing the activities of these structural genes.

The DNA of an organism is then made up of a number of different genes. Each gene during growth is repeatedly exactly replicated. When a gene mutates, its changed structure is thenceforward replicated, and if it is a structural gene this leads to the production of a protein with a different sequence of amino-acids. The mutant gene and the original gene are said to be *alleles* of (or *allelomorphic* to) each other. All the different forms that a given gene can be changed to as a result of mutation constitute a series of alleles.

*Genes and chromosomes.* Every cell of each individual of any plant or animal species usually has an identical set of a number of different chromosomes (bearing different genes). Every cell of an individual usually therefore has an identical set of genes (perhaps 10,000 in Drosophila). Individuals of the same species differ from each other in having different members of some of the series of alleles. Each chromosome has its genes arranged in single file ('linear order') along its length. Every specimen of a particular chromosome has its genes arranged in the same characteristic order along its length. The fixed position in the chromosome (relative to other genes) always occupied by one of a series of alleles is a *locus*. Only one member of a series of alleles can at any one time be present in one locus. Some genes, particularly those concerned with forming the RNA of the ribosomes are, however, repeated (*reiterated*) many times in identical or similar form within one set of chromosomes.

Before nuclear division by mitosis (q.v.) the genes in each chromosome are replicated, and the whole chromosome becomes double. Each of the two cells resulting from mitosis receives one of the replicas and has therefore exactly the same complement of genes and chromosomes.

In the body-cells of animals and higher plants chromosomes occur in pairs, the members of which have identical appearance (except sex-chromosomes, q.v.). The members of such a pair have the same arrangement of loci; and the genes in the two corresponding loci of a pair of chromosomes may either be identical, or two different members of an alellomorphic series. If identical, the individual is said to be *homozygous* for that locus; if alleles, *heterozygous*.

*Genes and the variety of individuals.* While every body-cell of a multi-cellular organism, with rare exceptions, has an identical set of genes, this is not true of the gametes produced by an individual, which are of enormous variety. A gamete, as the result of meiosis (q.v.), has only one member of each pair of chromosomes. But the two members of any pair of chromosomes usually differ from each other, because some of the loci are heterozygous, so that gametes receiving different members of a pair of chromosomes will be different. Since it is a matter of chance which member of each pair of chromosomes a gamete receives, a gamete may with equal probability have any of the possible combinations of one member of each pair of chromosomes, i.e. any of $2^x$ combinations where x is the number of chromosome pairs. This chance distribution is known as *independent assortment*. The number of different gametes produced by an individual is actually much further increased, by the phenomenon of *crossing-over* (q.v.), the resulting chromosomes being different, in the particular set of alleles they contain, from any possessed by the parent organism. A further, but much rarer, source of diversity in gametes is through mutation during their formation.

Knowing the laws governing the distribution of the chromosomes to the gametes, and assuming that it is a matter of chance which male gamete fertilizes which female gamete, we can calculate the probable distribution of one or more alleles amongst offspring of parents of given genetic constitution. The relative proportions of different kinds of offspring resulting are the *Mendelian ratios*, whose discovery in actual breeding experiments led Mendel to formulate the basic laws of inheritance.

The result of the variety of gametes produced by an individual is variety of offspring produced by any pair of parents. The chance of two such offspring being genetically alike is very remote, and (barring polyembryony, q.v.) probably no two individuals of a sexually reproducing population are genetically alike. This means that a great range of variation is always available for evolutionary change by natural selection (q.v.). This variety depends on the genes behaving as independent units, which segregate in gamete formation. If the genetic material received by an organism from its parents really blended together, then all the gametes produced by that organism would be alike, constituted of the same blend. All the variety within a population does not of course depend upon this diversity of chromosomal genes. Some depends on environmental differences during development of individuals. A small amount may depend on genetic material carried in cytoplasmic structures and not distributed by the segregating mechanism of the chromosomes. Differences between species are probably fundamentally of the same kind as differences within species.

For *operator gene, regulator gene, structural gene,* see *Operon.*

GENECOLOGY. Study of genetical composition of plant populations in relation to their habitats.

GENE EXCHANGE. Production of fertile offspring possessing new combinations of parental genes that occurs within a breeding population. Used by biosystematists in determining and defining limits of population units. See *Species, Ecotype, Ecospecies, Coenospecies.*

GENE FLOW. Movement of genes, as result of mating and gene exchange, within populations.

GENE FREQUENCY. Frequency of occurrence of a given kind of gene in a population in relation to frequency of all its alleles.

GENE POOL. Collective name for all the genes of a particular population.

GENERALIZED. Not specialized (q.v.).

GENERATION TIME. Mean time, within a population of cells, between a cell division and that of its daughter cells.

GENERIC. (Adj.). Of genus (q.v.).

GENETIC. Concerned with the genes (q.v.); or concerned with development.

GENETIC ASSIMILATION. See *Acquired characteristics, inheritance of*.

GENETIC DRIFT. Change in the genetic make-up of a population occurring, not as a result of natural selection, but by chance. Only happens in small, isolated, populations.

GENETICS. Study of heredity and variation; of the resemblances and differences between organisms. See *Gene*.

GENOME (GENOM). The set of chromosomes found in each nucleus of a given species.

GENOTYPE. Genetic constitution (the particular set of alleles present in each cell of an organism), as contrasted with the characteristics manifested by the organism (phenotype, q.v.).

GENUS. One of the kinds of group used in classifying organisms. Consists of a number of similar species; occasionally of one species only. Similar genera are grouped in a family. See *Binomial Nomenclature, Classification*.

GEOBOTANY. Branch of botany dealing with all aspects of relations between plants and the earth's surface; comprises plant ecology and plant geography.

GEOLOGICAL PERIODS AND EPOCHS. Main fossil-bearing geological periods and their ages (it must be emphasized that the latter are only approximate) are as follows:

| Era | Period | Million years since beginning of period |
|---|---|---|
| Cenozoic | Quaternary | 1.5 |
| | Tertiary | 65 |
| Mesozoic | Cretaceous | 135 |
| | Jurassic | 190 |
| | Triassic | 225 |
| Palaeozoic | Permian | 280 |
| | Carboniferous | 345 |
| | Devonian | 395 |
| | Silurian | 440 |
| | Ordovician | 500 |
| | Cambrian | 570 |

The Quaternary period is subdivided into the Recent (or Holocene) epoch (since the last glaciation) and the Pleistocene epoch. The Tertiary period is subdivided into the following epochs (in brackets, millions of years since beginning of epoch): Pliocene (7), Miocene (26), Oligocene (38), Eocene (54), Palaeocene (65). Sometimes the Pleistocene, Pliocene and Miocene are grouped into the Neogene, and the Oligocene, Eocene and Palaeocene into the Palaeogene. The Cambrian and all subsequent periods are known as the Phanerozoic; the pre-Cambrian as the Cryptozoic. The Upper Palaeozoic is Devonian to Permian, the Lower is Cambrian to Silurian, inclusive.

The fossil record begins in Pre-Cambrian times with the discovery of a few organisms resembling bacteria and blue-green algae in deposits dating back more than three billion years. A few green algae have been identified from an upper Pre-Cambrian formation approximately one billion years old. In Cambrian rocks, in addition to algae, a great variety of aquatic invertebrate animals (brachiopods, trilobites, etc.) occur as well as micro-organisms including fungi. There is little doubt that many fragile primitive organisms died without trace. Spores with wall markings like those of various land plants were also present. In Ordovician times fish-like vertebrates (Ostracoderms) made their appearance. Primitive land plants are known from the Silurian period. Colonization of land by plants was an event of enormous importance for animals making it possible for them too, dependent on green plants for food to live there permanently. By the late Devonian, arthropods, including insects, were established on land and the first terrestrial vertebrates, amphibians, had appeared. Club mosses, horsetails and ferns, many of them tree-like, were now abundant. They provided an enormously rich flora in Carboniferous times. Gymnosperms, mosses and liverworts, algae and fungi were also present. Tremendous accumulations of the remains of Carboniferous plants, partially decayed and subjected to intense pressure by overlying deposits, formed the coal seams of today. The Mesozoic era was the age of the great dinosaurian reptiles, and gymnosperms were the dominant plants. Angiosperms appeared in the Jurassic, became increasingly dominant towards the end of the Cretaceous as the gymnosperms declined, and remained the dominant plant group to the present day. The ascendancy of the mammals also began with the end of the Mesozoic.

GEOPHYTES. Class of Raunkiaer's Life Forms (q.v.).

GEOTAXIS. Taxis (q.v.) in which stimulus is gravitational force.

GEOTROPISM. (Bot.). Orientation of plant parts under stimulus of gravity. Main stems, *negatively geotropic*, grow vertically upwards and, if laid horizontal, elongation of cells in growth region at tip is increased on lower side and growing tip turns upwards, resuming vertical position. Main roots, *positively geotropic*, grow vertically

downwards and if laid horizontal, elongation of cells in apical
growth region is increased on upper side and root turns downwards
again. Generally accepted response mechanism is based on re-
distribution of auxin (q.v.) under stimulus of gravity, accumulation
of auxin on lower side of organ accelerating cell elongation in stem
and retarding it in root. Recent work suggests instead that effect
is due to unequal production of auxin on upper and lower side, i.e.
to changes in auxin metabolism. See also *Diageotropism* and *Plagiogeotropism*.

GEPHYREA. Class of annelids; a few genera of marine burrowing
worms. Coelom spacious; segmentation partially or completely
absent; chaetae present in some species.

GERM-CELLS. Gametes (q.v.)

GERMINAL EPITHELIUM. Epithelium lining seminiferous tubules o
vertebrate testis, from which during sexual maturity arise the
spermatogonia and the Sertoli cells that presumably nourish the developing sperm; applied also to epithelium covering coelomic
surface of vertebrate ovary, which probably forms follicle cells,
though it is now doubtful whether it forms oogonia throughout
sexual maturity.

GERMINAL VESICLE. Nucleus of animal oocyte during the period of
cytoplasmic growth. It is in prophase of the first meiotic division
and is enormously enlarged, with very little stainable chromatin
and with prominent nucleoli. Gene transcription is very active.
See *Lampbrush chromosome*.

GERM-LAYER. (Zool.). One of the main layers or groups of cells
which can be distinguished in an embryo during and immediately
after gastrulation (q.v.). These layers are roughly similar in
arrangement, and in ultimate differentiation, in most animals.
There are two in diploblastic animals, endoderm (q.v.) and ectoderm (q.v.). In triploblastic animals there is in addition the mesoderm (q.v.). There is general agreement as to which layer gives
rise to which tissues, e.g. nervous tissue is characteristically ectodermal, cartilage both mesodermal and ectodermal. (But it is not
agreed to which germ-layer the chordate notochord belongs.) It
is now known that the equating of the layers in different groups
cannot be pushed to extremes, as it formerly was, by supposing that
a given sort of tissue is in all groups of animals entirely derived from
a given germ-layer. Though the general architecture is similar,
there are also numerous differences between groups.

GERM-PLASM. A particular sort of protoplasm which Weismann
(1834–1914) suggested was transmitted substantially unchanged
from generation to generation via the germ-cells, giving rise in
each individual to the body-cells (soma) but itself remaining distinct and unaffected by the environment of the individual (*theory
of continuity of the germ-plasm*). Roughly equateable with modern
genes (q.v.) which however are not restricted to germ-cells but

occur in all cells. A special cytoplasm in ovum which during embryonic development becomes restricted to future germ-cells of adult, a sort of germ-plasm which does not however give rise to the soma, has been demonstrated in some animals, though not in others.

GESTATION PERIOD. Length of time from conception to birth in viviparous animal.

GIANT FIBRE. Nerve fibre (q.v.) of very large diameter (up to 1 mm. in squids) occurring in many invertebrates (e.g. annelids, crustaceans, cephalopods), and some vertebrates, providing very rapid conduction of impulses for sudden locomotion. Can be either a single enormous cell, or the result of fusion of many cells.

GIBBERELLINS. Class of plant hormones having spectacular effect in promoting stem elongation of certain plants (e.g. causes dwarf peas to grow to same height as tall varieties). Involved also in other processes of plant growth and development including some responses to light and temperature, dormancy, sex expression, flowering and fruit formation. Originally isolated from Ascomycete fungus *Gibberella fujikuroi* that causes abnormal elongation of infected host (rice) plants. Occurs in some other fungi and bacteria. Widely distributed in plants where major sites of concentration and, presumably, of synthesis, are regions of rapid development, e.g. apical buds, young leaves, root tips, developing seeds. Move through plant in both xylem and phloem.

GILL. (1) (Bot.). See *Lamella*, *Gill-fungi*. (2) (Zool.). Respiratory organ of aquatic animals: a projection of external surface of body or of internal layer of gut, well supplied with blood; through gill surface interchange by diffusion of oxygen and carbon dioxide between water and blood occurs. Often complex form, providing large surface area. Gills of most fishes are *internal gills* within gill slits, consisting of projections from wall of pharynx, i.e. endodermal. Gills of amphibian and dipnoan larvae, and of adults of some urodeles, are *external gills*, from epidermis of gill-slits, i.e. ectodermal.

GILL-BAR. Tissue separating adjacent gill-slits in chordates, containing blood-vessels, nerves, and skeletal support.

GILL-CLEFT. (1) Inpushing of epidermis corresponding to gill-pouch (q.v.); (2) Synonymous with gill-slit (q.v.).

GILL FUNGI. Fungi belonging to the family Agaricaceae of the Basidiomycetes; possessing a characteristic fruit-body consisting of a stalk (stipe) supporting a cap (pileus) on the under surface of which are radially arranged gills (lamellae) bearing the hymenium, e.g. mushrooms, toadstools.

GILL-POUCH. Outpushing of side-wall of pharynx towards epidermis in all chordate embryos, precursor of gill slit in fish and some Amphibia, but breaks through to exterior only temporarily or never in terrestrial vertebrates. A series of gill-pouches occurs on each side, one behind the other. See *Spiracle*. Term also used for gill-slit of adult when this is unusually sac-like (cyclostomes).

GILL-SLIT. Opening from side of pharynx to exterior in aquatic chordates. Usually vertically elongated, several lying in a series one behind the other on each side. Primitively probably concerned in filtering food particles from water pumped through them by action of cilia (as in tunicates and amphioxus). In fish and some Amphibia serve for respiration, the water, which is pumped through by muscular action, oxygenating blood in the gills (q.v.). Absent in adult tetrapod vertebrates, except in a few Amphibia, but occur in many tetrapod embryos. See also *Gill-Pouch*. Presence of gill-slits, or at least of gill-pouches and corresponding epidermal grooves at some stage of development, is a characteristic of phylum Chordata.

GINKGOALES. Order of Gymnospermae that flourished during the Mesozoic and now represented by one living member often referred to as a 'living fossil', *Ginkgo* (maidenhair tree). Leaves wedge-shaped, deciduous. Dioecious; microsporophylls arranged loosely in a catkin-like male cone; female cone consisting of a stalk bearing, usually, two ovules. Male gametes motile by cilia.

GIZZARD. Part of alimentary canal in many animals, where food is broken up. Precedes main digestion region. Very muscular walls; often contains hard 'teeth' attached to walls, e.g. Crustacea, or hard swallowed objects, as in birds.

GLAND. An organ (sometimes a single cell) whose main function is to build up one or more specific chemical compounds (secretions) which are passed to the outside of the gland.

(Bot.). Superficial, discharging secretion externally, e.g. glandular hair (lavender), nectary (q.v.), hydathode (q.v.); or embedded in tissue, occurring as isolated cells containing the secretion, or as layer of cells surrounding intercellular space (secretory cavity or canal) into which secretion is discharged, e.g. resin canal of pine. (Zool.). Most glands are *exocrine*, i.e. their secretions are discharged, usually through a tube or *duct*, on to a surface, either the outer (epidermal) surface of the body, e.g. sweat-glands of mammals, or the inner surface of the gut, e.g. digestive glands. There are also in some animals *endocrine glands*, secreting hormones (q.v.) directly into blood.

GLENOID CAVITY. Cup-like hollow on each side of pectoral girdle (on scapula and, when present, coracoid) into which head of humerus fits, forming shoulder-joint, in tetrapod vertebrate.

GLIA (NEUROGLIA). Supporting tissue of vertebrate central nervous system, consisting mainly of cells derived from embryonic neural tissue, some with long fibrous processes, others forming myelin by wrapping flattened processes in a spiral round nerve fibres. Glia also contains mesodermal cells (microglia) closely similar to macrophages.

GLOBIGERINA OOZE. Calcareous mud, covering huge areas of ocean-bottom (about ⅓ of whole sea floor) mainly formed from shells of Foraminifera (Protozoa), *Globigerina* being important genus.

GLOBULINS. Group of proteins, all heat-coagulable, soluble in dilute salt solution but not in water. Widely distributed in cells of plants and animals. Amongst globulins are the main proteins of plant seeds; and antibodies.

GLOMERULUS. Of vertebrate kidney; small bunch of capillaries, covered by thin epithelium, which projects into Bowman's capsule (q.v.). Capillaries are supplied with blood by an arteriole, and in birds and mammals discharge into another (efferent arteriole) which in turn supplies capillaries of uriniferous tubule (q.v.). Much of the dissolved substances, and much of the water, of blood flowing through glomerulus filters into capsule and passes down tubule (where most is reabsorbed into bloodstream again). Plasma proteins and blood corpuscles do not filter into capsule.

GLOSSOPHARYNGEAL NERVE. Ninth cranial nerve of vertebrates. In mammals mainly concerned with both sensory and motor aspect of the swallowing reflex, and taste-buds of back of tongue. A dorsal root (q.v.).

GLOTTIS. Opening of trachea into pharynx of vertebrate. Can usually be closed by muscles. In mammals, opening between vocal cords. See *Larynx, Epiglottis, Trachea.*

GLUCAGON. Hormone of vertebrates, produced by the islets of Langerhans (q.v.) of pancreas. It causes breakdown of glycogen in the liver, with release of glucose into the blood. Its effect on blood-sugar is hence the opposite of that of insulin. Chemically it is a small protein.

GLUCOCORTICOIDS. See *Adrenal gland.*

GLUCOSE (DEXTROSE). A 6-carbon-atom sugar (a hexose) widely distributed in plants and animals, particularly in compounds as disaccharides, e.g. sucrose, and polysaccharides, e.g. starch, cellulose, glycogen. Splitting of glucose, ultimately to $CO_2$ and water, involving intermediary combining with phosphate, is a major energy-source for metabolic processes. In green plants, glucose is product of photosynthesis, from $CO_2$ and water; it is stored as starch. In animals, glucose is obtained mainly from digestion of di- and polysaccharides and deamination of amino acids; it is stored as glycogen. See *Blood Sugar.*

GLUME (STERILE GLUME). Chaffy bract, pair of which occur at base of grass spikelet, enclosing it.

GLYCOGEN. 'Animal starch'. A soluble polysaccharide (q.v.) built up of numerous glucose molecules. Carbohydrate is stored by animals and fungi as glycogen. In vertebrates occurs especially in liver and muscles.

GLYCOLYSIS. First stage in the series of chemical reactions of respiration and fermentation. Conversion of glucose, by means of a complex system of enzymes and co-enzymes, into lactic acid (in animals, some fungi and bacteria) or pyruvic acid (in plants, yeast and some other fungi, few bacteria). Some energy in the form of ATP (q.v.) is made available for biochemical work, but this is small in comparison with that liberated in Krebs cycle (q.v.); it is of great importance in satisfying for short period energy demand beyond that provided by oxygen availability, e.g. in animals in short bursts of intense muscular activity.

GLYCOPROTEIN (MUCOPROTEIN). Compound of protein and polysaccharide. The protein forms a backbone with polysaccharide as one or many side-chains. These side-chains are of complex constitution but are shorter than those of mucopolysaccharides (q.v.) so that the protein tends to predominate.

GLYCOSAMINOGLYCAN. Mucopolysaccharide (q.v.).

GLYCOSIDE. Compound yielding by enzymatic or acid hydrolysis a sugar (most frequently glucose) and one or more other substances. Widely distributed in plants, e.g. anthocyanins (q.v.), amygdalin, sinigrin, digitalin, strophanthin, indican. Formation of some glycosides thought to render unwanted substances chemically inert; other functions ascribed to particular glycosides include formation of food reserves, control of invasion by pathogens. When the other substance is also a sugar, di- tri- or polysaccharides result.

GNATHOSTOMATA. Vertebrates with jaws. A grouping of vertebrate classes sometimes used in classification as a sub-phylum in contrast to Agnatha.

GNETALES. Order of Gymnospermae (q.v.) showing resemblances to Angiospermae in the presence of true vessels in the secondary wood and absence of archegonia in the ovule (except in *Ephedra*). Comprises three genera, *Ephedra*, *Welwitschia*, and *Gnetum*, which differ remarkably in habit and geographical distribution.

GOBLET CELL. Pear-shaped cell, present in some epithelia, the part near the free surface of the epithelium being swollen with mucin, which is secreted from time to time on to the surface.

GOLGI APPARATUS (G. BODY, G. MATERIAL). Local structure present in cytoplasm of animal and plant cells. Appears by electron microscopy as a group of paired membranes constituting a number of flattened sacs (cisternae) aligned roughly parallel, frequently with vesicular expansions, and associated with separate vesicles of various sizes. Vesicles seem to arise in some cells at the ends of tubules that extend as a meshwork from the margins of the cisternae. In cells of vertebrates there is usually one such complex body, in those of invertebrates and plants there may be several (*dictyosomes*, q.v.) scattered in the cytoplasm. Function imperfectly known, but concerned in secretion, e.g. in plants conspicuous in young cells and thought to be concerned in secretion of certain wall material. See Fig. 1, p. 51.

GONAD. Organ of animals which produces gametes. In some animals produces hormones too. See *Ovary; Testis; Ovotestis.*

GONAD HORMONES. Sex hormone produced by gonad. In vertebrates they are steroids. See *Androgen, Oestrogen, Progesterone.*

GONADOTROPIC (GONADOTROPHIC) HORMONES (GONADO-TROPINS). Hormones secreted by anterior lobe of pituitary (q.v.) of vertebrates, and by mammalian placenta, which control activity of gonads. Chemically they are glycoproteins. Their output from the pituitary is controlled by the hypothalamus (q.v.); changes in output are responsible for the onset of sexual maturity, for breeding season rhythms, and for oestrous cycles (q.v.). See *Follicle-Stimulating Hormone, Lactogenic Hormone, Luteinizing Hormone.*

GRAAFIAN FOLLICLE. Fluid-filled spherical vesicle in mammalian ovary containing an oocyte (q.v.) attached to its wall. Differs from ovarian follicle of other vertebrates in presence of cavity. Cavity first appears towards end of period of cytoplasmic growth of oocyte, amongst the follicle cells which closely surround oocyte. Cavity enlarges during early part of oestrous cycle (q.v.) of those mammals which have such a cycle, separating follicle cells into an external layer and a layer adherent to oocyte. Enlargement continues until follicle bursts on to surface of ovary, discharging the oocyte (ovulation, q.v.). A considerable number of follicles which grow during the first part of an oestrous cycle never ovulate, but degenerate. Growth of follicles is under influence of pituitary gland. See *Follicle-Stimulating Hormone.* Follicle cells are probably mainly responsible for oestrogen-production of ovary. After ovulation follicle becomes corpus luteum (q.v.) in most mammals.

GRAFT. (1) To graft is to induce union between tissues normally separate. (2) A graft is a relatively small part of a plant or animal which is grafted on to a relatively large part. The graft may be moved (transplanted) from its normal position to another place on the same organism (*autoplastic* grafting, autografting); or it may be moved to a different individual of the same species (*homoplastic* grafting, homografting) or of a different species (*heteroplastic* grafting, heterografting). In plants, the part grafted on is called the *scion,* that to which it is united the *stock.* In animals these individuals are respectively called *donor,* and *host* or *recipient.* See *Chimaera, Transplantation.*

GRAFT-HYBRID. See *Chimaera.*

GRAM'S STAIN. Stain used in bacteriology. Differentiates many kinds of (*gram-positive*) bacteria which take the stain, e.g. *Staphylococcus, Streptococcus,* from others (*gram-negative*) which do not, e.g. *Gonococcus,* typhoid bacteria.

GRANA. In chloroplasts (q.v.) groups of disc-shaped, flattened vesicles (thylakoids) stacked like coins in a pile, vesicle membranes bearing photosynthetic pigments. Most highly developed in chloroplasts of higher plants.

GRANULOCYTE. Polymorph (q.v.).

GRANULOPOIESIS. Formation of polymorphs. Occurs in myeloid tissue (q.v.).

GRAPTOLITES. Fossilized skeletons of extinct colonial animals found in Cambrian, Ordovician, and Silurian rocks. Relationships of the group are obscure; some zoologists regard them as Coelenterata; some as related to Hemichordata.

GREY MATTER. Tissue of vertebrate central nervous system containing numerous cell-bodies and dendrites of nerve cells; and terminations of nerve-fibres forming synapses with these; together with glia and blood-vessels. Occurs mainly as an inner layer surrounding central canal; but occurs also as a superficial layer (cortex) on cerebellum and cerebral hemispheres in some vertebrates. It is the tissue of the nuclei or centres. The co-ordinating work of the C.N.S. is done in grey matter by the large numbers of synapses present. Cf. *White Matter.*

GROOMING. Licking, scratching and picking over the fur of mammals; either of self or of other members of the species.

GROWTH. Increase in size. In botany usually includes also differentiation of cells, such as accompanies, or follows, increase in plant size, even though such differentiation contributes nothing to size change.

GROWTH, GRAND PERIOD OF. (Bot.). Expression applied to the total period of enlargement of a cell, an organ or part of an organ of a plant. During this period growth is slow at first, gradually increasing to a maximum and then falling off to zero as maturity is reached.

GROWTH HORMONE (SOMATOTROPIC HORMONE, STH). Hormone secreted by anterior lobe of pituitary. A protein. Promotes growth of the whole body.

GUARD CELLS. (Bot.). Specialized, crescent-shaped epidermal cells occurring in pairs surrounding stomata. Changes in shape of guard cells, due to changes in their turgidity, control opening and closing of stomata and hence affect loss of water vapour and gaseous exchange. See *Stoma.*

GUT. Alimentary canal (q.v.).

GUTTATION. Excretion of drops of water by plants through hydathodes (q.v.); occurring usually under condition of high humidity, and due to pressure built up within xylem by osmotic absorption of water by roots. See *Root Pressure.*

GYMNOPHIONA. Apoda (q.v.).

GYMNOSPERMAE. Conifers and their allies; sub-division of Spermatophyta. Primitive seed plants with many fossil representatives. Distinguished from the other group, Angiospermae, by having the ovules borne unprotected on surface of megasporophylls. Micro- and megasporophylls usually arranged in cones. Gametophyte generations reduced. Female gametophyte multicellular (female prothallus), with few exceptions, bearing archegonia. Male gametophyte initiated by pollen grain (microspore), consisting of varying number of prothallial cells and pollen tube containing male gametes; in some orders these are motile, in others non-motile. Characteristically without vessels in xylem (except in order Gnetales). See *Coniferales, Cycadales, Ginkgoales, Gnetales, Bennettitales, Cordaitales, Cycadofilicales.*

GYNANDROMORPH. Abnormal organism of mixed sex; some of tissues are genetically and structurally female, others genetically and structurally male. Can occur, e.g. through disturbance of genetic sex-determination mechanism during embryonic cleavage, as by loss of an X-chromosome (q.v.) in one blastomere and consequently in all its descendants. One half of such an organism can be male, one half female. Well-known in insects; occurs also in birds and mammals. Cf. *Intersex.*

GYNOBASIC (of a style), arising from base of ovary (due to infolding of ovary wall during development), e.g. white dead nettle.

GYNODIOECIOUS. Having female and hermaphrodite flowers on separate plants.

GYNOECIUM (PISTIL). Collective name for the carpels of a flower.

GYNOMONOECIOUS. Having female and hermaphrodite flowers on the same plant.

# H

HABITAT. Place with particular kind of environment inhabited by organism(s), e.g. the sea shore.

HABITUATION. Diminishing response to a stimulus as a result of its repetition.

HAEMOCOEL. Body cavity (q.v.) which is really expanded part of blood-system, containing blood. Well developed in Arthropoda and Mollusca where coelom is small. Unlike coelom it never communicates with exterior, and never contains germ-cells (cf. *Coelom*).

HAEMOCYANIN. Blue respiratory pigment (q.v.) present in blood of some molluscs and arthropods. It is a protein containing copper.

HAEMOGLOBIN. Respiratory pigment (q.v.) occurring in red blood cells of vertebrates and sporadically elsewhere among animals, e.g. in blood of earthworms, muscles of some roundworms. Occurs also in root-nodules of nitrogen-fixing leguminous plants. Scarlet in oxygenated form, bluish-red deoxygenated. Many haemoglobins are known, differing in molecular weight, absorption spectrum, oxygen-combining properties, etc. Each animal species has a different haemoglobin; and (in mammals) that of the foetus is different from that of the adult. A protein with iron in the prosthetic group; closely related to chlorophyll and to cytochrome. See *Myoglobin*.

HAEMOLYSIS. Escape of haemoglobin from red blood corpuscles owing to damage to surface membrane.

HAEMOPHILIA. Human disease in which blood-clotting is defective. Known only in males. Transmitted from mother to son. Determined by sex-linked recessive gene. Women homozygous for this gene are unknown.

HAEMOPOIESIS (HAEMATOPOIESIS). Formation of blood corpuscles. Occurs in lymphoid tissue and bone-marrow of adult vertebrates.

HAIR. (1) (Bot.). (*Trichome*). Single-celled or many-celled outgrowth from an epidermal cell. Functions various, e.g. absorbing (see *Root-hair*); secretory (see *Gland*); lowering transpiration rate. (2) (Zool.). Characteristic of mammal. Each hair consists of numerous cornified epidermal cells; grows at its base in hair-follicle where active cell-division occurs. See *Seta*.

HAIR-FOLLICLE. Deep pit of mammalian epidermis surrounding root of hair which projects far down into dermis. Receives duct of sebaceous gland. Muscle which erects hair is attached to it.

HALLUX. 'Big toe' of pendactyl hind-limb. On anterior or inner side (tibial side). Often shorter than other digits.

HALOPHYTE. Plant that tolerates very salty soil, a condition typical of shores of river estuaries.

HALTERE. Modified hind-wing of dipteran fly, consisting of a small projection from the body. Sensory function, probably concerned with maintaining equilibrium during flight.

HAPLOCHLAMYDEOUS. Monochlamydeous (q.v.).

HAPLOID. Having a single set of unpaired chromosomes in each nucleus. Characteristic of gametes; of some Sporozoa; of somatic nuclei of parthenogenetically produced males of some animals, e.g. bees; and of gametophytes and many spores of algae, fungi, Bryophyta, and vascular plants. See *Diploid, Alternation of Generations, Meiosis*.

HAPLONT. Haploid stage of an organism, ending with fertilization. Cf. *Diplont*.

HAPTEN. Small, separable, non-protein part of certain antigen molecules which carries the chemical group that combines specifically with an antibody. Unlike the whole antigen molecule, the separate hapten when injected does not cause production of anti body.

HAPTOTROPISM (THIGMOTROPISM). (Bot.). Tropism (q.v.) in which stimulus is a localized contact, e.g. a tendril in contact on one side with a solid object, a twig for instance, curves in that direction and coils round it.

HAUSTORIUM. (1) Specialized food absorbing organ characteristic of certain plant parasitic fungi, formed within living host cell at end of branch of hypha that penetrates cell wall. (2) Specialized organ of parasitic plant, e.g. dodder, which penetrates into and withdraws food material from tissues of host plant.

HAVERSIAN CANALS. Channels (roughly $50 \mu m$ diameter), carrying blood-vessels and nerves, which ramify throughout bone, communicating with its surface and marrow. Sheets (lamellae) of bone, and bone cells, are arranged concentrically around the canals.

HEARTWOOD. Central mass of xylem tissue in trunks of trees, with no living cells (such as xylem parenchyma and medullary ray) and no longer functioning in water conduction but only for mechanical support; with its elements frequently blocked by tyloses (q.v.) and often dark-coloured, e.g. oak, ebony, impregnated with various substances (tannins, resins, etc.) that render it more resistant to decay than surrounding sapwood.

HELIOTROPISM. Phototropism (q.v.).

HELMINTH. A worm, usually a parasitic one.

HELMINTHOLOGY. Study of parasitic worms.

HELOPHYTES. Class of Raunkiaer's Life Forms (q.v.).

HEMICELLULOSES. Heterogeneous group of long-chain polysaccharides distinct from cellulose (basic units are arabinose, xylose, mannose or galactose) forming part of the cell wall of plants, especially in lignified tissue; may function as reserve food materials especially in seeds, e.g. endosperm of date seeds.

HEMICHORDATA (ENTEROPNEUSTA). Small group of marine animals, included in the Protochordata; contains worm-like burrowing *Balanoglossus*, and sedentary ciliary feeders *Cephalodiscus* and *Rhabdopleura*. They have gill-slits; a structure sometimes regarded as notochord in anterior region only; nerve cord solid and superficial except in anterior region where it is hollow. Embryology suggests relationship with Echinodermata.

HEMICRYPTOPHYTES. Class of Raunkiaer's Life Forms (q.v.).

HEMIMETABOLA. Exopterygota (q.v.).

HEMIPTERA (RHYNCHOTA). Bugs. Large order of exopterygote insects, including scale-insects, leaf-hoppers, cochineal-insects, lac-insects, bed-bugs, green-flies. Usually two pairs of wings, anterior harder than the posterior. Parasites of plants and animals (whose juices they suck with their piercing mouth parts) and as such are of enormous economic importance, e.g. *Aphis* (q.v.).

HEMIZYGOUS. Term applied to a region of a chromosome of a diploid for which there is no homologue in the cell. The X-chromosome in organisms of the heterogametic sex is largely hemizygous.

HEPARIN. Substance which prevents blood clotting (q.v.) by stopping conversion of prothrombin to thrombin and by neutralizing thrombin. Extractable from various tissues, especially lung. Probably contained in mast cells, which occur in connective tissue. Sulphur-containing complex polysaccharide.

HEPATIC. (Adj.). Of the liver.

HEPATIC PORTAL SYSTEM. System of veins carrying blood from capillaries of intestine to liver in vertebrate (and amphioxus). Absorbed products of digestion (except fats, see *Lacteals*) thus go straight to liver cells which transform them chemically in various ways. See *Deamination*.

HEPATICAE. Liverworts, class of Bryophyta. Living in wet conditions, on soil or as epiphytes (q.v.), or in water. Consisting of a thin, prostrate plant body or a creeping central axis up to a few inches long, provided with leaf-like expansions; attached to soil by rhizoids growing from under surface. Sexual organs, antheridia and archegonia, variously grouped, male gametes motile by flagella. Fertilization is followed by development of a capsule containing spores which, being shed, germinate in most forms to form a short, thalloid *protonema* from which new liverwort plants arise.

HERB. Plant with no persistent parts above ground, as distinct from shrubs and trees.

HERBACEOUS. Having the characters of a herb.

HERBARIUM. Collection of preserved plant specimens for identification and reference purposes.

HERBIVORE. Plant-eater. Cf. *Carnivore, Omnivore*.

HERMAPHRODITE (BISEXUAL). (1) (Of a flowering plant or flower) having both stamens and carpels in the same flower. Cf. *Unisexual*. (2) (Of an individual animal) producing both male and female gametes. Among unisexual (q.v.) animals hermaphrodites may occur as aberrations.

HETEROCHLAMYDEOUS. (Of flowers), having two kinds of perianth segments (sepals and petals) in distinct whorls. Cf. *Homochlamydeous*.

HETEROCHROMATIN. Parts of chromosomes showing strongly basophilic staining in interphase. It apparently has little or no genetical activity. Sex chromosomes, especially the Y-chromosome of many animals, tend particularly to have large heterochromatic regions. Cf. *Euchromatin*.

HETERODONT. Having teeth of different kinds, as in most mammals, which have incisors, canines, molars. Cf. *Homodont*.

HETEROECIOUS. Of rust fungi (order Uredinales of Basidiomycetes), having certain spore forms of life-cycle on one host species and others on an unrelated host species. Cf. *Autoecious*.

HETEROGAMETIC SEX. The sex, individuals of which have within each of their nuclei a pair of dissimilar sex-chromosomes (q.v.) (one X- and one Y-chromosome); or an unpaired sex-chromosome (a single X-chromosome). Heterogametic sex is usually male, but is female in Lepidoptera, birds, reptiles, some amphibia and fish, and a few plants. Cf. *Homogametic sex*.

HETEROGAMY. (1) Synonym of anisogamy (q.v.); (2) Occasionally synonym of oogamy (q.v.); (3) (Zool.). Alternation of two forms of sexual reproduction in successive generations, e.g. of parthenogenesis and syngamy as in some aphids; or of hermaphrodite and dioecious, as in some nematodes.

HETEROGRAFT. Graft originating from an animal of a different species from that which receives it. Cf. *Allograft, Autograft, Homograft*.

HETEROKARYON (HETEROCARYON). Cell with more than one nucleus, not all of the same genetic constitution. In fungi, a cell, hypha or mycelium with haploid nuclei of different genetical constitution associated together in its cytoplasm; number of nuclei per cell may be stable (*dikaryon*, q.v.) or vary. In Fungi Imperfecti (see *Mycophyta*) variation in relative proportions of different nuclei on different substrates provides a system of somatic variation and adaptation. May be artificaly produced by fusion of different plant cells or animal cells. Cf. *Homokaryon*.

HETEROKONT. (Bot.) of a motile cell or spore, possessing two flagella of unequal length. Cf. *Isokont*.

HETEROMETABOLA. Exopterygota (q.v.).

HETEROMORPHIC. Used of alternation of generations (q.v.), particularly in algae, meaning generations vegetatively dissimilar, Cf. *Isomorphic*.

HETEROSIS (HYBRID VIGOUR). Increased vigour of growth, fertility, etc., in a cross between two genetically different lines, as compared with growth, etc. in either of the parental lines; associated with increased heterozygosity.

HETEROSPOROUS. Having two kinds of spores, microspores and megaspores, that give rise, respectively, to distinct male and female gametophyte generations; a condition found in certain Pteridophyta (where the term was first applied) and in Spermatophyta. In the former group there is a conspicuous difference in the size of the two kinds of spores, indicated in the terms applied to them, but this is not usually found in the Spermatophyta. Here the terms indicate homologies with the small and large spores of heterosporous pteridophytes rather than differences in size. Cf. *Homosporous.*

HETEROSTYLY. Condition in which length of style differs in flowers of different plants of a species, e.g. pin-eyed (long style) and thrum-eyed (short style) primroses. Anthers in one kind of flower are at same level as stigmas of other kind. Device for ensuring cross-pollination by visiting insects. Cf. *Homostyly.*

HETEROTHALLISM. (Of fungi, algae) condition in which sexual reproduction occurs only through participation of two thalli, each of which is self-sterile. In Fungi, includes *morphological heterothallism* where sexes are segregated, some thalli being male, others female; and *physiological heterothallism* where interacting thalli, often labelled plus and minus strains, show no morphological difference such as might be recognized as a difference in sex. Includes forms in which both thalli bear male and female sex organs and others which have no sex organs, union between strains depending on hyphal fusions. Cf. *Homothallism.*

HETEROTRICHOUS. Type of thallus found in many filamentous algae; consisting of a prostrate creeping system from which project branched filaments.

HETEROTROPHIC. (Of an organism) requiring a supply of organic material (food) from its environment. All animals and fungi, most bacteria and a few flowering plants are strongly heterotrophic, requiring organic food substances from which to make most of their own organic constituents. As herbivores, carnivores, saprophytes, or parasites they obtain this food from other organisms, living or dead. Ultimately almost all their organic material can be traced back to the synthetic activity of *autotrophic* organisms. Heterotrophic organisms commonly obtain their energy requirements also from organic food, i.e. they are chemotrophic (q.v.); but a few (particularly flagellates) are phototrophic (q.v.).

HETEROZYGOUS. Having two different allelomorphs in the two corresponding loci (q.v.) of a pair of chromosomes (q.v.). Cf. *Homozygous.* A heterozygous organism is a *heterozygote* for the locus in question; and with respect to that locus it produces two different kinds of gametes. Its phenotype is frequently identical with that of one of the two allelomorphs in the homozygous state (see *Dominant*); but it may be more or less intermediate between those of the two homozygotes.

HEXACANTH. Onchosphere (q.v.).

HEXAPODA. Insecta (q.v.).

HEXOSE. Sugar (monosaccharide) with six carbon atoms, e.g. glucose, fructose, galactose. Combinations of hexoses make up most of biologically important disaccharides and polysaccharides.

HIBERNATION. Dormancy during winter. Occurs in many mammals, most reptiles and Amphibia, and many vertebrates, of temperate and arctic regions. Metabolism is greatly slowed, and in mammals temperature drops to that of surroundings. Some, e.g. bats, wake to feed from time to time. See *Diapause, Aestivation*.

HILUM. Scar on seed coat marking point of former attachment of seed to funicle.

HIND-BRAIN. Hindmost of the three divisions marked out by constrictions in the embryonic vertebrate brain. Becomes during development medulla (q.v.) and cerebellum (q.v.).

HIP-GIRDLE (PELVIC GIRDLE). Skeletal support, situated in body-wall, for attachment of hind fins or limbs of Vertebrata. In fish consists fundamentally of a curved bar of bone or cartilage, situated transversely to long axis of body, one on each side in ventral region; the two bars usually fusing mid-ventrally to form a half-loop. At middle of the length of each bar is joint with the fin. Region dorsal to joint is *ilium*, region ventral is *ischio-pubis*. In tetrapods, except the earliest Amphibia, ischio-pubis forms two bones, an anterior pubis and posterior ischium; and the ilium, which extends much further dorsally than in fish, unites with one or more sacral vertebrae (q.v.) (compare shoulder girdle), forming a complete girdle round body in this region and giving rigid support to hind-limbs for locomotion (unnecessary in fish, which are propelled by tail). See *Acetabulum, Innominate Bone*. Fig. 10, p.265.

HIRUDINEA. Leeches, a class of annelids. Marine, freshwater or terrestrial; suckers at anterior and posterior ends; segmentation less clear than in chaetopods, as each segment is superficially subdivided into narrow rings; no chaetae; coelom partially obliterated; hermaphrodite; clitellum; fertilization internal; eggs develop in a cocoon. Some are blood-suckers.

HISTAMINE. A particular organic base, released from tissues when they are injured, causing dilatation of local blood-vessels.

HISTIOCYTE. See *Macrophage*.

HISTOCHEMISTRY. Study of distribution of particular chemical substances, by specific staining methods, etc., within sections or whole mounts of tissues.

HISTOCOMPATIBILITY ANTIGEN. Antigen on cell surface responsible for rejection of homografts (q.v.).

HISTOGENESIS. Differentiation of tissue.

HISTOGENS. Distinct tissue zones recognizable in apical meristems (q.v.) of many plants, especially in roots.

HISTOLOGY. Study of tissues.

HISTOLYSIS. Dissolution of tissue.

HISTONES. A class of basic proteins, with an unusually large proportion of the basic amino-acids arginine and lysine in their make-up,
associated with DNA in the chromosomes of eucaryotic (q.v.) cells.
Probably concerned with shutting off gene activity.

HOLARCTIC. Zoogeographical region amalgamating the Palaearctic
and Nearctic.

HOLOBLASTIC. (Of animal zygote) the whole zygote undergoing
cleavage (q.v.). Occurs in eggs with little or moderate amounts of
yolk. Cf. *Meroblastic*.

HOLOCARPIC. (Of fungi) having mature thallus converted in its
entirety into a reproductive structure. Cf. *Eucarpic*.

HOLOCENE (RECENT). Geological period consisting of recent times
since end of the last ice-age (about 10,000 years ago).

HOLOCEPHALI. A group of fish, including *Chimaera*. A sub-class or
order of Chondrichthyes. Differ from other Chondrichthyes (see
*Selachii*) in their large flat crushing teeth, and the fusion of upper
jaw (palatoquadrate) to skull, both associated with diet of molluscs;
and in having an operculum covering gill-slits. Rare fish now, but
with many fossil relatives. See *Elasmobranchii*.

HOLOGAMETE. See *Merogamete*.

HOLOMETABOLA. Endopterygota (q.v.).

HOLOPHYTIC. Feeding like a green plant, i.e. by synthesizing organic compounds from inorganic components, using the energy of
sunlight by means of chlorophyll. Cf. *Holozoic*. See *Autotrophic*.

HOLOTHUROIDEA. Sea-cucumbers; class of Echinodermata. Body
cylindrical, soft.

HOLOTYPE. Type specimen (q.v.).

HOLOZOIC. Feeding in an animal-like manner, i.e. by eating other
organisms or solid organic material elaborated by them. Cf.
*Holophytic*. See *Heterotrophic*.

HOMEOSTASIS. Maintenance of constancy of internal environment
(q.v.).

HOMINID. Man (*Homo*) and man-like fossils, e.g. *Pithecanthropus*. These
together make up the family Hominidae (order Primates).

HOMO. Genus of catarrhine primates whose only living representative
is man (*Homo sapiens*); but it contains several extinct species, e.g.
Neanderthal man. *H. sapiens* is distinguished anatomically from
living catarrhines by large brain (about 1500 ml.); absence of
brow ridges; chin prominence; teeth in each jaw arranged in a
smooth curve, with small canines; foot very different from hand,
with reduced toes, big-toe not opposable to others. Distinguished
in behaviour by walking upright or almost so, by using tools with
hands, by speech, and by the cultural tradition derived therefrom.
Extinct species possess some of these characters in nearly
human degree, while other characters are ape-like. See *Pithecanthropus*.

HOMOCHLAMYDEOUS. (Of flowers), having perianth segments of one kind (sepals) in two whorls. Cf. *Heterochlamydeous*.

HUMODONT. Having a set of teeth all of the same kind. As in most vertebrates other than mammals. Cf. *Heterodont*.

HOMOGAMETIC SEX. The sex, individuals of which have within each of their nuclei a pair of similar sex chromosomes (q.v.) (X-chromosomes). Cf. *Heterogametic sex*.

HOMOGAMY. Condition in which male and female parts of a flower mature simultaneously. Cf. *Dichogamy*.

HOMOGRAFT. Graft originating from an animal of the same species as, but of different genotype from, the recipient. Since it contains foreign antigens, the graft is liable to attack (rejection) by the immunity mechanisms of the recipient (the 'homograft reaction'). Cf. *Allograft, Autograft, Heterograft, Isograft*.

HOMOIOTHERMIC. 'Warm-blooded'. Maintaining a constant body temperature, independent of that of usual surroundings. Characteristic of birds and mammals. Cf. *Poikilothermic*.

HOMOKARYON (HOMOCARYON). A cell with more than one nucleus of identical genetic constitution. E.g. a fungal cell, hypha or mycelium may have more than one such haploid nuclei in its cytoplasm. Cf. *Heterokaryon*.

HOMOLOGOUS. An organ of one animal is said to be homologous with an organ of another when both have a fundamental similarity of structure and/or position relative to other organs, manifested especially during embryonic development; regardless of their functions in the adult, which may be very different; e.g. mammalian ear-ossicles (q.v.) are homologous with bones concerned in fish jaw attachment. The degree of similarity which constitutes 'fundamental similarity' is a matter of opinion, so that homology is not a clear-cut concept. The similarity is assumed to be due to descent of the organisms from a common ancestor. The presumption is that a developmental process that occurred in a common ancestor has become modified in two different directions in two descendant species, without the divergence obscuring the common origin. Evolution has evidently generally occurred, not by sudden origin of quite new embryonic processes, but by slight modification of existing ones, the changes taking effect particularly at later stages of development; resulting in the persistence of the similarities between related organisms, especially between their embryos, denoted by homology. Homology of organs implies relationship of the organisms bearing the organs, and it is the main concept of evolutionary comparative anatomy. Cf. *Analogous*.

HOMOLOGOUS CHROMOSOMES. Chromosomes which contain identical sets of loci (q.v.) ('homologous' is applied also to parts of chromosomes). The two chromosomes of each of the pairs normally found in all somatic cells of animals and of plant sporophytes are homologous. Two homologous chromosomes or parts of chromosomes have a strong attraction for each other during early stages of meiosis (q.v.) and undergo pairing.

HOMOSPOROUS. Having one kind of spore that gives rise to gametophyte generation bearing both male and female reproductive organs. Cf. *Heterosporous*. Characteristic of certain members of *Pteridophyta*. Exceptionally, as in Equisetales (q.v.), gametophyte plants may be dioecious in certain environmental conditions.

HOMOSTYLY. Condition (the common one) in which flowers of a species have styles of one length, as opposed to *Heterostyly* (q.v.).

HOMOTHALLISM. (Of fungi) condition in which sexual reproduction occurs in a colony derived from a single spore, i.e. each thallus is self-fertile. Cf. *Heterothallism*.

HOMOZYGOUS. Having identical genes (i.e. not having different allelomorphs) in the two corresponding loci of a pair of chromosomes (q.v.) Cf. *Heterozygous*. A homozygous organism is a *homozygote* for the loci in question. It has a phenotype characteristic of the particular allelomorph (but see *Penetrance*), whether or not the allelomorph is dominant or recessive to other allelomorphs.

HOOKWORMS. Nematode parasites of man (*Necator americanus* and *Ancylostoma duodenale*). Of very great medical and social importance. Common in parts of Africa, India, China, East Indies, South America, southern parts of North America. About 1 in. long; live in intestine; eggs, liberated in faeces, giving rise in suitable conditions to active larvae which penetrate human skin, chiefly of feet. Heavy infections cause anaemia and physical and mental retardation.

HORMONE. Organic substance produced in minute quantity in one part of an organism and transported to other parts where it exerts a profound effect.

Hormones (phytohormones) play a prominent role in *plant* growth. See *Abscisic acid, Auxins, Cytokinins, Gibberellin, Florigen*. Method of transport within plant not fully understood. Movement of auxins (e.g. in young stems) is active, i.e. it is under control of living cells and is not merely a simple diffusion process. Auxin transport is unidirectional, away from stem tip (basipetal). If applied to cut base of stem auxin will not move to the tip (unless e.g. plants have been treated with the antiauxin 2, 3, 5-tri iodobenzoic acid). An important recent concept is that of action and interaction of different types of phytohormones, e.g. relative amount of leaf and root formation in tissue culture can be varied by altering ratios of levels of kinetin and IAA. Hormone-like substances, liberated into water or air, have also been demonstrated to play an important role in sexual reproduction of certain fungi and algae.

In *animals* hormones are usually secreted by endocrine glands directly from gland cells into blood stream. Various hormones of different composition and activities are produced in different glands, e.g. see *Adrenal, Insulin, Pituitary, Thyroid, Secretin*. Occur conspicuously in vertebrates, but known in some invertebrates, e.g. see *Corpora allata*.

HORSETAIL. See *Equisetales*.

HOST. (1) Organism infected by a parasite. *Definitive host:* that in which an animal parasite attains sexual maturity. *Intermediate host:* one which is essential for the life cycle of an animal parasite, but in which it does not become sexually mature. (2) Animal (especially embryo) into which a graft (q.v.) is experimentally transplanted.

HUMERUS. Bone of proximal part of tetrapod fore-limb (bone of upper arm of man). (See Fig. 7, p. 213.)

HUMUS. Complex organic matter resulting from decomposition of plant and animal tissue in the soil, which gives to surface layer of soil its characteristically dark colour; of great importance for plant growth. Colloidal, improving texture and waterholding capacity of soil and forming a reservoir of mineral nutrients which are absorbed by humus and prevented from being leached away.

HYBRID. Plant or animal resulting from a cross between parents that are genetically unlike; often restricted to the offspring of two different species or of well-marked varieties within a species. Hybrid may be fertile (capable of producing offspring), or sterile. The more distant the genetical relationship between parents the greater is the probability that hybrids will be sterile; sterility is due to failures in pairing of chromosomes in meiosis.

HYBRID SWARM. Continuous series of forms resulting from hybridization of two species followed by crossing and backcrossing of subsequent generation. Very variable owing to segregation.

HYBRID VIGOUR. Heterosis (q.v.).

HYDATHODE. Water-excreting gland occurring on the edges or tips of leaves of many plants.

HYDATID CYST. A cyst formed by larva (cysticercus stage) of certain tapeworms in, e.g. sheep, man. Consists of a fluid-filled sac which may be large enough to hold a gallon. Contains innumerable larval heads each of which if swallowed by a dog may produce a tapeworm.

HYDRA. Genus of small freshwater hydrozoan coelenterates; ubiquitous, few species. No alternation of generations (q.v.).

HYDRANTH. See *Polyp*.

HYDROID. Member of one of the orders of Hydrozoa (q.v.). Colonial animals forming tuft-like growths on seaweeds, etc.

HYDROPHYTE. (1) Plant whose habitat is water or very wet places; characteristically possessing aerenchyma (q.v.). Cf. *Mesophyte*, *Xerophyte*. (2) Class of Raunkiaer's Life Forms (q.v.).

HYDROPONICS. System of large-scale plant cultivation developed from 'water-culture' methods of growing plants in the laboratory, in which their roots dip into a solution of nutrient salts or in which the plants are allowed to root in some relatively inert material. e.g. quartz sand, which is irrigated with the nutrient solution.

HYDROSERE. A sere (q.v.) commencing in water or moist sites.

HYDROTROPISM. Tropism (q.v.) in which the stimulus is water.

HYDROZOA. Hydroids, stinging corals, Portuguese-man-of-war, etc. Class of Coelenterata (of sub-phylum Cnidaria). Individual polyps and medusae usually quite small, though fairly bulky colonies occur; usually well-marked alternation of generations; coelenteron simple; gonads ectodermal. Cf. *Actinozoa, Scyphozoa.*

HYMENIUM. Layer of regularly arranged spore-producing structures found in fruit bodies of many ascomycete and basidiomycete fungi.

HYMENOPTERA. Order of endopterygote insects, including bees, wasps, ants. Two pairs of wings, membranous, coupled together; larva generally grub-like. Some members very highly specialized for social life; some others are, as larvae, parasites of insects, e.g. ichneumon flies.

HYOID ARCH. Visceral arch next behind jaws of vertebrates. Dorsal part forms hyomandibula (q.v.); ventral part in adult tetrapods forms *hyoid bone,* usually supporting tongue. Contains facial nerve; and forms many muscles of the face. See *Placodermi, Spiracle.*

HYOMANDIBULA. Dorsal element (bone or cartilage) of hyoid arch which takes part in jaw attachment in most fish (see *Hyostylic Jaw-Suspension*), and in tetrapods becomes columella auris (stapes).

HYOSTYLIC JAW-SUSPENSION. Found in most fish. Upper and lower jaws on each side are attached at their hinge to one end of the hyomandibula, the other end of which is anchored to the neuro-cranium. See *Autostylic jaw-suspension.*

HYPERPARASITE. Organism which lives parasitically in or on another parasite.

HYPERPLASIA. Increase in amount of tissue by increase in number of cells, which individually keep their usual size (cf. *Hypertrophy*), e.g. when part of mammalian liver is removed, rest undergoes hyperplasia. In plants, occurs in response to certain parasites.

HYPERTONIC. (Of a solution), having a concentration such that it gains water by osmosis (q.v.) across a semi-permeable membrane from some other specified solution. When the membrane and the other solution are unspecified, they are taken to be the plasma membranes and the interior of cells respectively. Cf. *Hypotonic, Isotonic.*

HYPERTROPHY. (1) Increase in size of tissue or organ by increase in size of individual elements (cells or collagen fibres) without increase of their numbers (cf. *Hyperplasia*), e.g. in exercised muscle; uterine muscle during later part of pregnancy; in plants, as response to certain parasites. (2) Sometimes, increase in size of tissue or organ, mechanism unspecified, but often hyperplasia. See *Compensatory Hypertrophy.*

HYPHA. Filament of a fungus thallus. Tubular, increasing in length by growth at its tip and giving rise to new hyphae by lateral branch-ing. Hyphae of Phycomycetes are usually without cross-walls (non-septate, aseptate). Those of other fungi possess cross-walls (septate) but each cross-wall has a minute central pore through which proto-plasmic continuity is maintained along the length of the hypha.

HYPOCOTYL. Part of seedling stem below cotyledons.

HYPODERMIS. Layer of cells immediately beneath epidermis of leaves of certain plants, often mechanically strengthened, c.g. pine, forming an extra protective layer; or forming water storage tissue.

HYPOGEAL. (Of cotyledons) remaining underground when the seed germinates, e.g. broad bean, pea. Cf. *Epigeal*.

HYPOGLOSSAL NERVE. Nerve of vertebrate supplying muscles below pharynx, or in amniotes, tongue. A ventral root (q.v.). Twelfth cranial nerve of amniote vertebrates and fossil amphibians, but arises from spinal cord in living anamniotes.

HYPOGYNOUS. See *Receptacle*.

HYPONASTY. (Bot.). More rapid growth of lower side of an organ, e.g. in a leaf, resulting in upward curling of leaf-blade. Cf. *Epinasty*.

HYPOPHYSECTOMY. Surgical removal of pituitary body.

HYPOPHYSIS. (1) (*Hypophyseal Pouch*) Median ectodermal inpushing of embryonic vertebrate head, just in front of buccal membrane, which fuses with infundibulum, forming pituitary body (q.v.). (2) Synonymous with pituitary body.

HYPOSTASIS. Interaction between non-allelic genes in which one (hypostatic) gene will not be expressed in presence of a second. Cf. *Epistasis*.

HYPOTHALAMUS. Floor and sides of brain of vertebrates just behind attachment of cerebral hemispheres. Derived from fore-brain. In mammals known to contain centres co-ordinating, amongst other things, manifestations of rage and mechanism of body temperature control, both of which predominantly involve sympathetic nervous system. The pituitary lies immediately below, and is partly con-trolled by, the hypothalamus; anti-diuretic hormone and oxytocin are probably supplied to the posterior lobe by the hypothalamus, and the anterior lobe is much influenced by hormones, including specific *releasing factors* for some of the anterior pituitary hormones, secreted by the hypothalamus and carried to the anterior lobes in portal veins.

HYPOTONIC. (Of a solution) having a concentration such that it loses water by osmosis (q.v.) across a semi-permeable membrane to some specified other solution. When the membrane and the other solution are unspecified they are taken to be the plasma mem-branes and interior of cells respectively. Cf. *Hypertonic, Isotonic*.

# I

IAA. Indole-3-acetic acid. Most common growth-regulating hormone (an auxin, q.v.) in plants.

IAN. Indole-3-acetonitrile. Growth-regulating hormone (an auxin, q.v.) occurring in plants.

ICHTHYOSAURIA. A fossil order of Reptilia. Lived during Mesozoic. Marine, fish-like in general appearance and mode of swimming, with paddle-like limbs, dorsal fin, large vertical fish-like tail-fin with spinal column extended into lower lobe. Up to forty feet long. Probably viviparous, reproducing entirely in the water, which they doubtless never left.

IDENTICAL TWINS. Monozygotic twins (q.v.).

IDIOBLAST. Cell distinctly different in form, structure or contents from others in same tissue, e.g. cystolith-containing parenchyma cell.

IDIOGRAM. See *Karyotype*.

ILEUM. That part of small intestine of mammals preceding the large intestine.

ILIUM. Dorsal part of hip-girdle, which in tetrapods is jointed to one or more sacral vertebrae (q.v.) so giving stability to attachment of hind-limbs. See Fig. 10, p. 265.

IMAGINAL DISC. Thickening of epidermis, together with underlying mesenchyme, in pupa of holometabolous insect which at metamorphosis gives rise to an adult organ, the larval structure being destroyed.

IMAGO. Adult sexually mature insect.

IMBRICATE. (Of leaves, petals, etc.), overlapping.

IMMUNITY. Ability of an animal or plant to resist infection by parasitic organisms. An essential requirement for survival, since most animals and plants are perpetually menaced by viruses, bacteria, fungi, and parasitic animals. Immunity of animals is due to many different mechanisms, such as impervious skin, antiseptic stomach (due to acid), activity of phagocytes (q.v.), and chemical defence by antibodies (q.v.) or interferon (q.v.). The terms immunity and immune and the subject matter of the science of immunology are usually restricted to the particular kind of reaction induced in vertebrates by the introduction into the body of certain foreign substances (antigens) which include, but are not confined to, parasites. An *immune reaction* in this sense involves the production of substances which combine specifically with the particular antigen introduced. These specific substances may be antibodies in the body fluids, or they may be carried by blood cells (lymphocytes). An animal that is protected by antibodies is said to be *immunized*. *Active immunity* is such immunity induced in an animal by an

antigen. *Passive immunity* is such immunity conferred by the transfer
to an animal of antibodies that have been induced in another
animal. Immunity in plants is (a) due to structural features, e.g.
waxy surface preventing wetting and consequently development of
pathogens, thick cuticle preventing entry of germ-tubes of fungus
spores; or is (b) protoplasmic, the protoplast being an unfavourable
medium for further development of a pathogen, see *Phytoalexins*; or
is (c) acquired immunity, used with respect to virus diseases and
applied to (1) recovery from an acute disease, and (2) resistance
conferred against virulent strains by presence of avirulent ones. (c)
is a non-sterile type of immunity which depends on persistence of
active virus in the recovered or protected plants. Freedom from a
second attack of an acute disease, or protection from the effects of
virulent strains, persists only as long as the plants are infected.
Plants are not known to produce antibodies.

IMMUNOGENIC. Able to cause antibody formation.

IMMUNOGLOBULIN. Globulin component of blood plasma consisting
of antibody.

IMPLANT. (Zool.). Material, whether tissue or not, artificially placed
in an embryo (an operation employed to discover an induction or
evocation) or in an adult.

IMPLANTATION (NIDATION). Attachment of mammalian embryo
(blastocyst, q.v.) to lining of uterus, preparatory to forming
placenta. In primates embryo dissolves lining epithelium of uterus,
and embeds itself in substance of uterine wall.

IMPRINTING. Rapid learning, during a sensitive period in early life,
to react to a particular object (commonly a parent) by attempting
to stay near it.

IMPULSE. The 'message' which is conducted along a nerve-fibre. It
is fundamentally the same in all nerve-fibres. It is a travelling wave
of chemical and physical events involving particularly the surface
membrane of the fibre. It moves at between 1 and 100 metres per
second (speed depending on species of animal and on the diameter
of, and amount of myelin around, the nerve-fibre; and on temperature and other conditions at the time). The energy for the impulse
is provided locally along the course of the nerve-fibre, and not by
the stimulus which sets the impulse going. Consequently the
characteristics of the impulse (action potential (q.v.), speed, etc.)
are unaffected by the nature or intensity of the stimulus. See *All-or-
None Law*. The impulse runs without loss of vigour; and wherever
in the nerve cell it starts, it travels right through all the branches of
that nerve-cell (see *Nerve-Net*). Each impulse occupies up to an
inch or two of the length of the nerve-fibre at any instant. When
it has passed a given place in the nerve, that place is, for a few
thousandths of a second, refractory, i.e. it will not transmit another
impulse. A succession of impulses in one nerve-fibre must therefore
be spaced out, never being closer than the refractory zone. Most

stimuli, including stimulation via a receptor, set off a train of successive impulses in a nerve-cell, rather than a single impulse; and different stimuli can therefore produce different conduction in a nerve-fibre by affecting not the individual impulse, but the number and frequency of successive impulses in a train of impulses.

INBREEDING. Reproduction by the mating of closely related individuals as opposed to *Outbreeding* by the mating of less related individuals.

INCISOR. Chisel-shaped tooth in front of mouth of mammals. Primitively three on each side of upper and lower jaws. Gnawing teeth of rodents which continually grow in length and tusks of elephants are modified incisors.

INCLUSION BODIES. Microscopically visible bodies produced in cytoplasm of cells, sometimes in nucleus, of many plants and animals as result of virus infection. Often consist largely of virions, which may form crystals.

INCOMPATIBILITY. (1) In flowering plants, failure to set seed (i.e. of fertilization and subsequent development of embryo) after pollination (self or cross) has taken place. Due to inability of pollen tubes to grow down style. In physiologically heterothallic (q.v.) fungi, failure to reproduce sexually in single or paired cultures. In both cases the incompatibility is genetically determined – it is due to the possession by the individual plants or thalli of genes which prevent the fusion of likes; and the result is the same, namely, to promote outbreeding (q.v.). (2) Also used in horticulture to mean inability of scion to make a successful union with stock.

INCUS. Mammalian ear-ossicle (q.v.) representing quadrate of other vertebrates.

INDEHISCENT. (Of fruits), not opening spontaneously to liberate their seeds, e.g. hazel-nut.

INDEPENDENT ASSORTMENT. The chance distribution to the gametes of alleles, the distribution of members of one pair having no influence on distribution of members of another. So that if an individual has one pair of alleles, A and a, and another pair, B and b, it will form approximately equal numbers of gametes of the four possible chance combinations of one member from each pair: A and B, A and b, a and B, a and b. Mendel's Second Law asserts this, but it requires the qualification that independent assortment does not apply to linked genes (see *Linkage*), but only to those lying on different chromosomes, since it is due to the independent behaviour of chromosome pairs during meiosis (q.v.).

INDIGENOUS. (Of organisms) native to a particular area, not introduced.

INDUCIBLE ENZYME. Adaptive enzyme (q.v.).

INDUCTION. Influence of one embryonic tissue (or of an artificial implant) on another embryonic tissue, directing its differentiation. A tissue whose differentiation is induced by another shows dependent differentiation (q.v.). See *Evocation*. For enzyme induction, see *Enzyme*. For prophage induction, see *Lysogeny*.

INDUSIUM. Membranous outgrowth from underside of leaf which in certain ferns covers and protects a group (sorus) of developing sporangia.

INDUSTRIAL MELANISM. Occurrence of dark forms of moths in industrial districts, shown to be due to natural selection by predators of moths against a background of blackened vegetation.

INFERIOR OVARY. See *Receptacle*.

INFLAMMATION. The local response to any local injury in a vertebrate. Consists of (i) dilatation of blood-vessels; (ii) invasion by leucocytes; (iii) passage of blood proteins and fluid through capillary walls into tissue spaces. Functions probably as protective mechanism (by means of leucocytes and antibodies) against any invading bacteria.

INFLORESCENCE. Flowering shoot. Inflorescences are grouped according to method of branching as (*a*) *indefinite* or *racemose*; (*b*) *definite* or *cymose*.

In (*a*) branching in monopodial. The inflorescence consists of a main axis increasing in length by growth at tip and giving rise to lateral branches bearing flowers. The flowers open in succession from below upwards, or, if inflorescence axis is short and flattened, from outside inwards. Following types of indefinite inflorescence are recognized: *Raceme*, with a main axis bearing stalked flowers; e.g. lupin, foxglove; *Panicle*, compound raceme, e.g. oat; *Corymb*, a raceme with flowers borne at same level, due to elongation of stalks (pedicels) of lower flowers, e.g. candytuft; *Spike*, a raceme with sessile flowers, e.g. plantain; *Spadix*, a form of spike with thick fleshy axis, e.g. cuckoo pint; *Catkin*, a spike of unisexual, reduced flowers, often pendulous, e.g. hazel, birch; *Umbel*, a raceme in which the axis has not lengthened so that the flower stalks arise at the same point, the flowers in a head with the oldest at the outside, youngest in the centre, e.g. carrot, cow parsley; *Capitulum*, in which axis of inflorescence is flattened, laterally expanded with growing point in centre, and bearing closely crowded, sessile flowers, the oldest at the margin, the youngest in the centre, e.g. dandelion.

In (*b*) branching is sympodial. The main axis ends in a flower and further development takes place by growth of lateral branches, each of which behaves in the same way. The cyme is described as a *Monochasium* when each branch of the inflorescence bears one other branch, e.g. iris, and as a *Dichasium* when each branch gives rise to two other branches, e.g. stitchwort.

Many inflorescences are mixed, partly indefinite, partly definite, e.g. horse-chestnut, a raceme of cymes. See Fig. 5, p. 148.

INFUNDIBULUM. Outpushing from floor of brain (of diencephalon) of embryo vertebrate which meets hypophysis (q.v.) and with it develops into pituitary body (q.v.).

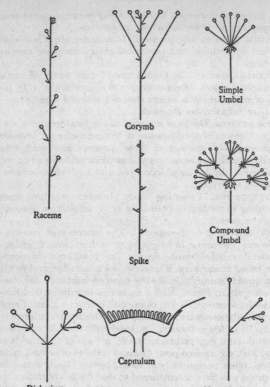

Raceme

Corymb

Spike

Simple
Umbel

Compound
Umbel

Dichasium

Capitulum

Monochasium

*Fig. 5. Diagrams of different types of inflorescence.*

INFUSORIA. Term formerly applied to microscopic organisms found
in infusions of organic substances, including various Protozoa and
Rotifera; has also been used in a restricted sense for the Ciliophora.

INHIBITION. (Nervous). Prevention, as a result of the influence of
nerve impulses, of activation of an effector. May occur in central
nervous system: e.g. when a muscle is stimulated by its motor nerve-
fibres to contract, the tonus of antagonistic muscles is simultaneously relaxed by inhibition of their motor nerve-cells (*reciprocal
inhibition*); or a reflex can be inhibited by stimulating both the
sensory nerve-fibres of the reflex and certain other sensory nerve-
fibres at the same time. Such *central* inhibition is one of the most

important ways in which the central nervous system (q.v.) produces its flexible control of activities, by preventing action of effectors in unsuitable circumstances. In Crustacea *peripheral* inhibition occurs, special inhibitory nerve-fibres as well as excitatory ones running to the muscles. Similar peripheral inhibition occurs in autonomic system of vertebrates, e.g. vagus nerve inhibits heart beat, sympathetic stimulates it.

INITIAL(S). (Bot.). Cell or cells from which, by division or differentiation, tissues or organs develop. E.g. in apical meristems (q.v.); or cell from which antheridium develops in Bryophyta.

INNERVATION. Nerve supply (to a particular organ).

INNOMINATE. (1) Short *artery* arising from aorta and giving rise to a subclavian artery (to fore-limb) and a carotid artery (to head), in many birds and mammals. (2) *I. bone*. Each lateral half of the hip-girdle, when pubis, ilium, and ischium are fused into a single bone, as in adult reptiles, birds, and mammals.

INSECTA (HEXAPODA). Class of Arthropoda containing springtails, silverfish, cockroaches, earwigs, termites, flies, green-flies, bugs, lice, fleas, butterflies, beetles, bees, ants. (Some animals commonly referred to as 'insects' do not belong to this group.) Most insects are terrestrial and breathe air by means of tracheae. They have one pair of antennae, three pairs of legs, three distinct parts of the body (head, thorax, and abdomen) and most have wings. See *Anoplura, Aphaniptera, Apterygota, Coleoptera, Dermaptera, Diptera, Ephemeroptera, Homiptera, Hymenoptera, Isoptera, Lepidoptera, Mallophaga, Neuroptera, Odonata, Orthoptera, Plecoptera, Psocoptera, Thysanoptera, Trichoptera*.

INSECTIVORE. Any member of the Insectivora, an order of placental mammals; a primitive insect-eating group, resembling in many respects the Cretaceous ancestors of all placentals. E.g. mole, hedgehog, shrew.

INSECTIVOROUS. Insect-eating.

INSTAR. Stage in larval development of an insect, between two ecdyses (q.v.).

INSTINCT. An elaborate pattern of successive reflexes, which occurs as a whole in response to certain stimuli.

INSULIN. Hormone of vertebrates, affecting the amount of glucose in the blood; secreted by islets of Langerhans in pancreas. A protein. Secretion is stimulated by high glucose concentration in blood, which insulin decreases by suppressing breakdown of liver glycogen to glucose, and encouraging building up of glycogen from glucose in liver and muscle, and building up of fat from glucose in fat cells. It also stimulates protein synthesis. Antagonized by adrenaline, adrenal glucocorticoids, and glucagon. See *Blood-sugar*.

INTEGUMENT. Skin. (Of seed plants), layer enclosing nucellus of ovule (q.v.) and ultimately forming seed coat. Most flowering plants have two integuments, inner and outer.

INTERCALARY. (Of a meristem) situated between regions of per-

manent tissue, e.g. at base of nodes and leaves in many monocotyledons. Cf. *Apical*.

INTERCELLULAR. Between the cells. *I. bridges* (plasmodesmata in
plants), cytoplasmic connections between cells present in some
plant and animal tissues. *I. fluid* (interstitial fluid, tissue fluid), fluid
between tissue cells of animals, bathing the plasma-membranes (to
be distinguished from blood; see *Internal environment*). *I. material*, is
chiefly skeletal, e.g. in animals, material external to the plasma
membranes, such as reticulin, collagen, elastin, bone salts, matrix
of cartilage and connective tissue; in plants the middle lamella,
composed of pectic compounds, is intercellular material binding
together adjacent cells (cellulose also may be regarded as equivalent to the intercellular material of animals, but is considered as
part of the plant cell). *I. spaces*, in plants air-filled cavities between
walls of neighbouring cells, e.g. in cortex and pith, forming internal
aerating system; spaces may be large, rendering tissue light and
spongy as in aerenchyma (q.v.). In animals filled with intercellular
fluid.

INTERFASCICULAR CAMBIUM. Cambium (q.v.) arising between
vascular bundles. Cf. *Fascicular cambium*.

INTERFERON. Protein produced in an animal cell when it is infected
by a virus; interferon inhibits non-specifically the multiplication of
viruses.

INTERNAL ENVIRONMENT. Medium in which body cells are
bathed i.e. the intercellular fluid. In equilibrium with blood-stream
in vertebrates, it is normally kept highly constant in composition
(homeostasis) e.g. in respect of osmotic pressure, content of individual ions, acidity and alkalinity (pH), and glucose concentration,
by sensitive mechanisms which control these conditions in the
blood, and hence in the intercellular fluid. Deviations from constancy have rapidly deleterious influence on cells, particularly on
brain cells. Constancy is not always so complete in invertebrates.

INTERNODE. (1) Part of plant stem between two successive nodes
(q.v.). (2) Part of a nerve-fibre between two successive nodes of
Ranvier (q.v.).

INTEROCEPTOR. (1) Receptor (q.v.) which detects stimuli arising
inside the body. Cf. *Exteroceptor*. (2) In more restricted sense, receptor in lining of gut and respiratory organs, detecting stimuli from
substances introduced from outside.

INTERPHASE. State of cell when not undergoing mitosis; i.e. in the
$G_1$ (or $G_0$), S and $G_2$ phases of the cell cycle (q.v.).

INTERSEX. (Zool.). Abnormal individual which is intermediate
between the two sexes in characteristics (it may or may not be
hermaphrodite, q.v.), having all its cells of identical genetical composition (cf. *Gynandromorph*). May occur through failure of sex-
determining mechanism of genes (see *Sex chromosomes*); or through
hormonal or other influence during development (see *Free-martin*).

INTERSTITIAL CELLS. Of vertebrate gonads; those which lie between the ovarian follicles or between the testis tubules. Those of
the testis probably secrete the testicular sex-hormones (chiefly
testosterone, q.v.).

INTERSTITIAL FLUID. See *Intercellular fluid*.

INTESTINE. Alimentary canal between stomach and anus or cloaca.
In vertebrates practically all absorption of products of digestion
occurs in intestine, and a great deal of digestion; and undigested
residue is converted there to faeces. Frequently coiled, so that much
longer than body (about 8 metres long in man). Internal surface
usually increased by folds and projections (see *Spiral valve*, *Villus*).
Lined by simple epithelium, containing mucus-secreting glands;
its anterior part has digestive enzyme-secreting glands and special
absorptive powers. Smooth muscle in walls churns up contents and
gradually passes them towards anus. Anterior part receives ducts
of large digestive glands, liver and pancreas. Usually anterior part
is of smaller diameter than posterior, in which faeces are stored;
and in amniotes there is a clear division into *small intestine* and
*large intestine*, with a valve and often a *caecum* at their junction.
Small intestine is concerned with digestion, and absorption of the
products into blood and lymph capillaries (see *lacteals*) in the wall.
Large intestine is mainly concerned with preparation of faeces by
removal of water, valuable on dry land. Small and large intestines
of amniotes are not always homologous with those of anamniotes.

INTIMA. Endothelium (q.v.) lining vertebrate blood vessels.

INTRACELLULAR. Within a cell. Cf. *Extracellular*.

INTRASPECIFIC. Amongst members of the same species. *I. selection*,
natural selection (q.v.) of one kind of individual at the expense of
another kind of the same species, the two kinds directly competing
with each other for limited supplies of some requirement. E.g.
selection of a character of a male animal (such as large antlers)
which gives advantage over other males in reproduction.

INTROGRESSIVE HYBRIDIZATION. Infiltration of genes of one
species into genotype of another. When two species come into
contact under conditions favouring one or the other, if hybrids are
produced they tend to back cross with the favoured (more abundant) species. This process, continually repeated, results in a
population of individuals most of which resemble the predominant
parent but which possess also some characters of the other parent.

INTRORSE. (Of dehiscence of an anther), towards centre of flower.
Cf. *Extrorse*.

INTUSSUSCEPTION. (Bot.). Increase in surface area of cell wall by
interpolation of new particles between existing particles of extending wall. Cf. *Apposition*.

INULIN. Soluble polysaccharide, built of fructose molecules, occurring as stored food material in many plants, e.g. members of Compositae, dahlia tubers. Absent in animals.

INVAGINATION. Pushing inwards of part of a sheet of cells so as to form a pocket opening on to original surface. A common process in embryonic development of animals (see *Blastopore*).

INVERSION. Reversal of part of a chromosome so that genes within that part lie in inverse order.

INVERTASE. See *Sucrose*.

INVERTEBRATA. Collective term for all animals which are not members of the Vertebrata (e.g. *Amoeba*, sponges, jelly-fishes, worms, snails, flies, starfishes, sea-squirts).

IN VITRO. By derivation, means 'in glass'. In general, applied to biological processes when they are experimentally made to occur in isolation from the whole organism (which usually means within a glass vessel). E.g. the activities of cells in tissue culture (q.v.) occur *in vitro*. Cf. *In Vivo*.

IN VIVO. Within the living organism. Cf. *In Vitro*.

INVOLUCRE. Protective investment; (1) in thalloid liverworts, scale-like upgrowth of thallus over-arching archegonia; (2) in leafy liverworts and in mosses, group of leaves surrounding sexual organs; (3) in many flowering plants, e.g. family Compositae, group of bracts enveloping young inflorescence.

INVOLUTION. (1) Production of abnormal bacteria, yeasts, etc., e.g. in old cultures. (2) (Atrophy). Decrease in size of an organ, opposite of hyperplasia and hypertrophy, e.g. of thymus and other lymphoid tissue after puberty.

IRIS. Structure controlling amount of light admitted to vertebrate eye. The iris is the coloured part of human eye. It is a thin sheet of tissue, forming a pigmented diaphragm in front of lens with central opening (pupil) through which light passes to retina. Attached at outer margin to ciliary body (q.v.). Contains radiating muscles which enlarge pupil and a ring of muscles at its free inner margin which narrows pupil. Light, stimulating retina and optic nerve, reflexly controls size of pupil, narrowing for strong, enlarging for dim light. Accommodation for near vision is also accompanied by narrowing. See Fig. 3, p. 107. A structurally and functionally similar iris occurs in Cephalopod eye.

IRRITABILITY. Responsiveness to change in environment by complex, usually adaptive activity; a universal property of living things. Manifested in, e.g. changes of cell turgor, protoplasmic movements, growth curvatures of plants, nervous activity of animals.

ISCHIUM. Ventral, backward-projecting, part of hip-girdle (q.v.). Ischia bear the weight of a sitting primate. See Fig. 10, p. 265.

ISLETS OF LANGERHANS. Groups of cells, scattered throughout pancreas of gnathostome vertebrates, which secrete insulin (q.v.) (from B cells) and glucagon (q.v.) (from A cells).

ISOANTIGEN. Antigen present in only some members of a given species.

ISOBILATERAL. (Of leaves), having same structure on both sides.

Characteristic of leaves of monocotyledons, e.g. iris, where leaf-blade is more or less vertical and the two sides are equally exposed. Below epidermis on both sides of the leaf, lying regularly side by side with their long axes at right-angles to it, are elongated cells of palisade mesophyll and between them, loosely arranged cells of spongy mesophyll. Cf. *Dorsiventral*.

ISOENZYMES (ISOZYMES). Variants of a given enzyme, occurring within a single organism, having the same specificity for substrate, hence catalysing the same reaction, but with slight differences in molecular structure which make it possible to separate them. They may differ quantitatively in activity. Several isoenzymes of an enzyme may occur within a single cell.

ISOGAMY. Condition in which gametes are similar, i.e. not differentiated into male and female; found in some green algae, fungi, and Protozoa, but uncommon. Cf. *Anisogamy*.

ISOGENEIC (SYNGENEIC). With the same set of genes. Cf. *Allogeneic*.

ISOGRAFT. Graft originating from an animal other than, but of the same genotype as, the recipient; e.g. between two animals of a highly inbred strain. See *Autograft*, *Homograft*.

ISOKONT. (Bot.). Of a motile cell or spore, possessing two flagella of equal length. Cf. *Heterokont*.

ISOLATING MECHANISM. Mechanism restricting the exchange of genes between populations, by diminishing cross-breeding. Necessary for the evolutionary divergence of populations from each other.

ISOMORPHIC. Used of alternation of generations (q.v.), particularly in algae, meaning generations vegetatively identical. Cf. *Heteromorphic*.

ISOPODA. Order of Crustacea, including woodlice, water-slaters, pill-bugs, etc.

ISOPTERA. Termites (white ants); order of exopterygote insects. Live in huge colonies with elaborate system of castes, resembling that of true ants, though independently evolved.

ISOTONIC. (Of a solution), having a concentration such that it neither gains nor loses water by osmosis (q.v.) when separated by a semi-permeable membrane from a specified other solution. When the membrane and the other solution are unspecified, they are taken to be the plasma-membranes and interior of cells respectively. Cf. *Hypertonic*, *Hypotonic*.

ISOTYPE. Duplicate of type specimen (q.v.).

ISOZYME. *Isoenzyme* (q.v.).

# J

**JEJUNUM.** Part of small intestine succeeding duodenum and preceding ileum in mammals. Main absorptive region. Larger diameter and larger villi than rest of small intestine.

**JUGULAR.** Main vein returning blood from head (particularly brain) in vertebrates. See *Cardinal veins*.

**JURASSIC.** Geological period (q.v.); lasted approximately from 190 till 135 million years ago.

# K

**KARYOKINESIS.** Mitosis (q.v.).

**KARYOLOGICAL.** Concerned with the nucleus, particularly with the chromosomes.

**KARYOTYPE.** The characteristics of the set of chromosomes (chromosomal sizes, shapes and number) of a typical somatic cell of a given species, individual or cell strain. A diagrammatic representation of a karyotype may be called a *karyogram* or *idiogram*.

**KATABOLISM.** Catabolism (q.v.).

**KEEL (CARINA).** Thin plate-like projection of bone, from ventral surface of breast-bone (sternum) of birds and bats, to either side of which the powerful wing-muscles are attached.

**KERATIN.** Tough fibrous protein containing much sulphur, occurring in epidermis of vertebrates, forming resistant outermost layer of skin, and also hair, feathers, horny scales, nails, claws, hooves, and outer coating of horns of cows, sheep, etc. *Keratinization* is transformation of epidermal cells into keratin, which occurs in formation of above structures.

**KIDNEY.** Organ of excretion and/or water regulation in vertebrates, consisting of numerous nephrons (q.v.) and their blood supply. See also *Coelomoduct, Nephridium.*

**KILOCALORIE.** See *Calorie.*

**KINAESTHETIC.** Detecting movement. Refers, e.g. to sense-organs of vertebrate muscles, tendons, and joints. See *Proprioceptor.*

**KINESIS.** Locomotory movement of an organism or cell in response to a stimulus, such that the speed, or frequency of turning, depends on strength of stimulus; but stimulus does not control direction of movement. Cf. *Taxis.*

**KINETIN.** See *Cytokinins.*

**KINETOCHORE.** Spindle attachment (q.v.).

**KINETOPLAST, KINETOSOME.** See *Centriole.*

**KININS.** (Bot.). Cytokinins (q.v.). (Zool.). Polypeptides producing contraction of smooth muscle.

**KINOMERE.** Spindle attachment (q.v.).

**KREBS CYCLE (CITRIC ACID CYCLE).** Complex cycle of enzyme-controlled reactions by which pyruvic acid is broken down in presence of oxygen to carbon dioxide, and ATP (q.v.), a source of energy, is synthesized. The cycle provides the final step in oxidation of carbohydrates, glycogen or glucose having been broken down during glycolysis to pyruvic acid. It also deals with the final phases of fat oxidation and is concerned in synthesis of some amino acids. The cycle is associated with the mitochondria, which contain the system of enzymes.

# L

**LABIAL.** (Adj.). Of the lip.

**LABIUM.** (Bot.). (1) Lower lip of flowers of family Labiatae. (2) Lip subtending ligule in lycopod *Isoetes* (Zool.). Lower lip of insect. Consists of the paired appendages of one segment fused together in mid-line.

**LABRUM.** Plate of exoskeleton, hinged to the head above the mouth, which forms the upper lip of insects.

**LABYRINTH, MEMBRANOUS.** See *Ear, inner*.

**LABYRINTHODONTIA.** The main group of fossil Amphibia. Late Devonian to Triassic. Contains forms closely related to certain fish (Crossopterygii) and others transitional to reptiles.

**LABYRINTHULALES.** Net slime moulds. Group (Order) of colonial organisms, cells naked, spindle-shaped, secreting an extracellular membrane-limited matrix in the form of a network of tubes (slimeways), through which they move. Aquatic, mostly marine. Affinity uncertain. See *Myxomycophyta*.

**LAC.** Resinous exudation covering females of an insect, *Tachardia* (Hemiptera). The main constituent of shellac.

**LACERTILIA (SAURIA).** Lizards. A sub-order of Squamata (sometimes a separate order), class Reptilia. Unlike the other squamate sub-order, the Ophidia (snakes), lizards have normal-sized jaw gape, movable eyelids, and eardrums; and most have normal limbs.

**LACHRYMAL GLAND.** Tear gland of eye of tetrapod vertebrate. Lies beneath upper eyelid of man and other mammals. Continually secretes small amounts of sterile, and slightly antiseptic, tears which keep cornea moist. Tears drain into nose through *lachrymal duct* from inner corner of eye.

**LACTASE.** See *Lactose*.

**LACTATION.** Production of milk. See *Mammary gland, Lactogenic hormone*.

**LACTEALS.** Lymph vessels draining villi (q.v.) of intestine in vertebrates. Into them passes fat absorbed from intestine, and the fat globules give milky appearance to contained lymph.

**LACTIC ACID.** Organic acid formed as product of splitting up of glucose (glycolysis), which is an essential process in utilization of energy of food by many animal cells, and particularly during contraction of vertebrate striped muscle. Also formed in metabolism of many bacteria, e.g. from lactose in souring of milk (hence its name).

**LACTOGENIC HORMONE (PROLACTIN, LUTEOTROPIC HORMONE, LTH).** Gonadotropic hormone (q.v.) secreted by anterior lobe of pituitary in vertebrates. In mammals, promotes secretion of

progesterone by corpus luteum, and is largely responsible for onset
of milk production in mother after parturition; also stimulates cropmilk (q.v.) production in pigeons; and is probably responsible for
maternal, broody and related behaviour in mammals, birds,
amphibia and fish.

LACTOSE. Sugar (disaccharide, with twelve carbon atoms) occurring
in mammalian milk. Compound of a molecule of glucose and a
molecule of galactose (into which it is split by intestinal enzyme
*lactase*).

LAMARCKISM. View that acquired characters (q.v.) are inherited,
first systematically propounded by Lamarck (1744–1829). Lamarck however was principally concerned with a supposed evolutionary effect of *habits* acquired during the life of an animal. The
rather different modern theories of the inheritance of responses to
environmental influence are hence often called Neo-Larmarckism.

LAMELLA. Thin layer, membrane or plate-like structure, e.g.:
(1) One of spore-bearing gills in fruit-body of mushroom or related
fungus, attached to underside of cap and radiating from centre to
margin. (2) One of series of double membranes within chloroplast
which bear the photosynthetic pigments. (3) Of bone. One of
thin layers (roughly five micrometres thick) in which the calcified
matrix (q.v.) of bone occurs. Frequently disposed concentrically
around Haversian canal (q.v.), or parallel to surface of bone.

LAMELLIBRANCHIATA (PELECYPODA). Bivalves; class of molluscs
with bivalve shells, including mussels, clams, oysters. Aquatic;
elaborate mechanism of feeding by ciliary currents.

LAMINA. Leaf-blade.

LAMINARIN. Polysaccharide reserve food material characteristic of
brown algae (Phaeophyta).

LAMPBRUSH CHROMOSOME. The form that the chromosomes take
in the oocytes of many animals, and in some other situations. They
are usually long (up to 1 mm.) and are covered by a profusion of
very fine hair-like lateral projections, which are actually loops, each
loop with a core of DNA.

LAMP SHELLS. Brachiopoda (q.v.).

LANUGO. Crop of very fine hair covering human foetus, which disappears before birth.

LARVA. The pre-adult form in which some animals hatch from the
egg; capable of fending for itself though usually in a way different
from adult; but usually incapable of sexual reproduction (see
*Paedogenesis*); and distinctly different from sexually mature adult
in form. Turns into adult, usually by a rather rapid metamorphosis
(q.v.). E.g. tadpole of frog, caterpillar of butterfly; and many
marine invertebrates (Echinodermata, Mollusca, Annelida) have
planktonic, transparent, ciliated larvae quite unlike adults (see
*Trochophore, Veliger*).

LARYNX. Dilated region of upper part of trachea of tetrapods, just at its junction with pharynx. 'Adam's apple' of man. Has plates of cartilage in its walls, movable by muscles which open and close glottis (q.v.). In some tetrapods, including most mammals, a dorso-ventral fold of membrane (vocal cord), situated within larynx, projects into its lumen from each side wall. Vibration of cords produces vocal sounds. Movement of the cartilage plates varies stretch of vocal cords, and hence alters pitch of voice. See *Syrinx*.

LATENT PERIOD. Time between application of stimulus and first detectable response in an irritable tissue (e.g. muscle or nerve, where it is a fraction of a millisecond). Also applied to a nervous reflex; but term *reaction time* is more often used for reactions of a whole animal or plant.

LATERAL LINE SYSTEM (ACUSTICO-LATERALIS SYSTEM). System of sense organs, present in aquatic vertebrates (Agnatha, fish, and aquatic Amphibia), in pores or canals arranged in a line down each side of the body, and in complicated pattern of lines on head. Detects pressure changes including vibrations (low-frequency sounds) in water. Canals in dermal bones of head lodge the system, and are important in establishing homologies of these bones in different fish. Inner ear is probably a modified part of system. Supplied entirely by cranial nerves.

LATERAL PLATE. Mesoderm on lateral and ventral sides of verte-brate embryos. Unsegmented (cf. *Somitic Mesoderm*). Within it the perivisceral coelom arises. Forms peritoneum, smooth muscle of gut, heart, pericardium, muscle and bone of tetrapod limb, etc.

LATEX. Fluid produced by a number of flowering plants characteris-tically exuding from cut surfaces as a milky juice, e.g. dandelions, lettuce. Contains a number of substances including proteins, sugars, mineral salts, alkaloids, oils, caoutchouc, etc., and rapidly coagulates on exposure to air. Function of latex not clearly under-stood but thought to be concerned in nutrition and in protection and healing of wounds. Latex of a number of species is collected and used in manufacture of several commercial products, most important being rubber.

LATIMERIA. The only known living representative of the great group of fossil fish, Crossopterygii. A coelacanth.

LEAF BLADE. Thin, flattened, conspicuous portion of leaf, seat of photosynthesis (q.v.), for which it is admirably adapted; may be simple, consisting of one piece, or compound, divided into separate parts or leaflets. Typical dicotyledon leaf presents large surface area with photosynthesizing cells arranged immediately below upper epidermis allowing maximum absorption of light energy. It is provided with a system of veins bringing water and mineral nutrients and removing products of photosynthesis; and with a system of intercellular spaces opening to the atmosphere through stomata and permitting gaseous exchange.

LEAF GAP. Localized region in vascular cylinder of stem immediately

above point of departure of a leaf trace (leaf trace bundle) (q.v.)
where parenchyma is differentiated instead of vascular tissue. In
some plants where there are several leaf traces (leaf trace bundles)
to a leaf these are associated with a single leaf gap. Leaf gaps are
characteristic of ferns, gymnosperms and angiosperms (Pteropsida).

LEAF-SCAR. Scar marking position where a leaf was formerly
attached to the stem.

LEAF-SHEATH. Base of leaf modified to form a sheath round the
stem, e.g. grasses, sedges.

LEAF-TRACE. (1) Vascular bundle extending between vascular
system of stem and leaf base; where more than one occurs each
constitutes a leaf trace. (2) Vascular supply extending between
vascular system of stem and leaf base, consisting of one or more
vascular bundles, each known as a *leaf trace bundle.*

LECITHIN. Fatty substance (phospholipid) containing gycerol, fatty
acid, choline, and phosphoric acid, present in all animal and plant
cells, particularly as a constituent of unit membranes (q.v.).

LECTIN. Plant protein with specific combining groups, which reacts
much as an antibody does with chemical groups of animal cells.

LECTOTYPE. Specimen selected from the original material to serve
as the type specimen (q.v.) when this was not designated at the
time of publication or is missing. Cf. *Neotype.*

LEGUME. (1) A pod. Fruit of members of family Leguminosae (peas,
beans, gorse, laburnum, etc.). Dry fruit formed from a single carpel
that liberates its seeds by splitting open along both sutures into two
parts or valves. (2) Used by agriculturists for a particular group of
fodder plants belonging to this family, clovers and allied plants.

LEMMA (INFERIOR PALEA). Glume-like bract of grass spikelet
bearing in its axil a flower, which, with palea (q.v.), it encloses.

LEMUR. One of a group of primitive primates, found in Old World
tropics.

LENS. Of eye of vertebrates, transparent structure just behind pupil,
lying in aqueous humour, attached by collagen fibres to ciliary
body. See Fig. 3, p. 107. In land-living forms, including man, not
as important as cornea in the refraction which produces image on
retina; function is accommodation (q.v.) by change of shape. In
fish, spherical, and responsible for both refraction and accommodation. In embryonic development of vertebrate originates from
epidermis, as an induction (q.v.) by retina. Consists largely of
elongated inert cells (*lens fibres*) which contain large amounts of
special lens proteins, the crystallins. Lenses and lens-like structures
occur in eyes of many invertebrates.

LENTICEL. Small raised pore, usually elliptical in shape, developing
in woody stems when epidermis is replaced by cork; packed with
loosely arranged cells and allowing exchange of gases between
interior of stem and atmosphere.

LEPIDOPTERA. Butterflies, moths. Order of endopterygote insects. Two pairs of large wings; wings and body covered with scales; larva a caterpillar. Adults feed on nectar of flowers using a highly specialized proboscis; larvae usually feed on plants, and include some serious pests.

LEPIDOSIREN. South American lungfish (member of Dipnoi, q.v.).

LEPTOCEPHALUS. Oceanic larva of European eel. Migrates more than 2000 miles across Atlantic from breeding-ground of eels near West Indies to reach European fresh-waters, where becomes adult. Quite transparent.

LEPTOSPORANGIATE. (Of sporangia in vascular plants), arising from a single parent cell and possessing a wall of one layer of cells. Spore production low in comparison with *eusporangiate* (q.v.) type.

LEPTOTENE. Stage in early prophase of first division of meiosis (q.v.) in which the chromosomes appear as a tangled mass of very slender threads bearing bead-like structures, the chromomeres, along their length.

LETHAL GENE. Gene which kills individual bearing it. If individuals heterozygous for it are killed it is a dominant lethal; if only individuals homozygous for it are killed, it is a recessive lethal.

LEUCOCYTE. White blood cell (q.v.).

LEUCOCYTOSIS. Presence of unusually large number of white blood cells in blood, a response to infection of tissue damage.

LEUCOPHYTE. Colourless, non-photosynthetic alga. Change from photosynthetic form has been achieved experimentally in some species and has proved to be irreversible. Structurally like pigmented (chlorophyll-containing) forms but physiologically heterotrophic, like protozoa. Lends support to suggestion of evolutionary origin of protozoa from algae.

LEUCOPLAST. Colourless plastid found in cells of plant tissues not normally exposed to light. Include *amyloplasts*, storing starch, *elaioplasts*, storing oil and *aleuroplasts*, storing protein.

LEUCOSIN. Chrysolaminarin (q.v.).

LH. Luteinizing hormone (q.v.).

LIANES. Climbing plants found in tropical forests, with long, woody, rope-like stems of anomalous anatomical structure.

LICHENES. Lichens, dual organisms formed from symbiotic association of two plants, a fungus and an alga. The fungus partner is usually an Ascomycete, sometimes a Basidiomycete, the algal partner a green (Chlorophyta) or blue-green (Cyanophyta) alga. A cosmopolitan group of plants occurring on tree trunks, old walls, on the ground, exposed rock, etc., and providing the dominant flora in large areas of mountain and arctic regions where few other plants can live. Lichens play an important part with liverworts and mosses in the primary colonization of bare areas.

Lichens are *crustose*, forming a thin, flat crust on the substratum, *foliose*, flat with leaf-like lobes, or *fruticose*, upright, branched forms. Very slow growing and vary greatly in size, e.g. from a millimetre to several metres across. Reproduce vegetatively by *soredia*, groups of fungal hyphae enclosing algal cells, cut off and dispersed in large numbers. Sexual reproduction is confined to fungus partner and in majority of lichens it is by the development of apothecia or perithecia. On germination of the ascospores new lichen plants are formed if the algal partner happens to be present but in its absence the fungus dies.

In arctic regions certain lichens are valuable as a source of food, e.g. Iceland moss, reindeer moss. Other lichens provide dyes, e.g. *Roccella*, providing litmus.

LIFE CYCLE. Progressive series of changes undergone by an organism or lineal succession of organisms, from fertilization to the death of that stage producing the gametes which begin an identical series of changes. In vertebrates this would simply be from union of gametes to death of the resulting individual; but in many plants and animals there is a succession of individuals, with sexual or asexual reproduction connecting them, in the entire cycle, e.g. in flukes (q.v.). See *Alternation of generations*.

LIGAMENT. Strong band of collagen connecting the two bones at a joint. Helps restrict movement to that provided for by shape of joint, preventing dislocation.

LIGNIN. Complex aromatic compound, chemistry of which is not fully understood (considered to be a polymer of phenyl propane units), which is deposited in cell walls of sclerenchyma, xylem vessels and tracheids, making them strong and rigid. Forms 25–30 per cent of the wood of trees.

LIGULE. Membranous outgrowth arising (1) from junction of leaf-blade and leaf-sheath in many grasses and (2) from base of the leaves of certain lycopods.

LIMITING FACTOR. Any variable factor of the environment whose particular level is at a given time limiting some activity of an organism or population of organisms. E.g. temperature may limit photosynthesis when other conditions would favour a higher rate, or may similarly limit population growth.

LIMNOLOGY. The study of fresh waters and their inhabitants.

LIMULUS. King-crab, an aquatic arachnid, only living representative of its order (Xiphosura). Apparently identical animals existed in the Triassic.

LINGUAL. (Adj.). Of the tongue.

LINKAGE. Association of two or more non-allelomorphic genes, so that they tend to be passed from generation to generation as an inseparable unit, and fail to show independent assortment (q.v.). Due to their being in same chromosome. Separation of such genes into different chromosomes occurs from time to time as a result of crossing-over (q.v.). The nearer such genes are to each other on a chromosome the less often they are separated by crossing-over and the more *closely linked* they are said to be. All the genes in one chromosome form one *linkage-group*.

LINKAGE MAP. See *Chromosome map*.

LINOLEIC ACID (VITAMIN F). Unsaturated fatty acid required by various insects and mammals, probably including man.

LIPASE. Enzyme which splits esters of fatty acids, e.g. true fats, into alcohol and acid.

LIPID (LIPIDE). See *Fat*.

LIPIN, LIPINE. Fat (q.v. meaning (1)) containing nitrogen, and often phosphorus (phospholipin) or sulphur. Always complicated compound, e.g. lecithin (q.v.).

LIPOID. (1) Substance resembling fat (q.v.) in solubility, but not containing fatty acid (e.g. steroid, carotene, terpene); (2) Substance, resembling fat in solubility, which may contain fatty acid (e.g. phospholipin); but excluding neutral fats. (3) Occasionally, fat (q.v. meaning (1) or (2)).

LITHOSERE. A sere (q.v.) originating on exposed rock surface.

LITTORAL. Inhabiting bottom of sea or lake near shore, roughly within a depth to which light and wave action reach. For sea, usually taken as between high tide mark and 200 metres (i.e. approximately to limit of continental shelf). For lakes, approximately down to 10 metres.

LIVER. Gland whose duct opens into gut, usually with digestive function. Not homologous in different phyla. Liver of vertebrates has many functions, e.g. secretion of bile (q.v.); storage of glycogen (see *Blood-sugar*); synthesis of plasma albumin.

LIVER-FLUKE. Of sheep, cattle, etc., fluke (q.v.) which lives in bile ducts and causes liver-rot, disease which leads to great losses. Common in wet meadows where the intermediate host, a water snail, flourishes and infects the pastures with cercaria larvae.

LIVERWORTS. Hepaticae (q.v.).

LOCULICIDAL. (Bot.). Describing dehiscence of multilocular capsule by longitudinal splitting along dorsal suture (midrib) of each carpel, e.g., iris. Cf. *Septicidal*.

LOCUS. The position occupied, in all homologous chromosomes, by a particular gene or one of its alleles. Homologous chromosomes contain identical sets of loci in the same linear order. Loci pair in meiosis.

LODICULES. Reduced perianth of grass flowers; two small, scale-like structures below ovary which at time of flowering swell up, forcing open the enclosing bracts (pales), exposing stamens and pistil.

LOMASOME. See *Mesosome*.

LOMENTUM. Form of legume fruit (q.v.) constricted between the seeds and breaking into one-seeded portions when ripe, e.g., birds-foot.

LONG-DAY PLANT. See *Photoperiodism*.

LTH. Lactogenic Hormone (q.v.).

**LUMBAR VERTEBRAE.** Vertebrae of the waist region; without ribs; situated between the rib-bearing thoracic and the sacral vertebrae. Present in most amniotes.

**LUMEN.** Cavity. Space within tube or sac, or enclosed by cell-wall.

**LUNG.** Organ for breathing air. (1) In vertebrates. Embryologically a diverticulum of the gut. Present in early fishes before origin of Amphibia, probably as an accessory breathing organ adapted to oxygen-poor fresh waters in which earliest vertebrates probably lived. A functional lung occurs in some living fishes (*Polypterus*, Dipnoi). In others it has evolved into swim-bladder (q.v.). Present in almost all amniotes. See *Bronchus, Bronchiole, Alveolus*. (2) In land molluscs, highly vascular part of mantle.

**LUNG BOOK.** Respiratory organ of some air-breathing arachnids (spiders and scorpions); consists of projections, containing blood and arranged like leaves of a book, in a depression of the body wall.

**LUTEAL PHASE.** See *Oestrus Cycle*.

**LUTEAL TISSUE.** Tissue which fills cavity of a ruptured Graafian follicle, constituting a corpus luteum (q.v.). Derived from follicle cells. Secretes progesterone.

**LUTEINIZING HORMONE (LH).** Gonadotrophic hormone (q.v.) secreted by anterior lobe of pituitary in vertebrates. In females, activates the oestrogen-producing tissue of the ovaries, probably promotes the final stages of development of ovarian follicles, produces ovulation, and in mammals initiates corpus luteum development. In males, activates the androgen-producing tissue of the testes, and in some vertebrates produces transfer of sperm from testis to ducts.

**LYCOPODIALES.** Club mosses. Order of Pteridophyta with fossil history extending back to Palaeozoic. Attained their highest development in Carboniferous and included tree-like forms, e.g. *Lepidodendron*, *Sigillaria*. Existing representatives small, evergreen plants with upright or trailing stems bearing numerous small leaves. Sporangia borne singly in axils of leaves, sporophylls occurring in groups at intervals along stem or forming terminal cones. Homosporous, e.g. *Lycopodium*, with small prothalli, wholly or partly subterranean, mycotrophic; or heterosporous, with reduced prothalli remaining largely enclosed by spore wall, e.g. *Selaginella*.

**LYCOPSIDA.** Group (Subdivision) of Tracheophyta (q.v.) including clubmosses (Lycopodium) and related plants, living and extinct.

**LYMPH.** Fluid drained by lymph vessels from intercellular spaces; its water-content ultimately derived from blood by filtration through capillary walls. Colourless, containing small amount of protein, and varying numbers of cells, chiefly lymphocytes. See *Lymphatic system*.

**LYMPHATIC (L. VESSEL).** Lymph-carrying vessel, lined by smooth endothelium like a blood-vessel; but always with thin walls, which in larger vessels contain smooth muscle and connective tissue.

Many have valves. The smallest vessels are *lymphatic capillaries*. In Anura some of the vessels are enlarged into very big *lymph spaces*. See *Lymphatic system, Lacteal*.

LYMPHATIC SYSTEM. System of fluid-containing tubes present in vertebrates. A blindly-ending meshwork of small tubes (lymph capillaries) permeates most tissues (not nervous system), and connects up into ever larger vessels (but not usually larger than 2-3 mm. diameter) which finally join venous system usually near the heart. Lymph (q.v.) is drained from the tissues into the blood by this system. Because of high permeability of lymph capillaries, large molecules and particles from the intercellular spaces, including invading bacteria, which cannot get through blood capillary walls, are carried away with the lymph. In the course of the lymphatic vessels in some vertebrates are lymph nodes, which filter out and destroy bacteria in the lymph, and supply lymphocytes to it. The lymph moves by contractility of vessels; or by squeezing of lymphatic vessels by neighbouring skeletal muscles, the larger vessels having valves which ensure flow in one direction; or (except in birds and mammals) by lymph hearts.

LYMPH HEART. Enlarged part of lymphatic vessel with muscular pulsating wall, present in many vertebrates, but not in birds or mammals. Pumps lymph.

LYMPH NODE (LYMPH GLAND). Organ on the course of a main lymphatic vessel, consisting of lymphoid tissue (q.v.). Its macrophages remove foreign bodies from lymph. If these foreign bodies are bacteria, it may become inflamed ('swollen glands'). It is an important source of antibodies. Occurs in mammals, and, not so well-developed, in birds; not in other vertebrates.

LYMPHOCYTE. Kind of white blood cell (q.v.) of vertebrates. Rather small and usually spherical (6–8 micrometres diameter in man) with relatively little cytoplasm. Forms 20–25 per cent of white blood cells in man. Non-phagocytic, actively amoeboid, produce or carry antibodies. Lymphocytes are continuously made in lymphoid tissue.

LYMPHOID TISSUE (LYMPHATIC TISSUE). Tissue of vertebrates which produces lymphocytes (q.v.) by division of some of its cells; it also contains macrophages (q.v.). Widely distributed in body. Occurs especially in spleen, lymph nodes, thymus, tonsils.

LYSIGENOUS. (Of secretory cavities in plants), originating by dissolution of secreting cells, e.g. oil-containing cavities in orange peel. Cf. *Schizogenous*.

LYSIS. Destruction of cells through damage to or rupture of plasma membrane, allowing escape of cell contents.

LYSOGENY. Relationship between bacteriophage of a non-virulent (temperate) kind and bacterium. The temperate bacteriophage does not multiply after entering bacterial cell, nor cause lysis, but instead its genetic material, DNA, becomes attached to that of the bacterium and is reproduced with it at each division of the bacterial cell. This attached condition, the *prophage* state, may continue through many generations of the bacterial cells. Bacteria carrying prophage are said to be lysogenic; with rare exceptions their other characteristics are unaltered. Spontaneous change to production of complete bacteriophage particles, with lysis of the bacterial cell, occurs occasionally in a lysogenic cell, and can be induced (*prophage induction*) by treatments that induce mutations in other organisms. Prophage, and other kinds of genetic elements having similar relationship with bacteria are termed *episomes* (q.v.).

LYSOSOME. Sub-microscopic, membrane-bounded, particle, lacking internal structure demonstrable by electron microscope, containing hydrolytic enzymes. Present in large numbers in cytoplasm of animal cells. Liberate their enzymes in injured cells and assist in digestion and removal of dead cells. Believed to be involved in autolysis (q.v.) and in controlled selective destruction of tissues that occurs in many developmental processes, conspicuously in metamorphosis (q.v.). Comparable structures have been observed in plants and fungi.

LYSOZYME. Class of enzymes that destroy or weaken cell wall of many bacteria, leading to rupture and death of protoplast. Hydrolyse complex polymers of amino acids and amino sugars present in the walls. Secreted by skin and mucous membranes and present in tears, saliva and other body fluids of mammals; and in bird egg white; providing protection against bacterial invasion.

# M

**MACROGAMETE (MEGAGAMETE).** Female gamete, distinguished from male gamete by larger size and/or by structure. See *Anisogamy*.

**MACROMOLECULE.** Molecule of very many atoms, with molecular weight in thousands or millions of units. E.g. proteins, nucleic acids, polysaccharides.

**MACRONUCLEUS (MEGANUCLEUS).** Members of Ciliophora have two kinds of nucleus; one is the large macronucleus, which is polyploid, divides amitotically and is apparently concerned with the ordinary protein synthesis of the organism; and the other the smaller *micronucleus*, which divides mitotically and provides the gametes during conjugation. The macronucleus disappears during conjugation, and is reconstituted from the zygote nucleus, i.e. from micronuclear chromosomes. More than one macronucleus and micronucleus may occur in each organism.

**MACROPHAGES.** Phagocytic cells widely distributed in vertebrate body. Occur in all connective tissue, where after injury they become active in removing the debris. The resting, connective tissue forms are often called *histiocytes*. Occur also (forming the reticulo-endothelial system) in contact with lymph (in lymph-nodes) or blood (in bone-marrow, spleen, liver), removing by phagocytosis from these fluids any foreign particles. Can be readily demonstrated by injecting an animal with Indian ink or certain dyes, the particles of which are engulfed by, and mark, the macrophages. Move by membrane-like pseudopodia. See *Reticulo-endothelial system, Monocyte*.

**MACROPHAGOUS.** (Of animals). Feeding on pieces of food large relative to their own size. Feed at intervals. All land animals are macrophagous. Cf. *Microphagous*.

**MACROSPORANGIUM.** Megasporangium (q.v.).

**MACROSPORE.** Megaspore (q.v.).

**MACROSPOROPHYLL.** Megasporophyll (q.v.).

**MACULA (OF EYE).** See *Fovea*.

**MAGGOT.** Worm-like larva of certain insects (dipteran flies) with no appendages and without well-marked head.

**MALARIA PARASITE.** Genus of sporozoan Protozoa (*Plasmodium*), causing malaria in man.

**MALLEUS.** Mammalian ear-ossicle (q.v.) representing articular bone of other vertebrates.

**MALLOPHAGA.** Biting lice, bird lice. Order of small exopterygote insects. Live on birds as scavengers, eating bits of feather, skin, etc.; they cannot pierce and suck. Cf. *Anoplura*.

**MALPIGHIAN BODY (M. CORPUSCLE).** Filtering unit of vertebrate kidney; a Bowman's capsule with its glomerulus.

**MALPIGHIAN LAYER.** Layer of epidermis next to dermis; in it active

cell-division goes on; some of the new cells thus formed leave
the layer, becoming keratinized and replacing the outer cells of the
epidermis which are continually wearing away. Contains most of
the melanin responsible for dark skin.

MALPIGHIAN TUBULES. Tubular glands, excretory in function,
opening into anterior part of hind gut of insects, arachnids, and
myriapods.

MALTASE. See *Maltose*.

MALTOSE. Sugar (disaccharide, with twelve carbon atoms) formed
as a result of starch breakdown. Occurs, e.g. in germinating seed
(such as barley) and during digestion. A maltose molecule is a
compound of two molecules of glucose (into which it is split by
enzyme *maltase*).

MAMMA. Mammary gland (q.v.).

MAMMAL. Any member of the Mammalia, a class of tetrapod vertebrates. E.g. man, dog, whale. Contains three living sub-classes,
Monotremata, Marsupialia, and Placentalia, the latter two sub-
classes containing also numerous fossils; and some other, imperfectly known, fossil groups dating as far back as Triassic. Peculiar
to mammals are: hair; milk secretion; diaphragm used in respiration; lower jaw of single pair of bones; presence of only left systemic arch (q.v.); three bones (auditory ossicles) in each middle
ear connecting ear-drum and inner ear.

MAMMARY GLAND. Milk-producing gland on ventral surface, peculiar to female mammals. Probably represents modified sweat-
glands. Growth and activity is affected by gonad hormones (q.v.)
and state of the gland usually varies with oestrous cycle (q.v.);
actual milk production depends on several hormones, including
pituitary lactogenic hormone (q.v.).

MANDIBLE. (1) Of vertebrates, lower jaw. (2) Of insects, Crustacea,
and Myriapoda, one of the pair of mouth-parts (q.v.), which
usually does most of the work of biting and crushing food.

MANTLE. Of molluscs, fold of skin covering whole or part of body.
Outer surface secretes shell. Protects feeding and/or respiratory
organs, which lie in space between body and mantle. A similar
structure is found in brachiopods.

MANUS. Hand. Carpus, metacarpus, and digits of tetrapod fore-
limb. See *Pentadactyl Limb*, *Pes*.

MARSUPIALIA (METATHERIA, DIDELPHIA). A sub-class of Mammalia, living in Australia and North and South America. Like
placental mammals, the young develop inside uterus of mother,
but usually with a placenta (q.v.) connected with the yolk sac instead of with the allantois. Born in a very undeveloped state, and
usually sheltered in a pouch (marsupium) which contains the teats
of the milk glands. Includes opossum and a few other species in
New World, kangaroo and many other animals of Australia; much
more widespread as fossils.

**MARSUPIUM.** Pouch of many marsupials and *Echidna*. Fold of skin supported by epipubic bones of hip girdle, forming pouch containing mammary glands, into which the new-born (or eggs of *Echidna*) are placed. Young are attached to teats in marsupials; lick milk in *Echidna* which has no teats.

**MASS FLOW.** Hypothesis of transport of materials in phloem. Sieve-tubes (q.v.) and contents are regarded as forming an osmotic system continuous throughout the plant connected, via plasmodesmata (q.v.), with other tissues. A gradient of osmotic and hence turgor pressure exists within the sieve-tube system as a result of entry into it of synthesized materials, e.g. sugars, from the leaf mesophyll (increasing pressures), and their removal for consumption in areas of growth and storage (lowering pressures). This pressure gradient results in mass flow of water and dissolved substances through the system from regions of high to regions of low pressure. Circulation of water is completed via the xylem with which the phloem is intimately connected.

**MAST CELL.** Granular cell of vertebrate connective tissue, secreting histamine and heparin.

**MASTIGONEMES.** Exceedingly fine lateral projections along the length of certain flagella ('tinsel flagella'). Thought to increase mechanical efficiency of flagellum by increasing surface area.

**MASTIGOPHORA.** Flagellata (q.v.).

**MASTOID PROCESS.** Excrescence of human skull (of periotic bone) just behind ear, containing air-spaces which communicate with middle ear.

**MATRIX.** (Zool.). Intercellular substance in which cells are embedded, e.g. in cartilage, or connective tissue. Bone matrix is intercellular substance in which bone salts are deposited.

**MATURATION OF GERM-CELLS.** (Zool.). Process of development of mature sperm and ova, from normally sized and proportioned precursor cells, which occurs in testis and ovary respectively. It includes reduction division or meiosis of the nucleus, which halves number of chromosomes; and extensive changes in cytoplasm, quite different in the two sorts of gametes. See *Oocyte, Spermatocyte*.

**MAXILLA.** (1) One of the (dermal) bones of the upper jaw of vertebrates (and of the face in man) which carries all of the upper teeth, except incisors. (2) Sometimes used for the whole upper jaw of vertebrates. (3) One of a pair of mouth-parts in insects, Crustacea, and Myriapoda, lying behind the mandibles (q.v.); assists in eating.

**MEATUS.** A passage. E.g. external auditory meatus (see *Ear, outer*).

**MECKEL'S CARTILAGE.** Bar of cartilage, one forming each side of lower jaw of embryo gnathostome vertebrate, and of adult elasmobranch. In most other adult vertebrates it becomes reduced, and partly ossified as articular, which (except in mammals, see *Ear ossicles*) always forms hinge of lower jaw, rest of lower jaw being composed of dermal bones. Represents part of a visceral arch (q.v.).

MECONIUM. Contents of intestine of mammalian foetus. Derived from secretions of glands discharging into gut, and swallowed amniotic fluid.

MEDIAN. Situated in or towards the plane which divides a bilaterally symmetrical organism or organ into right and left halves.

MEDIASTINUM. Median space in the chest of mammals; a narrow dorsoventrally extended cleft between the two pleural cavities (q.v.), containing the heart in its pericardium, aorta, trachea, oesophagus, thymus, etc.

MEDULLA. Central part of an organ. (1) *of plants*, pith; central core of usually parenchymatous tissue in those stems in which the vascular tissue is in the form of a cylinder; functioning in food storage. May occur in some roots where central tissue develops into parenchyma instead of xylem. (2) *Adrenal m.* see *Adrenal gland*. (3) Of brain, see *Medulla oblongata*.

MEDULLA OBLONGATA. Often called simply medulla. Most posterior part of the brain of vertebrates, merging into the spinal cord. Thick-walled and floored, but with thin roof; its internal cavity is fourth ventricle. Primitively concerned with co-ordination of impulses from lateral line, ear, taste, and touch receptors. Contains important centres for respiratory movement, control of blood-vessels and heart, etc. Glossopharyngeal and vagus nerves arise from it.

MEDULLARY RAY. Thin, vertical plate of parenchyma cells, one to several cells wide, running radially through tissues of stele (q.v.). Medullary rays are either *primary*, passing from pith (medulla) to cortex between the primary vascular bundles, or *secondary*, formed from cambium during process of secondary thickening and ending blindly in secondary xylem and phloem. Since these latter have no connection with the pith (medulla) they are called by some authorities *vascular* (phloem or xylem) *rays*. Large numbers of medullary rays are present in the vascular cylinder and they form system of radiating plates of living tissue connected with each other by living parenchyma cells. The function of the medullary rays is in storage and radial conduction of synthesized food material.

MEDULLATED NERVE FIBRE. Synonym of myelinated nerve fibre. See *Nerve fibre, Myelin*.

MEDUSA. Free swimming form of coelenterate (of sub-phylum Cnidaria, e.g. jelly-fish). Bell or umbrella shaped, swimming by pulsations of body. Generally do not reproduce by budding. Reproduce sexually, fertilized eggs giving rise to polyps. Are themselves produced asexually by polyps (q.v.). See *Alternation of generations*.

MEGAGAMETE. Macrogamete (q.v.).

MEGANUCLEUS. Macronucleus (q.v.).

MEGAPHYLL. Type of leaf possessing branched system of veins and with leaf trace generally associated with one or more leaf gaps in stele of stem. Associated (with few exceptions) with siphonostelic vascular system in stem. Characteristic of ferns and seed plants. Cf. *Microphyll*.

MEGASPORANGIUM (MACROSPORANGIUM). Sporangium within which megaspores are formed. In flowering plants known as the ovule. Cf. *Microsporangium*.

MEGASPORE (MACROSPORE). Larger of the two kinds of spore produced by heterosporous ferns; the first cell of female gametophyte generation of these plants and of seed plants. In flowering plants becomes embryo sac (q.v.). Cf. *Microspore*.

MEGASPOROPHYLL (MACROSPOROPHYLL). Leaf or modified leaf bearing megasporangia. In flowering plants, the carpel. Cf. *Microsporophyll*.

MEIOSIS (REDUCTION DIVISION). Two successive cell divisions of special kind, starting in a diploid cell. Both divisions resemble mitoses, but the chromosomes are duplicated only once, before the first division, so that the number of chromosomes present in each of the four daughter-cells is half that of diploid cell (i.e. the daughter-cells are haploid). Meiosis occurs at some time in the life cycle of all sexually reproducing organisms, because gametes must be haploid to compensate for the chromosome doubling produced by fertilization. In animals, and some algae, it occurs during formation of gametes. In many fungi and green algae and in Sporozoa, it occurs immediately after fertilization or on germination of zygote. In most other plants it occurs some time after fertilization but some time before gamete formation, during formation of spores (see *Alternation of generations*).

The course of meiosis is extremely similar wherever it occurs. Chief differences from two successive mitoses are as follows (Cf. *Mitosis*; Figs. 6A, 6B, pp. 180, 181). When chromosomes first appear (in prophase) they are separate fine threads; this is the *leptotene* (q.v.) stage. The two homologous members of each pair of chromosomes then associate closely side by side, corresponding loci adhering together, a process called *pairing* or *synapsis*; each associated pair is a *bivalent*; Fig. 6B (2b); this is the *zygotene* (q.v.) stage. The bivalents shorten and thicken. Each individual chromosome is now manifestly double (the actual doubling occurred in the previous interphase); hence each bivalent consists of four *chromatids* (2c) (*pachytene* (q.v.) stage). The two chromatids derived from one chromosome remain paired but they separate from the other two chromatids derived from the homologous chromosome (*diplotene* (q.v.) stage, followed by *diakinesis* (q.v.) ). At certain places, however, they are held together by interchanges (chiasmata) occurring between chromatids derived from homologous chromosomes. Chiasmata are the visible expression of crossing-over (q.v.) of genes. There are usually one or more chiasmata per chromosome pair per meiosis. In a chiasma two chromatids, one from each of the original chromosomes, have apparently broken at corresponding places; and the broken ends of one chromatid have fused with the broken ends of the other, Fig. 6B (2c). Where there is more than one chiasma in a single bivalent they may involve different pairs of chromatids, but always one from each of the original chromosomes. At anaphase two of the four chromatids from each bivalent go to one pole of the spindle, and the other two to the other pole. The chromatids go in pairs because the spindle attachment of each original chromosome has not yet duplicated, so that two chromatids are united at that point. Owing to the effects of chiasmata, however, the united chromatids are not usually derived throughout their length from the same chromosome (though they always are in the immediate neighbourhood of the spindle attachment) but are mixtures of one or more pieces from each of the original chromosomes. It is a matter of chance, and quite uninfluenced by behaviour of other bivalents, which spindle attachment with its chromatids, goes to which pole of the spindle (Fig. 6B (4) ).

After anaphase there may be a short telophase (5) and resting stage, or the second meiotic division may follow immediately, usually in both the daughter-cells formed by the first division. It is like a mitosis, except that it starts prophase with only half the normal number of chromosomes, each already divided into two chromatids before the previous prophase. These two chromatids separate at anaphase (4′), one going to each daughter-cell. Again, the distribution of the chromatids is a matter of chance, except that the two from each chromosome must go to opposite poles. On this chance distribution of the chromatids at both anaphases depends the law of Independent Assortment (q.v.). Each daughter-cell therefore eventually receives only the haploid number of chromosomes (5′). The reduction from the diploid number of the original cell to the haploid number of the four products is one of the bases of genetic segregation (q.v.).

MEIOSPORE. Spore produced as a result of meiosis.

MELANIN. Dark-brown pigment present in many animals which in different concentrations gives brown and yellow coloration. Occurs as graules in cells. Colour of human hair is mainly due to melanin. See DOPA.

MELANOPHORE. Chromatophore (q.v.) containing melanin as pigment.

MELATONIN. See *Pineal body*.

MEMBRANE BONE. Dermal bone (q.v.).

MEMBRANOUS LABYRINTH. See *Ear, inner*.

MENDELISM. Science of the behaviour of genes (q.v.) in inheritance studied by breeding experiments.

MENDEL'S LAWS. First Law, of Segregation (q.v.). Second Law, of Independent Assortment (q.v.).

MENINGES. Membranes covering the vertebrate central nervous system; dura mater (q.v.) outside pia-arachnoid (q.v.).

MENSTRUAL CYCLE. Modified oestrous cycle (q.v.) of catarrhine primates (Old World monkeys, anthropoid apes, and man) which has special feature of sudden destruction of mucosa of uterus at end of luteal phase of cycle, producing bleeding; and absence of any well-marked period of oestrus (q.v.).

MENTAL PROMINENCE. Chin. Projection at front of lower jaw bone (dentaries) of man. Not to be confused with intellectual eminence, another peculiarity of *Homo sapiens*.

MERICARP. One-seeded portion of a schizocarp (q.v.).

MERISTELE. See *Dictyostele*.

MERISTEM. Localized region of active cell-division in plants from which permanent tissue is derived. New cells formed by activity of a meristem become variously modified to form characteristic tissues of the adult (epidermis, cortex, vascular tissue, etc.). A meristem may have its origin in a single cell, e.g. in ferns, or in a group of cells as in flowering plants. The principal meristems in the latter group occur at tips of stems and roots (apical meristems or growing points), between xylem and phloem of vascular bundles (cambium) in the cortex (cork cambium), in young leaves, and, e.g. in many grasses, at bases of internodes (intercalary meristems). Meristems may also arise in response to wounding.

MEROBLASTIC. (Of animal zygote), only a part undergoing cleavage (q.v.). Occurs in yolky eggs (e.g. chick), the yolk-rich part remaining undivided into cells. Cf. *Holoblastic*.

MEROGAMETE. Of Protozoa, gamete formed by multiple division, and smaller than the ordinary organism, as distinct from holo-gamete which is as large as the ordinary organism and only one of which is produced from each individual. When male and female gametes are strongly differentiated (e.g. malaria parasite) male gametes are merogametes and female hologametes.

-MEROUS. As a suffix, referring to the number of parts, e.g. corolla pentamerous, consisting of five petals.

MEROZYGOTE. Partial zygote. Result of sexual process in certain bacteria in which transfer of genetic material from donor to recipient of two conjugating cells is almost always incomplete. Unlike zygotes of higher organisms recipient cell carries one complete set of genes (its own) and an incomplete set from donor cell. Also results from other forms of transfer of genetic material in bacteria, namely transduction (q.v.) and transformation (q.v.).

MESENCEPHALON. Mid-brain (q.v.).

MESENCHYME. Embryonic connective tissue consisting of rather widely scattered, irregularly branching cells in a jelly-like matrix. Gives rise to connective tissue, bone, cartilage, blood, etc.

MESENTERY. (1) Double layer of peritoneum attaching stomach, intestines, spleen, etc., to dorsal wall of peritoneal cavity. Contains blood, lymph, and nerve supply to these organs. (2) More strictly, the same double layer attaching small intestine only. (3) Vertical partitions in coelenteron of Actinozoa.

MESODERM (MESOBLAST). Germ-layer of triploblastic animal embryo composed, like endoderm, of cells which have moved from surface of embryo into its interior during gastrulation; developing into tissues between gut and ectoderm (muscle, blood, connective tissue, etc.). Term is usually applied to the germ-layer while it is still a demarcated region of the embryo, after gastrulation but before differentiation into the derived tissues; and all the tissues at later stages derived from the embryonic layer may be called mesodermal. See *Germ-layer*, *Ectoderm*, *Endoderm*.

MESOGLOEA. Layer of jelly-like material between external and internal cellular layers of the body of a coelenterate. It may be thin and contain prolongations of cells of these layers, as in *Hydra* and delicate hydroids; or bulky and tough (fibrous), containing many cells (which do not however form organs), as in sea-anemones or large jelly-fish.

MESONEPHROS. Part of kidney of vertebrates which arises in embryonic development later than, and posterior to, the pronephros (q.v.) and discharges into pronephric (Wolffian) duct. There is one on each side. The testes connect with them, and in adult sperms pass through them and down the Wolffian ducts to the exterior. Become functional kidneys of adult anamniotes. In amniotes they function as kidneys in embryo; but later in development are superseded in this function by metanephros (q.v.) and they degenerate except for part connected with testis in male. See *Epididymis*, *Vas efferens*, *Metanephros*.

MESOPHILIC. (Of a micro-organism) with optimum temperature for growth between 20 and 45°C.

MESOPHYLL. Internal tissue of leaf-blade differentiated into *palisade* and *spongy* mesophyll. In dorsi-ventral leaves palisade mesophyll consists of elongated cells immediately below upper epidermis with their long axes at right-angles to leaf surface; these cells contain numerous chloroplasts and are chiefly concerned in photosynthesis. Spongy mesophyll is a tissue of irregular, loosely arranged cells, containing fewer chloroplasts, with large air spaces between the cells, communicating through stomata with atmosphere outside.

MESOPHYTE. Plant growing under average conditions of water supply. Cf. *Hydrophyte*, *Xerophyte*.

MESOSOME. Infolding, often highly complex, of plasma membrane of certain bacteria. Similar organelles, termed *lomasomes*, occur in hyphae and sporing structures of certain fungi, and in some algae and higher plants.

MESOTHELIUM. Layer of flattened cells, a simple squamous epithelium (q.v.) in appearance, derived from mesoderm; lines coelomic cavities of vertebrates (see *Pericardium, Pleura, Peritoneum*), and some other spaces, e.g. synovial sacs.

MESOTHORAX. Middle of the three segments of the insect thorax. Bears a pair of walking-legs and (in winged insects) a pair of wings.

MESOZOIC. See *Geological Periods and Epochs*. This era (the age of great reptiles) lasted approximately from 225 till 65 million years ago.

MESSENGER RNA. Ribonucleic acid molecule that conveys from the DNA the information that is to be translated into the structure of a particular polypeptide molecule. Every different polypeptide that a cell makes requires a corresponding species of messenger RNA (mRNA) molecule. The mRNA, which is a single strand of nucleotides, is built up on a length of DNA (a cistron), its sequence of nucleotides matching (by base-pairing, q.v.) that of one strand of the DNA. The polypeptide molecule is then built up by means of the mRNA (which has become freed from the DNA and attached to ribosomes, q.v.), the sequence of amino-acids in the polypeptide being determined by the sequence of nucleotides in the mRNA (see *Transfer RNA*). mRNA in bacteria, in which it has been most studied, is short-lived and is continuously produced.

METABOLA. Pterygota (q.v.).

METABOLISM. (1) In general the chemical processes occurring within an organism, or within part of one. They involve breaking down of organic compounds from complex to simple (catabolism) with liberation of energy available for the organism's many activities; and building up of organic compounds from simple to complex (anabolism) using energy liberated by catabolism and, in the case of autotrophic organisms, energy from external non-organic sources (particularly from sunlight). Catabolism is by no means confined to the breaking down of the 'food-material' necessary for the organism's energy requirements. It involves, continuously, very many constituents of the organism, though they are broken down at various rates (DNA in resting cells is one of the constituents that seems to remain quite stable); and correspondingly anabolism involves, continuously, synthesis of many constituents. These processes go on even in an apparently static tissue like bone. This metabolic whirlpool, whose extent has become apparent only since the use of 'tracers' (q.v.) is a system of reactions predominantly controlled by enzymes (q.v.). In most of the aspects of metabolism which have been sufficiently investigated, such as catabolism of carbohydrates, there is a fundamental similarity throughout a wide variety of organisms, including plants, animals, and bacteria. Correspondingly, there are close similarities between the enzymes of these organisms. See *Metabolite, Respiration*. (2) Metabolism of some constituent of an organism (e.g. 'fat metabolism'); the part of total metabolism involving that constituent.

METABOLISM, BASAL. The rate of energy expenditure of an animal at rest, usually expressed per unit weight. In man, basal metabolic rate (BMR) is expressed as the output of Calories per square metre of body surface per hour. Measured directly, or indirectly by calculation from the amount of oxygen consumed or carbon dioxide given off.

METABOLITE. Substance which takes part in a process of metabolism (q.v.). Most metabolites are made by the organism in the course of metabolism; others must be taken in from the environment, the organism being unable to make them itself; in still other cases part of the supply of a particular metabolite may be made by the organism, part taken in. Autotrophic organisms need to take in only inorganic metabolites, e.g. water, carbon dioxide, nitrates, and a number of trace elements (q.v.) from the environment. Heterotrophic organisms need, as well as inorganic metabolites, a wide range of organic metabolites from the environment, varying much from species to species, but including certain amino-acids and vitamins.

METACARPAL BONES. Bones of the fore-foot of tetrapod vertebrates (palm-region of man). Rod-like bones, usually one corresponding to each digit. Articulate with wrist bones (carpals) proximally, finger-bones (phalanges) distally. See Fig. 7, p. 213.

METACARPUS. Region of fore-foot of tetrapods, containing metacarpal bones. Palm-region of man.

METACHROMATIC. When stained with a dye, taking a colour different from that usually produced by the dye. E.g. heparin stains purple with thionin, instead of the usual blue. Such staining with basic dyes is commonly an indication of the presence of sulphated polysaccharides.

METACHRONAL RHYTHM. Pattern of beating of cilia (as in ciliated epithelium) or multiple limbs (as in Polychaeta). If the effective stroke is defined as occurring backwards, then each cilium or limb is at a slightly earlier stage in the beat cycle than the one behind it, slightly later than the one in front of it. The effective beat therefore appears to pass as a wave *forwards* in the series of cilia or limbs, though the surrounding fluid is driven *backwards*.

METAMERIC SEGMENTATION (METAMERISM). See *Segmentation*.

METAMORPHOSIS. Period of rapid transformation from larval to adult form. Often involves considerable destruction of larval tissues (see *Lysosome*). E.g. transition of frog tadpole to adult.

METANEPHROS. Part of kidney of amniote vertebrates which arises in embryonic development later than, and posterior to, mesonephros (q.v.), one on each side. Acquires special duct, ureter, which grows into it from the original pronephric duct. Functional kidney of late embryo and adult. See *Pronephros*, *Renal Portal System*.

METAPHASE. Stage of mitosis (q.v.) and of meiosis (q.v.) when chromosomes are arranged on equator of spindle. See Figs. 6A, 6B, pp. 180, 181.

METAPHYTA. See *Embryophyta*.

METAPLASIA. Transformation of one sort of normal adult tissue into another.

METATARSAL BONES. Bones in the hind-foot of tetrapod vertebrates. Rod-like bones, usually one corresponding to each digit. Articulate with ankle bone (tarsals) proximally, toe-bones (phalanges) distally. See Fig. 7, p. 213.

METATARSUS. Region of hind-foot of tetrapods containing metatarsal bones.

METATHERIA. Marsupialia (q.v.).

METATHORAX. Hindmost of the three segments of insect thorax. Bears a pair of walking legs and (in many winged insects) a pair of wings.

METAXENIA. Influence of male (pollen) parent on maternal tissue (i.e. outside embryo and endosperm), e.g. variation in time of maturity of dates with different pollen parents. This particular effect is thought to be brought about by hormones secreted by developing embryo and endosperm.

METAXYLEM. Elements of primary xylem differentiated from procambium (q.v.), after protoxylem; wider, with thicker, more heavily lignified walls; inextensible.

METAZOA. Animals whose bodies consist of many cells, as distinct from Protozoa, which are unicellular; all animals commonly recognized as animals, including man. Sponges (Parazoa, q.v.) though also multicellular, differ so much from other multicellular animals that they are not usually included in the Metazoa.

MICROBE. Microscopic organism, many pathogenic.

MICROBODIES. Cytoplasmic organelles, spherical or oval, 0.1 to 1.5 micrometres across, bounded by membrane. Contain various enzymes; one kind of microbody (*peroxisome*) contains oxidases and catalase (enzyme destroying hydrogen peroxide). Found in a number of different plant and animal cells.

MICRODISSECTION. Technique of doing operations on minute objects (e.g. living cells) while viewed through a microscope, by mechanically operated instruments.

MICROGAMETE. Male gamete, differentiated from female gamete by smaller size and/or by structure. See *Anisogamy*.

MICRO-INCINERATION. Method of examining distribution of minerals in sections of tissues, or whole micro-organisms, by placing on a slide, burning away all organic constituents in a high-temperature furnace, and determining the nature and position of the ash microscopically.

MICROMETRE (MICRON). Unit of length for microscopic objects. One thousandth of a millimetre. Usually written $\mu$m. The limit of resolution of a microscope using visible light is about one-fifth of a micrometre. A nanometre (formerly millimicron), one thousandth of a micrometre, is written nm, and is ten Angstroms (the physicists' unit of small distance).

MICRONUCLEUS. See *Macronucleus*.

MICRO-NUTRIENT. Substance which an organism must obtain from its environment to maintain health, though necessary only in minute amounts; either vitamin (q.v.) or trace element (q.v.).

MICRO-ORGANISM. Microscopically small organism; unicellular plant, animal, or bacterium.

MICROPHAGOUS. Of animals, feeding on particles minute relative to their own size. E.g. barnacle, right whale. Such animals tend to feed continually; and particularly by sieving particles from water drawn to them by ciliary action, or by movements of appendages. Plankton is main source of such particles; these feeders are all aquatic. Cf. *Macrophagous*.

MICROPHYLL. Type of leaf, usually very small, but not always, e.g. *Isoetes*, with very simple vascular system consisting of single, un-branched vein. Leaf trace not associated with leaf gap in stele of stem. Associated with protostelic vascular system in stem. Characteristic of club mosses, horsetails and related forms, and of Psilotales, Psilophytales. Cf. *Megaphyll*.

MICROPYLE. (Bot.). Canal formed by extension of integument(s) of ovule beyond apex of nucellus; recognizable in mature seed as a minute pore in seed coat through which water enters when seed begins to germinate. (Zool.). Pore in egg-membranes of an ovum, through which sperm reaches and fertilizes the ovum, e.g. in many insects.

MICROSCOPE. The ordinary microscope of the laboratory is a *compound microscope* with two sets of lenses (objective and eye-piece) which magnify the object in two steps. Biologists work with various magnifications, achieved by using objectives of different powers, commonly a 'low-power' or 'two-thirds' objective (giving a final magnification including that of the eye-piece of roughly 60–100 times), a 'high-power' or 'sixth' objective (final magnification of roughly 200–400 times) and an oil immersion (q.v.) 'twelfth' objective (final magnification 600–1000 times, sometimes up to 1,500 times). 'Two-thirds', 'sixth' and 'twelfth' indicate the focal length of the objective in inches. About 1,500 times is the maximum degree of magnification it is useful to have with ordinary light, because it is sufficient to make it easy to look at the finest detail that can possibly be seen ('resolved'). Further magnification reveals nothing more; the details merely look bigger and vaguer. This is because it is physically impossible with a microscope, however great its magnification, to see that two points are really two and not a single point when they are nearer together than approximately half the wavelength of the light used to illuminate them. Detail finer than this cannot be resolved. A modern compound microscope can almost reach this physical limit. Only by decreasing the wave-length of the illumination used can finer detail be resolved; and that is how the electron microscope achieves its immense power of detecting minute detail, the 'illumination' being by electrons, which have a very short wavelength.

MICROSOMES. Particles isolated from cytoplasm for biochemical study by mechanically breaking up (homogenizing) cells and differentially centrifuging the result. They are largely artefacts, consisting mostly of vesicles with attached ribosomes formed from the broken up endoplasmic reticulum.

MICROSPORANGIUM. Sporangium within which microspores are formed. In flowering plants, pollen sac. Cf. *Megasporangium*.

MICROSPORE. Smaller of the two kinds of spore produced by heterosporous ferns; first cell of male gametophyte generation of these plants and of seed plants. In flowering plants, becomes pollen grain. Cf. *Megaspore*.

MICROSPOROPHYLL. Leaf or modified leaf bearing microsporangia. In flowering plants the stamen. Cf. *Megasporophyll*.

MICROTOME. Machine for cutting extremely thin slices of tissue (usually 3 to 20 micrometres; for the electron microscope, with special techniques, 100 times thinner than this). Such slices (*sections*) are easily stained and examined with a microscope. Tissue for cutting is either frozen, or, more usually, embedded in a firm but easily-cut supporting substance, generally paraffin wax for the light microscope, or araldite for the electron microscope.

MICROTUBULE. Fibrous structure in cytoplasm, which in electronmicrographs looks like a long tubule roughly 250 Angstroms in outside diameter. Many are found in most cells. See *Spindle*, *Flagellum*, *Colchicine*.

MICROVILLI. Minute finger-like projections from a cell surface, around a tenth of a micrometre in diameter. Closely-packed regularsized microvilli on free surface of epithelium constitute a *brush border*.

MID-BRAIN (MESENCEPHALON). Middle of the three divisions marked out by constrictions in the embryonic vertebrate brain. Becomes during development very thick-walled, with small central cavity. Particularly concerned with sight and hearing.

MIDDLE EAR. See *Ear, middle*.

MIDDLE LAMELLA. See *Cell-wall*.

MILDEW. (1) Plant disease caused by a fungus that produces a superficial, powdery, or downy growth on surface of host; (2) Fungus causing such a disease; (3) often used synonymously with mould (q.v.).

MILK TEETH. Deciduous teeth (q.v.).

MILLIMICRON. See *Nanometre*.

MILLON'S TEST. Test for phenols, including the amino acid tyrosine which is present in most proteins.

MIMETIC. Mimicking species, see *Mimicry*.

MIMICRY. Protective similarity in appearance of one species of animal to another. In *Batesian mimicry* one of the two is poisonous, distasteful, or otherwise protected from predators, and often conspicuously marked (warning or aposematic coloration); the other, innocuous, gaining protection from predators by similarity to the first. In *Müllerian mimicry* both species are protected from predators, and they gain mutually from having the same warning coloration since predators can learn to avoid both species by tasting one. Mimicry occurs particularly amongst insects.

MIOCENE. Geological epoch (q.v.), sub-division of Tertiary, lasted approximately from 26 till 7 million years ago.

MIRACIDIUM. Ciliated larva of fluke (q.v.). Emerges from egg, which is released from vertebrate host in excreta, and parasitizes a snail, in which it reproduces asexually.

MITES. Members of the order Acarina other than ticks (q.v.). Some mites are free-living (e.g. cheese mite), others parasitic (e.g. *Sarcoptes*), causing scabies and mange.

MITOCHONDRIA (CHONDRIOSOMES). Microscopic bodies occurring in cytoplasm of every cell in varying numbers (up to 2500 per cell in rat liver) except in bacteria and blue-green algae. Most are granular, rod, or thread-shaped, about 0.5 micrometre in width or diameter; thread-like forms up to 10 micrometres or more long. Stain specifically in living cell with Janus Green (due to presence of cytochrome oxidase system which keeps dyes in oxidized (coloured) form. Bounded on outside by double membrane ('unit membrane'); within is a dense matrix. Inner component of the double membrane is folded inwards at a number of places so as to project into the matrix as lamellae termed *cristae* (crests), which are covered by so-called *elementary particles* containing components of oxidative enzyme systems. Cristae vary in number, may be branched, tubular rather than lamellate, and may be arranged parallel with long axis of mitochondrion, not, as is usual, at right-angles. Mode of mitochrondrial multiplication not yet resolved; possibly by division. Contain DNA and many oxidative enzyme systems; comprise power plant of cell, producing energy (in form of ATP) for many cell functions. Plastids of green plants are possibly related to mitochondria. See Fig. 1, p. 51.

MITOSIS (KARYOKINESIS). The usual process by which a nucleus divides into two. Each chromosome duplicates before beginning of mitosis, and mitosis involves separation of the resulting duplicates so that one goes into each daughter nucleus. As a result the two daughter nuclei have an identical complement of chromosomes and hence of genes. The process is divided into four stages: prophase, metaphase, anaphase, telophase (Fig. 6A, p. 180). *Prophase* (2): Within the optically largely homogeneous resting nucleus chromosomes appear, at first as very long threads (the whole tangle is sometimes called a spireme) which shorten and thicken steadily by

180

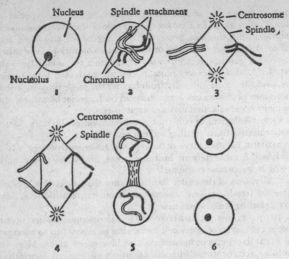

*Fig. 6A. Diagram of mitosis in a nucleus showing only one pair of chromo-somes (one chromosome black, other white). There are usually many pairs in each nucleus. Cytoplasm is not shown. Note that centrosomes do not occur in cells of most plants. 1, Resting stage. 2, Prophase, each chromosome already double (consisting of two chromatids). 3, Metaphase. 4, Anaphase. 5, Telo-phase. 6, The two daughter nuclei in resting stage.*

each coiling into a close spiral. Each chromosome is already double at its earliest appearance. *Metaphase* (3): Nuclear membrane dis-solves. A spindle (q.v.) forms where the nucleus was, between the centrioles (q.v.) if these are present. The chromosomes lie (as an 'equatorial plate') at the equator of the spindle, attached to it by their spindle attachments (q.v.). They pause in this position. *Ana-phase* (4): The duplicates of each chromosome (chromatids) separ-ate and move rapidly towards the poles of the spindle. They do not reach the poles, but the spindle itself elongates, pushing the two groups of chromosomes further apart. *Telophase* (5): The chromo-somes uncoil, elongating and finally disappearing. A new nuclear membrane forms. Spindle gradually disappears. The cytoplasm, if it divides, does so at this stage (see *Cell-division*).

Time taken for mitosis varies a good deal but is usually between half and three hours. See *Meiosis, Amitosis.*

MITOSPORE. Spore produced as result of mitosis.

MITRAL VALVE. Valve between left auricle and left ventricle of mammalian heart, consisting of two membranous flaps.

ML. Millilitre, one thousandth part of a litre.

181

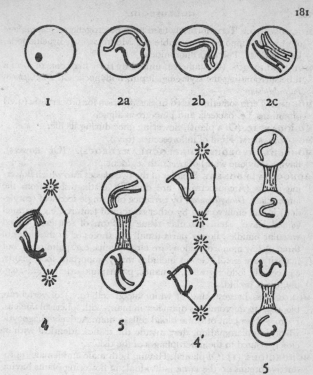

*Fig. 6B. Diagram of certain stages of meiosis, in nucleus like that of fig. 6A. Stages are numbered to correspond to those of mitosis shown in fig. 6A. Prophase in three stages, 2a (appearance of chromosomes), 2b (pairing), 2c (separation of chromatids with chiasma formation). 4 and 5, first anaphase and telophase, two chromatids having mixed constitution due to chiasma. 4' and 5', second anaphase and telophase. Four nuclei result from the whole process of meiosis.*

MOLARS. Those crushing back teeth of mammals which, unlike premolars, have no predecessors in the milk teeth. They have usually several roots, and a complicated pattern of ridges and projections on biting surface. See *Dental Formula*.

MOLLUSCA. Large phylum of animals including mussels, snails, octopuses, etc., mostly aquatic; soft bodied, often with a hard shell; unsegmented; with a head and muscular foot. Includes classes Amphineura, Gastropoda, Scaphopoda, Lamellibranchiata, Cephalopoda.

**MOLLUSCOIDA.** Term formerly used for a heterogeneous assemblage of animals supposed to resemble the Mollusca, e.g. Brachiopoda, Urochordata, Polyzoa, Phoronidea.

**MONADELPHOUS.** (Of stamens), united by their filaments to form a tube surrounding the style, e.g. lupin, hollyhock. Cf. *Diadelphous, Polyadelphous.*

**MONERA.** Term sometimes used in classification for procaryotic (q.v.) organisms, i.e. bacteria and blue-green algae.

**MONOCARPIC.** (Of a plant), flowering once during its life.

**MONOCHASIUM.** Kind of inflorescence (q.v.).

**MONOCHLAMYDEOUS (HAPLOCHLAMYDEOUS).** (Of flowers), having only one whorl of perianth segments.

**MONOCOTYLEDONEAE.** Smaller of the two classes into which flowering plants (Angiospermae) are divided; distinguished from the larger class, *Dicotyledoneae*, by presence of a single seed leaf (cotyledon) in the embryo and by other structural features, e.g. parallel veined leaves, stem vascular tissue in form of scattered closed vascular bundles, flower parts usually in threes or in multiples of three. A few monocotyledons are large plants, e.g. palm trees, but majority are small. Group includes many important food plants, e.g. cereals, fodder grasses, bananas, palms; and ornamentals, e.g. lily, tulip, orchid.

**MONOCYTE.** Largest kind of white blood cell (q.v.) of vertebrate blood (9–12 micrometres diameter in man), with spherical nucleus. Form 3–8 per cent of white blood cells in man. Actively phagocytic when, in inflammation, they invade the tissues. Identical with or closely related to the macrophages of the tissues.

**MONOECIOUS.** (1) (Of plants). Having both male and female reproductive organs on the same individual; in flowering plants having unisexual, male and female, flowers on same plant, e.g. hazel. Cf. *Dioecious, Hermaphrodite.* (2) (Of animals) hermaphrodite (q.v.). Cf. *Dioecious, Unisexual.*

**MONOKARYON (MONOCARYON).** A fungus hypha or mycelium composed of cells each containing one haploid nucleus, all genetically identical, i.e. a homokaryon with one nucleus per cell. Characteristic of early phase of life-cycle in many Basidiomycete fungi. Cf. *Dikaryon.*

**MONOPHYLETIC.** (Of a taxon) consisting of individuals descended from a common ancestor which is a member of the same taxon. Cf. *Polyphyletic.*

**MONOPODIUM.** Axis produced and increasing in length by apical growth, e.g. trunk of pine tree. Cf. *Sympodium.*

**MONOSACCHARIDE.** Simplest sugar; ceases to have the properties of a sugar when split up. See *Hexose, Pentose, Disaccharide.*

**MONOSOMIC.** Abnormal chromosome complement in which one chromosome of the somatic (diploid) set is missing. Type of aneuploidy (q.v.).

MONOTREMATA. A sub-class of Mammalia, containing the duck-billed platypus and two genera of spiny anteater. Live in Australia and New Guinea. A very primitive group, only distantly related to all other known mammals: from which they differ in laying eggs, and in possessing many other reptilian features. But have hair and secrete milk. Fossil history unknown.

MONOZYGOTIC TWINS (IDENTICAL TWINS, UNIOVULAR TWINS). Twins due to fission into two, at some stage of its develop-ment, of the embryo derived from a single fertilized egg. Such twins are genetically identical and therefore of same sex. Cf. *Dizygotic twins, Polyembryony*.

MORPHACTINS. Group of synthetic plant growth-regulating com-pounds, derived from fluorenecarboxylic acid, that reduce and modify growth, especially new growth. Internally, orientation of spindle axes of dividing cells is altered. Most striking external effect is development of dwarf, bushy habit due to shortening of internodes and loss of apical dominance (see *Auxin*). Other effects include inhibition of phototropism and geotropism, seed germina-tion, lateral root development.

MORPHALLAXIS. See *Blastema*.

MORPHOGENESIS. Development of form or structure in ontogeny or in regeneration.

MORPHOGENETIC MOVEMENTS. Displacements of masses of cells in embryonic development of animals, particularly conspicuous dur-ing gastrulation (q.v.).

MORPHOLOGY. Study of form.

MORULA. (Zool.). Embryo during process of cleavage, before blastula stage; consists of a number of blastomeres.

MOSAIC. (1) (Bot.). Symptom of many virus diseases of plants, a patchy variation of normal green colour. (2) (Genetics). Synonym of chimaera (q.v.). Animals of this kind (i.e. a mixture of cells of different genetic composition), such as gynandromorphs, are more usually called mosaics, plants usually chimaeras. (3) (Zool.). *Mosaic development*; development when determination is complete but before functional differentiation (q.v.) starts, each region of the embryo differentiating almost independently of influence from other regions. Little regulation (q.v.) can occur. Time of onset of mosaic development varies much. In vertebrates does not start till after gastrulation; in many invertebrates (e.g. groups with spiral cleavage) zygotes or early cleavage stages show mosaic development, and hence are known as *mosaic eggs*.

MOSSES. Musci (q.v.).

MOTOR. Concerned with stimulation of effector organs. *M. cortex*. Part of cerebral cortex controlling nerves to striped muscles. *M. end-plate*. End-organ (q.v.) of a motor nerve-fibre on a muscle fibre, consisting of an accumulation of muscle cytoplasm and nuclei, within which the nerve-fibre branches, and through which its nerve-impulses stimulate the muscle fibre. *M. nerve.* Peripheral nerve consisting of nerve-fibres of motor neurones. *M. nerve-fibre.* Nerve-fibre of motor neurone. *M. neurone* (motoneurone). Nerve-cell whose nerve-fibre connects with effector organ; conducts impulses from central nervous system (q.v.) which stimulate effector to activity. See *Nerve-root.*

MOTOR ROOT. Nerve-root, synonymous with ventral root (q.v.).

MOULD. (1) Any superficial growth of fungus mycelium (mildew); (2) popular name for fungus.

MOUTH-PARTS. Structures which surround the mouth of arthropods and are concerned in feeding. They are mostly modified paired appendages of the head segments (see *Labrum, Mandible, Maxilla, Labium*).

MUCIN. Mucoprotein forming mucus (q.v.) in solution.

MUCOPOLYSACCHARIDE (GLYCOSAMINOGLYCAN). Compound of protein and polysaccharide. The protein forms a backbone to which long but relatively simple polysaccharide chains are attached; polysaccharide tends to predominate. See *Glycoprotein.*

MUCOPROTEIN. Glycoprotein (q.v.).

MUCOSA. Mucous membrane (q.v.).

MUCOUS MEMBRANE. General name for a moist epithelium (q.v.). and its immediately underlying connective tissue, in vertebrates. Particularly applied to lining of gut and urino-genital ducts. Epithelium is usually simple, though stratified near openings to exterior; often ciliated; often contains goblet cells (q.v.) secreting mucous.

MUCUS. (1) Slimy solution of mucin, secreted by goblet cells of vertebrate mucous membrane. (2) Any viscous, sticky or slimy fluid (usually of unknown composition) secreted by invertebrates.

MÜLLERIAN DUCT. Oviduct of female gnathostome vertebrate. A pair in most species, only one in birds. A tube, at one end opening into coelom by a ciliated funnel, at other end joining cloaca (or, with urethra, joining remnant of cloaca in placental mammals). Muscular and ciliary movements pass eggs down the tube; and where fertilization is internal, pass sperm up it. In marsupial and placental mammals it is differentiated into fallopian tube, uterus, and vagina (but q.v.). In all placentals the posterior parts of the pair of ducts fuse, so that there is a single median vagina, and often, as in humans, a single median uterus. The duct has no representative, or only a vestige, in males. Embryonically arises from mesothelium of coelom in close association with Wolffian duct (q.v.); it is therefore mesodermal.

MULTICELLULAR. Consisting of many cells. Cf. *Unicellular.*

MULTINUCLEATE. Of a cell (q.v.), containing many nuclei.

MULTIPLE ALLELOMORPHS. A set of more than two genes, all allelomorphs (q.v.). Only two of the set can be present at the same time in somatic cells of an animal or a vascular plant (except in polyploids, q.v.). Multiple allelomorphs originate from each other by mutation.

**MULTIPLE FACTORS (MULTIPLE GENES).** Polygenes (q.v.).

**MUSCI.** Mosses, class of Bryophyta. World-wide in distribution, occurring in damp habitats, e.g. moist woodland, in water, and under drier conditions, e.g. on heaths, walls. A moss plant consists of a prostrate or erect stem, a fraction of an inch to a foot in length, bearing closely arranged leaves and anchored to the substratum by rhizoids. Internally the stem possesses a distinct central conducting strand of elongated cells. Sexual organs (antheridia and archegonia) are borne in separate groups at tips of stems. Male gametes are motile by flagella. Fertilization is followed by development of a capsule, containing spores, each of which, on germination, gives rise to a filamentous or thalloid *protonema*, from which new moss plants develop as lateral buds.

**MUSCLE.** Tissue consisting of cells which are highly contractile. Most of edible parts of animals (flesh) is muscle. See *Actin, Myosin, Cardiac muscle, Smooth muscle, Striped muscle.* **MUSCLE FIBRE** see *Striped muscle.*

**MUSCULO-EPITHELIAL CELL.** Cell characteristic of coelenterates, forming greater part of body of a simple member of the group such as *Hydra*. Columnar cell, arranged with others in a continuous sheet, each cell with one or two processes which are contractile, and which extend into the mesogloea. The main parts of the cells form the epithelial outer or inner layers of the body. In some coelenterates (jelly-fish) epithelial part may be reduced so that the cell looks more like a smooth muscle cell.

**MUSHROOM.** Popular name for edible fruit-bodies of fungi belonging to family Agaricaceae of Basidiomycetes, especially of species of *Agaricus*.

**MUTAGENIC.** Causing mutations.

**MUTANT.** Gene which has undergone mutation within the particular stock of organisms under observation; or organism bearing such a gene; or character due to such a gene.

**MUTATION.** Sudden change in chromosomal DNA. The most important mutations are those occurring in the gametes or their precursors, since they can produce an inherited change in the characteristics of the organisms developing from them, such changes being the raw material of evolution. The majority of mutations are changes of individual genes (gene-mutations), but some are gross structural alterations of chromosomes (e.g. inversion, translocation) or changes in numbers of whole chromosomes per nucleus (e.g. polyploidy). Mutation is normally a very infrequent event, though it can be greatly speeded up by irradiation with X-rays, gamma-rays, neutrons, etc., and by some chemicals (e.g. mustard gas). From the standpoint of adaptation of the organism, mutations are random. Evolution has occurred by natural selection of mutations, not by directed mutation. They are merely the raw material for evolutionary change. The great majority of mutations are deleterious, upsetting the balanced mechanism of embryonic development of the organism; and on the whole the larger the change they induce the more deleterious they are.

Mutation in the restricted sense of gene-mutation is a sudden change in an individual gene, probably the substitution of a different nucleotide for an existing one in the DNA, which alters the amino acid sequence of the protein normally dependent on that gene, with many possible repercussions in structure and function of the organism. The changed gene is allelomorphic to the old. It reproduces itself, in the changed form, many times (perhaps of the order of a million) before undergoing another mutation, which may be back to the original gene, or to a new allele. The same kind of gene-mutation, i.e. a change from one particular allele to another particular allele, occurs repeatedly within a population of organisms, probably over long periods of time. E.g. in the human population the gene for haemophilia (q.v.) has arisen repeatedly by mutation from a normal allele. An entirely new gene-mutation is therefore a much rarer event than the mutation rate would suggest.

A mutation may occur in a body-cell (*somatic mutation*) and is then transmitted to all cells derived by mitosis from that cell.

MYCELIUM. Collective term for mass of hyphae that constitutes vegetative part of a fungus, e.g. mushroom spawn.

MYCETOCYTE. Specialized insect cell containing symbiotic micro-organisms (bacteria or yeasts). In different insect species scattered within a particular tissue or localized in discrete organs known as *mycetomes*.

MYCETOZOA. Myxomycophyta (q.v.).

MYCOLOGY. Study of fungi.

MYCOPHYTA. Fungi – mushrooms, moulds, rusts, yeasts, etc. Group (Division) of simple eucaryotic (q.v.) organisms lacking chlorophyll. Unicellular, or possess tubular filaments, hyphae; reproducing asexually and sexually with formation of spores, often produced in enormous numbers. Many fungi are microscopic; some, especially their fruit-bodies, e.g. mushroom, puff-ball, reach a fair size. Lacking chlorophyll, fungi live either as saprophytes or as parasites of plants and animals. They are extremely important as agents of plant disease (they also cause a few animal diseases), and in the decay of food, fabrics and timber. In soil they take part with other organisms in decomposition of plant and animal residues. Various fungi are used in industrial processes, e.g. brewing and baking, others provide valuable sources of certain food proteins and vitamins. The development of antibiotics from fungi, particularly of penicillin from certain species of *Penicillium*, has been responsible for important advances in medical practice.

Division is sub-divided into four classes; (1) *Phycomycetes*, possessing hyphae usually without cross walls (non-septate, aseptate), reproducing asexually by zoospores, aplanospores or conidia, and sexually with formation of thick-walled resting spores; (2) *Ascomycetes*, possessing hyphae with cross walls (septate), with asexual reproduction by conidia and sexual reproduction with formation of ascospores in an almost spherical or cylindrical cell, the ascus. In most Ascomycetes the asci are grouped within fruit-bodies (cleistocarp, apothecium, perithecium) visible to the naked eye; (3) *Basidiomycetes*, with septate hyphae and sexually produced spores, *basidiospores*, borne externally on a club-shaped or cylindrical cell, the *basidium*. In some members the basidia are grouped together in highly-organized fruit-bodies, e.g. mushroom, puff-ball, stink-horn, bracket-fungus; (4) *Fungi Imperfecti*, a group of fungi with septate hyphae that lack a sexually reproducing stage, thought to be mostly asexual forms of Ascomycetes in which sexual stage has been lost during evolution or has not yet been identified.

MYCOPLASMAS. Smallest free-living micro-organisms. Procaryotic (q.v.), lacking cell wall, variable in form and able to pass through bacteria-retaining filters. Grouped in genus *Mycoplasma* and usually classified with bacteria. Some are saprophytic, others cause diseases of animals and man. Earlier known as pleuro-pneumonia-like (PPLO) organisms after disease caused in cattle by first member to be described. Recently shown to be cause of certain plant diseases formerly attributed to viruses.

MYCORRHIZA. 'Fungus root'; an association of a fungus with root of a higher plant. Mycorrhizas are of common occurrence. Two main types exist. (1) *endotrophic*, in which fungus is within cortex cells of root, e.g. orchid, and (2) *ectotrophic*, in which it is external, forming a mantle that completely invests the smaller roots, e.g. pine tree. Mycorrhizas are believed to constitute an example of a mutually beneficial symbiotic association, probably evolved from an original host/parasite relationship. It has been clearly shown (a) that mycorrhizal plants benefit from the association, e.g. under natural conditions presence of fungus partner is vital for establishment and growth of seedling trees of a number of different species, e.g. pines, and (b) that association of fungus with tree is necessary for development and reproduction by fungus.

MYCOSIS. Disease of animals caused by fungal infection, e.g. ringworm.

MYCOTROPHIC. (Of plants), having mycorrhizas.

MYELIN. Fatty substance (phospholipid, cholesterol, etc.) with protein, making a sheath to larger nerve fibres (q.v.) of vertebrates and Crustacea; formed by lamellar extensions of Schwann or glial cells wrapping spirally around each nerve fibre.

MYELOID TISSUE. Tissue producing myeloid elements (polymorphs and red blood cells) of vertebrate blood, which are formed throughout life. Except in embryo, usually located in bone marrow. In adult man mainly in ribs, sternum, skull, hip girdle, vertebrae.

MYOFIBRIL. Bundle of filamentous contractile protein found in smooth and striped muscle cells. See *Actin, Myosin.*

MYOGLOBIN. A variety of haemoglobin (q.v.) occurring in muscle fibres.

MYONEME. Contractile fibril of Protozoa.

MYOSIN. Protein that in conjunction with actin (q.v.) provides the structural framework of the contractile mechanism in muscle and probably in other cells. A myosin molecule has an attachment site for actin, and an enzymic site that breaks down ATP with liberation of energy for contraction. The generally accepted *sliding filament hypothesis* ascribes contraction to myosin molecules sliding along actin filaments.

MYOTOME. That part of somitic mesoderm (q.v.) which forms striped muscle.

MYRIAPODA. Centipedes and millipedes. Class of Arthropoda with long bodies and many legs, distinct head, one pair of antennae, mandibles, at least one pair of maxillae; live on land and breathe air by means of tracheae. Centipedes (Chilopoda) have one pair of legs per segment; are usually more or less flattened; carnivorous. Millipedes (Diplopoda) have two pairs of legs per segment (each segment representing two embryonic segments fused together); are usually cylindrical; and herbivorous. There are several important differences between these two groups which indicate that they are not very closely related, and they are sometimes put into separate classes.

MYXAMOEBA. Naked cell, capable of amoeboid movement, characteristic of vegetative phase of slime-fungi (Myxomycophyta) and certain simply organized fungi.

MYXOBACTERIA. Small group of rod-shaped bacteria that are distinguished by gliding movement in contact with solid surface and by delicate, flexible cell wall. In many myxobacteria vegetative cells mass together to form minute 'fruiting bodies'.

MYXOMYCETES (MYCETOZOA). See *Myxomycophyta.*

MYXOMYCOPHYTA. Slime moulds. Group (Division) of very simple organisms with both plant and animal characteristics. Taxonomic position uncertain; in past have been grouped with fungi (in Myxomycetes) and with Protozoa (in Mycetozoa). In the vegetative condition members of the largest group (Class Myxomycetes) consist of naked, multinucleate masses of protoplasm known as *plasmodia.* These show amoeboid movement and ingest food (animal characteristics). They reproduce by spores, shown in some genera to have cellulose walls, formed within sporangia (a plant characteristic). Meiosis is presumed to occur before spore formation. The spores germinate to form one or more myxamoebae, or biflagellate swarm cells which may either behave as gametes and copulate in pairs soon after their formation, or may first lose their flagella, undergo a series of divisions and then copulate. Growth of the zygote results in formation of a plasmodium. Plasmodia may also be formed by coalescence of many zygotes or small plasmodia. Widely distributed, occurring under damp conditions on decaying vegetable matter. One of the commonest species, *Fuligo septica* (flowers of tan), forms yellow plasmodia up to eight inches in diameter and frequently occurs on tanner's bark. The group includes *Acrasiales* (q.v.) and *Labyrinthulales* (q.v.).

MYXOPHYTA. Cyanophyta (q.v.).

# N

NAD. Nicotinamide adenine dinucleotide. Co-enzyme I. Oxidizing-reducing co-enzyme. Reduced form is expressed as $NADH_2$. NAD is also referred to as DPN (diphosphopyridine nucleotide).

NADP. Nicotinamide adenine dinucleotide phosphate. Co-enzyme II. Oxidizing-reducing co-enzyme. Reduced form is expressed as $NADPH_2$. NADP is also referred to as TPN (triphosphopyridine nucleotide).

NANOMETRE (NM). One-thousandth of a micrometre; 10 Angstroms. Formerly called a millimicron.

NARES. Nostrils of vertebrates. Opening from olfactory organ: *external nares* on to surface of head, or *internal nares* into mouth. See *Choanae*. Usually paired.

NASAL CAVITY. Cavity of tetrapod head containing olfactory organ communicating with mouth and with surface of head by internal and external nares respectively; lined by mucous membrane. See *Palate*.

NASTIC MOVEMENT. (In plants) response to a stimulus that is independent of direction of stimulus. May be a growth curvature, e.g. opening and closing of many flowers in response to changes in light intensity; or a sudden change in turgidity of particular cells causing a rapid change in position of particular plant organs, e.g. rapid folding of leaflets and drooping of leaves of sensitive plant (*Mimosa pudica*) when lightly struck. Nastic movements are classified according to nature of stimulus, e.g. *photonasty*, response to alteration in light intensity, *thermonasty*, to alteration in heat intensity, *seismonasty*, to shock. Cf. *Tropism*.

NATIVE PROTEIN. Protein that is not denatured. See *Denaturation*.

NATURAL ORDER. See *Family*.

NATURAL SELECTION. The principal mechanism of evolutionary change, originally suggested by Darwin in 1859. The theory that evolution occurs by natural selection asserts that, of the range of different individuals which make up the population of a given species, individuals having certain characteristics contribute more offspring to the succeeding generation than those having other characteristics; and if such characteristics have an inherited basis, the composition of the population is thereby changed.

If one considers the zygotes produced within a population of a species, usually only a minority will develop to maturity and still fewer will succeed in producing offspring. Within such a population there is always variation between individuals. The theory of natural selection asserts that the contribution of offspring to the next generation is not entirely random, but is correlated with this variability. Some kinds of variant individual are consistently more successful in leaving offspring than other kinds. The successful variants and their progeny are said to be 'selected', by a natural process. In other words different variations (q.v.) have different 'survival value' in the face of the hostile circumstances in which all organisms live. Of these variations, only those which are inherited are important for evolution. Natural selection is thus the main agent controlling the composition of a population during the course of time, eliminating certain variants and thus preventing change in some directions, making other variants more prevalent and hence producing evolutionary change in other directions.

NATURE AND NURTURE. Synonymous with genotype and environment respectively. Differences in either or both of these may be responsible for differences in character (variation, q.v.) between organisms. Variations due to 'nurture' are not usually inherited.

NAUPLIUS. Kind of larva of many crustacean species. Oval, unsegmented, three pairs of appendages.

NEANDERTHAL MAN. *Homo neanderthalensis*, a rather recently (perhaps 50,000 years ago) extinct species of hominid from Pleistocene (mainly from early part of fourth glaciation about 100,000 years ago). Human brain size, but heavy brow ridges, low forehead, no chin prominence, did not walk fully erect. Its remains are associated with more than one culture, but particularly Mousterian, which had ritual burial of dead.

NEARCTIC. Zoogeographical region consisting of North America southwards to the middle of Mexico, and Greenland.

NECTARY. Gland secreting sugary fluid (*nectar*) attractive to insects in many insect pollinated flowers.

NEKTON. Swimming animals of pelagic zone of sea or lake. Includes, e.g. fishes and whales. Cf. *Plankton, Benthos, Pelagic*.

NEMATOCYST. See *Thread-cell*.

NEMATODA. Round-, thread-, eel-worms. Phylum of animals not closely related to any other, with many peculiarities of, e.g. muscular, excretory and reproductive systems, body cavity, and development. Includes minute free-living forms, e.g. vinegar eels; plant parasites, e.g. eelworm of potatoes; and animal parasites, e.g. hook-worm.

NEMERTEA. Ribbon worms; a small phylum of marine worms sharing several characteristics with the Platyhelminthes, but differing from them in having a tube-like gut with mouth and anus, a peculiar proboscis, a simpler reproductive system and a circulatory system.

NEO-DARWINISM. Name sometimes given to modern evolution theory which combines the theory of natural selection with the discoveries of Mendelian genetics.

NEOGEA. Neotropical (q.v.).

NEOGENE. See *Geological Periods and Epochs*.

NEO-LAMARCKISM. See Lamarckism.

NEOLITHIC. Phase of human history during which plants were cultivated and animals domesticated, and many other technical advances on previous (palaeolithic) period made. Started approximately 10,000 years ago in Middle East and spread slowly over the world (though there was probably independent discovery of cultivation in America).

NEOPALLIUM. That part of roof of cerebral hemispheres of vertebrates which is not particularly connected with sense of smell, but serves more general co-ordination. Forms main mass of cerebral cortex of man.

NEOPLASM. Tumour. Abnormal localized multiplication of some type of cell. *Malignant* if the growing cells infiltrate surrounding tissue and are carried by blood or lymph to other localities in the body, there continuing their growth; otherwise *benign*.

NEOTENY. Persistence of the form of a larval or of other early stage of development. Either temporary, e.g. climatically delayed development; or permanent, in which case the animal must breed in juvenile form (paedogenesis, e.g. axolotl, and many other animals which as adults resemble juvenile stages of related species). Neoteny may be applied to retarded development of individual structure, e.g. ostrich feathers resembling down-feathers of flying birds. Neoteny has probably been very important in evolution of many groups, including man, who has resemblances to young stages of apes.

NEOTROPICAL (NEOGEA). Zoogeographical region consisting of South and most of Central America. See *Nearctic*.

NEOTYPE. Specimen selected to replace the type specimen (q.v.) when all the original material is lost or destroyed. Cf. *Lectotype*.

NEPHRIDIUM. Organ present in many invertebrates (Platyhelminthes, Nemertea, Rotifera, Annelida, larvae of some Mollusca) and in amphioxus. Probably excretes, and helps to control water content of body. Consists of a tube of ectodermal origin opening to the exterior at one end. The other end may be closed (*protonephridium*) with flame cells opening into it; or it may open into the coelom. A nephridium may combine with a coelomoduct (q.v.) forming a *nephromixium*.

NEPHRON. Excretory unit of vertebrate kidney, consisting of a Malpighian corpuscle (q.v.) and its attached uriniferous tubule (q.v.).

NERITIC. Inhabiting the sea over the continental shelf; arbitrarily taken to be sea where it is shallower than 200 metres. Cf. *Oceanic*.

NERVE. Bundle of motor and/or sensory nerve-fibres with accompanying connective tissue and blood-vessels, in a common sheath of connective tissue. Each nerve-fibre conducts impulses independently of its fellows. See *Cranial Nerve*, *Spinal Nerve*.

NERVE-CELL (NEURON, NEURONE). (1) Cell of nervous tissue which conducts the impulses (q.v.) by which the nervous system functions. Each has a nucleus surrounded by a mass of cytoplasm, constituting the cell-body or perikaryon; and projecting from this, thread-like processes, very various in length and number, which carry the impulses from place to place. A commonly occurring arrangement of these processes is a single long *axon* (q.v.) which carries impulses away from the cell-body to other nerve-cells or to effectors; and numerous short *dendrites* (q.v.) which receive impulses from the axons of other nerve-cells. Transfer of impulses from nerve-cell to nerve-cell takes place at synapses (q.v.). Central nervous system (q.v.) of all animals contains very numerous nerve cells. Some are entirely confined within it, forming an elaborate interconnecting system. Others are only partly within it, their thread-like processes running out of it to all parts of the body, some to effectors (motor nerve fibres), some to receptors (sensory nerve fibres). Other nerve cells are situated mainly or wholly outside the central nervous system, e.g. those in nerve nets (q.v.) or sensory nerve cells. (2) Term is sometimes used synonymously with cell-body (q.v.).

NERVE CORD. Solid strand of nervous tissue, forming part of central nervous system (q.v.) of invertebrates. In Annelida and Arthropoda there are two parallel ventral nerve cords, each bearing a row of segmentally arranged ganglia.

NERVE ENDING. The structure at the peripheral end of a fibre of the peripheral nervous system, in which impulses start (in a sensory fibre) or finish (in a motor fibre). May be merely the bunch of fine branching twigs by which the fibre itself ends (*free nerve ending*); or may be a distinct end-organ (q.v.).

NERVE-FIBRE. The axon of a nerve-cell (q.v.), or the similar process (but carrying impulses towards the cell body) of many peripheral sensory nerve cells, together with the various special membranes which may surround it. Many nerve-fibres of vertebrates and some of Crustacea and annelid worms are *myelinated* (*medullated*): i.e. the axon is covered by a relatively thick fatty sheath of myelin except at periodically-spaced nodes of Ranvier. Fibres which lack a myelin sheath are called *unmyelinated* or *non-medullated*; their axons are bounded merely by the usual plasma-membrane of all cells. Surrounding the axons of fibres of the vertebrate peripheral nervous system lie the Schwann cells, of which the myelin is really a part; and each single myelinated fibre is further enclosed in a reticulin neurilemmal tube. In the central nervous system Schwann cells and neurilemmal tubes are absent. The diameter of nerve fibres varies in any vertebrate animal from 1 to 20µm; in some invertebrates giant nerve fibres occur and may reach 1 mm. diameter in squids and burrowing worms. A nerve-fibre commonly branches into many small-diameter twigs at its termination. An increased diameter gives greater conduction velocity; the same velocity is also produced in smaller space by a myelin layer, the impulses then

apparently leaping from node to node along a fibre instead of
travelling continuously along it. A nerve may be nearly as long as
the whole animal, so that in large vertebrates fibres may occur up
to a million times longer than they are thick.

NERVE IMPULSE. See *Impulse*.

NERVE-NET. Network of nerve-cells, diffusely distributed through
tissues, which in some phyla (e.g. Coelenterata, Echinodermata)
makes up all or most of the nervous system, though usually
associated with some concentration of the cells into major strands
providing through ways for conduction. In phyla with well-
developed central nervous systems (e.g. Arthropoda, Vertebrata,
Cephalopoda) a nerve-net may hardly exist (usually only in gut
wall). Consists of separate nerve-cells communicating with each
other by contact only (synapses). Conduction in a nerve-net is slow
and often in all directions. In Coelenterata a strong stimulus,
eliciting more impulses, has a more extensive effect than a weak
one, because impulses are used up in producing summation at the
synapses; not, as previously thought, because of any fading of
impulses within the nerve-fibres.

NERVE ROOT. In vertebrates, each spinal nerve arises from the
spinal cord by two roots; a *dorsal* (posterior in human anatomy)
and a *ventral* (anterior in human anatomy) which join to form the
spinal nerve as they pass through the wall of the vertebral column.
The dorsal roots contain all the sensory nerve fibres, their cell-
bodies (q.v.) being in a ganglion on the course of each root; in
some vertebrates they may also contain a few motor fibres. Through
the ventral roots pass the motor fibres, their cell-bodies being in the
spinal cord. Cranial nerves can also be classified into dorsal and
ventral roots, which do not however join, remaining separate
nerves; cranial dorsal roots have ganglia and contain, besides
sensory, numerous motor fibres running to face, jaw, and gill
muscles, and motor fibres of the parasympathetic system; cranial
ventral roots contain some sensory (proprioceptor, q.v.) fibres.
Dorsal and ventral roots are a characteristic feature of all vertebrates, and occur in amphioxus, though in this chordate motor
fibres to the viscera go through dorsal roots, and (as also in some
Cyclostomes) the two roots do not join to form spinal nerves.

NERVOUS SYSTEM. A mechanism which co-ordinates the various
activities of an animal with each other and with events in the external world, by means of messages rapidly conducted from part to
part. Present in all multicellular animals except sponges. It consists of numerous cells of special kind (nerve-cells, q.v.), with
branching thread-like processes. Every nerve-cell is in contact with
others by means of these processes, the points of contact being
called synapses (q.v.). The nerve-cells and their processes, linked
by synapses, form a system which permeates the whole body. Some
of the processes of the nerve-cells terminate at sense-organs, some

at muscles or other effectors (q.v.), while many end at synapses with other nerve-cells. The nervous system functions by 'messages' (impulses, q.v.), which run along the nerve-cell processes and are able to cross synapses. Impulses are started by sense-organs, and they can set a muscle or other effector in operation when they reach it. But the nervous system does not simply provide a means by which the stimulation of a certain sense-organ automatically activates a certain effector. That would limit the number of possible activities to the number of direct receptor-effector connections. There usually are many fairly direct connections of this type. See *Reflex*. But the work of the nervous system co-ordinates activities in a far more subtle and complicated way, by means of the synapses. A synapse discriminates which impulses it passes through to the succeeding nerve-cell according to what impulses are arriving at other synapses involving that nerve cell. See *Summation* and *Inhibition*. These other synapses link up with other parts of the nervous system. Consequently, an impulse started by a sense-organ is not limited to the two possibilities of activating or failing to activate a given receptor. It can, by means of connecting synapses, promote or inhibit numerous other activities, according to the state of other parts of the nervous system. Very complicated co-ordination is, therefore, possible with suitably complex connections. In most animals, the elaborate co-ordination for which the synapses are an essential basis occurs in the central nervous system (q.v.). Here most of the synapses are located, and the rest of the nervous system (peripheral nervous system, q.v.) consists mainly of nerve-cell processes running directly to sense-organs or effectors. The nervous system is not the only co-ordinating system. There is a much more slowly acting and less flexible one based on hormones (q.v.).

NERVOUS TISSUE. Nerve cells (q.v.) and/or their nerve fibres; together with the accessory cells which closely surround them, e.g. Schwann cells of vertebrate nerve fibres; and supporting connective tissue or glia (q.v.) with blood-vessels.

NEURAL. Concerned with the nervous system. *N. arch*, a bony arch resting on centrum of each vertebra, forming tunnel (*N. canal*) through which spinal cord runs. *N. crest*, embryonic material of vertebrates, found initially at both sides of the neural plate as this rolls up and sinks beneath epidermis; gives rise to extraordinary variety of tissues, probably including dorsal root ganglia, Schwann cells, sympathetic ganglia, melanophores, cartilage of visceral arches. *N. fold*, raised ridge of neural plate, neural crest, and epidermis along edge of neural plate, beginning the formation of neural tube. *N. plate*, flat expanse of neural tissue, first-formed embryonic rudiment of nervous system of vertebrate. See *Organizer*. *N. spine*, median dorsal bony projection from neural arch, serving usually as muscle attachment. *N. tissue*, embryonic nervous tissue, in vertebrates a simple epithelium of columnar cells which only later differentiate into glia and nerve cells. *N. tube*, longitudinal tube of neural tissue in vertebrate embryos, formed by rolling up of neural plate until the neural folds join in the mid-dorsal line to form a tube and the epidermis fuses above; expanded in front as the rudiment of the brain, the narrower posterior part being that of spinal cord; forms central nervous system, and motor nerve fibres of peripheral nervous system.

NEURAL TRANSMITTER (NEUROHUMOUR). Chemical substance released in minute amounts by the ending of a nerve fibre; either at a synapse, when it excites the adjacent nerve-cell, or at a motor nerve-ending, when it excites the adjacent effector organ. Acetyl choline, adrenaline and noradrenaline are the best known. See *Cholinergic, Adrenergic*.

NEUROBLAST. Embryonic cell that will develop into a nerve-cell.

NEUROCRANIUM. The part of the skull surrounding brain and internal ear, as distinct from the part composing jaws and their attachments (*splanchnocranium*).

NEUROGLIA. Glia (q.v.).

NEUROHUMORAL. Acting by means of a neural transmitter (q.v.).

NEUROHYPOPHYSIS. See *Pituitary*.

NEURONE (NEURON). Nerve-cell (q.v.).

NEURONE THEORY. Theory that nervous system is made up of numerous discrete nerve cells, each originating from single cell of embryonic neural tissue, which merely make contact with each other at synapses; in contrast to the view (now largely discarded) that there is protoplasmic continuity throughout the nervous system.

NEUROPIL. The mass of interwoven dendrites and axons within which the nerve cell-bodies of the central nervous system are embedded.

NEUROPTERA. Order of endopterygote insects including alderflies, lacewings. Two similar pairs of membranous wings which when at rest are held up over body. Larvae of some are aquatic, others, e.g. lacewing larvae, feed on aphides and help to control these pests.

NEURULA. Stage of vertebrate embryo after most of the gastrulation movements have ceased, when determination is far advanced and differentiation, manifested externally by neural plate, is proceeding fast. Stage ends when neural tube is complete.

NEUTER. Sexless. Without reproductive organs but with other parts more or less normal.

NICHE. A particular role (or set of relationships) of organisms in an ecosystem, which may be filled by different species in different geographical areas. E.g. grass-eaters may be kangaroos in Australia, cattle on the pampas.

NICOTINIC ACID (NIACIN, P-P FACTOR). A vitamin of the B

group, lack of which is part of the cause of pellagra in man. Forms part of a respiratory coenzyme, widely (universally?) distributed. Required as a vitamin by those vertebrates and insects tested. Synthesized by many micro-organisms. See *NAD*.

NICTITATING MEMBRANE. Transparent fold of skin forming a third eye-lid. When open, lies at inner (anterior) corner of eye or below lower eye-lid. Occurs in some sharks and amphibia, and widespread in reptiles and birds. Well-developed in few mammals.

NIDATION. Implantation (q.v.).

NIDICOLOUS BIRDS. Those which hatch in relatively undeveloped state and stay in nest some time after hatching.

NIDIFUGOUS BIRDS. Those which hatch well-developed, and leave the nest immediately.

NIT. Egg of human louse, which is cemented on to hair.

NITRIFICATION. Conversion by soil bacteria of organic compounds of nitrogen, unavailable to green plants, into available nitrates. Occurs in several steps, involving different kinds of bacteria. See *Nitrogen Cycle*.

NITROGEN CYCLE. Circulation of nitrogen atoms brought about mainly by living things. In outline, inorganic nitrogen compounds (chiefly nitrates), are absorbed from soil or water and built up into organic compounds by autotrophic plants. These die or decay or are eaten by animals and the nitrogen, still as organic compounds, returns to soil or water in their excreta or by their death and decay. Bacteria then convert them to inorganic nitrogen compounds. Some nitrogen is lost to the atmosphere as gas, and some is extracted from the atmosphere by nitrogen-fixing (q.v.) bacteria and blue-green algae.

NITROGEN FIXATION. Conversion of atmospheric nitrogen into organic nitrogen compounds, a process that can be carried out only by certain soil-inhabiting bacteria and certain blue-green algae (*Cyanophyta*). Some nitrogen-fixing bacteria live symbiotically with leguminous plants (peas, beans, clover, etc.) in nodules on roots, others live independently in soil. By their activity soil is enriched in nitrogen, a fact of considerable practical importance. See *Nitrogen Cycle*.

NODE. (1) Part of plant stem where one or more leaves arise. Cf. *Internode*. (2) Nodes of Ranvier. Constrictions regularly repeated along myelinated peripheral nerve fibres.

NOMENCLATURE. See *Binomial Nomenclature*.

NON-DISJUNCTION. Failure of the two homologous chromosomes of a pair to go to opposite poles at the first meiotic division, so that one daughter-cell has both chromosomes and the other neither.

NORADRENALINE (NOREPINEPHRINE). See *Adrenaline*. Lacks a methyl group present in adrenaline.

NOTOCHORD. Skeletal rod (of large vacuolated cells packed within a firm sheath) lying lengthwise, between C.N.S. and gut. Present in some stage of development of all chordates. In most vertebrates occurs complete only in embryo (or larva), though remnants usually persist, between the vertebrae which replace it, in the adult. Occurs in larval and adult amphioxus, in larval tunicates, and (it is often held) is represented in adult Hemichordata.

NOTOGEA. Australian (q.v.).

NUCELLUS. Central tissue of ovule (q.v.), containing embryo sac and surrounded by integument(s).

NUCLEIC ACID. Long chain molecule formed from a large number of nucleotides; universally found in living things. See *DNA*, *RNA*.

NUCLEO-CYTOPLASMIC RATIO. Ratio of volume of nucleus to volume of cytoplasm; may be fairly constant for any given cell-type of a given species.

NUCLEOLUS. Small dense body containing RNA (q.v.) and protein, one or more of which occurs inside the resting nucleus and is visible during life. Disappears during mitosis. Produced by certain regions of chromosomes (nucleolar organizers). Concerned in synthesis of ribosomes. See Fig. 1, p. 51.

NUCLEO-PROTEINS. Compounds of nucleic acid and protein.

NUCLEOTIDE. Compound formed from sugar (with 5 carbon atoms), phosphoric acid, and a nitrogen-containing base (purine or pyrimidine). Found free in cells (e.g. ATP, q.v.) and as part of various coenzymes, and as the building-blocks of nucleic acids (q.v.).

NUCLEUS. Body containing the chromosomes (q.v.) present in nearly all cells of plants and animals (eucaryotic organisms). Every nucleus has originated from a previous nucleus, usually by mitosis (q.v.) or meiosis (q.v.), occasionally by amitosis (q.v.). Variously shaped, usually spherical or ovoid with firm superficial membrane (*nuclear membrane*). In the non-dividing cell it usually appears homogeneous in living state, except for one or more nucleoli and granules of heterochromatin; and when fixed contains a darkly staining (basophilic) irregular meshwork. It is highly probable that the organization of the chromosomes is intact in resting cells, and that the homogeneity is deceptive and the meshwork an artefact. At onset of mitosis or meiosis, chromosomes become visible in both living and fixed cell, separating out from a non-basophilic *nuclear sap*. Nucleus is essential for continued life of most cells (but see *Red Blood Cell*); if it is removed (as by microdissection) remaining cytoplasm soon dies. See Fig. 1, p. 51. In procaryotic organisms the DNA is not contained within a nuclear membrane.

NUCLEUS (OF BRAIN). Demarcated mass of nerve cell-bodies, i.e. of grey matter, in vertebrate brain. A very large number of such nuclei have been anatomically distinguished, though their function is often uncertain. Nuclei are connected by tracts of nerve-fibres. The term is anatomical, not physiological. Cf. *Centre*.

NULLISOMIC. Abnormal chromosome complement in which both members of a pair of chromosomes are missing from the somatic (diploid) set. Type of aneuploidy (q.v.).

NUNATAK. See *Refugium*.

NUT. Dry, indehiscent, one-seeded fruit, somewhat similar to an achene but product of more than one carpel and usually larger with a hard, woody wall, e.g. hazel nut.

NUTATION (CIRCUMNUTATION). Spiral course pursued by apex of a plant organ during growth due to continuous change in position of most rapidly growing region of the organ; most pronounced in stems but also occurs in tendrils, roots, flower-stalks, sporangiophores of some fungi.

NYCTINASTY. Response by plants to periodic alternation of day and night, e.g. opening and closing of many flowers, 'sleep-movements' of leaves. Related to changes in temperature, light intensity. See *Photonasty, Thermonasty*.

NYMPH. Young stage of exopterygote insect; resembling the adult in, e.g. kind of mouth parts, and in having compound eyes (cf. *Larva*); different in being sexually immature, and wingless or having wings incompletely developed.

# O

OBDIPLOSTEMONOUS. (Of stamens), in two whorls, outer opposite petals (instead of alternating with petals, the general condition), inner opposite sepals, e.g. stitchwort.

OCCIPITAL CONDYLE. Bony knob at back of skull articulating with first vertebra. See *Condyle*, *Atlas*. Absent in most fish, whose skull is not movable on vertebral column. Double in Amphibia and mammals, single in reptiles and birds.

OCCIPUT (OCCIPITAL REGION). (1) In vertebrates, an inexactly delimited region of the head in neighbourhood of joint between skull and vertebral column. (2) In insects, plate of exoskeleton forming back of the head.

OCEANIC. Inhabiting sea where it is deeper than 200 metres. Cf. *Neritic*.

OCELLUS. Simple light-receptor occurring in many invertebrates.

OCTOPODA. Sub-order of Mollusca (class Cephalopoda); octopus, argonaut.

OCULOMOTOR NERVE. Third cranial nerve of vertebrates. Almost entirely motor, supplying four of the extrinsic eye-muscles (q.v.; the inferior oblique muscle, and all rectus muscles except external); and, by nerve fibres of parasympathetic system, intrinsic eye-muscles of accommodation and pupil constriction. A ventral root.

ODONATA. Dragon-flies. Order of exopterygote insects with aquatic nymphs. Carnivorous; have large eyes; two pairs of similar wings. Strong fliers, Some fossil (Carboniferous) dragon flies had a wing span of two feet.

ODONTOBLASTS. Cells which lie in pulp cavity of vertebrate tooth and send processes into adjacent dentine (q.v.) which they take part in forming.

ODONTOID PROCESS. See *Atlas*.

OEDEMA (EDEMA). Swelling of tissue through increase of its (chiefly intercellular) fluid content, due to passage of extra amounts of water out from capillaries, e.g. in inflammation. Also used of generalized overdevelopment of plant cells.

OESOPHAGUS (ESOPHAGUS). Part of gut between pharynx and stomach, concerned simply in passing food along by peristalsis.

OESTROGEN (ESTROGEN). Any substance producing changes in the female sexual organs similar to those produced by the naturally-occurring hormone of the vertebrate ovary, oestradiol. Oestrogenic activity is usually tested on mouse vagina (q.v.). Oestradiol, a steroid, affects the growth and physiological activity of much of the female reproductive system, and is responsible for development and maintenance of many female secondary sexual characters. It is also produced by the adrenal cortex and testis, in small amounts, and

by the mammalian placenta. Synthetic oestrogens are not necessarily steroids.

OESTROUS (ESTROUS) CYCLE. Reproductive cycle of short duration
(usually between five and sixty days according to species) occurring in sexually mature females of many species of mammal, in
absence of pregnancy (and only during breeding season, where
such occurs). Each cycle consists of a brief period (usually a day or
two) of *oestrus* (*estrus*) or 'heat' at which time and at no other the
female will copulate with a male, ovulation (q.v.) coinciding with
this oestrus; and, preceding and succeeding oestrus, there are
various changes throughout the body, particularly in the uterus,
which may be regarded as preparations for pregnancy. The whole
set of changes is controlled by hormones. In outline the phases
of the cycle are typically (*a*) *follicular* with growth of Graafian
follicles (q.v.) in ovary, proliferation of lining of uterus (endometrium), increasing secretion of oestrogen (q.v.) by ovary; (*b*)
*ovulation*, with activation of mating reflexes; (*c*) *luteal*, with corpus
luteum (q.v.) formation in ovary, great development of uterine
glands, secretion of progesterone (q.v.) by corpora lutea, oestrogen
secretion diminishing; (*d*) regression of corpus luteum, beginning
of new follicular growth, return to unproliferated state of uterine
lining, diminution of oestrogen and cessation of progesterone
secretion. If fertilization occurs in phase (*b*) then phase (*d*) is
omitted, and the cycle is suspended in the luteal phase for the
duration of pregnancy. If there is no fertilization then the cycle
usually immediately repeats, but in some species there is only one
cycle per breeding season. Cycle depends on cyclical production of
gonadotrophic hormones (q.v.) by pituitary gland, these hormones
controlling changes in the ovary which in turn controls all the other
changes by means of the cycles of oestrogen and progesterone
production. There is considerable variation according to species
in the characteristics of the cycle; the luteal phase may for instance
be omitted (mouse); and another variant is the menstrual cycle
(q.v.).

OIL-IMMERSION OBJECTIVE. Objective of light microscope (q.v.),
space between which and the cover-slip over the object examined
is filled with drop of oil of same refractive index as glass; system
used for finest resolution and highest magnification with the light
microscope.

OLECRANON PROCESS. Bony process on ulna of mammals extending beyond elbow joint, for attachment of muscles which straighten
fore-limb.

OLFACTORY. (Adj.). Of sense of smell. *O. bulb*, terminal part of cerebral hemisphere of vertebrates, from which springs *O. nerve* (first
cranial nerve) running to organs of smell.

OLIGOCENE. Geological epoch (q.v.), subdivision of Tertiary, lasted
approximately from 38 till 26 million years ago.

OLIGOCHAETA. Order of annelids (class Chaetopoda) including earthworms. Freshwater and terrestrial; chaetae few; no parapodia; head without special appendages; hermaphrodite; copulation, but fertilization external; clitellum present; eggs develop in a cocoon. Cf. *Polychaeta*.

OLIGOTROPHIC. (Of lakes) poorly productive in terms of organic matter formed, nutrient supply low. Cf. *Eutrophic*.

OMMATIDIUM. See *Eye, Compound*.

OMNIVOROUS. Eating a diet of both plants and animals. Cf. *Carnivore, Herbivore*.

ONCHOSPHERE. (Hexacanth.) Six-hooked embryo of tapeworms. Develops from egg, and if it gets into suitable host, grows into larva (cysticercus, cysticercoid, or plerocercoid).

ONCOGENIC. Cancer-producing.

ONTOGENY. The whole course of development during an individual's life history.

ONYCHOPHORA. Small group of animals all belonging to one genus, *Peripatus*. Worm-like, with many short unjointed legs. Found in warmer parts of the world. With some arthropod characters, e.g. tracheae, but have thin unjointed cuticle and other characters which they share with annelids. Sometimes classified as a subphylum or class of Arthropoda, sometimes as a separate phylum.

OOCYTE. (Zool.). Cell which undergoes meiosis and thereby forms ovum. *Primary oocyte* undergoes greater part of cytoplasmic growth involved in ovum formation, and first of two meiotic divisions. As a result of this division it gives rise to one cell with very little cytoplasm (polar body, q.v.) and one *secondary oocyte* with massive cytoplasm. Latter undergoes second meiotic division, giving rise to another polar body and an ovum. Fertilization frequently occurs in one of the two oocyte stages. Cf. *Spermatocyte*.

OOGAMY. Sexual reproduction in which a large, non-motile egg is fertilized by a small male gamete. Occurs in all Metazoa and some plants. See *Anisogamy*.

OOGENESIS. (Zool.). Formation of ova. See *Maturation of Germ-Cells, Oocyte*.

OOGONIUM. (1) (Bot.). Female sex organ of certain algae and fungi, containing one or more oospheres. (2) (Zool.). Cell of animal ovary which undergoes repeated mitosis and eventually gives rise to oocytes (q.v.).

OOSPHERE. (Bot.). Large, naked, spherical, non-motile female gamete (egg); formed within an oogonium.

OOSPORE. (Bot.). Thick walled resting spore formed from a fertilized oosphere.

OPERCULUM. (1) Lid, e.g. of moss capsule, egg shell of fluke. (2) Cover of gill-slits of fish and Amphibia. (3) Exoskeletal plate of some gastropods, e.g. snail, which can close opening of shell when animal withdraws into the latter.

OPERON. Group of closely linked genes responsible for the synthesis of a group of enzymes functionally related as members of one enzyme system; the activity of this group of genes in synthesizing messenger RNA being switched on or off by a single *operator gene*, which is also a part of the operon, but specializing in this controlling function. The genes controlled by the operator are called *structural genes*. The operator gene is itself controlled in one of two ways. Either it is switched off by a repressor substance, which is produced by a *regulator gene* (not part of the operon) and which can be inactivated by some metabolite or signal substance (an effector) coming from elsewhere in the cell or from outside the cell; so that the presence of the effector results in the operon becoming active. Or it is switched off by a repressor which is a combination of a substance (itself inactive) from the regulator gene with an effector from elsewhere; so that the presence of the effector results in the operon becoming inactive. Operon systems are concerned in the control of gene activity in bacteria, as in the formation of adaptive enzymes; and may be concerned in other organisms.

OPHIDIA. Snakes. A sub-order of Squamata, or sometimes made a separate order of Reptilia. Limbless; with exceptionally wide jaw gape due to mobility of bones; eyelids immovable, nictitating membrane fused over cornea; no ear drums.

OPHIUROIDEA. Brittle-stars; class of Echinodermata; star-shaped; long and sinuous arms radiating from clearly delineated central disc; easily break up by autotomy.

OPHTHALMIC. Optic (q.v.).

OPSONIN. Antibody reacting with surface component of bacteria, promoting their phagocytosis.

OPTIC. (Adj.). Of the eye. *O. chiasma*, structure formed beneath vertebrate forebrain by nerve-fibres of right optic nerve crossing to left side of brain and vice versa. In most vertebrates all the nerve-fibres cross. In mammals, however, 50 per cent remain on their original side, 50 per cent cross. *O. nerve*. second cranial nerve of vertebrate, really part of brain wall. See *Retina*.

ORAL. (Adj.). Of the mouth.

ORBIT. Cavity or depression in skull of vertebrates housing eyeball.

ORDER. One of the kinds of group used in classifying organisms. Consists of a number of similar families (sometimes of only one family). Similar orders are grouped into a class. 'Natural orders' of flowering plants are equivalent to Families (q.v.). See *Classification*.

ORDOVICIAN. Geological period (q.v.), lasted approximately from 500 till 440 million years ago.

ORGAN. Muticellular part of an animal or plant which forms a structural and functional unit, e.g. leaf, kidney.

ORGAN CULTURE. Maintenance alive of a whole organ, after removal from the organism, by partial immersion in a nutrient fluid.

The organ must be small, hence is usually embryonic, because nutrients must diffuse into it from outside.

ORGANELLE. A persistent structure with specialized function forming part of a cell, e.g. a mitochondrion or flagellum; an organelle in a cell is analogous to an organ in a whole organism.

ORGANIZER. (1) Dorsal lip of blastopore of amphibian embryo, consisting of material which will become notochord and somites; and corresponding region of other vertebrate embryos. When transplanted to blastula of same or related species, performs a complex of inductions (q.v.) as a result of which the transplanted organizer and the surrounding host tissues develop into a complete embryonic axis; the best-known amongst these inductions is the evocation (q.v.) of neural plate. (2) Any part of an embryo which performs an induction on another part.

ORGANOGENESIS. Formation of organs during development.

ORIENTAL. Zoogeographical region consisting of India and Indo-china southwards to Wallace's Line (q.v.).

ORNITHINE CYCLE. Probable method of urea formation in ureotelic (q.v.) vertebrates. Carbon dioxide and ammonia combine with the amino acid ornithine to give the amino acid arginine, which is split by enzyme arginase into ornithine and urea. Occurs in liver. See Uricotelic.

ORNITHISCHIA. Fossil order of Reptilia, formerly part of order Dinosauria which is now divided into Ornithischia and Saurischia. Lived during Mesozoic. Contains only herbivorous species and none reaching the gigantic size of the biggest Saurischia.

ORNITHORHYNCHUS. The Duckbilled Platypus, a very primitive monotreme mammal of Australia.

ORTHOGENESIS. Steady trend of evolution in a given direction over a prolonged period of time, affecting related groups of organisms, due to the working out of inherent trends within the inherited material. It is not generally accepted that orthogenesis is the proper explanation of the many known instances of persistent evolutionary trends.

ORTHOPTERA. Order of exopterygote insects including cockroaches, locusts, grasshoppers. Mostly large, terrestrial insects with biting mouth parts; narrow, hardened forewings, and membranous hind wings. Good runners and jumpers, many flightless.

ORTHOSTICHY. See Phyllotaxy.

ORTHOTROPOUS. (Of ovule), erect on funicle, micropyle pointing away from placenta. Cf. Anatropous, Campylotropous.

OSCULUM. Of sponges, an opening through which the water taken in through ostia leaves the body.

OSMIUM TETROXIDE (OSMIC ACID). $OsO_4$. Component of all the best fixatives for light microscopy of cells, since it produces little distortion. Blackens fat. Also an important fixative for electron microscopy.

OSMO-REGULATION. Control of osmotic pressure within an organism. See *Contractile vacuole, Internal environment*.

OSMOSIS. When a solution of, say, sugar in water is separated from pure water by a membrane permeable to water but not to sugar (*semi-permeable membrane*), water passes across the membrane into the sugar solution. This movement of water is *osmosis*. If external pressure is applied to the sugar solution, the movement of water into it will be opposed. The pressure required to stop the movement completely is called the *osmotic pressure* of the sugar solution. It is greater the more concentrated the solution. Water will similarly pass by osmosis from any solution having a weaker osmotic pressure to any having a stronger (involving the same or different dissolved substance) provided the membrane separating them is of the appropriate semi-permeable kind, until the two solutions attain equal osmotic pressures. And if the membrane is merely *more* permeable to water than to the dissolved substance, water will still move from weak solution to strong, while the dissolved substance moves more slowly in the opposite direction, until the two solutions have equal osmotic pressures. The amount of osmotic pressure produced by solutions (in standard conditions) depends on the *number* of dissolved particles (molecules or ions), whatever their size, in a given amount of water. Proteins, and other substances with large molecules, develop therefore a small osmotic pressure relative to the weight of them which is dissolved. More or less semi-permeable membranes are very widespread in living organisms, e.g. they surround all cells; and so osmosis plays a great part in controlling the distribution of water in living organisms.

OSTEICHTHYES. Bony fish, often treated as a single class of Vertebrata. Contains *Actinopterygii, Crossopterygii* and *Dipnoi*.

OSTEOBLAST. Cell responsible for formation of calcified intercellular substance of bone. Cells within bone (*osteocytes*) are osteoblasts which have become included as the bone developed, and have ceased to divide and to form bone substance.

OSTEOCLAST. Multinucleate cell which breaks down the calcified intercellular substance of bone. Activity stimulated by parathyroid hormone. Remodelling of bone shape by such breaking down constantly accompanies bone growth.

OSTIOLE. Pore in fruit bodies (pycnidia and perithecia) of certain fungi and in conceptacles of brown algae through which, respectively, spores or gametes are discharged.

OSTIUM. Of sponges, an opening through which water is drawn into the body. Much more numerous than oscula (q.v.).

OTIC. Concerning the ear. See *Auditory*.

OTOCYST. Statocyst (q.v.).

OTOLITH. Granule of calcium carbonate in vertebrate inner ear. Several such granules are attached to fine processes of sensitive cells, the latter communicating via nerves with the brain. The pull of gravity on the gránules and therefore on the cell-processes registers the position of the animal with respect to gravity. Similar arrangement in some invertebrates. See *Statocyst*.

OUTBREEDING. See *Inbreeding*.

OVARIAN FOLLICLE. Sac of cells which invests developing oocyte of many Metazoa. Probably concerned in nourishment of growing oocyte, and in vertebrates secretes oestrogen. See *Graafian Follicle*.

OVARY. (1) (Bot.). Hollow basal region of a carpel, containing one or more ovules. In a flower which possesses two or more united carpels the ovaries are united to form a single compound ovary. (2) (Zool.). Organ which produces ova. In vertebrates it also produces sex hormones. See *Oestrogen, Progesterone*.

OVIDUCT. (Zool.). Tube carrying ova from ovary, or from coelom into which ova are shed, to the exterior. See *Müllerian Duct*.

OVIPAROUS. Laying eggs in which the embryos have as yet developed little if at all. Cf. *Ovoviviparous, Viviparous*.

OVIPOSITOR. Organ at hind end of abdomen in female insects, through which eggs are laid (*oviposition*). Formed from modified parts of paired appendages; consists of several separate but inter-locked parts. Frequently long and sometimes capable of piercing animals or plants, permitting eggs to be laid in otherwise inaccessible places, such as inside other organisms. Sting of bees and wasps is a modified ovipositor.

OVOGENESIS. Oogenesis (q.v.).

OVOTESTIS. Organ of some hermaphrodite animals, e.g. snail, which functions both as ovary (q.v.) and testis (q.v.).

OVOVIVIPAROUS. Having embryos which develop within the maternal organism, from which they may derive nutriment, though they are separated from it by the persistence, through most or all of development, of egg-membranes. E.g. many insects, snails, fish, lizards, and snakes. Cf. *Oviparous, Viviparous*.

OVULATION. Bursting of ripe egg from ovarian follicle. In vertebrates the egg (actually a secondary oocyte) is discharged on to surface of ovary and thence passes into oviduct; and ovulation is frequently result of stimulation by pituitary hormone. See *Oestrous Cycle*.

OVULE. Structure found in seed plants (gymnosperms and angiosperms) that develops into a seed after fertilization of an egg-cell within it. In gymnosperms the ovules are unprotected; in angiosperms protected by the megasporophyll which forms a closed structure (carpel) within which they are formed, singly or in numbers. Each ovule is attached to the carpel wall by a stalk or funicle which arises from its base (chalaza). A mature angiosperm ovule consists of a central mass of tissue, the nucellus, surrounded by one or two protective layers, the integuments, from which the seed coat is ultimately formed. Integuments enclose nucellus except at apex, where there is a small passage, the micropyle. Within the nucellus is a large oval cell, the embryo sac (q.v.) developed from megaspore, containing the naked egg-cell.

OVUM. Unfertilized egg-cell. A single large immobile cell, containing a haploid nucleus. In many animals, it is the oocyte (q.v.) which is fertilized by the sperm and in these animals, strictly speaking, an unfertilized ovum does not therefore exist.

OXIDASE. Enzyme (a kind of dehydrogenase, q.v.) which catalyses oxidation of a substrate by removal of hydrogen which combines with molecular oxygen.

OXIDATIVE PHOSPHORYLATION. Coupling of phosphate with ADP to make ATP (q.v.), utilizing energy released during respiration.

OXYGEN DEBT. Oxygen deficit when an organism or part of an organism has been doing work with inadequate oxygen supply; e.g. after hard muscular work oxygen consumption of man remains above normal for some time, until the debt has been repaid.

OXYHAEMOGLOBIN. Oxygenated haemoglobin. See *Respiratory Pigment*.

OXYTOCIN. Hormone secreted by pars nervosa of the pituitary (q.v.). Produces strong contraction of uterine muscle and ejection of milk in mammals. Function in non-mammalian vertebrates unclear. A polypeptide.

# P

$P_1$. Parental generation, consisting of the parents from which a breeding experiment starts; all the males being uniform as regards the allelomorphs under observation, and all the females likewise.

PACEMAKER. Region of vertebrate heart where contraction at each beat is started: the sinus venosus (a contractile chamber of heart); or its homologue in mammals and birds the sino-auricular node (a small group of muscle and nerve cells in auricle wall). A wave of electro-negativity spreads at each beat from pacemaker first to auricle(s) then to ventricle(s), activating them to contract in turn. If pacemaker removed, rest of heart beats, but at slower rate. Heart muscle has therefore intrinsic power of rhythmical contraction, normally masked by more rapid pacemaker stimulation.

PACHYTENE. Stage in prophase of first division of meiosis (q.v.), following zygotene, in which each of the paired chromosomes of the bivalents begins to shorten and thicken and now appears doubled as two chromatids. The group of four associated chromatids formed from each pair of chromosomes is known as a tetrad.

PAEDOGENESIS. Reproduction in larval or other pre-adult form. See *Neoteny*.

PAIRING (OF CHROMOSOMES (SYNAPSIS) ). Side by side association of homologous chromosomes at meiosis (q.v.). See Fig. 6B, p 181.

PALAEARCTIC. Zoogeographical region, consisting of Europe, North Africa, and Asia southwards to the Himalayas and Red Sea.

PALAEOBOTANY. Study of fossil plants.

PALAEOCENE. Geological epoch (q.v.), earliest subdivision of Tertiary, lasted approximately from 65 till 54 million years ago.

PALAEOGENE. See *Geological Periods and Epochs*.

PALAEOLITHIC. Phase of human history during which, though tools were manufactured, food was obtained solely by hunting, fishing, or collecting, with no cultivation. Lasted from at least half a million years ago up to beginning of Neolithic stage (q.v.) about 10,000 years ago.

PALAEONTOLOGY. Study of fossils.

PALAEOZOIC. Geological era lasting approximately from 570 till 225 million years ago. See *Geological Periods and Epochs*.

PALATE. Roof of vertebrate mouth. In mammals and crocodiles roof of mouth is not homologous with that of other vertebrates; a new (false) palate has developed beneath original palate, by bony shelves projecting inwards from bones of upper jaw. The nasal cavity is thus extended and its internal opening (choana, q.v.) placed right back in the throat. In mammals the bony part of the false palate or *hard palate* is continued backwards by a fold of mucous membrane and connective tissue, the *soft palate*.

PALEA (SUPERIOR PALEA, PALE). Glume-like bract of grass spikelet on axis of individual flower which, with lemma, it encloses.

PALISADE. See *Mesophyll*.

PALMELLA. Stage or growth form of certain algae, in which numerous cells are embedded within a gelatinous matrix.

PALPS. Of polychaete annelid worms, tactile appendages on the head; of bivalve molluscs, ciliated flaps of tissue around mouth concerned in production of feeding currents; of Crustacea, distal parts of appendages which carry mandibles, may be locomotor, or may help in feeding; of insects, parts of first and second maxillae, shown to be olfactory in some insects.

PALYNOLOGY. Pollen analysis (q.v.).

PANCREAS. Sweetbread. Gland of gnathostome vertebrate situated in mesentery near duodenum, into which it discharges through pancreatic duct an alkaline mixture of digestive enzymes (trypsinogen, lipase, amylase, maltase, etc.). Stimulated to secrete this mixture by hormone secretin (q.v.). Also contains groups of cells (islets of Langerhans) of quite different function, secreting into blood of portal system the hormones insulin (q.v.) and glucagon (q.v.) according to the level of the blood sugar (q.v.). In cyclostomes the components of the pancreas are not anatomically separate from the intestinal wall.

PANCREATIN. Extract of pancreas containing digestive enzymes.

PANICLE. Kind of inflorescence (q.v.).

PANTOTHENIC ACID. Vitamin of B group, forming a co-enzyme; required by a variety of organisms, e.g. some yeasts, some bacteria, insects, vertebrates.

PAPAIN. Intracellular proteolytic enzyme (or mixture of enzymes), found in plant (paw-paw), which splits proteins in neutral solution.

PAPILLA. A projection. *Dermal papillae*, projections of dermis into epidermis of vertebrates, increasing surface of contact between the two tissues. *Tongue papillae*, variety of projections on upper surface of mammalian tongue, on which lie taste-buds, and which may be cornified to form a rasping surface, e.g. in cat.

PAPPUS. Ring of fine, sometimes feathery hairs, developed from calyx crowning the fruits of flowering plants of family Compositae, e.g. dandelion; acting as a parachute and aiding in wind dispersal of fruits.

PARABIOTIC TWINS. Artificial 'siamese twins' produced by surgically joining two animals, so that their blood circulations become continuous.

PARAFFIN SECTIONS. Sections of tissues cut by microtome (q.v.) after embedding in paraffin wax. Usual method of preparing tissues for microscopical study.

PARAMECIUM. Genus of ciliate Protozoa. 'Slipper-animalcule.'

PARAMORPH. Any taxonomic variant within a species; used particularly when, because of lack of data, its status cannot be defined more precisely.

PARAPHYSIS. (Bot.). Sterile filament, numbers of which occur in mosses and in certain algae, interspersed amongst the sex organs; and in the hymenium of ascomycete and basidiomycete fungi.

PARAPODIUM. Paired, segmentally arranged, muscular lateral projection of body of polychaete worms, bearing chaetae and sometimes other structures; locomotor in free-living forms.

PARASEXUAL CYCLE. Breeding system of certain fungi (including both those with normal sexual reproduction and those with only asexual reproduction) that involves genetic recombination outside the sexual cycle. System comprises the following steps: (1) rare (1 in $10^6$ to $10^7$) fusion of two, genetically unlike nuclei in a heterokaryotic mycelium to produce a diploid heterozygous nucleus which (2) multiplies by mitosis during which crossing over occasionally occurs followed, again at rare intervals (1 in $10^3$) by (3) formation of haploid nuclei from the diploids (haploidization) in which whole chromosomes reassort at random producing new genetic combinations. Starting from a culture containing a mixture of genetically different haploid nuclei the result of the parasexual cycle is a much more varied mixture of nuclei consisting of haploids like the originals, haploid recombinants, homozygous and heterozygous diploids. Little is yet known of natural significance of the parasexual cycle but it has already been shown to determine variation in pathogenicity in certain plant pathogens.

PARASITE. Organism living in or on another organism (its host) from which it obtains food. *Facultative p.*, an organism which can live entirely as a saprophyte (q.v.) but can live as a parasite under certain conditions. *Obligate p.*, an organism which can live only parasitically. Parasites may or may not be harmful to the host. Cf. *Symbiosis, Saprophyte*.

PARASTICHY. See *Phyllotaxy*.

PARASYMPATHETIC SYSTEM. Part of autonomic nervous system (q.v.).

PARATHYROID. Endocrine gland of tetrapod vertebrates, usually paired, lying near or, in some species, within thyroid. Developed from gill pouches. Its hormone (a protein) controls distribution of calcium and phosphate in the body. Administration of hormone transfers calcium from bones to blood (see *Osteoclast*); deficiency lowers blood calcium, producing tetany.

PARATONIC. (Of plant movements), induced by external stimuli, e.g. nastic movements, taxes and tropisms (q.v.). Alternatively described as induced or aitiogenic. Cf. *Autonomic*.

PARATYPE. Any specimen, other than the type specimen (q.v.) or duplicates of this, cited with the original taxonomic description and naming of an organism.

PARAZOA. Grade of organization exemplified only by Porifera (q.v.), which are multicellular animals separately evolved from all others (Metazoa, q.v.).

PARENCHYMA. (Bot.). Tissue consisting of living, thin-walled cells, often almost as broad as long, and permeated by a system of inter-cellular spaces containing air. Cortex and pith are typically composed of parenchyma. (Zool.). (1) Loose tissue consisting of irregularly-shaped vacuolated cells, forming a large part of body of Platyhelminthes. (2) The specific cells of an organ, as opposed to the blood-vessels, connective tissue, etc.

PARIETAL. (1) Of coelomic lining (peritoneum or pleura), that covering inside of body-wall, as opposed to *visceral* part covering organs within coelom. (2) *P. bones*, pair of membrane-bones which in most vertebrates covers large part of upper surface of brain, behind frontal bones. (3) *P. organ*, see *Pineal apparatus*. (4) (Bot.). See *Placentation*.

PARTHENOCARPY. Formation of fruit without fertilization. In most plants development of a fruit from the ovary can proceed only after fertilization has occurred, but in a number of plants fruit develop-ment regularly takes place from unfertilized flowers. Such fruits, e.g. banana, pineapple, are seedless but otherwise normal in appearance. Parthenocarpy can also be induced in unfertilized flowers, e.g. in tomato, by application of certain auxins (q.v.). It has been suggested that fertilization provides a stimulus for pro-duction of hormone which, in turn, induces development of fruit tissue, and that where natural parthenocarpy occurs, sufficient hormone to enable fruit development to proceed is produced by the plant independently of stimulus of fertilization.

PARTHENOGENESIS. Development of ovum without fertilization (q.v.) into a new individual. In many animals it may be induced artificially. See *Artificial Parthenogenesis*. In some plants (dandelion), and animals (aphids, rotifers, where males may be absent), is of normal occurrence. Ova which develop in this way are usually diploid, in which case all offspring are genetically identical with the parent. Frequently in such animals ordinary sexual reproduc-tion, providing genetic recombination, together with employment for males, occurs from time to time (heterogamy, q.v.). See *Apomixis*.

PASSAGE CELLS. Cells of endodermis, characteristically of older monocotyledonous roots, opposite protoxylem groups of stele, that remain unthickened, with casparian strips (q.v.) only, after thick-ening (involving deposition of suberin, cellulose, and lignification) of all other endodermis cells; allowing transfer of material between cortex and vascular cylinder.

PASSERINE. A member of the Passeriformes, a group of birds. A perching bird, with large first toe directed back, other three toes forward. The group includes about half the known species of bird, including most of our common inland ones.

PASTEURIZATION. Method of partial sterilization named after famous pioneer of microbiology, Louis Pasteur, who found that heating at temperature well below boiling point destroyed bacteria

causing wine spoilage without affecting its flavour. Now widely
used to kill some disease-causing bacteria in food. Best known
example is pasteurization of milk (heating for 30 minutes at 62° C.)
which kills tubercle and other harmful bacteria.

PATELLA. Knee-cap. A bone (sesamoid bone, q.v.) over the front of
the knee joint in tendon of (extensor) muscles which straighten the
hind-leg, present in most mammals, some birds and reptiles.

PATHOGEN. Parasite which causes disease.

PATHOLOGY. Study of disease or of diseased tissues.

PATRISTIC. (Of similarity of plants) due to common ancestry. See
Cladistic.

PEAT. Accumulated dead plant material that has remained incompletely decomposed owing, principally, to lack of oxygen, as in
moorland and fen where land is more or less completely water-
logged; often forming a layer many feet deep.

PECTIC COMPOUNDS. Acid polysaccharide carbohydrates present
in cell walls of unlignified tissue; comprising pectic acid and pec-
tates, pectose (protopectin), pectin. Form gels under certain conditions. Principal constituents are galacturonic acid, galactose,
arabinose, and methyl alcohol.

PECTORAL FIN. See Fin.

PECTORAL GIRDLE. Shoulder girdle (q.v.).

PEDICEL. Stalk of an individual flower of an inflorescence.

PEDIPALP. Second head appendage of arachnids; may be locomotor
(kingcrabs); clawed and used for seizing prey (scorpions); sensory; or modified in the male for fertilization (spiders).

PEDUNCLE. Stalk of an inflorescence.

PELAGIC. Inhabiting the mass of water of sea or lake, in contrast to
the sea or lake bottom. See Benthos. Pelagic animals and plants are
divided into plankton and nekton (q.v.).

PELECYPODA. Lamellibranchiata (q.v.).

PELVIC FIN. See Fin.

PELVIC GIRDLE. Hip-girdle (q.v.).

PELVIS. (1) The pelvic girdle. (2) The lower part of the abdomen
surrounded by the pelvic girdle. (3) P. of kidney, funnel-shaped expansion of ureter as it joins the concave side of kidney.

PENETRANCE. Proportion of organisms bearing a particular dominant gene, or homozygous for a recessive, which show the effect of
that gene. Penetrance of many genes is practically 100 per cent
but in the case of other genes it is much less, the value being affected
by environment or genotype.

PENIS. Organ associated with ducts from testis, used to introduce
sperm from male into female.

PENTADACTYL LIMB. The kind of limb found in four classes of
vertebrates: Amphibia, reptiles, birds, and mammals, collectively
called the tetrapods. Evolved as an adaptation to life on land, and
therefore not found in fishes or other primitively aquatic verte-

brates. The limb is in three parts: upper-arm or thigh; fore-arm or shank; hand or foot. The latter bears five terminal fingers or toes (digits), hence the name pentadactyl. The first part contains one long bone (humerus in arm, femur in leg); the second two long more or less parallel bones (radius and ulna in arm, tibia and fibula in leg); the third many small bones in a fairly uniform pattern (carpals, metacarpals, and phalanges successively in arm;

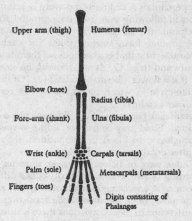

Upper arm (thigh)     Humerus (femur)

Elbow (knee)

Radius (tibia)

Fore-arm (shank)     Ulna (fibula)

Wrist (ankle)     Carpals (tarsals)

Palm (sole)     Metacarpals (metatarsals)

Fingers (toes)

Digits consisting of
Phalanges

*Fig. 7. Diagram of skeleton of pentadactyl limb of vertebrate, giving names of parts of fore-limb, and (in brackets) of hind-limb. On left, common name of whole part; on right, names of bones.*

tarsals, metatarsals, and phalanges in leg). See Fig. 7, above. Many modifications of this fundamental pattern occur, through loss or fusion of elements, especially in the terminal parts.

PENTOSE. Sugar (monosaccharide) with five carbon atoms, e.g. ribose. Important constituents of nucleic acids (q.v.); make up various plant polysaccharides, e.g. pectin, gum arabic.

PEPSIN. Enzyme (peptidase, q.v.) splitting proteins in acid solution. Secreted in vertebrate stomach, along with hydrochloric acid.

PEPTIDASE. An enzyme splitting peptides, and in many cases proteins, by attacking certain peptide links. *Exopeptidases* split off terminal amino-acids of a peptide chain. *Endopeptidases* split peptide chains by attacking links between certain amino-acids anywhere they occur in the chain; e.g. trypsin, pepsin, papain; since they break up proteins into large fragments they are often called *proteinases*.

PEPTIDE. Compound formed of two or (polypeptide) more amino acids, by amino ($NH_2$) group of one joining with carboxyl (COOH) group of the next, forming *peptide bond* (—NH—CO—) with elimination of water.

PEPTONE. Product of protein splitting, consisting of large fragments.

PERENNATION. (Of plants) survival from year to year by vegetative means.

PERENNIAL. Plant that continues its growth from year to year. In *herbaceous* perennials aerial parts die away in autumn, replaced by new shoots in following year from underground structures, e.g. rhubarb, delphinium; in *woody* perennials, permanent woody stems above ground form starting point for each new year's growth, a characteristic that enables some of them to reach a large size, e.g. shrubs and trees. Cf. *Annual, Biennial, Ephemeral.*

PERFECT. (1) (Of a flower), hermaphrodite; (2) (Of fungi), applied to stage of life-cycle in which spores, formed as result of sexual reproduction, are produced.

PERFUSION. Artificial passage of fluid through blood-vessels of an organ or animal. Fluid may be fixative; saline to wash out blood; or may approximate to blood in composition, in order to keep organ alive after isolation from animal.

PERIANTH. Outer part of flower enclosing stamens and carpels, usually consisting of two whorls. In dicotyledons differentiated as an outer green *calyx* consisting of a whorl of *sepals*, and an inner, usually conspicuous, often coloured *corolla* consisting of a whorl of *petals*, e.g. buttercup. In monocotyledons there is usually no differentiation of calyx and corolla, both whorls being alike. In some flowers perianth is reduced, e.g. in stinging nettle where only calyx is present, and grasses where perianth is represented by two tiny scales (*lodicules*); or it is absent altogether, e.g. willow.

PERIBLEM. See *Apical Meristem.*

PERICARDIAL CAVITY (P. SAC). Cavity within which heart lies. In vertebrates, a coelomic space, separated from perivisceral part of coelom (incompletely in elasmobranchs). In Arthropoda and Mollusca, a haemocoelic space supplying blood to heart.

PERICARDIUM. (1) Serous membrane forming wall of pericardial cavity in vertebrates. (2) Sometimes synonymous with pericardial cavity (q.v.).

PERICARP. (Bot.). Wall of an ovary after it has matured into a fruit; may be dry, membranous, or hard, e.g. achene, nut; or fleshy, e.g. berry.

PERICHAETIUM. Distinct whorl of leaves surrounding sex organs in mosses.

PERICLINAL. (Bot.). (Of planes of division of cells), running parallel to surface of plant part. Cf. *Anticlinal.*

PERICYCLE. Tissue of vascular cylinder lying immediately within endodermis, consisting of parenchyma cells and sometimes fibres.

PERIDERM. Cork cambium (phellogen) and its products, i.e. cork and secondary cortex (phelloderm).

PERIGYNOUS. See *Receptacle*.

PERIKARYON. Cell-Body (q.v.).

PERINEUM. Region of body wall between anus and urinogenital openings of placental mammals.

PERIOSTEUM. Layer of connective tissue tightly investing vertebrate bones, to which muscles and tendons are attached. Contains active or (in adult) potential osteoblasts, which in the embryo, and in the adult after fractures, are important in formation of bone.

PERIPATUS. See *Onychophora*.

PERIPHERAL NERVOUS SYSTEM. All the rest of the nervous system when the central nervous system is excluded. It consists mainly of *nerves* (q.v.) of various sizes (up to half-inch diameter in man). The major nerves branch repeatedly after leaving the central nervous system to distribute their numerous nerve fibres (perhaps 100,000 in a big vertebrate limb nerve) to the many different effectors and receptors they serve. There are no synapses in the course of most nerves; the nerve fibres are usually continuous right through from the receptors to the central nervous system (in the case of sensory nerve fibres) or from the central nervous system to the effectors (in the case of motor nerve fibres). Though they may run side by side in the nerve, sensory and motor fibres do not usually interact except via the synapses in the central nervous system. But synapses do occur in certain parts of the peripheral nervous system; see *Autonomic Nervous System*, *Nerve Net*.

PERISPERM. Nutritive tissue surrounding embryo in some seeds, e.g. stitchwort; derived from nucellus (q.v.). Cf. *Endosperm*.

PERISSODACTYLA. Odd-toed ungulates. An order of mammals containing horses, tapirs, and rhinoceros. Walk on their toes which are hoofed, and are characterized by fact that weight-bearing axis of foot lies along third toe. The third toe is usually larger than the others (some of which may disappear); e.g. horses have a very large third toe, and minute second and fourth toes ('splint bones'). One of the two great groups of hoofed mammals (ungulates), other being the Artiodactyla.

PERISTALSIS. Waves of contraction passing along tubular organs, particularly intestine, mixing contents and moving them along. Produced by surrounding coats of smooth muscle.

PERISTOME. (1) (Bot.). Fringe of pointed appendages round mouth of dehiscent capsule in mosses, concerned in spore liberation. (2) (Zool.). Spirally twisted groove leading to mouth of some ciliate Protozoa.

PERITHECIUM. Rounded or flask-shaped fruit-body of certain ascomycete fungi and lichens, with an internal hymenium of asci and paraphyses and with an apical pore (ostiole) through which the ascospores are discharged.

PERITONEAL CAVITY. Abdominal cavity. Coelomic cavity of mammals posterior to diaphragm, containing liver, spleen, most of gut, and other viscera which almost completely fill it. Term sometimes also used for perivisceral cavity of other vertebrates.

PERITONEUM. Serous membrane lining peritoneal or perivisceral cavity covering surface of viscera within it, and forming mesentery (q.v.).

PERITRICHOUS. (Of bacterial flagella) arising at many places over surface of cell. Cf. Polar.

PERIVISCERAL CAVITY (COELOM). The main body cavity (q.v.). See *Coelom, Haemocoel.*

PERMANENT TEETH. The second of the two sets of teeth of most mammals. See *Deciduous Teeth.*

PERMEABILITY. Of membrane, extent to which molecules of a given kind can pass through it. Substances differ greatly in the ease with which they pass through a given membrane, e.g. water or fatty substances pass easily, many ions and proteins with great difficulty, through plasma-membrane (q.v.). Permeability of any biological membrane is itself variable within wide limits. The very numerous membranes of animals and plants, e.g. plasma-membranes or sheets of cells such as the endothelium lining of blood capillaries, produce many osmotic effects (see *Osmosis*) and are of great importance in determining local differences in composition of the organism.

PERMIAN. Geological period (q.v.); lasted approximately from 280 till 225 million years ago.

PEROXIDASE. Enzyme (a kind of dehydrogenase, q.v.) which catalyses the oxidation of a substrate by removal of hydrogen which combines with hydrogen peroxide. Occurs particularly in plants.

PEROXISOME. See *Microbodies.*

PES. Foot of hind leg of tetrapod vertebrate. Consists of tarsus, metatarsus and digits. See *Pentadactyl Limb, Manus.*

PETAL. One of parts forming corolla of a flower, usually brightly coloured and conspicuous. See *Flower.*

PETIOLE. Leaf-stalk.

pH. A quantitative expression for acidity or alkalinity of a solution, i.e. concentration of hydrogen or hydroxyl ions. Scale ranges from 0 to 14, $p$H7 being neutral, less than 7 acid, more than 7 alkaline. Concentration of hydrogen or hydroxyl ions increases or decreases ten times for each unit of change in $p$H. Theoretically $p$H= $-\log$ cH, where cH is the concentration of hydrogen ions in grams per litre.

PHAEOPHYTA. Brown algae (seaweeds). Division of algae. Brown to olive-green in colour. Possess chlorophylls a and c, $\alpha$-, $\beta$-carotene and xanthophylls, including brown pigment fucoxanthin which masks other pigments. Main food reserve is polysaccharide *laminarin.* Cell wall of two layers, inner of cellulose, outer of mucilaginous pectic material. Very diverse in form, ranging from minute (less than 1 mm long), filamentous, to very long and complex, differentiated into a disc or root-like basal attachment part, and a stem-like part of varying lengths, bearing a branched or unbranched, ribbon or leaf-like part, often provided with air bladders, e.g. bladder wrack; up to 60–70 metres in length in largest forms with relatively complex internal structure. Asexual reproduction by fragmentation of thallus or by mostly laterally biflagellate zoospores. Sexual reproduction isogamous, gametes motile, or anisogamous, by fusion of small, motile, male gamete with large, non-motile egg. Marine (with rare exceptions), usually abundant in cold water. Benthic, common inhabitants of inter-tidal zone. A species of *Sargassum* is exceptional in being pelagic, accumulating in large quantities in the Sargasso sea near the West Indies.

PHAGE. Bacteriophage (q.v.).

PHAGOCYTE. A cell which engulfs into its cytoplasm particles from its surroundings, by a process of flowing all round them called *phagocytosis*. Phagocytes are an important defence mechanism of most Metazoa against invading bacteria. In man and other mammals, polymorphs (q.v.) and macrophages (q.v.) are particularly phagocytic.

PHALANGES. Bones of digit (finger or toe). Each finger has one to five phalanges (more in whales) joined end-to-end in a row, the proximal of each row being jointed to a metacarpal bone. See Fig. 7, p. 213.

PHANEROGAMIA. Name given by early systematic botanists to seed plants (Gymnospermae and Angiospermae); so called because organs of reproduction, e.g. cones or flowers, are clearly evident. Equivalent to Spermatophyta. Cf. *Cryptogamia*.

PHANEROPHYTES. Class of Raunkiaer's Life Forms (q.v.).

PHARYNX. (1) Part of vertebrate gut between mouth and oesophagus into which open glottis in tetrapods, and gill-slits in fish. In man and other mammals, throat and back of nose; partly divided by soft palate into upper (nasal) section and lower (oral or throat) section. Contains sensory receptors setting off swallowing reflex. (2) Part of gut into which gill-slits open internally in ascidians and amphioxus.

PHELLEM. Cork (q.v.).

PHELLODERM. Secondary cortex tissue; formed by cork cambium.

PHELLOGEN. Cork cambium (q.v.).

PHENETIC. (Of relationship or classification) based on maximum observable similarity. Cf. *Phylogenetic*.

PHENOCOPY. A non-inherited departure from the normal phenotype, induced by an environmental influence usually acting on an organism during its development, that mimics the effect of a known gene-mutation.

PHENOLOGY. Study of periodicity phenomena of plants, e.g. time of flowering in relation to climate.

PHENOTYPE. The sum of the characteristics manifested by an organism, as contrasted with the set of genes possessed by it (genotype, q.v.). It is possible for organisms to have the same genotype but different phenotypes (owing to environmentally-produced variation); or the same phenotype with different genotypes (e.g. in heterozygotes and homozygotes with a dominant allelomorph; or through incomplete penetrance).

PHEROMONE. Chemical substance the release of which into its surroundings by an animal influences the behaviour or development of other individuals of the same species. E.g. sexual attractants in many insect species; queen-bee substance, produced by a queen and inhibiting development of other queens.

PHLOEM. Vascular tissue that conducts synthesized foods, e.g. sugars, proteins, and some mineral ions, through the plant. Characterized by presence of sieve-tubes (q.v.) and in some plants, companion cells, fibres, and parenchyma cells. Or two kinds, *primary*, formed by differentiation from procambium and *secondary*, additional phloem produced by activity of cambium.

PHORONIDEA. Small phylum of worm-like animals. Sedentary, live in tubes. Have a ring of ciliated tentacles with which they feed, and superficially resemble certain Polyzoa.

PHOSPHAGEN. Phosphate of creatine, or of arginine (an amino acid). Reversible splitting off of phosphate from phosphagen plays important part in providing readily available store of energy-rich phosphate for ATP (q.v.) in muscle contraction. Creatine phosphate is the phosphagen of ophiuroids, Acrania, and vertebrates; arginine phosphate of most invertebrates and of tunicates; and both phosphagens occur in echinoids and Hemichordata.

PHOSPHATASES. Enzymes splitting phosphate from its organic compounds (esters).

PHOSPHATIDE. See *Phospholipid*.

PHOSPHOLIPID (PHOSPHOLIPIN, PHOSPHOLIPOID, PHOSPHATIDE). Lipine containing phosphoric acid and nitrogenous base. E.g. lecithin.

PHOSPHORESCENCE. Light given out by living things does not depend on previous illumination and should therefore not be called phosphorescence. It is known as bioluminescence (q.v).

PHOSPHORYLATION. Bringing about the combination of an organic acceptor molecule (e.g. sugar) with phosphate. In phosphorylation of some substances 'high energy bonds' (indicated by ∼) are formed; the resulting compounds are highly reactive in water with other organic molecules in the presence of appropriate enzymes; when their phosphate is transferred energy becomes available for biochemical and other work. Such processes form the fundamental energy-transfer system in metabolism. Most important high-energy compound is ATP (q.v.), universally present in living organisms.

**PHOTIC ZONE.** Surface zone of sea or lake sufficiently illuminated for photosynthesis.

**PHOTONASTY.** Response to a general non-directional illumination stimulus, e.g. closing or opening of flowers at night-time, seen respectively in wood sorrel and evening primrose.

**PHOTOPERIODISM.** Response of plants to relative length of day and night. Although flowering display is best known example of photoperiodism many other plant responses are controlled by photoperiod. Photoperiodic responses are regulated by the photo-reversible pigment phytochrome (q.v.). Circadian rhythms (q.v.) are considered to be a fundamental basis of photoperiodism. *Short-day* plants, e.g. chrysanthemum, cosmos, soybean, usually flower only in response to photoperiods (day lengths) that are shorter than a certain critical length in each 24-hour cycle, i.e. they respond inductively to a 'long night'. In contrast to these are *long-day* plants, e.g. radish, lettuce, henbane, that usually flower only in response to photoperiods that are longer than a certain critical level in each 24-hour cycle, i.e. they respond inductively to a 'short-night'. All gradations between short and long-day types exist; in some, *day-neutral* plants, e.g. tomato, flowering is virtually unaffected by photoperiod. Photoperiodic response varies with age of plant and with temperature. The photoperiodic stimulus is perceived by leaves and is transmitted, probably in form of a hormone (tentatively named *florigen*) to growing points where it induces flower initiation. Similar effects of day-length regulate the timing of the breeding season in many vertebrate animals.

**PHOTOPHILE.** Literally 'light-loving'; light receptive phase of circadian rhythm (q.v.), lasting about 12 hours. Cf. *Skotophile.*

**PHOTOPHOSPHORYLATION (PHOTOSYNTHETIC PHOSPHORYLATION).** Coupling of phosphate with ADP to make ATP, using light energy absorbed in photosynthesis. May be *cyclic* or *non-cyclic*; former results in formation of ATP only, latter in formation of ATP and hydrogen (used in $CO_2$ reduction). See *Photosynthesis.*

**PHOTORECEPTOR.** Receptor (q.v.) detecting light, e.g. vertebrate eye.

**PHOTORESPIRATION.** Type of respiration characteristic of certain plant species that is activated by light. Biochemically different from normal respiration, involving glycolate metabolism. Plants displaying photorespiration, e.g. sugar beet, tobacco, wheat, have higher $CO_2$ compensation points, fix carbon dioxide by the Calvin cycle (see *Photosynthesis*) and, photosynthetically, are less efficient than those which do not, e.g. maize, sugar cane, sorghum. The latter fix carbon dioxide by the oxaloacetic acid pathway. These two types of plant also differ in other significant and apparently interrelated respects. The chloroplasts of plants of the first type are distributed evenly throughout the mesophyll and are absent around veins. Those of plants of the second type are strikingly concentrated around the veins; and translocation from the leaves is relatively rapid.

PHOTOSYNTHESIS. In green plants, synthesis of organic compounds from water and carbon dioxide using energy absorbed by chlorophyll from sunlight. Source of most of the oxygen in the atmosphere. Takes place within chloroplasts. Basic for existence of virtually all other forms of life (exceptions being photosynthetic and chemosynthetic bacteria) since products form raw materials on which, directly or indirectly, all plants and animals depend for provision of energy for all the reactions that constitute metabolism. Photosynthesis may be summarized by the empirical equation

$$CO_2 + 2H_2O \xrightarrow[\text{Green plant}]{\text{Light energy}} (CH_2O) + O_2 + H_2O$$

Absorption of light energy initiates a series of light (photochemical) reactions, a unique feature of photosynthesis. Oxygen is released from oxidation of water; a reducing agent $NADPH_2$ is generated; light energy is converted in *photophosphorylation* to chemical energy in the form of the energy-rich compound ATP. These reactions take place in the grana of chloroplasts (q.v.). They are followed, in the grana, by chemical reactions described, in contrast to photochemical reactions, as 'dark' reactions. Using the reducing power of $NADPH_2$ and the energy of ATP, $CO_2$ is reduced to carbohydrate (reductive $CO_2$ fixation). Two pathways are known. In some plants $CO_2$ is combined in the Calvin (its discoverer) cycle with a 5-carbon compound, ribulose diphosphate, which subsequently gives rise to two molecules of the 3-carbon compound phosphoglyceric acid. This in turn gives rise to phosphoglyceraldehyde, triosephosphate, hexose phosphate and hexose. From phosphoglyceric acid, fatty acids and amino acids may be subsequently derived. ADP, NADP and phosphate are released for reincorporation into the cycle. In other plants the pathway to phosphoglyceric acid involves combination of carbon dioxide with the 3-carbon pyruvic acid to form the 4-carbon dicarboxylic acid oxaloacetic acid (with rapid interconversions with malic and aspartic acids). A carboxyl (COOH) group is transferred from oxaloacetic acid to an acceptor (possibly a 2 or 5-carbon sugar phosphate) forming phosphoglyceric acid. Thereafter hexose is formed by a series of reactions similar to those of the Calvin pathway.

Photosynthetic bacteria differ conspicuously from green plants in the source of hydrogen used in photosynthesis, being unable to use water and hence unable to produce oxygen. Most, in fact, are anaerobic. In the purple and green sulphur bacteria, hydrogen is derived from hydrogen sulphide and sulphur is a by-product. In the purple non-sulphur bacteria, organic compounds are used as hydrogen sources under anaerobic conditions, but some species, growing in the presence of oxygen and in darkness, use organic compounds as food directly, i.e. they behave as heterotrophs. See *Chloroplast, Chlorophyll.*

PHOTOTAXIS. Taxis (q.v.) in which stimulus is light.

PHOTOTROPHIC. Of organisms, recently internationally defined as obtaining energy from sunlight. Cf. *Autotrophic, Heterotrophic, Chemotrophic.*

PHOTOTROPISM (HELIOTROPISM). Tropism (q.v.) in which stimulus is light. E.g. bending of stems of indoor plants towards a window. Brought about by increased elongation of cells in growth region at tip of stem on shaded side. Generally accepted that effect is due to greater concentration of auxin (q.v.) on that side than on side facing light but some recent evidence suggests as the explanation asymmetric distribution of some cofactor that influences auxin effect.

PHRAGMOPLAST. In plant cells, equatorial region of the spindle between the two groups of chromosomes separating from one another at anaphase of mitosis. Across it at telophase, in equatorial plane, cell-plate (q.v.) develops.

PHYCOBILINS (BILIPROTEINS). Red (*phycoerythrin*) and blue (*phycocyanin*) pigments present with chlorophyll in red and blue-green algae. Like carotene (q.v.) assist in photosynthesis by transferring light energy that they absorb to chlorophyll. Proteins (globulins) combined with prosthetic pigment groups; structurally similar to bile pigments in animals.

PHYCOCYANIN. See *Phycobilins.*

PHYCOERYTHRIN. See *Phycobilins.*

PHYCOLOGY. Study of algae.

PHYCOMYCETES. A group of fungi (see *Mycophyta*).

PHYLLOCLADE. Cladode (q.v.).

PHYLLODE. Flattened, leaf-life petiole.

PHYLLOTAXY (PHYLLOTAXIS). Arrangement of leaves on stem, whorled, opposite, alternate or spiral. In spiral phyllotaxy a line connecting points of attachment of successive leaves forms a spiral. Position of leaves in spiral is regular. In most simple, truly alternate arrangement leaves are 180° apart and to pass from one leaf to that precisely above it involves one circuit of the stem and two leaves, a phyllotaxy of 1/2. Various forms of phyllotaxy occur, 1/3, 2/5, 3/8, 5/13, etc., each fraction representing angle made by successive leaves with stem (looking vertically downwards). At end of each spiral a leaf is directly above the one at the beginning. Looking down on a stem these points of superimposition are identified as vertical rows of leaves known as *orthostichies*. At growing point, though leaf primordia are spirally arranged, orthostichies do not

occur, but looking down at apex, primordia are arranged in a series
of descending curves or *parastichies*, some clockwise, others anticlockwise. Parastichy in an apex, may become orthostichy
in a mature shoot by straightening out of spirals during elongation.

PHYLOGENETIC (PHYLETIC). (Of relationship or classification),
based on closeness of evolutionary descent. Cf. *Phenetic*.

PHYLOGENY. Evolutionary history.

PHYLUM. One of the major kinds of group used in classifying animals,
e.g. phylum Chordata. Consists of one class or a number of similar
classes. Phylum is not often used in plant classification, the term
Division being substituted. See *Classification*.

PHYSIOLOGICAL SALINE. Solution of salts in water used for temporarily preserving cells alive. It must be isotonic (q.v.). The
simplest is isotonic sodium chloride (0.9 per cent for mammals), but
most cells cannot survive long in a solution of a single salt. A more
usual saline is therefore Ringer (q.v.) in which potassium, calcium
and magnesium chlorides are also present. For optimum survival,
Ringer must be buffered (q.v.) to the right $pH$, usually with
phosphates or bicarbonate. Salines do not provide the food requirements of cells (though some contain glucose) so survival in
them is limited.

PHYSIOLOGIC SPECIALIZATION (BIOLOGIC SPECIALIZATION).
Existence within a particular species of a number of genetically
different races or forms, which, though indistinguishable in
structure, show differences in physiological, biochemical, or pathogenic characters. Of great significance in pathology. E.g. where a
number of races of a plant pathogen exist, differing in their pathogenicity towards varieties of the host plant, the problem of breeding
a resistant variety is complicated, more so when new races, showing
new differences in pathogenicity, may continually be produced.
This is the case, e.g. with *Puccinia graminis tritici*, causing Black
Stem Rust of wheat, one of the most serious of all plant diseases.
More than 300 physiologic races of this fungus have so far been
demonstrated.

PHYSIOLOGY. Study of the processes which go on in living organisms.

PHYTOALEXINS. Non-specific fungitoxic substances, generally
phenolic in nature, synthesized de novo or in greatly increased
concentration by plants in response to infection by fungi. Believed
to play a primary role in disease resistance, preventing development in a particular plant of all but those fungi relatively insensi-
tive to the phytoalexin(s) produced and thus enabled to become
pathogenic to it.

PHYTOCHROME. Photoreversible, proteinaceous plant pigment,
present in very low concentration, energized by red light (wave
length c. 660 m$\mu$) to a chemically active form and functioning as
an enzyme to initiate reactions that profoundly affect plant growth,

e.g. germination, growth of roots, stems, and leaves, flowering, pigment formation, and other displays that are controlled by photoperiod. After activation by red light phytochrome is gradually lost and/or reconverted into the original, inactive form in darkness or, more quickly, in far-red light (wave length c. 730 m$\mu$). Relative amounts of red and far-red light determine amount of phytochrome activated and thus response of plant.

PHYTOGEOGRAPHY. Plant Geography (q.v.).

PHYTOKININS. Cytokinins (q.v.).

PHYTOPATHOLOGY. Study of plant diseases.

PHYTOPHAGOUS. Plant-eating.

PHYTOPLANKTON. Plants of plankton (q.v.). Cf. *Zooplankton*.

PHYTOSOCIOLOGY. Plant Sociology (q.v.).

PHYTOTRON. Building in which plants can be grown on a large scale in a range of rigidly controlled conditions – of light, temperature of air and soil, humidity and composition of air, water and nutrient content of soil, etc. Individual controlled environment chambers, a common feature of most botanical laboratories, provide more limited, small scale control of environment. Both types of facility can be of immense value in experimental investigations of plant growth.

PIA-ARACHNOID MEMBRANES. Delicate membranes ensheathing vertebrate central nervous system: *pia mater* immediately covering central nervous system, containing many blood-vessels; *arachnoid* outside that, in contact with dura mater (q.v.) and separated from pia by spaces filled with cerebrospinal fluid. See *Meninges*.

PIGEON'S MILK. Crop milk (q.v.).

PILEUS. Cap of mushroom type of fungus fruit-body, bearing the hymenium on its under surface.

PILI. Hair-like appendages present at times on cells of many bacteria, sometimes more than one kind per cell, revealed by electron microscopy. Majority much thinner than flagella. Composed of protein subunits helically arranged around a hollow core. Cause cells to stick together. Shown to be associated with conjugation in some bacteria.

PILIFEROUS LAYER. That part of the epidermis of a root which bears root-hairs. Extends from near the root tip (behind zone of active cell division) backwards for varying distance depending on species.

PINEAL APPARATUS. Primitively consists of two outgrowths of roof of fore brain lying within skull, one behind the other (though may represent right and left of a pair). Anterior is *parietal organ* which forms an eye-like structure (*pineal eye*, q.v.) in some lizards and *Sphenodon*, a vestigial eye in lamprey (Cyclostomata), and is reduced or absent in other vertebrates. Posterior forms a second, functional eye-like structure in lamprey, and the glandular *pineal body* (q.v.) or *epiphysis* of other vertebrates.

PINEAL BODY (EPIPHYSIS). See *Pineal apparatus*. Its function is un-known, but often assumed to secrete a hormone concerned with colour-change; and *melatonin*, which strongly concentrates pigment within melanophores, lightening colour, can be extracted from pineal body.

PINEAL EYE. See *Pineal apparatus*. Pineal eye is a vesicle, formed as diverticulum of brain. In most complete form outer layer of vesicle becomes a lens (unlike vertebrate paired eyes, see *Lens*), inner layer a retina connected by nerve to brain. There is a gap in skull above the eye, and skin covering is almost transparent. Nerve however usually degenerates in adult reptile, though not in lam-prey. Function unknown.

PINNA. (1) Leaflet, primary division of a leaf. (2) See *Ear, outer*.

PINNIPEDIA. Seals, walruses, etc. Specialized aquatic branch of the order Carnivora of placental mammals.

PINOCYTOSIS. Ingestion of surrounding fluid by cell. Local invagina-tion of plasma membrane completely surrounds minute drop of fluid, which is thus engulfed by cytoplasm, forming a vesicle.

PISCES. Fish. Formerly regarded as a single class of vertebrates, are now resolved into (usually) five distinct classes; Placodermi, Acanthodii, Chondrichthyes, Actinopterygii, Choanichthyes. The latter two are united by some zoologists as the Osteichthyes.

PISTIL. (Bot.) (1) Each separate carpel of an apocarpous gynoecium. (2) The gynoecium as a whole whether it is apocarpous or syn-carpous.

PISTILLATE. (Of flowers), possessing carpels but not stamens; i.e. female. Cf. *Staminate*.

PITH. See *Medulla*.

PITHECANTHROPUS. Java ape-man. Lower Pleistocene. Brain of human type but small; walked erect; ape-like in heavy brow ridges and absence of chin prominence. See *Sinanthropus*.

PITHECOIDEA. Anthropoidea (q.v.).

PITRESSIN. Extract of posterior lobe of pituitary, causing when in-jected constriction of capillaries and arterioles (which raises arterial pressure); and diminished urine formation (see *Anti-diuretic hormone*).

PITS. Small, sharply defined areas in walls of plant cells that remain thin while rest of wall becomes thickened; appear as depressions in wall. Coincide in position with pits in walls of adjacent cells and separated from them by pit membrane consisting of middle lam-ella and a very thin layer of primary wall material on either side. *Simple* pits, as described, occur in living cells and through them pass strands of cytoplasm, the *plasmodesmata* connecting one cell with another. Simple pits also occur in stone cells and some fibres. In *bordered* pits, characteristic of xylem vessels and tracheids, the pit cavity is partly enclosed by over-arching of the cell wall and the pit membrane may possess a central, thickened impermeable area (*torus*), which closes aperture of pit if pit membrane is laterally displaced.

PITUITARY BODY (P. GLAND, HYPOPHYSIS CEREBRI). Endocrine gland beneath floor of brain, within skull, of vertebrates. Secretes a number of hormones (9 identified with fair reliability), all proteins or glycoproteins. Has two main components: the *neurohypophysis* (*pars nervosa*), embryologically derived from the brain (see Infundibulum); and the *adenohypophysis* (*pars distalis* and *pars intermedia*), embryologically derived from the hypophysis (q.v.) in the narrow sense. The term *anterior pituitary* or *anterior lobe* means the pars distalis; the term *posterior pituitary* or *posterior lobe* means the pars nervosa often plus the pars intermedia, these two parts being closely fused. The pars nervosa secretes oxytocin and antidiuretic hormone (ADH); these hormones are formed in neurones of the hypothalamus (q.v.) and passed down axons into the pars nervosa where they are stored. The pars distalis produces 6 hormones: follicle-stimulating, luteinizing, lactogenic, ACTH, thyrotropic and growth hormone (somatotropic hormone, STH); its activities are influenced by hormones from the hypothalamus. The pars intermedia (absent in birds and some mammals) produces intermedin, concerned with changing skin colour in fish, amphibia and reptiles.

PLACENTA. (Bot.). Part of ovary wall (fused margins of carpel(s)) on which ovules are borne. (Zool.). Organ, consisting of embryonic and maternal tissues in close union, by which embryo of viviparous animal is nourished. In placental mammals the embryonic tissue

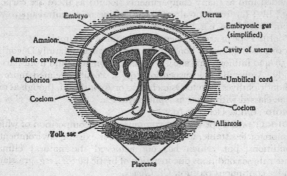

*Fig. 8. Diagrammatic section through foetus of a mammal in the uterus, showing relation to placenta, and extra-embryonic membranes. Mesoderm stippled. Arrangement of extra-embryonic membranes is fundamentally the same in all amniotes; though relative size of allantois and yolk-sac vary, and in birds and reptiles placenta is absent, and chorion is enclosed by albumen and shell instead of by uterus.*

concerned is the chorion, with blood vessels supplied via allantois or occasionally via yolk-sac. In ungulates the trophoblast of the chorion merely fits closely against endometrium of uterus; but in most mammals the endometrium becomes much altered (decidua, q.v.) and in parts eroded, so that the trophoblast is in contact with maternal blood-vessels (carnivores) or maternal blood (other mammals including man). There is exchange of small molecules through the trophoblast between maternal and embryonic blood in the mammalian placenta; oxygen and food-substances enter the embryo, urea and carbon dioxide leave it. Only minute amounts of proteins are exchanged. The placenta produces hormones (gonadotropic, oestrogen, progesterone) which keeps uterus adapted to the pregnancy. At birth the umbilical cord (q.v.), which connects placenta to embryo, is broken, and the placenta is discharged from the uterus after the embryo. See Fig. 8.

PLACENTALIA (EUTHERIA, PLACENTAL MAMMALS). A sub-class of Mammalia, containing the great majority of living mammals. Characteristic of placentals is that the embryo develops in the maternal uterus, attached to the maternal tissues by a highly organized placenta. The cerebral cortex is larger and more complex than in the other mammals.

PLACENTATION. (Bot.). Type of arrangement of placentas in a syncarpous ovary; (a) parietal; carpels are fused only by their margins, placentas then appearing as internal ridges on ovary wall, e.g. violet; (b) axile; margins of carpels fold inwards, fusing together in centre of ovary to form a single, central placenta. Ovary is divided into as many compartments (loculi) as there are carpels, e.g., lily; (c) free central; placenta arising as a central upgrowth from ovary base, e.g. primrose.
(Zool.). Type of arrangement of placenta in mammals.

PLACODERMI. Group of bony fish entirely fossil and mainly Devonian (350–400 million years ago). Bony shields on head and front part of body. Autostylic jaw suspension (q.v.). Possibly related more to Chondrichthyes than to Osteichthyes or Acanthodii, though at one time classed with latter as Aphetohyoidea.

PLACOID SCALE. Denticle (q.v.).

PLAGIOCLIMAX. Type of plant community the composition of which is more or less stable, in equilibrium under existing environmental conditions, but which has not achieved the natural climax under those conditions due to action of biotic factors, e.g. grassland under continuous pasture. Cf. *Climax.*

PLAGIOGEOTROPISM. Orientation of plant part by growth curvature in response to stimulus of gravity so that its axis makes an angle other than a right-angle with the line of gravitational force; exhibited, e.g. by branches of a main root which make an acute angle with the vertical. Also used in a wider sense to mean orientation of an organ so that its axis makes a constant angle with the vertical and including diageotropism (q.v.) as a special type. See *Geotropism*.

PLAGIOSERE. Succession (q.v.) of plants deflected into a new course by biotic factor or factors. Cf. *Prisere*.

PLANKTON. Animals and plants of sea or lake which float or drift almost passively. They are mostly very small; the smallest are *nannoplankton*, e.g. diatoms. Plankton occurs mainly near the surface, where the plants get suitable illumination. Of great ecological and economic importance, providing food for fish and whales.

PLANONT (PLANOSPORE). Zoospore (q.v.).

PLANT GEOGRAPHY (PHYTOGEOGRAPHY). Study of ranges of plants over the earth and of the causes, present and past, underlying their characteristic distributions. Closely allied to ecology but broader in concept, concerned also with aspects of genetics, taxonomy, evolution, palaeontology, geology.

PLANTIGRADE. Walking on ventral surface of whole foot, i.e. of metacarpus or metatarsus and of digits (cf. *Digitigrade, Unguligrade*). E.g. man is plantigrade.

PLANT SOCIOLOGY (PHYTOSOCIOLOGY). Study of plant communities that make up vegetation, their origin, formation, composition and structure.

PLAQUE. Clear zone in a bacterial culture on an agar plate caused by localized destruction of bacterial cells by activity of bacteriophage (q.v.). Similarly applied to zone of lysis by virus in tissue culture of animal cells. Counting plaques provides simple technique for estimating concentration of infective virus in a fluid applied to the culture.

PLASMA. Blood plasma (q.v.). Applied also to lymph minus its cells.

PLASMA CELL. Vertebrate cell, with basophilic cytoplasm due to extensive endoplasmic reticulum, which is believed to synthesize antibody.

PLASMAGEL. See *Ectoplasm*.

PLASMAGENE. Particle in cytoplasm having the properties of a gene in that it is self-reproducing, shows inheritance from cell to daughter-cell, and affects the character of the cell bearing it; but unlike a gene in that it is not inherited in mendelian fashion through the gametes.

PLASMALEMMA. Plasma-membrane (external plasma membrane in plants).

PLASMA-MEMBRANE (CELL-MEMBRANE). Extremely thin membrane (about one-hundredth micrometre thick) mainly of fat and protein covering surface of all cells (or protoplast in plants). Responsible for restricted penetration of many substances into interior of cell and in the reverse direction (see *Permeability*). Severe damage to membrane at once destroys cell. In plants plasma-membranes occur both at outer surface of protoplast (external, ectoplast, plasmalemma) surrounded by cell wall, and bordering vacuole (internal, tonoplast).

PLASMA PROTEINS. Dissolved proteins of vertebrate blood plasma (about seven per cent of weight of human blood) which are responsible for holding fluid in blood-vessels by osmosis (see *Capillary*). To them is due the value of transfusion of plasma in increasing the volume of circulating blood. Amongst plasma proteins are antibodies and blood-clotting (q.v.) substances.

PLASMASOL. See *Endoplasm*.

PLASMID. See *Episome*.

PLASMODESMATA. Extremely fine cytoplasmic threads one to few tenths of a micrometre wide passing through walls of living plant cells and connecting cytoplasm of adjacent cells; may be scattered, or grouped in membranes of pits (q.v.). See *Cell-wall*.

PLASMODIUM. (1) Vegetative stage of slime-fungi (Myxomycophyta, q.v.). Multinucleate, amoeboid mass of protoplasm bounded by plasma membrane, without a definite size or shape. Cf. *Coenocyte*, *Syncytium*. (2) Generic name of malaria parasite, a Sporozoan.

PLASMOLYSIS. (Bot.). Shrinkage of cell protoplasm away from its cellulose wall when placed in hypertonic (q.v.) solutions, due to osmotic withdrawal of water from its large central vacuole.

PLASMON. The total complement of extra-chromosomal hereditary factors (plasmagenes, q.v.) in a cell.

PLASTACHRON. Time interval between two of a series of periodic events, e.g. development of leaf primordia, in plant growth.

PLASTIDS. Small, variously shaped bodies in cytoplasm of plant cells (excluding bacteria, blue-green algae, fungi, slime-fungi), one to many per cell in different plants, containing pigments and/or reserve food materials. Develop from *pro-plastids* (q.v.). Some contain pigments chlorophyll, carotenoids, some are centres of accumulation of starch, proteins, oils. Comprise colourless *leucoplasts* (q.v.) and pigmented *chromoplasts* (q.v.) including *chloroplasts* (q.v.).

PLASTOGENE. Plastid (q.v.) carrying a factor having properties of a gene (q.v.) but, unlike a gene, not inherited in mendelian fashion. A plasmagene (q.v.).

PLATELET. Blood platelet (q.v.).

PLATYHELMINTHES (FLATWORMS). Phylum containing eddy-worms, flukes, tapeworms. Resemble coelenterates in that the gut, when present, has only one opening, and there is no coelom, nor blood system; but differ in that they are bilaterally, not radially, symmetrical; have bulky parenchymatous tissue derived from the mesoderm; flame cells; and a very complex hermaphrodite reproductive system. Includes classes Turbellaria, Trematoda, Cestoda; some parasites of great economic and medical importance.

PLATYRRHINES. The New World monkeys, members of group

Platyrrhini (order Primates). Characterized by broad nasal septum. Often have prehensile tails. E.g. marmoset, howler. See *Catarrhine*.

PLECTOPTERA. Stone-flies. Small order of exopterygote insects with aquatic nymphs.

PLECTENCHYMA. Tissue of fungal hyphae. Of two types, *prosenchyma*, in which component hyphae, loosely woven, can be recognized as such and *pseudoparenchyma*, consisting of closely packed cells, no longer distinguishable as hyphae, resembling parenchyma (q.v.) of higher plants.

PLEIOMORPHISM (PLEOMORPHISM). Occurrence in a number of different forms; e.g. in life cycle, as in the succession of different spore forms in the life cycle of rust fungi. Cf. *Polymorphism*.

PLEIOTROPIC. (Of a gene), affecting more than one characteristic in the phenotype.

PLEISTOCENE. Geological epoch (q.v.); lasted approximately from one and a half million till ten thousand years ago. During it four major ice ages occurred. Succeeded by Recent epoch.

PLEROCERCOID. Larva of certain tapeworms in which there is no bladder, the body being solid (cf. *Cysticercus*, *Cysticercoid*). See *Onchosphere*.

PLEROME. See *Apical meristem*.

PLESIOSAURIA. A fossil order of Reptilia; lived during Jurassic and Cretaceous. Marine; swam by large paddle-like limbs; long neck, short tail; up to 50 ft in total length.

PLEURA. Serous membrane lining pleural sac, and covering surface of lung, in mammals.

PLEURAL CAVITY (P. SAC). Coelomic space surrounding lung in mammal, separated from rest of perivisceral coelom by diaphragm. There is a pair of pleural sacs separated from each other by mediastinum and pericardial sac. Actual space of sac is normally a thin layer of fluid between pleura of lungs and body-wall, which are almost in contact.

PLIOCENE. Geological epoch (q.v.), sub-division of Tertiary, lasted approximately from seven till one and a half million years ago.

PLUMULE. (Zool.). Down feather. Temporary feather of nestling bird, persisting in some adult birds between contour feathers. No barbules (q.v.). (Bot.). Terminal bud of well-differentiated embryos in seed plants.

PLUTEUS. Larva of echinoid or ophiuroid; ciliated, planktonic.

PNEUMATOPHORE. Special root branch produced in large numbers by some vascular plants growing in water or in tidal swamps, e.g. mangrove; grows erect, projecting into the air above and contains well developed intercellular system of air spaces in communication with atmosphere through pores on aerial portion.

PNEUMOGASTRIC NERVE. Vagus nerve (q.v.).

PODIA. Tube-feet (q.v.).

POIKILOTHERMIC. 'Cold-blooded', but actually with varying body temperature, which approximately follows that of surroundings. Cf. *Homoiothermic*. Characteristic of all animals except birds and mammals. Aquatic poikilotherms keep very close to temperature of surrounding water. Terrestrial ones may differ considerably from surrounding air, either cooling by evaporation, or heating by sun's radiation or muscular exercise.

POLAR. (Of bacterial flagella) arising at one or both ends of cell. Cf. *Peritrichous*.

POLAR BODY (POLOCYTE). Minute cell produced during development of oocyte (q.v.) containing one of the nuclei derived from first or second division of meiosis (q.v.) but practically no cytoplasm.

POLARITY (POLAR BEHAVIOUR). Differentiation, morphological or physiological, or both, between the two ends of an axis, e.g. shoot and root, head and tail. Characteristic of most organisms, unicellular and multicellular, and of many cells within organisms.

POLLEN. Microspores of seed plants (Gymnospermae and Angiospermae) each containing a greatly reduced male gametophyte. Carried by wind or insects, or more rarely by water, to ovules (Gymnospermae) or to the stigmas of the carpel (Angiospermae), where they germinate with production of pollen tubes carrying male nuclei to eggs within ovules.

POLLEN ANALYSIS (PALYNOLOGY). Method of reconstructing floras of the past based on observations on pollen grains (and other spores) preserved in ancient peat and sedimentary deposits. The resistance to decay of the outer coats of pollen grains with their distinctive sculpturing makes possible both qualitative and quantitative estimates of species occurring thousands of years ago.

POLLEN TUBE. Tube formed on germination of pollen grain that carries male gametes to egg. In flowering plants each pollen tube penetrates tissues of stigma and style into ovary. After entering ovary pollen tube grows towards an ovule, passing down micropyle to nucellus and finally penetrating nucellus tissues into embryo sac where it ruptures at the tip, setting free two male gametes one of which fuses with egg nucleus. The second male nucleus fuses with the central fusion nucleus; the resulting nucleus is known as the endosperm nucleus and from it arises endosperm.

POLLEX. 'Thumb' of pentadactyl fore-limb. The lateral digit on side of fore-foot corresponding to the radius. Often shorter than other digits.

POLLINATION. Transference of pollen from anther to stigma. See *Anemophily*, *Entomophily*.

POLLINIUM. Coherent mass of pollen grains, as in orchids.

POLOCYTE. Polar body (q.v.).

POLYADELPHOUS. (Of stamens), united by their stalks (filaments) into several groups, e.g. St John's Wort. Cf. *Monadelphous, Diadelphous*.

POLYCHAETA. Order of annelids (class Chaetopoda) including bristleworms, tube-worms, fan-worms. Marine; chaetae numerous, borne on projections of body (parapodia); usually well-marked head with special appendages; unisexual; fertilization external. Cf. *Oligochaeta*.

POLYDACTYLOUS. Having more than the normal number of digits.

POLYEMBRYONY. (Bot.) Formation of more than one embryo per ovule, often by vegetative budding from pro-embryo (q v.). (Zool.). Formation of more than one embryo per zygote by fission at some early stage of development. E.g. an armadillo (*Dasypodus*) always has identical quads from a single ovum. Most striking cases are in parasitic Hymenoptera, where up to 2,000 embryos may spring from one zygote. Monozygotic twins (q.v.) are the simplest form of polyembryony.

POLYGENES (MULTIPLE FACTORS). Genes with individually a very small effect on phenotype differences, systems of which are associated in producing quantitative variation of particular characters, e.g. stature. Quantitative variation is also environmentally produced. See *Quantitative Inheritance*.

POLYMORPH (POLYMORPHONUCLEAR LEUCOCYTE, GRANULO-CYTE). Kind of white blood cell of vertebrates. 7–9 micrometres diameter in man, with darkly staining nucleus constricted into a number of lobes (lobation of nucleus may be absent in some vertebrates). Cytoplasm usually contains conspicuous granulations, which are the equivalent of large lysosomes (q.v.). Polymorphs form 65–75 per cent of white blood cells in man. Actively phagocytic especially when, in inflammation (q.v.), they invade the tissues. Produced continually in bone marrow (myeloid tissue, q.v.) each polymorph having only a short life. In man, granulations of most polymorphs (neutrophils) stain preferentially with neither acid nor basic dyes, those of some (eosinophils, q.v.) stain strongly with acid dyes, those of a few (basophils) with basic dyes.

POLYMORPHISM. Having several different forms. Particularly used of distinct kinds of individual belonging to one species, occurring in fairly constant proportions within a freely interbreeding population. E.g. within some species of butterfly there co-exist individuals which mimic other species and individuals which do not; another example is human blood groups. Dimorphism of the two sexes is exactly analogous. The different types are commonly controlled by different genes of one allelomorphic set. Insect castes (q.v.) are a special case of polymorphism. Cf. *Pleiomorphism*.

POLYP (HYDRANTH). Sedentary form of coelenterate, e.g. *Hydra*, sea-anemone. Cylindrical trunk, fixed at one end; mouth at other end, surrounded by ring of tentacles. Many polyps reproduce themselves by budding, and may form colonies. Some reproduce sexually, fertilized eggs giving rise to new polyps (*Hydra*, sea-anemone). Others do not produce sexually, but produce medusae (q.v.) by budding and these reproduce sexually, their fertilized eggs giving rise to new polyps (e.g. hydroids; jelly-fish).

POLYPEPTIDE. Peptide (q.v.) formed of three or more amino-acids.

POLYPETALOUS. (Of flower), with petals free from one another, e.g. buttercup. Cf. *Gamopetalous.*

POLYPHYLETIC. A group of species classified together is polyphyletic when some of its members have had quite distinct evolutionary histories, not being descended from a common ancestor which was also a member of the group; so that, if the classification is to correspond with phylogeny, the group should be broken up into several distinct groups. E.g. phylum Polyzoa is generally regarded as being polyphyletic and is therefore better split into two phyla Endoprocta and Ectoprocta. Cf. *Monophyletic.*

POLYPIDE. Member of a colony of Polyzoa.

POLYPLOID. Having three or more times the haploid number of chromosomes. Polyploid individuals, sub-species and species are fairly common in plants (especially angiosperms) but rare in animals. This is mainly because polyploid organisms are sterile when crossed with diploids, and a polyploid suddenly arising in a diploid population can therefore only reproduce vegetatively, parthenogenetically, or by self-fertilization. These ways are commonly open to plants, but not commonly to animals. See *Allotetraploid.* Polyploid cells and tissues occur in otherwise diploid organisms (see *Endomitosis*).

POLYPTERUS. Primitive actinopterygian fish of tropical Africa, with well developed lungs and ganoid scales.

POLYRIBOSOME. See *Ribosome.*

POLYSACCHARIDE. Carbohydrate produced by combination of many molecules of monosaccharide; e.g. starch, cellulose. Some kinds, e.g. chitin, have other constituents besides such simple sugars. Large, often fibrous, molecules. Important structural and reserve energy-rich material in organisms.

POLYSEPALOUS. (Of a flower), with sepals free one from another, e.g. buttercup. Cf. *Gamosepalous.*

POLYSOME. See *Ribosome.*

POLYSPERMY. Penetration of numerous sperm into one ovum at time of fertilization. Occurs normally in very yolky eggs (e.g. shark, bird); only one sperm nucleus fuses with egg nucleus, the rest taking little further part in development. May occur abnormally in other eggs, upsetting development.

POLYTENE. (Of a chromosome), consisting of many parallel identical chromatids, through repeated duplication without division, the chromatids remaining exactly paired. Salivary gland chromosomes (q.v.) are polytene.

POLYTHETIC. (Of classification), system in which membership

of taxon is based on possession of large number of common characters.

POLYTOPIC. (Of a taxon), occurring in two or more separate areas.

POLYZOA (BRYOZOA). Sea-mats, corallines. Phylum of small, aquatic, usually fixed and colonial animals, superficially resembling hydroid coelenterates but considerably more complex. Have ciliated tentacles with which they feed; anus; coelom; some have horny or calcareous skeletons. Contains two classes, Ectoprocta and Endoprocta, which are usually regarded as distinct phyla.

POME. False 'fruit' greater part of which is developed from receptacle of flower, not from ovary; e.g. apple, edible, fleshy part representing receptacle and the core, ovary.

POPULATION CYCLE. Rise and fall of population numbers with regular periodicity. E.g. the 10-year cycle of the snowshoe rabbit and other mammals and birds of N. America.

PORIFERA. Sponges. Non-mobile animals consisting of many cells but built on a different plan from the Metazoa; hence grouped separately from all other multicellular animals as Parazoa. They have for instance, no nervous system, and possess collar cells (choanocytes, q.v.) which are found otherwise only in a certain group of flagellates, the choanoflagellates, from which sponges have probably evolved. Currents of water are drawn into the body through small pores (ostia) and passed out through larger pores (oscula), food particles being collected en route. In most sponges the body is supported by skeleton of lime, silica, or spongin (a collagen-like protein).

PORTAL VEIN. Vein carrying blood from one capillary network to another. (See *Hepatic portal system*, *Renal portal system*).

POSITION EFFECT. Influence, on characters produced by a given gene, of change of its position in the chromosomes relative to other genes (e.g. by translocation).

POSTCAVAL VEIN. Vena Cava Inferior (q.v.).

POSTERIOR. (Bot.). Of lateral flowers, part nearest the main axis. See *Floral diagram*. (Zool.). Situated at or relatively nearer to the hind end, i.e. usually the end directed backwards when the animal is in motion. (In human anatomy, the posterior side is the back, which is equivalent to *dorsal* side of other mammals.)

POSTERIOR ROOT. Nerve-root, synonymous with dorsal root (q.v.).

PRECAVAL VEIN. Vena Cava Superior (q.v.).

PRECIPITIN REACTION. *In vitro* reaction between solutions of antigen and antibody (q.v.), with formation of a precipitate. Important technique in diagnosis of human pathogens and plant pathogenic viruses and the basis for serological identification of microorganisms in general.

PREDATOR. Animal that feeds on other animals, i.e. is a secondary consumer (see *Food-chain*); but not including a parasite.

PREFORMATION. Hypothetical pre-existence of entire adult diversity of structure in the fertilized egg; embryonic development supposedly consisting merely of enlargement and manifestation of this structure. Cf. *Epigenesis.*

PREMAXILLA. Dermal bone forming front part of upper jaw in most vertebrates, bearing teeth (incisors in mammals). Forms most of upper beak in birds.

PREMOLARS. Those crushing cheek teeth of mammals which (unlike molars) have predecessors in deciduous (milk) set of teeth. They have usually more than one root, and a pattern of ridges and projections on biting surface. (See *Dental Formula.*)

PRESUMPTIVE. (Zool.). Embryological term applied to tissues before their differentiation, meaning 'becoming in the course of normal development'. E.g. if a tissue is 'presumptive epidermis' it means that in normal development it would become epidermis, regardless of whether or not it is already determined (q.v.) as epidermis. A *presumptive region* is part of an embryo consisting of all the cells which will, in normal development, become a particular organ or tissue. Maps of presumptive regions have been prepared for early stages of many species.

PRIMARY MERISTEM. Region of active cell division, that has persisted from origin in embryo or young plant, e.g. growing points (apical meristems) of root and stem, cambium. Cf. *Secondary Meristem.*

PRIMARY PRODUCTION. The total amount of organic material synthesized in a given time by the autotrophic organisms of an ecosystem. See Productivity.

PRIMATE. A member of the Primates, an order of placental mammals, containing man, apes, and monkeys. A primarily arboreal order, rather primitive in structure. Usually climb by grasping; nails commonly present instead of claws, and big toe and often thumb usually well-developed and opposable to other digits. Tree-life has also involved particularly well-developed eye-sight, often with binocular vision (see *Fovea*). Relatively large brain. First appear at beginning of Tertiary. Includes three sub-orders, Lemuroidea, Tarsioidea, and Anthropoidea.

PRIMITIVE. At an early stage in the evolutionary history of a given group; or similar to an organism (or part thereof) at such an early stage.

PRIMITIVE STREAK. Longitudinal thickening in disc-like early embryo of bird or mammal during the stage of gastrulation (q.v.). The streak is produced by the accumulation of mesoderm as this material moves from its originally superficial position into the interior of the embryo. See *Blastopore.*

PRIMORDIAL GERM CELLS. Large cells in vertebrates, appearing early in embryonic life, which migrate to the developing gonads and there give rise to the gametes.

PRIMORDIAL MERISTEM. Promeristem (q.v.).

PRISERE. Primary sere. Complete, natural succession of plants, from bare habitat to climax. Cf. *Plagiosere*.

PROBOSCIDEA. Elephants. An order of placental mammals, modern ones characterized by proboscis (trunk), large size, pillar-like legs, greatly lengthened incisors (tusks), and huge grinding molars only two pairs of which are in use at one time.

PROCAMBIUM. Tissue of elongated, narrow cells grouped into strands, differentiated in the plerome just behind growing point in stem and root of vascular plants; gives rise by further development to vascular tissue.

PROCARYOTIC (PROKARYOTIC). (Of cells or organisms), having the genetic material in the form of simple filaments of DNA (see *Chromosome*), and not separated from the cytoplasm by a nuclear membrane. The cells of bacteria and of blue-green algae are of this type, distinguishing these organisms sharply from all others (cf. *Eucaryotic*).

In one bacterium, *Escherichia coli*, the DNA consists of a single thread, when straightened out many times longer than the cell diameter, in the form of a closed loop. Division of the DNA during cell division is not by means of a spindle as in the mitosis of eucaryotic cells. Mitochondria and chloroplasts, the membrane-bounded organelles associated in other organisms with respiration and photosynthesis, are lacking. In swimming forms (which occur only in bacteria) organs of locomotion are either flagella, much simpler than those of eucaryotic cells, consisting of a single fibril; or, in spirochaetes, consist of a bundle of fibrils, the axial filament, that is wound round the cell protoplast and embedded in the cytoplasm at each end. Cell wall of procaryotic organisms is unique in containing *mureins*, distinctive polymers composed of certain amino acids and carbohydrates.

PROCHORDATA. Protochordata (q.v.).

PROCTODAEUM. An intucking of ectoderm of embryo meeting endoderm of posterior end of gut, forming anus or cloacal opening.

PRODUCTIVITY. (Of an ecosystem), primary productivity is the rate at which energy from light is absorbed and utilized with carbon dioxide in the production of organic matter in photosynthesis. Net productivity is given by the amount of organic matter formed in excess of that used in respiration. It represents food potentially available to the consumers of the ecosystem (q.v.). It can be measured approximately by sampling vegetation at intervals and measuring the dry weight produced per unit area; or on a small scale in appropriate conditions by measuring rates of photosynthesis and respiration of whole plants or of small areas of vegetation.

PRO-EMBRYO. In seed plants, group of cells formed by initial divisions of fertilized egg-cell which by further development is differentiated into suspensor and embryo proper.

PROGESTERONE. Hormone (a steroid) secreted by corpus luteum (q.v.) of mammalian ovary, responsible for preparing reproductive organs for pregnancy, in luteal phase of oestrous cycle (q.v.); and for maintaining uterus in special state for nourishment and protection of embryo during pregnancy, when it is also produced by placenta.

PROGESTOGEN. General term for substance with progesterone-like effects.

PROGLOTTIS (plural PROGLOTTIDES). One of the string of segments of which a tapeworm consists; when mature each has at least one set of reproductive organs.

PROLACTIN. Lactogenic hormone (q.v.).

PROLEGS. Stumpy appendages with no joints, on ventral surface of abdomen of caterpillar.

PROLIFERATION. Growth by active cell-division.

PROMERISTEM. Extreme tip of apical meristem (q.v.) consisting of actively dividing cells which have not yet begun to show morphological differentiation.

PRONATION. Position, or rotation towards the position, of fore-limb such that fore-foot (hand) is twisted through 90 degrees relative to elbow, the radius and ulna being crossed. Men and other primates can untwist the fore-arm (*supination*).

PRONEPHROS. The first part of kidney of vertebrates to arise in embryonic development. It appears at border of somites and lateral plate, just behind heart, as a number (varying according to species) of nephrons (q.v.) segmentally arranged (i.e. one per somite). Commonly the nephrons communicate with the coelom, and they join a tube (*pronephric duct*) which grows back from their neighbourhood to the cloaca, putting coelom into communication with exterior (see *Coelomoduct*). It is the functional kidney of larvae of anmniotes (e.g. tadpole); but small and non-functional in those without larvae (e.g. elasmobranchs) and vestigial in amniotes. Its duct becomes Wolffian duct (q.v.). See *Mesonephros, Metanephros*.

PRONUCLEUS. Sperm nucleus (male pronucleus) after its entry into ovum at fertilization, but before fusion with ovum nucleus; or ovum nucleus (female pronucleus) after completion of meiosis but before fusion with sperm nucleus. Pronuclei are haploid.

PROPAGULE. (Bot.). Any part of a plant capable of growing into a new organism; e.g. spore, seed, gemma, cutting.

PROPHAGE. Bacteriophage DNA when it is associated with the DNA of its host bacterium, and is reproduced as part of its host DNA through many generations of bacteria. See *Lysogeny*.

PROPHASE. Initial stage of mitosis (q.v.) or meiosis (q.v.) during which chromosomes appear within the nucleus, and in meiosis undergo pairing. See Figs. 6A, 6B, pp. 180, 181.

PRO-PLASTIDS. Immature, colourless plastids occurring in cells of meristematic tissues. Consist of a double membrane enclosing granular stroma. Multiply by division. Give rise in mature cells to *leucoplasts* (q.v.) or *chromoplasts* (q.v.).

PROPRIOCEPTOR. (1) Receptor (q.v.) which detects position and movement, e.g. kinaesthetic receptors such as those of muscle of vertebrates and skeleton of insects recording passive stretch, or contraction; or balancing organs of internal ear. Usually do not show sensory adaptation. Cf. *Interoceptor*. (2) In wider sense, receptor which detects changes within the body other than those caused by substances taken into gut or respiratory tract; including, e.g. deep pain receptors, and receptors detecting pressure in blood-vessels, as well as those included under (1).

PROSENCEPHALON. Fore-brain (q.v.).

PROSENCHYMA. See *Plectenchyma*.

PROSTATE GLAND. Gland of male reproductive system of mammals which contributes substances to semen, of unknown function. Its size and secretory powers are controlled by androgens.

PROSTHETIC GROUP. Non-protein substance when it is combined with a protein, e.g. nucleic acid in nucleo-protein.

PROTANDROUS. (Of flowers), anthers maturing before carpels, e.g. dandelion. See *Dichogamy*. (Of animals), producing first sperm, and then eggs, e.g. certain roundworms. Cf. *Protogynous*.

PROTEASE. See *Proteolytic enzyme*.

PROTEIN. Very complex organic compound, composed of numerous amino-acids (q.v.). Proteins of innumerably many different kinds are present in all living things, making a considerable proportion of their dry weight. A protein molecule is made of hundreds or thousands of amino-acid molecules joined together by peptide links (q.v.) into one or more chains, which are variously folded. There are 20 different kinds of amino-acid commonly found in proteins, and most of these usually occur in any one protein molecule; they are arranged in the chain in a sequence which is exactly the same in all molecules of a given kind of protein. The possible different arrangements of the amino-acids are evidently practically infinite, and the diversity is fully exploited by living things, every species having kinds of protein molecule peculiar to itself. A protein molecule is very large (most have a molecular weight from about 20,000 up to several million), and dissolved proteins form therefore colloidal solutions. Proteins are not soluble in fat solvents. Many are soluble in water or dilute salt solutions (e.g. globulins); others, with elongated (*fibrous*) molecules, are insoluble in these solvents (e.g. scleroproteins, myosin). Proteins are synthesized from amino-acids by all living things; the precise sequence of the amino-acids being determined by the sequence of nucleotides in nucleic acids. Only autotrophic organisms make them from inorganic substances. They are destroyed by proteolytic enzymes (q.v.) (see *Peptone, Polypeptide*). Proteins are frequently combined with other substances, especially nucleic acid (nucleo-proteins), carbohydrates (muco- or glycoproteins), fats (lipoproteins).

PROTEINASE (ENDOPEPTIDASE). See *Peptidase*.

PROTEOLYTIC ENZYME. Any enzyme taking part in breaking down of proteins. A system of several peptidases (q.v.) is necessary to break proteins down to constituent amino acids; and such frequently occurs, e.g. in plant and animal cells (see *Cathepsin*), and in plant seeds and animal digestive juices.

PROTHALLUS. Independent, gametophyte plant of Pteridophyta (ferns and related plants). Small, green parenchymatous thallus bearing antheridia and archegonia; shows little differentiation. Usually prostrate on soil surface attached by rhizoids; may be subterranean, mycotrophic.

PROTHORAX. Most anterior of the three segments which make up insect thorax. Bears a pair of walking-legs, but no wings.

PROTHROMBIN. See *Blood clotting*.

PROTISTA. Group (Kingdom) originally proposed for all unicellular organisms. More recently enlarged to include all organisms of simple biological organization, unicellular, coenocytic or multicellular, and including algae, bacteria, fungi, slime-fungi and protozoa.

PROTOCHORDATA (PROCHORDATA). Term sometimes applied to a heterogeneous group of animals of phylum Chordata, related to the vertebrates, which they resemble in possessing gill slits, notochord, and dorsal hollow nerve cord, or at least traces of these. Includes Acrania, a group consisting of various species of amphioxus, a small animal which looks fish-like, but has no skeleton, brain, or eyes; Urochordata (sea-squirts, etc.), which in the adult form have little resemblance to vertebrates: and Hemichordata (e.g. *Balanoglossus*) worm-like forms whose vertebrate affinities are much more remote.

PROTOGYNOUS. (Of flowers), carpels maturing before anthers, e.g. plaintain. See *Dichogamy*. (Of individual animals), producing first eggs, and then sperms. Cf. *Protandrous*.

PROTONEMA. Branched, multicellular, filamentous or less commonly thalloid structure produced on germination of spore in members of Bryophyta from which new plants develop as buds.

PROTONEPHRIDIUM. Organ thought to be excretory, present in Platyhelminthes, Nemertea, Rotifera, and some trochophore larvae; consisting of one or more flame cells (q.v.), at the inner end of tubes which open to the exterior.

PROTOPLASM. Substance within and including plasma-membrane of a cell (q.v.) or protoplast (q.v.) but usually taken to exclude large vacuoles, or masses of secretion, or ingested material. In animals and plants differentiated into nucleus (q.v.) and cytoplasm (q.v.).

PROTOPLAST. (Bot.). The actively metabolizing part (i.e. the protoplasm) of a cell (q.v.) as distinct from the cell-wall (q.v.). Equivalent to what a zoologist means by a cell.

PROTOPTERUS. African lungfish (Dipnoan).

PROTOSTELE. Most simple, primitive type of stele (q.v.), consisting of central core of xylem surrounded by cylinder of phloem. Includes *haplostele*, simplest form with xylem in form of a rod; *actinostele*, with xylem ribbed, appearing star-shaped in transverse section; and *plectostele*, with xylem in form of several longitudinal parallel strips embedded in phloem. Present in stems of certain ferns, club mosses; almost universally in roots.

PROTOTROPH. Strain of a micro-organism (alga, bacterium or fungus) having no nutritional requirements in addition to those of the wild type (q.v.) from which it was derived. Cf. *Auxotroph*.

PROTOXYLEM. First xylem elements to be differentiated from procambium (q.v.); extensible. Described as *endarch* when internal to the later-formed metaxylem, e.g. in stems of angiosperms; *exarch* when external to metaxylem, e.g. in roots; and *mesarch* when surrounded by metaxylem, e.g. in stems of ferns.

PROTOZOA. Group (phylum or sub-kingdom) of animals differing from the rest (Metazoa and Parazoa) in consisting of one cell only, but resembling them and plants, and differing from bacteria, in having at least one well-defined nucleus. Contains classes Flagellata, Rhizopoda, Ciliophora, Sporozoa. Unicellularity does not necessarily imply close relationship; the fungi and algae also include unicellular forms. The status of the Flagellata (q.v.) is particularly complicated. Protozoa are ubiquitous, and of great significance in the economy of nature; some parasitic forms are important economically and medically (e.g. malaria parasite).

PROVENTRICULUS. (1) Anterior part of stomach of birds, where digestive enzymes are secreted; the posterior part of stomach being the gizzard. (2) Of some invertebrates (Crustacea, Insecta) the gizzard.

PROXIMAL. Situated towards point of attachment or of origin. Cf. *Distal*.

PSEUDO-ALLELES. Alleles in the sense that they affect the same process in the organism, and involve homologous cistrons as judged by the cis-trans effect; but nevertheless, because they have originated as mutations in different parts of the cistron, show recombination by crossing-over within the cistron.

PSEUDOGAMY. Development of ovum into a new individual as a result of stimulation by a male gamete, whose nucleus however does not fuse with that of ovum, and contributes nothing to hereditary constitution of embryo. Occurs in some nematodes, and in some higher plants.

PSEUDOPARENCHYMA. See *Plectenchyma*.

PSEUDOPODIUM. Temporary protrusion of the cell, associated with flowing movements of protoplasm, occurring in rhizopod and other

Protozoa, white blood cells, etc. Serves locomotion and feeding (phagocytosis). Physiology of such movement is not understood.

PSEUDOPREGNANCY. Occurrence in female mammal of changes closely resembling those of pregnancy, but in absence of embryos; due to hormone secretion by corpus luteum (q.v.) of ovary. Occurs in species where active corpus luteum is formed as a result of copulation, when such copulation is sterile (e.g. rabbit, mouse); or where normal oestrus cycle (q.v.) includes a pronounced luteal phase (e.g. bitch),

PSILOPHYTALES. Order of extinct, palaeozoic Pteridophyta (q.v.) that flourished in the Devonian (q.v.). Oldest land plants known, with very primitive organization. Small, rhizomatous plants with dichotomously branched aerial shoots a few mm. to about a cm. in diameter, leafless or with many small leaves, with simple protostelic, vascular system; bearing apical sporangia.

PSILOPSIDA. Group (Sub-division) of Tracheophyta (q.v.) including Psilophytales and Psilotales.

PSILOTALES. Order of Pteridophyta (q.v.) related to extinct and most primitive Pteridophytes (Psilophytales, q.v.); represented by two genera, *Psilotum* and *Tmesipteris*. Usually found as sub-tropical or tropical epiphytes. Small, rhizomatous plants with dichotomously branched aerial shoots, vascular system protostelic to siphonostelic. Sporangia borne in groups of two or three in axils of small, two-lobed sporophylls. Homosporous, gametophytes subterranean, lacking chlorophyll, mycotrophic; bearing antheridia and archegonia scattered indiscriminately.

PSOCOPTERA. Booklice. Order of exopterygote insects. Small, some wingless. Common booklouse, found in damp rooms, feeds mainly on fungus.

PSYCHROPHILIC. (Of a micro-organism), with optimum temperature for growth below 20° C.

PTERIDOPHYTA. Division of plant kingdom comprising ferns, horsetails, clubmosses, etc. A prominent group of the Carboniferous era, when tree-like forms were common; living representatives forming a small, widely distributed group attaining its greatest development in the tropics. Largely terrestrial; characterized by possession of true stems, leaves, and roots; a well-developed vascular system (but no cambium); sporangia borne on leaves (*sporophylls*) and by separate, small, inconspicuous sexual plants (*prothalli*), bearing antheridia and archegonia. Sporophylls resembling ordinary foliage leaves, e.g. bracken, or much modified, arranged in a cone, e.g. horsetail. The sporangia liberate spores which germinate to give rise to prothalli. Fertilization of egg in archegonium is effected by male gametes motile by flagella. Zygote develops into a new plant. Alternation of generations (q.v.) is well marked. The fern plant, the sporophyte, is the dominant generation; the prothallus is the gametophyte. Contrasted with lower plants the out-

standing feature of the pteridophytes is the development of an
independent sporophyte, with roots, stems, leaves, and well-
developed vascular system. In most ferns the sporophyte gives rise
to only one kind of spore and one kind of gametophyte (prothallus)
bearing both antheridia and archegonia; they are *homosporous*.
In other, *heterosporous* members, e.g. *Selaginella*, the sporophyte produces small *microspores* and larger *megaspores*. The microspores give
rise to extremely reduced male prothalli, each bearing an antheridium containing a small number of spermatozoids. The
megaspores, which may be reduced to one per sporangium, produce slightly larger female prothalli, each bearing a few archegonia. During their development these gametophytes are retained
within the spores. In some species with a single, large megaspore
per sporangium, development of gametophyte, fertilization of egg
and embryo formation takes place while the megaspore is enclosed
within the sporangium which maintains its physiological connection with the sporophyte. This condition foreshadows that in seed
plants where the megaspore is permanently retained within the
megasporangium, on the sporophyte. Living representatives are
in four orders, Filicales (ferns), Equisetales (horsetails), Lycopodiales (clubmosses), Psilotales. Fossil forms include orders Psilophytales and Sphenophyllales. These groups are now frequently
classified in Subdivisions of Division Tracheophyta (q.v.): Psilotales and Psilophytales in Psilopsida, Lycopodiales in Lycopsida,
Equisetales and Sphenophyllales in Sphenopsida, and Filicales in
Pteropsida (with seed plants).

PTERIDOSPERMAE. See *Cycadofilicales*.

PTERODACTYLA (PTEROSAURIA). Fossil order of flying reptiles.
Lived during Jurassic and Cretaceous. Membraneous wings supported mainly by greatly elongated fourth finger, and also by rest
of arm. Many analogies in structure with birds, but independently
developed, though both birds and pterodactyls evolved from the
same group of non-flying reptiles.

PTEROPODA. Sea butterflies; a few families of gastropod molluscs,
highly modified for pelagic life, with or without a shell.

PTEROPSIDA. Group (Sub-division) of Tracheophyta (q.v.) including
ferns, conifers and flowering plants.

PTERYGOTA (METABOLA). Sub-class of insects including all except
a few primitively wingless forms (Apterygota). Some members of
the Pterygota are wingless (e.g. fleas) but are believed to have been
derived from winged ancestors. Cf. *Apterygota*, *Endopterygota*,
*Exopterygota*.

PTYALIN. An amylase present in saliva of some mammals, including
man.

PTYXIS. Way in which leaves are folded or rolled up in the bud.

PUBIC SYMPHYSIS. Joint or fusion formed mid-ventrally between
pubic bones of two halves of pelvic girdle. In most mammals, in

*Archaeopteryx* (but not in living birds except ostrich) and in many reptiles. See *Symphysis*.

PUBIS. Ventral, forward-projecting part of hip girdle (q.v.) of tetrapods. See Fig. 10, p. 265.

PUFF. Swollen region of salivary gland chromosome (q.v.) a few micrometres long, believed to represent a gene or group of genes actively synthesizing RNA, which makes up a considerable proportion of the mass of the puff.

PULMONARY. (Adj.) Of the lung (q.v.). *P. artery* of vertebrates, carries de-oxygenated blood from heart (from right ventricle in crocodiles, birds, and mammals) to capillaries of lungs. *P. vein* carries oxygenated blood back to heart (to left auricle in all tetrapods).

PULMONATA. Order of gastropod molluscs, members of which have a lung, e.g. snails, slugs.

PULP-CAVITY. Internal cavity of vertebrate tooth or denticle, open by usually a narrow channel to tissues in which tooth is embedded, containing connective tissue, nerves, and blood-vessels, with odontoblasts lining the dentine wall of the cavity. *Persistent pulp*, pulp-cavity widely open, tooth growing continuously from below, e.g. rodent incisor.

PULSE. Wave of raised pressure which passes rapidly (much faster than rate of flow of blood) from heart outwards among all the arteries, every time the ventricle discharges its contents of blood into the aorta. The increased pressure dilates the arteries, and this can be felt; the dilation also relieves the pressure somewhat, so that the pulse dies away as it proceeds and has quite disappeared in the capillaries.

PULVINUS. Localized enlargement of base of leaf-stalk and/or of base of leaflets in certain plants, concerned in movement of leaves or leaflets in response to stimuli.

PUPA (CHRYSALIS). Stage between larva and adult of endopterygote insect, in which locomotion and feeding cease but great developmental changes occur.

PUPIL. Opening in iris (q.v.) at front of eye. See Fig. 3, p. 107.

PURE LINE. Succession of generations of organisms homozygous for all genes. All variation (except for occasional mutation) in a pure line is due to environmentally produced modifications, which are not inherited. Selection of certain of these modifications for breeding does not therefore alter the characteristics of the pure line; it breeds true. Pure lines are obtained by intensive inbreeding, most efficiently by self-fertilization.

PUTREFACTION. Type of bacterial decomposition of protein-containing substrate (largely anaerobic) with formation of evil smelling amines rather than ammonia.

PYCNIDIUM. Minute, globose or flask-shaped fungus fruit body, with apical ostiole, lined internally with conidiophores.

**PYCNOSIS.** Contraction of nucleus into compact strongly-staining mass, occurring as cell dies.

**PYLORUS.** Junction between stomach and duodenum of vertebrate. Has a sphincter muscle within a fold of mucous membrane which closes off the junction during digestion of food in stomach.

**PYRENOID.** Small, spherical, often highly refractive protein bodies found singly or in numbers embedded in chloroplasts of many algae but absent in majority of brown and red algae. In green algae associated with starch synthesis and surrounded by starch deposits.

**PYRIDOXINE (VITAMIN B6).** Vitamin of B group, forming a co-enzyme (pyridoxal phosphate); required by variety of organisms, e.g. some of the yeasts, bacteria, insects, birds, and mammals.

**PYRROPHYTA.** Fire algae. Division of algae. Possess chlorophylls a and c, $\beta$-carotene, xanthophylls. In different forms, store reserve food as starch, fats, oils. Not completely autotrophic, requiring vitamins. Cellulose cell wall. *Dinophyceae* (dinoflagellates) is most important class. Mostly unicellular, some colonial, motile by two, laterally inserted, flagella. Walls of many (armoured) forms consist of interlocking plates often bearing long processes possibly an adaptation to pelagic life. Other forms occur: naked and amoeboid; sessile palmelloid colonies; branched filaments. Asexual reproduction various, by cell division, zoospores. Colourless forms also occur and provide link with protozoa. Constitute a major component of marine and fresh-water plankton. With diatoms (*Bacillariophyceae* q.v.) and a few other algae provide basis of all other life in sea.

**PYXIDIUM.** Type of capsule (q.v.).

# Q

$Q_{10}$. Temperature coefficient. The increase in rate of a process (expressed as a multiple of initial rate) produced by raising temperature 10° C. Often between two and three for biological, as for many chemical processes.

$QO_2$. Term used in measurement of respiration. Oxygen uptake in microlitres ($\mu$l.) per milligram dry weight per hour.

QUADRAT. Square of vegetation (standard size is one metre square) chosen at random for study of composition of vegetation in a selected area.

QUADRATE. Cartilage-bone of posterior end of vertebrate upper jaw (developing in palato-quadrate cartilage), attached to neurocranium (brain case), and in most vertebrates articulating with lower jaw. In mammals becomes incus (q.v.).

QUALITATIVE INHERITANCE. Type of inheritance in which expression of a particular character differs sharply amongst individuals of a species (discontinuous variation), e.g. sex. Depends on action of a few genes of major effect. Cf. *Quantitative Inheritance*.

QUANTASOMES. Regularly arranged sub-units observed by electron microscopy in thylakoid (q.v.) lamellae. Estimated each contains approximately 300 chlorophyll molecules which are believed to function as a unit (photosynthetic unit) in absorption of light quanta.

QUANTITATIVE INHERITANCE. Type of inheritance in which expression of the character concerned differs only in degree amongst individuals of a species, characteristically showing every gradation from one extreme to the other (continuous variation), with a predominance of intermediate types; e.g. stature in man. Depends on associated action of a number of genes each producing a small effect. See *Polygene*. Cf. *Qualitative inheritance*.

QUATERNARY. Geological period comprising both Pleistocene (q.v.) and Recent.

# R

RACEME. Kind of inflorescence (q.v.).

RACHIS. (1) Main axis of an inflorescence. (2) Axis of a pinnately compound leaf to which leaflets are attached.

RADIALLY SYMMETRICAL. Capable of being halved in either of two (or more) planes so that the halves are approximately mirror images of each other. Characteristic of many animals, e.g. coelenterates, echinoderms; and of many flowers. See *Actinomorphic*, *Bilaterally Symmetrical*.

RADICAL. (Bot.). Arising from the root or crown of the plant.

RADICLE. Root of embryo of seed plants.

RADIOLARIA. Group of marine planktonic rhizopod Protozoa. Their skeletons of silica have been important in forming flint, and oozes of the ocean bottom.

RADIUS. The anterior of the two bones (other is ulna) of fore-arm of tetrapod vertebrate fore-limb. Articulates with the side of the hand (fore-foot) on which lies the thumb. See Fig. 7, p. 213.

RADULA. 'Tongue' of molluscs; a horny strip, continually renewed, with teeth on its surface used for rasping food. It is absent in lamellibranchs, which feed on very small particles of food.

RAMENTA. Brown, chaffy, scaly epidermal hairs covering young leaves and stems of ferns.

RAMET. An independent individual of a clone (q.v.).

RAPHE. (1) In seeds formed from anatropous (q.v.) ovules, longitudinal ridge marking position of adherent funicle (q.v.). (2) In Diatoms, longitudinal slit in valve (q.v.), varying in form and structure; associated with power of movement of these organisms.

RAPHIDE. Needle-shaped crystal of calcium oxalate occurring in bundles in certain plant cells.

RATITES. Living flightless birds. Cf. *Carinates*. Wings reduced in size, without barbules on feathers, or keel on sternum for attachment of wing muscles. E.g. emu, cassowary, kiwi, ostrich, rhea. Term is not now usually used in classification of birds.

RAUNKIAER'S LIFE FORMS. System of classification of vegetation based on position of perennating buds in relation to soil level. Indicates how plants pass the unfavourable season of their annual cycle. The following classes are recognized. *Phanerophytes*: woody plants with perennating buds borne more than 25 cm above soil level. Includes trees and many shrubs. Taller trees, more than 8 m. high are *Mega-* and *Meso-phanerophytes*; trees and shrubs between 2 and 8 m. are *Microphanerophytes*, and shrubs between 25 cm. and 2 m. are *Nanophanerophytes*. *Chamaeophytes*: woody or herbaceous plants with perennating buds above soil level but below 25 cm. *Hemicryptophytes*: herbs with perennating buds at soil level, protected by soil itself, or by dry, dead portions of the plant. *Geophytes*: herbs with perennating buds below soil surface. *Helophytes*: herbs with perennating buds lying in mud. *Hydrophytes*: herbs with perennating buds lying in water. *Therophytes*: herbs which survive the unfavourable season as seeds.

REACTION TIME. See *Latent period*.

RECAPITULATION. Occurrence in the embryonic development of an individual, of stages repeating the structure of ancestral adult forms, successively later embryonic stages corresponding to successively more recent ancestors. Hence 'ontogeny repeats phylogeny' (though in condensed form, and with special embryonic adaptations). E.g. the gill-slits of an embryo bird repeat the gill slits of its fish ancestors. Though historically important, recapitulation in this sense is largely discredited now; but it is probably true that the earlier embryonic stages of an organism resemble the corresponding *embryonic* stages of its ancestors, more than do the later stages, and recapitulation of ancestral embryonic characters, in this sense, occurs. Thus the gill slits of a bird embryo resemble the embryonic gill slits of its fish ancestors, the developmental mechanism for this region of the body having changed relatively little in the course of evolution.

RECENT. Holocene (q.v.).

RECEPTACLE. (1) (*Thalamus, Torus*) Apex of flower-stalk bearing

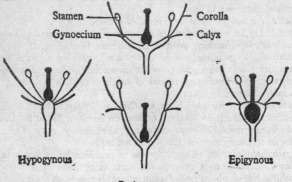

*Fig. 9. Diagram of different types of floral receptacle, showing the position of the gynoecium (black) relative to the other flower parts.*

flower parts (perianth, stamens, carpels); axis of flower. Variously shaped in different flowers, conical to concave, and according to its form the gynoecium may be *superior* or *inferior* and the flower *hypogynous, perigynous,* or *epigynous*. When the carpels are at apex of a conical receptacle and other flower parts inserted in turn below level of carpels the gynoecium is *superior* and the flower *hypogynous*, e.g. buttercup, Fig. 9. When carpels are at apex (centre) of a concave receptacle with other flower parts borne around its margin, the gynoecium is *superior* and the flower *perigynous*, e.g. bramble, rose, Fig. 9 (upper and lower figures). When receptacle completely encloses carpels and other flower parts arise from receptacle above, the gynoecium is *inferior* and the flower *epigynous*, e.g. apple, dandelion, Fig. 9. In this condition the carpel walls are intimately fused with wall of the receptacle. (2) Also used to describe the shortened axis of the inflorescence (q.v.) (capitulum) in Compositae.

RECEPTACULUM SEMINIS. Spermatheca (q.v.).

RECEPTOR (SENSE-ORGAN). That part of an animal which, in co-operation with the nervous system, detects what goes on (i.e. receives stimuli from) outside or inside the animal. Of different kinds, each especially sensitive to a specific sort of stimulus, such as temperature, light, or muscular movement. When a stimulus of sufficient intensity affects an appropriate receptor, the latter influences the behaviour of the animal by sending impulses through the nervous system, nerve-cell(s) of which connect with it.

RECEPTOR SITE. Part of a cell or molecule that specifically combines with some agent, e.g. with a hormone molecule or a virus.

RECESSIVE. (Genetics.) Converse of dominant (q.v.). A recessive gene has no effect on phenotype unless homozygous.

RECIPROCAL CROSSES. Crosses between two plants in which the source of male and female gametes are reversed.

RECOMBINATION. Formation in offspring of gene combinations that are not present in either parent; occurs by independent assortment (q.v.) of chromosomes and their genes during gamete production followed by random union of different sorts of gamete at fertilization.

RECTUM. Terminal part of intestine, opening to exterior by anus or cloacal opening. In vertebrates, rather narrower than colon (q.v.).

RECTUS MUSCLES OF EYE. See *Eye-muscles*.

RED BLOOD CELLS OR CORPUSCLES (ERYTHROCYTES). Cells of vertebrate blood, containing haemoglobin (q.v.). Carry nearly all the oxygen contained in the blood. Smooth-surfaced, flattened discs, round in cyclostomes and most mammals, oval in other vertebrates. Easily distorted but elastic. Incapable of movement on their own. In mammals have no nuclei, except in embryo. In other vertebrates the nucleus does not synthesize RNA. An individual r.b.c. has a relatively short life (average about four months in man) and r.b.c.s. are formed (in myeloid tissue of bone marrow) and perish (the remains being taken up by reticulo-endothelial system, q.v.) continuously in enormous numbers (over a million a second in man). In man each is a circular biconcave disc, eight

micrometres in diameter after fixation, and there are roughly five
million per cubic millimetre of blood. See *Reticulocyte*.

RED CELL GHOST. Red blood cell whose haemoglobin has leaked
away.

REDIA. One of the kinds of larva produced asexually by a previous
larval stage of flukes; parasitic in snails; rediae reproduce asexually
giving rise either to more rediae or to cercariae (q.v.).

REDUCTION DIVISION. Meiosis (q.v.).

REFLEX. Very simple form of behaviour occurring in almost all
animals with a nervous system, in which a certain kind of stimulus
almost invariably evokes, with hardly perceptible delay, one
specific kind of simple response. E.g. a pin stuck in one's foot evokes
an immediate withdrawal. The constancy and immediacy of
response depends on an inborn nervous pathway (i.e. one which is
independent of experience), the *reflex arc*, along which the impulses
travel. It involves the central nervous system. In the instance cited
the stimulus causes groups of impulses to travel along a number of
sensory nerve fibres into the spinal cord, where they are relayed
through other nerve fibres, and impulses are set going down a
group of motor nerve fibres which activate the muscles whose contraction withdraws the foot. Even the simplest reflex involves
synapses in the central nervous system, and these provide opportunity for interaction of the nerve-cells involved in the reflex with
other events in the central nervous system, allowing for example
development of conditioned reflexes (q.v.), or inhibition (q.v.).

REFUGIUM. Locality which has escaped drastic alteration following
climatic change, in contrast to the region as a whole, e.g. a driftless
area (usually a tableland or mountain, known as a *Nunatak*) within
a region that has undergone general glaciation. Usually forms a
centre for relic (q.v.) species. Exist widely over earth's surface
because although, owing to glacial advance and recession, changes
of climate affecting the survival of plants have occurred, no general
climatic change affects a large area uniformly, with the result that
relic colonies, of species or communities, are left behind.

REGENERATION. Restoration by an organism of tissues or organs
which have been removed. Power of regeneration is highly variable
between different groups of organisms; in some Platyhelminthes
a minute fragment can regenerate the whole animal; in mammals
limited to wound-healing, regrowth of peripheral nerve fibres, and
compensatory hypertrophy (q.v.). Very common in plants occurring, e.g. in higher plants by growth of dormant buds, formation of
secondary meristems and production of adventitious buds, roots.
Exploited on large scale in plant propagation.

REGULATION. Normal development of an animal embryo, or part of
an embryo, occurring although its structure has been disturbed in
some way, as by removing some of it, or adding to it, or rearranging
it. E.g. half a sea-urchin embryo, at a sufficiently early stage, will

develop into a normally proportioned though small larva. Regulation is a widespread feature of the early stages of animal development. In some species powers of regulation practically disappear at the time of fertilization (*mosaic eggs*, q.v.) while in others the fertilized egg, and later stages, easily regulate (*regulation eggs*).

REGULATOR GENE. See Operon.

REINFORCEMENT. (In animal behaviour) reward.

RELEASER. Stimulus which sets off an instinctive act. A *social releaser* is a releaser emanating from a member of the same species as the reactor.

RELIC. Surviving organism, population, or community, characteristic of an earlier time. See *Refugium*.

RELIC (OR RELICT) DISTRIBUTION (R. FAUNA, R. FLORA). Spatial distribution which represents localized remains of an originally much wider distribution. E.g. organisms widespread in glacial times now confined to mountain tops. See *Relic*, *Refugium*.

RENAL PORTAL SYSTEM. In fish and Amphibia blood is brought from capillaries of posterior end of body (hind limbs, tail) to kidneys by a pair of renal portal veins (really part of posterior cardinal veins), which break up into capillaries in kidney mainly around tubules. Blood is collected up again either into posterior cardinal veins (fish) or renal veins and vena cava inferior (Amphibia). This portal system is slightly or not at all developed in amniotes, which have a different sort of kidney (metanephros, q.v.). See *Portal vein*.

RENNIN. Enzyme secreted in the stomach of young mammals which clots milk (converting soluble protein caseinogen into casein which forms insoluble calcium-casein compound). Rennet is impure rennin.

REPLACING BONE. Cartilage-bone (q.v.).

REPLICATION. Production of exact copies of complex molecules, such as must occur during the growth and reproduction of any living thing. The only biological molecules in which the original molecule serves as a direct model for the construction of the new are those of DNA, and in some cases possibly RNA. The mechanism of this self-replication involves the separation of the two strands of DNA (when, as is usual, the DNA is double-stranded) and the construction on each of a new 'complementary' strand by base pairing (q.v.). Each new double strand of DNA thus consists half of new and half of old DNA; the process is called *semi-conservative* replication.

REPRESSION. (Of enzyme). Where a pathway of successive enzymes leads to the formation of an important metabolite, the amount of the latter present may control the activity of all the enzymes involved by inhibiting their synthesis. See *Enzyme*. Cf. *End-product inhibition*.

REPTILIA. Reptiles, a class of vertebrates. Includes many orders, the living ones being Chelonia (turtles and tortoises), Rhyncocephalia (the tuatara), Squamata (lizards and snakes), Crocodilia (crocodiles); and the entirely extinct ones being, amongst others, Orni-

thischia and Saurischia (both dinosaurs), Pterodactyla, Ichthyosauria, Plesiosauria, Therapsida (the ancestors of the mammals).
Reptiles are poikilothermic (q.v.) tetrapods, mostly living and reproducing entirely on land, though some have become aquatic.
They were the dominant terrestrial animals in the Mesozoic.
Modern ones are distinguished from Amphibia by horny skin,
metanephric kidney, and by the embryo being enclosed in an egg-
shell and having a protective amnion and an allantois; and from
birds and mammals by absence of the special features, such as
feathers or hair, of those groups. But in the fossil record there are
intermediates between them and both amphibia and mammals,
and no sharp dividing line is possible. The distinction for most
fossils is made on the structure of the vertebral column, and other
skeletal features.

RESOLUTION. See *Microscope*.

RESPIRATION. (1) Breathing, e.g. pumping air in and out of lungs,
or water over gills. (2) Taking oxygen from the environment and
giving off carbon dioxide. (1) and (2) are sometimes referred to as
*external respiration* in contrast to (3) *internal, tissue* or *cell respiration*,
i.e. the chemical reactions from which an organism derives
energy. In most organisms internal respiration is accompanied
by consumption of free oxygen and production of carbon dioxide
(the external manifestation of which is (2); in some organisms
(2) being facilitated by (1)). This kind of respiration is called
*aerobic*. If glucose, for instance, is being used as basis for aerobic
respiration, it is oxidized to carbon dioxide and water, and the
same amount of energy is liberated as if that glucose were burnt
in air. In the organism a complicated chain of oxidation-reduction
reactions is involved, various substances being alternately oxidized
and reduced under the influence of various enzyme systems (see
*Cytochrome, Dehydrogenase, Oxidase*). Energy can be liberated by the
break-down of substances without molecular oxygen being concerned in the reaction; this is known as *anaerobic respiration*, e.g.
breakdown of glycogen to lactic acid in vertebrate muscle; or of
glucose to ethyl alcohol and carbon dioxide by yeast. Such processes do not liberate as much energy as does aerobic respiration.
Many organisms (or parts of them) respire anaerobically for some
time when their supply of oxygen is insufficient for aerobic respiration, in which case they may acquire an oxygen debt (q.v.). A few
bacteria are strictly anaerobic, i.e. they do not use free oxygen
at all.

RESPIRATORY ENZYME. Enzyme which catalyses oxidation-reduction reactions. See *Dehydrogenase, Oxidase*.

RESPIRATORY MOVEMENT. Movement of part of an animal by
which the air or water from which the animal obtains oxygen and
to which it gives off carbon dioxide is frequently renewed at the
surfaces where this exchange of respiratory gases occurs (i.e. at

the respiratory organ). There is great variety of respiratory organs among animals, and great variety of respiratory movement. E.g. breathing movements of chest and diaphragm in man and other mammals; telescopic movements of the abdomen of a wasp; baling of water past the gills in a lobster.

RESPIRATORY ORGAN. Organ across whose surface interchange of respiratory gases (carbon dioxide and oxygen) occurs, between body fluids of animal and the environment; lung, gill.

RESPIRATORY PIGMENT. Substance which combines reversibly with oxygen, thus acting as a carrier or store of it. E.g. haemoglobin of human blood becomes loaded with oxygen in the lungs, where it comes into equilibrium with air; and it gives up this oxygen when it comes into contact with tissues having a low oxygen pressure. Respiratory pigments change colour according to the degree of oxygenation (e.g. haemoglobin is scarlet oxygenated, purple deoxygenated) and many have characteristic absorption spectra; these properties have facilitated their investigation. Respiratory pigments are frequently present in blood, either in plasma (haemocyanin, chlorocruorin, haemoglobin of several invertebrates) or in blood corpuscles (haemoglobin of vertebrates; a few other pigments of invertebrates).

RESPIRATORY QUOTIENT (R. Q.). Ratio of the volume of carbon dioxide expired to the volume of oxygen consumed during the same time. A theoretical R.Q. can be calculated for the oxidation of various foodstuffs. For carbohydrates it is 1, for fats 0.7, and for proteins 0.8. It was formerly thought that the R.Q. of an organism or tissue gave direct information concerning the kind of foodstuff being oxidized; but in practice the interpretation of an R.Q. is not so simple, for cells can oxidize more than one of the three foodstuffs at the same time, and certain other metabolic processes may use oxygen or produce carbon dioxide.

RESPONSE. Change in an organism or part of it, usually adaptive, produced by a stimulus (q.v.). See *Irritability*.

RESTING CELL (R. NUCLEUS). Cell or nucleus which is in interphase (q.v.).

RESTING EGGS (WINTER EGGS). Eggs which can only develop after a dormant period, during which they are resistant to adverse conditions; produced by some fresh water animals, e.g. rotifers, certain crustacea (water fleas); may differ considerably from other eggs of the same species, in e.g. being fertilized instead of parthenogenetic, having more yolk, or thicker shell.

RESTING POTENTIAL. See *Action Potential*.

RETICULAR FORMATION. See *Arousal*.

RETICULATE (THICKENING). Internal thickening of wall of a xylem vessel or tracheid in the form of a network.

RETICULIN FIBRES. Very fine, almost inextensible intercellular fibres forming a network around and amongst the cells in many vertebrate tissues, e.g. muscle, nerve, kidney, liver, and other glands. They hold the tissues together. They stain selectively with special silver impregnation methods (hence name *argyrophil fibres*) and they are more resistant to chemical treatment and high temperature than the thicker collagen fibres of connective tissue. Nevertheless their material (*reticulin*) consists largely of collagen, and transitional states are frequently found. Indeed in formation of collagen fibres (in embryo or after wounding), reticulin fibres appear first and change to collagen.

RETICULOCYTE. Immature mammalian red blood cell, which has lost its nucleus, but shows some staining due to RNA.

RETICULO-ENDOTHELIAL SYSTEM. Those phagocytic macrophages of vertebrates in contact with blood (in bone-marrow, spleen, liver) or lymph (in lymph nodes); they free these fluids from foreign particles, e.g. bacteria. See *Macrophage*.

RETINA. Layer lining interior of vertebrate eye, except in front (in region of ciliary body); it is sensitive to light. It has an outer pigmented layer, next to the choroid; and an inner transparent nervous layer next to cavity of eye-ball. The nervous layer contains light-sensitive rods (q.v.) and/or cones (q.v.) in contact with pigmented layer; and nerve-fibres, intermediary nerve cells, blood-vessels and glia, interposed between incoming light and rods and cones. Embryologically part of the brain. Develops as hollow outpushing of brain wall, whose outer end becomes dinted in to form a stalked cup; the double-walled cup forms the two layers of the retina, the stalk forms optic nerve. See Fig. 3, p. 107; *Fovea*; *Blind spot*. In molluscs the retina is formed not from the nervous system but from the external ectoderm, and the light-sensitive cells are external to the nerve-fibres, etc.

RH FACTOR (RHESUS FACTOR). Substance (an antigen; there are actually several, closely related) occurring in blood corpuscles of a high proportion of human beings (85 per cent in Great Britain and U.S.A.). Depends on a complex of linked genes. The rest of the population is without the factor (Rh-negative). Rh-negative individuals do not normally possess antibodies against the antigen they have not got (as they do in the classical blood-groups, q.v.). But they can acquire such antibodies, as by blood transfusion; or in the case of a woman by bearing Rh-positive children, whose antigen crosses the placenta. The antibody thus formed in a Rh-negative mother may cross the placenta again and if in sufficient concentration, which usually requires at least one preceding pregnancy with Rh-positive child, it may damage a Rh-positive foetus.

RHIZOID. Single or several-celled hair-like structure serving as a root. Rhizoids are present at base of moss stems and on under-surfaces of liverwort plants and fern prothalli and in some algae and fungi.

RHIZOME. Underground stem, bearing buds in axils of reduced scale-like leaves; serving as a means of perennation and vegetative propagation, e.g. mint, couch grass.

RHIZOMORPH. Root-like structure composed of fungus hyphae, increasing in length by apical growth, that serves for transport of food materials from one part of thallus to another and assists in spread of fungus through or over substratum. A complex, internally differentiated and highly co-ordinated structure and distinguished from mycelial strands, in which one or more main hyphae are ensheathed by their lateral branches in varying degrees of complexity. Term is also used to include both rhizomorph and strand as defined.

RHIZOPLANE. The root-surface component of the rhizosphere (q.v.).

RHIZOPODA (SARCODINA). Class of Protozoa characterized by the possession of pseudopodia; includes *Amoeba*; Foraminifera; Radiolaria, etc.

RHIZOSPHERE. Zone of soil immediately surrounding roots which is modified by their activity. It is characterized by enhanced micro-biological activity and often by changes in relative proportions of types of organisms present compared with surrounding soil; due to changes in nutrient status of soil arising from removal of nutrients by root absorption and release of others in root exudation and by sloughing off of dead cells. Within the rhizosphere a further micro-environment is often distinguished, namely, the *rhizoplane* or root surface.

RHODOPHYTA. Red algae (seaweeds). Division of algae. Possess chlorophyll a and d, α-, β-carotene, xanthophylls, phycocyanin (blue) and phycoerythrin (red) pigments. Usually red in colour because of predominance of phycoerythrin. Main food reserve is a form of starch (amylopectin). Relatively small compared with brown algae (*Phaeophyta*, q.v.), but also very diverse. Thallus in a few forms microscopic, in others filamentous, often highly branched, or flattened, membranous. Cell wall two-layered, inner of cellulose, outer of pectic material, gelatinous. Motile reproductive cells absent. Mostly marine, especially in warmer seas, widely distributed, benthic (often epiphytic) in lower part of intertidal zone. Some coralline forms are important in reef building, some yield agar (q.v.), others (Irish moss) are eaten.

RHYNCHOCEPHALIA. A small order of reptiles, containing only *Sphenodon* (the tuatara) and a number of extinct forms. Lizard-like but with many primitive features.

RHYNCHOTA. Hemiptera (q.v.).

RHYTIDOME. See *Bark*.

RIBOFLAVIN (LACTOFLAVIN, VITAMIN B₂). Vitamin of B group. Forms part of co-enzymes concerned in cellular oxidation (FAD, FMN), widely (universally?) distributed in living organisms. Liver, muscle, yeast are important sources. Required as vitamin by those vertebrates (including man) and insects tested, and by some bacteria. Synthesized by many bacteria, including those present in human intestine.

RIBONUCLEIC (RIBOSENUCLEIC) ACID. RNA (q.v.).

RIBOSOMES. Granules of protein and RNA present in the cytoplasm of all types of organism, about 100Å in diameter and hence invisible with a light microscope. In eucaryotic cells they are often attached to endoplasmic reticulum. Their RNA is synthesized in nucleoli. They are the site of protein synthesis; messenger RNA (q.v.) attaches to them, and there receives molecules of transfer RNA (q.v.) bearing amino acids. Ribosomes are often linked together in a chain probably by a long molecule of messenger RNA; such groups are called polyribosomes, polysomes or ergosomes. Number of ribosomes in a polysome is probably related to length of messenger RNA molecule, and this in turn to the length of polypeptide chain to be formed.

RICKETTSIAS. Group of minute rod-shaped bacteria, obligate intra-cellular parasites of certain arthropods, particularly of fleas, lice and ticks. Do not appear to harm arthropod hosts but can be transmitted via bites to man and other mammals in which they may cause severe, often fatal disease, e.g. in man, typhus.

RINGER (RINGER'S FLUID). Physiological saline (q.v.) containing sodium, potassium, and calcium chlorides (and sometimes other salts), these being main salts in fluid which normally bathes cells. Much used in physiological experiments for temporarily maintaining cells or organs alive in vitro (q.v.).

RNA. Ribonucleic acid, a molecule consisting of a large number of nucleotides attached together to form a long strand one nucleotide thick. Each nucleotide contains the sugar ribose, and one of the four different bases found in DNA (q.v.) except that uracil replaces thymine. In some viruses RNA is the inherited material, and may possibly undergo self-replication; but in most organisms it occurs mainly as ribosomes (q.v.), to a lesser extent as *Transfer RNA* (q.v.) and less still as *Messenger RNA* (q.v.), in all these forms being concerned in translating the structure of DNA into the structure of protein molecules. In eucaryote cells there are also various kinds of nuclear RNA.

ROD. Kind of light-sensitive nerve-cell present in vertebrate retina. The rod-shaped outer segment of the cell, which is the light-sensitive part, consists largely of a stack of flat and parallel unit membranes (q.v.), at right angles to the cell length; this develops embryologically from a cilium, and retains its characteristic 9+2 pattern of fibrils (see *Flagellum*). Rods do not discriminate fine detail or probably colour differences, but they are sensitive to very dim light, which cones (q.v.) are not. There are about 120 million in one retina of a primate. Response to light depends on visual purple (q.v.).

RODENT. Any member of the order Rodentia, e.g. rat, squirrel (rabbit and hare are now put in a separate order, Lagomorpha). Gnawing mammal, with a pair of large continually growing chisel-like incisors in upper and lower jaws. Grinding molars. Most widespread and numerous of all mammal orders.

ROGUE. (1) Variation from standard type of variety, etc.; (2) to remove such variants from a growing crop; (3) used also in a wider sense meaning to remove any undesirable plants from a variety in the field, including genetic variants, those affected by disease, etc.

ROOT. That part of vascular plants that usually grows downwards into the soil, anchoring plant and absorbing water and nutrient salts. Roots cannot be distinguished from stems on basis of their position with respect to soil since roots of some plants may be wholly or partly above ground, while other plants possess underground stems. Externally, roots differ from stems principally in that they do not bear leaves and buds; they also possess at their tip a protective layer of cells, the root-cap. Internally, roots differ from stems in arrangement of vascular tissue in a central core and with protoxylem (q.v.) exarch.

ROOT-CAP. Cap of loosely arranged cells covering apex of growing point of root and protecting it as it is forced through soil. Formed from promeristem (q.v.), dermatogen, or from a meristematic layer external to dermatogen known as *calyptrogen*.

ROOT HAIR. Tubular outgrowth of epidermal cell of root; with thin delicate wall having intimate contact with soil particles. Produced in large numbers behind region of active cell division at tip of root forming root-hair zone. Greatly increases absorbing surface of root. Short-lived, collapsing after few days but continually replaced from new root tissue formed by activity of apical meristem.

ROOT NODULES. Small swelling on roots of leguminous plants (pea, bean, clover, etc.) produced as a result of infection by nitrogen-fixing bacteria. See *Nitrogen Fixation*.

ROOT PRESSURE. Pressure under which water passes from living cells of root into xylem; demonstrated by exudation of liquid from cut end of decapitated plant. May continue for long periods. Due to maintenance of osmotic gradients through active transport of solutes.

ROTIFERA. Wheel animalcules. Phylum of minute Metazoa which swim and feed by means of a ciliated band, the 'wheel'. Formerly confused with ciliate Protozoa and included in Infusoria.

ROUNDWORMS. Nematoda (q.v.).

R.Q. Respiratory quotient (q.v.).

RUDERAL. Plant living in waste places near habitations.

RUMEN. Storage compartment of complicated stomach (rumen is really a diverticulum of oesophagus) of ruminants, into which newly eaten, but unchewed, food is passed and from which it (the 'cud') is subsequently returned to mouth for chewing. Some digestion of food (especially cellulose), and much synthesis of B vitamins which are absorbed by the animal, occurs by bacterial action in rumen; some products of cellulose digestion are absorbed by rumen.

RUMINANT. Mammal belonging to the sub-order Pecora of the order Artiodactyla. Deer, giraffes, sheep, goats, antelopes, oxen. No upper incisor teeth. Often with bone-cored horns. Stomach usually complicated. See *Rumen*.

RUNNER. Stolon that roots at tip forming new plant that eventually is freed from connection with parent by decay of runner. Also used horticulturally of the daughter plant itself.

# S

**S PHASE.** See *Cell cycle.*

**SACCHARASE.** See *Sucrose.*

**SACCHAROMYCES.** Genus of ascomycete fungi that includes those used in production of bread and alcoholic drinks. See *Yeasts.*

**SACCULE.** See *Ear, inner.*

**SACRAL VERTEBRA.** Vertebra of tetrapods which articulates by means of rudimentary ribs with ilia of hip-girdle (q.v.). One in Amphibia, two or more fused together (sacrum) in other tetrapods.

**SACRUM.** Group of sacral vertebrae fused together, the ilia of the hip-girdle being united to some or all of them. See *Hip-Girdle.*

**SAGITTAL.** In the plane extending longitudinally (antero-posteriorly), and dorso-ventrally in the mid-line. Divides bilaterally symmetrical animal into two similar (right and left) halves.

**SALIVA.** Fluid secreted into mouth. In terrestrial vertebrates, fluid containing mucus (q.v.), and in some of them ptyalin (q.v.), secreted from salivary glands into mouth as a reflex response to presence there of food. Provides lubrication for swallowing. In insects, fluid secreted on to mouth-parts, often containing digestive enzymes; used for dissolving or lubricating food, and in blood-suckers may contain an anti-coagulant.

**SALIVARY GLAND CHROMOSOMES (SALIVARIES).** Giant chromosomes occuring in salivary glands (and some other tissues) of dipterous insects (including *Drosophila*). Nuclei of these tissues have their chromosomes microscopically visible, unlike normal resting nuclei. Each pair of homologous chromosomes is closely adherent together (paired). The chromosomes are stretched out to a much greater length than usual (up to $\frac{1}{5}$ mm.) and greatly thickened by repeated duplication, i.e. they are polytene. They are marked by an elaborate pattern of transverse basophilic bands, formed by homologous regions of the numerous chromosome strands lying side by side. The pattern is due to the arrangement of the genes along the chromosomes. From genetic differences associated with changes in the pattern, numerous genes have been localized. See *Chromosome Map.*

**SALTATION.** Abrupt, often permanent change in character of whole, or more usually, part, of fungus thallus. In culture, generally appearing as a sector differing, e.g. in rate of growth, colour, degree of spore production. May be due to mutation (q.v.) or to somatic segregation of homokaryons (q.v.) from a heterokaryon (q.v.).

**SAMARA.** Winged achene (q.v.).

**SAPROPHYTE.** Organism which obtains organic matter in solution from dead and decaying tissues of plants or animals. Activities of

innumerable saprophytic bacteria and fungi are of immense importance to life on this planet in making available to the living the
carbon, nitrogen and other elements of the dead (and some, the
yeasts, through their activities in producing alcohol, give us
more immediate pleasure though questionable benefit). Cf.
*Parasite.*

SAPWOOD. Outer region of xylem of tree trunks, containing living
cells, e.g. xylem parenchyma and medullary ray cells, and functioning in water conduction and food storage as well as providing
mechanical support. Cf. *Heartwood.*

SARCODINA. Rhizopoda (q.v.).

SAURIA. Lacertilia (q.v.).

SAURISCHIA. An order of fossil reptiles, one of the two into which the
group Dinosauria has now been split (the other being Ornithischia).
Lived during the Mesozoic. Contained carnivorous and herbivorous species. Many bipedal. Some, but by no means all, were
extremely large (up to fifty tons).

SAUROPSIDA. Term not usually used in classification but denoting a
natural group: the majority of reptiles including all the living
forms and many fossil forms, e.g. dinosaurs, pterodactyls, together
with the birds, all of which are closely related; as distinct from the
extinct mammal-like reptiles (Therapsida, q.v.) and the mammals,
which form another natural group (Theropsida).

SCALARIFORM THICKENING. Internal thickening of wall of a
xylem vessel or tracheid, in the form of more or less transverse bars,
suggestive of ladder rungs.

SCAPE. Leafless flowering stem arising from ground level, e.g. dandelion, daffodil.

SCAPHOPODA. Elephant's tusk shells; small class of molluscs.
Marine; specialized for burrowing; tubular shell open at both
ends.

SCAPULA. Dorsal part of shoulder girdle (q.v.). Shoulder-blade in
man and other mammals. See Fig. 10, p. 265.

SCHISTOSOMA (BILHARZIA). Genus of blood-flukes (of class Trematoda, Platyhelminthes) including human parasites of very great
medical importance, in e.g. parts of Africa (expecially Egypt),
South America, China.

SCHIZOCARP. Dry fruit formed from a syncarpous ovary that splits
at maturity into its constituent carpels forming a number of partial
fruits, usually one-seeded, resembling achenes (q.v.) and called
mericarps, e.g. hollyhock, mallow, geranium, cow parsley.

SCHIZOGENOUS. (Of secretory cavities in plants), originating by
separations of cells, e.g. oil-containing cavities in leaves of St John's
wort. Cf. *Lysigenous.*

SCHIZOMYCOPHYTA. Bacteria (q.v.).

SCHWANN CELL. Kind of cell which ensheaths every nerve-fibre of
vertebrate peripheral nervous system. In a myelinated fibre one

cell occurs between every pair of adjacent nodes (q.v.) and forms the myelin (q.v.). Probably largely derived from neural crest.

SCION. Twig or portion of a twig of one plant that is grafted on to a stock of another.

SCLEREID. See *Sclerenchyma*.

SCLERENCHYMA. Tissue giving mechanical support to plants. Cells thick walled, usually lignified, inelastic, sometimes consisting of cellulose, often so thick as to leave only a very small lumen; usually without living protoplasm at maturity. Two types of cell occur in sclerenchyma, *fibres* and *stone-cells* (*sclereids*). Fibres are very elongated cells with tapering ends, occurring singly or variously grouped into strands. They are extracted from such plants as flax (cellulose fibres) and hemp (lignified fibres) and used in manufacture of rope, linen, paper, etc. Stone cells are usually not much longer than they are broad, occurring singly or in groups; common in fruits, e.g. pear, nuts, and in seed coats. Cf *Collenchyma*.

SCLEROPROTEINS. Very stable fibrous proteins, insoluble in water or salt solutions; present mainly as surface covering of animals, e.g. keratin, collagen, or as fibres binding cells together, e.g. collagen, elastin.

SCLEROSIS. Hardening. E.g. in vertebrate tissues after injury, by increase in concentration of collagen.

SCLEROTIC. Fibrous or cartilaginous firm outer coat of eye-ball in vertebrates, continuous with cornea in front of eye. See Fig. 3, p. 107.

SCLEROTIUM. Compact tissue-like mass of fungus hyphae, often with a thickened rind, varying in size from that of a pin's head to that of a man's head; capable of remaining dormant for long periods, e.g. during conditions unfavourable to normal fungus growth, and commonly giving rise to fruit bodies, e.g. ergot (q.v.).

SCOLEX. Part of tapeworm which is attached to wall of gut of host by suckers and/or hooks; sometimes called the 'head'.

SCROTUM. Pouch of skin of pelvic region in many mammals which contains testes (at least during breeding season) keeping them cooler than body temperature (latter inhibits development of sperm).

SCUTELLUM. Cotyledon of grass embryo.

SCYPHISTOMA. The fixed (polyp) stage of jelly-fish (scyphozan Coelenterata), usually quite small and insignificant, which by horizontal splitting gives rise to free-swimming jelly-fish.

SCYPHOMEDUSAE. Scyphozoa (q.v.).

SCYPHOZOA (SCYPHOMEDUSAE). Jelly-fish. Class of coelenterates (of sub-phylum Cnidaria). Polyp stage (scyphistoma, q.v.) small and inconspicuous or absent; medusae large and more complexly organized than those of Hydrozoa; gonads endodermal. Cf. *Hydrozoa*, *Actinozoa*.

SEAWEEDS. Red, brown, or green algae (q.v.), living in or by the sea.

SEBACEOUS GLAND. Skin gland of mammals nearly always opening into a hair-follicle, secreting fatty substance (*sebum*). Formed from epidermis, but projects deep into dermis.

SECONDARY MERISTEM. Region of active cell division that has arisen from permanent tissues, e.g. cork cambium (phellogen), wound cambium. Cf. *Primary meristem*.

SECONDARY SEXUAL CHARACTER. A characteristic of animals which differ between the two sexes; but excluding the gonads, and the ducts, with their associated glands, which convey the gametes.

SECONDARY THICKENING. Formation of additional, secondary, vascular tissue by activity of cambium (q.v.) with accompanying increase in diameter of stems and roots of dicotyledons and gymnosperms; providing additional conducting and supporting tissue for growing plant and, in most cases, making up greater part of mature structure.

SECRETIN. Hormone which stimulates secretion of digestive juices by pancreas, and of bile by liver. Produced in epithelium of wall of duodenum and jejunum under stimulus of acid and products of digestion coming through pylorus from stomach. A peptide.

SECRETION. (1) The passage of (usually complex) material elaborated by a cell from the inside to the outside of its plasma membrane; the material (itself called a secretion) having a special function in the organism. Secretion is probably an activity of most cells, but is specialized in gland-cells. Usually takes place by extrusion of material, but may involve destruction of whole cell (holocrine secretion, e.g. sebaceous gland). (2) Secretion, when used in contrast to simple diffusion, means that the cell does work in passing the secretion through its plasma-membrane against the forces of diffusion, e.g. secretion of hypotonic fluid such as sweat. See *Active Transport*.

SECTION. See *Microtome*.

SECTORING. (Of a fungus colony), formation of an area (sector) distinctly different from rest of colony, e.g. in growth-rate, colour, form, reproduction; often wedge-shaped. Due to segregation of nuclei of one genetic type in that part of the colony. See *Saltation*.

SEED. Product of a fertilized ovule, consisting of an embryo enclosed by protective seed coat(s) derived from the integument(s). Some seeds (castor oil, pine) are provided with food material in the form of *endosperm* tissue surrounding the embryo, in other (*non-endospermic*) seeds food material is stored in cotyledons, e.g. pea. Seed habit is culmination of an evolutionary development involving, in sequence, heterospory, reduction of a free-living female gametophyte generation dependent on water for sexual reproduction, and its retention within tissues of sporophyte by which it is protected and supplied with food. Occurred early in geological history and in more than one group of plants (present in Carboniferous in Cycadofilicales and in some fossil lycopods, as well as in present day conifers and flowering plants). Of equal importance was evolution of male gametophyte to pollen grain germinating by pollen tube, thus avoiding necessity for water in fertilization. Independence of water in sexual reproduction increased immensely the range of environments open for colonization. Biological advantages of seed habit include, further, protection and nutrition of embryonic plant during its development, provision of dispersal mechanisms, provision of food to tide over critical period of growth of embryo and its establishment as an independent plant after seed is shed.

SEGMENTATION. (1) (Zool.). *Metameric segmentation, Metamerism.* Repetition of a pattern of elements belonging to each of the main organ systems of the body, along the antero-posterior axis of the body; or a comparable repetition along the axis of an appendage. Most strongly marked in Annelida and Arthropoda. The repetition produces a series of units, called *segments* (or *metameres*), of fundamentally similar structure, e.g. in the earthworm each of the externally visible rings is a segment; each segment contains a pattern of blood-vessels, epidermal structures, nervous system, excretory organs, etc., which is repeated with some variation in every other segment. It should be noted that the similarity beween different segments of a given animal may be very imperfect. In particular the segments at the anterior end, which form the head, are very different from each other and from other segments. Vertebrates show segmentation most clearly in embryonic development, but it is almost confined to parts of the muscular, skeletal, and nervous systems. See *Somitic Mesoderm.* It does not appear in the epidermis, as in Annelida and Arthropoda. (2) In embryology, a synonym for cleavage (q.v.) applied to both plants and animals.

SEGREGATION. Separation into different gametes, and thence into different offspring, of the two members of any pair of allelomorphs possessed by an individual; the two allelomorphs having previously been brought together in the individual, one from each of its parents; and having in no way blended or altered each other while associated together in the individual. What is known as Mendel's first law asserts that allelomorphs segregate. Segregation is the result of the relatively unchanging nature of genes; of their separate carriage in chromosomes; of the mechanism of meiosis which provides each gamete with only one member of each pair of chromosomes; and of fertilization by which pairs of chromosomes are formed again.

SEISMONASTY. (Bot.). Response to a non-directional shock stimulus, e.g. rapid folding of leaflets and drooping of the leaves in *Mimosa pudica* when lightly struck or shaken.

SELACHII. a sub-class or order of Chondrichthyes, containing the sharks, dogfish, skates, and rays. Sharp, rapidly replaced teeth, and upper jaw not fused to skull (cf. *Holocephali*). Occasionally extended to cover various fossil groups of Chrondrichthyes also; occasionally restricted solely to sharks and dogfish.

SELECTION PRESSURE. Measure of the effectiveness of natural selection in altering the genetic composition of a population.

SELECTIVE ADVANTAGE. To have a selective advantage is to have or confer increased fitness (q.v.).

SELF-DIFFERENTIATION. Of a region, tissue or feature of an embryo; differentiation, independently of influence of other parts of embryo. Cf. *Dependent differentiation*.

SELF-FERTILIZATION. Fusion of male and female gametes from same individual. Cf. *Cross-Fertilization*.

SELF-POLLINATION. Transference of pollen from anther to stigma of the same flower, or to stigma of another flower on same plant. Cf. *Cross-Pollination*.

SELF-STERILITY. Of some hermaphrodites (q.v.) inability to form viable offspring by self-fertilization. See *Incompatibility*.

SEMEN. Product of male reproductive organs, consisting of sperm together with secretions of various accessory glands, e.g. of prostate gland in mammals.

SEMICIRCULAR CANALS. Semicircular tubes, projecting from and joined at both ends to the inner ear (q.v.) of vertebrates. Gnathostomes have three on each side, occupying the three planes of space, two vertical at right-angles to each other, one horizontal. Agnatha have only the two vertical (in some only one). Angular acceleration (e.g. rapid turning) of the animal in any direction produces currents of fluid (endolymph) along the corresponding canal, which are detected by fine projections from sensory cells, and communicated to brain via auditory nerve.

SEMINAL VESICLE (VESICULA SEMINALIS). Organ which stores sperm in the male.

SEMINIFEROUS TUBULES. Coiled tubes (each about 50 cm. long and $\frac{1}{8}$ mm. diameter in man), several hundreds of which are present in vertebrate testis. Made of germinal epithelium. During sexual activity all stages of spermatogenesis occur in them, up to almost mature sperm. Supposedly nutritive Sertoli cells, to which developing spermatids are attached, are also present. Correspond to ovarian follicles (q.v.) of ovary. See *Follicle-Stimulating Hormone*.

SENSE-ORGAN. Receptor (q.v.).

SENSORY. Concerned with receptors (q.v.). *S. nerve*. Peripheral nerve consisting of nerve-fibres of sensory nerve-cells. *S. nerve-fibre*. Nerve-fibre of a sensory nerve-cell. *S. nerve-cell* (*S. neurone*). Nerve-cell whose fibres connect with receptor, transmitting impulses started by receptor to central nervous system (q.v.). In vertebrates the cell-body of such a nerve-cell is attached to its nerve-fibre at a point along its course situated in dorsal root ganglion, and there are no dendrites. In invertebrates cell-body is situated at (peripheral) end of nerve-fibre furthest away from central nervous system. *S. Root.* Of vertebrates, nerve-root (q.v.) containing the sensory nerve-fibres.

SEPAL. One of the parts forming calyx of dicotyledonous flowers; usually green and leaf-like. See *Flower.*

SEPTICIDAL. (Bot.). Describing dehiscence of multilocular capsule by longitudinal splitting along septa between carpels, separating carpels from each other, e.g., St John's Wort. Cf. *Loculicidal.*

SEPTUM. Partition or wall.

SERE. Particular example of plant succession (q.v.). Seres originating in water are known as *hydroseres*; those arising under dry conditions as *xeroseres*, of which those developing on exposed rock surfaces are known as *lithoseres*.

SEROLOGY. Study of antigen-antibody reactions. See *Antibody, Complement, Precipitin Reaction.*

SEROUS MEMBRANE. Mesothelium and underlying connective tissue lining coelomic spaces (pericardial, perivisceral, pleural, peritoneal cavities) in vertebrates.

SERTOLI CELLS. See *Germinal Epithelium; Seminiferous Tubule.*

SERUM. Blood serum (q.v.).

SESAMOID BONE. Bone developed within tendon of vertebrate, occurring especially in mammals, particularly where tendon works over ridge of underlying bone, e.g. patella (knee-cap).

SESSILE. (1) Of parts of plants or eyes of Crustacea; without a stalk. (2) Of animals, fixed to the substratum; sedentary.

SETA. (Bot.). Stalk of sporogonium (q.v.) in mosses and liverworts. (Zool.). Bristle or 'hair' of invertebrates. (True hair (q.v.) is a feature of mammals only.) Produced by epidermis, consisting either (*a*) solely of cuticular material, or (*b*) of hollow projection of cuticle enclosing an epidermal cell or part of one. Type (*a*) also known as chaetae (q.v.) are characteristic of Polychaeta and Oligochaeta. Setae of insects are of type (*b*).

SEX CHROMATIN (BARR BODY). Small heterochromatin body characteristic of some interphase nucleus of homogametic sex of some animals including human females. Derives from one of the two X chromosomes. Number of bodies is one less than number of X chromosomes. Particularly evident in cases of abnormalities amongst sex chromosomes, an XXX individual having two, an XXXX three.

SEX CHROMOSOME. Chromosomes of which there is a homologous pair in the nuclei of one sex (the homogametic sex, q.v.), and a dissimilar pair (or an unpaired chromosome) in those of the other (the heterogametic sex, q.v.). The sex chromosomes which occur as a pair in the homogametic sex are called X-chromosomes. The heterogametic sex has an X-chromosome and either a Y-chromosome or none. The homogametic (or XX) sex produces gametes which are identical in their sets of chromosomes, all containing one X-chromosome. The heterogametic (XY or XO) sex produces equal

numbers of two different sorts of gametes, one with and one without an X-chromosome. Union of the gametes of the XX sex with
those of the XY (or XO) sex therefore results in offspring consisting of approximately equal numbers of the two sexes. The
presence or absence of a Y-chromosome determines sex in mammals; in insects it is determined by the number of X-chromosomes
in relation to the number of autosomes. The sex-determining
mechanism is of course absent in hermaphrodite animals and
plants.

SEX-DETERMINATION. See *Sex-chromosomes*.

SEX-LIMITED CHARACTER OR GENE. Gene expressed in only one
of the two sexes, e.g. a gene controlling characteristic of milk production.

SEX LINKAGE. Of a gene or character, having special distribution
with reference to sex as a result of (in the case of a gene) being
carried on the X-chromosome (q.v.) or (in the case of a character)
controlled by a gene so carried. A man, for instance, receives his
X-chromosome and therefore all his sex-linked genes from his
mother; and he hands them on to his daughters (who also get an
X-chromosome from their mother), not to his sons. Since in a man
there is no partner to the X-chromosome, recessive genes on it cannot be masked by a dominant allelomorph, so that men manifest a
larger number of recessive genes (like those for haemophilia or red-
green colour-blindness) than women; and conversely a smaller
number of dominant genes. What is true for men is true for the
heterogametic sex of any organism. Sex-linkage must be distinguished from sex-limitation (q.v.). Both sexes manifest a full set
of sex-linked genes; but the homogametic sex, unlike the heterogametic sex, will only manifest a recessive gene if it has received it
from both parents, which will be a rare event if the gene is uncommon in the population.

SEX RATIO. Relative proportion of the numbers of males and females
in a population. Usually expressed as number of males per 100
females. *Primary* sex ratio is that immediately after fertilization;
*secondary*, that at birth (or hatching); *tertiary* at maturity.

SEXUAL REPRODUCTION. Reproduction involving fusion of haploid
nuclei, usually of gametes (q.v.).

SEXUAL SELECTION. A possible mode of evolution suggested by
Darwin. The females of a population are supposed to select for
mating only males having certain characteristics and thereby to
transmit these characteristics to future generations to the exclusion
of characteristics of rejected suitors. Darwin explained the origin of
many secondary sexual characters in this way, especially brilliant
adornment and courtship behaviour. In Darwin's strict sense
sexual selection is probably of rather limited importance since even
where a female has a choice between males, which is infrequent, the
rejected males will usually find a mate elsewhere and so their

characteristics will not be eliminated. The evolution of secondary sexual characters is probably more a matter of natural selection (q.v.), one pair (male and female) of animals reproducing more successfully than another because of the characters they possess, including those characters serving sexual stimulation.

SHELLFISH. Fishmonger's term for shelled molluscs and crustaceans.

SHIP-WORM. Wood-boring member of the Lamellibranchiata (genus *Teredo*) which does great damage to wooden wharves, ships, etc.

SHORT-DAY PLANT. See *Photoperiodism*.

SHOULDER GIRDLE (PECTORAL GIRDLE). Skeletal support in body-wall for attachment of front fins or limbs of vertebrate. Consists primitively of a curved bar of cartilage or bone on each side of the body, the two often fusing ventrally, forming a hoop, incomplete dorsally, transverse to long axis. Each bar bears a joint with fin or limb. See *Glenoid Cavity*. Region dorsal to joint is *scapula*, region ventral is *coracoid*. Extra dermal bones, notably *clavicle*, usually occur on ventral side. Scapula forms no joint with or bony attachment to vertebral column or ribs (unlike pelvic girdle). Coracoid and clavicle are joined mid-ventrally to breast bone (sternum) in tetrapods. See Fig. 10.

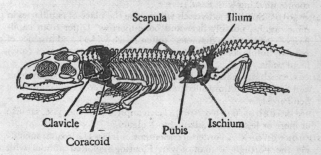

*Fig. 10. Skeleton of a tetrapod vertebrate, showing arrangement of shoulder and hip-girdles.*

SIBLINGS (SIBS). Brothers and/or sisters; offspring of same male parent and same female parent.

SIEVE-PLATE. See *Sieve-Tube*.

SIEVE-TUBE. Characteristic element of phloem functioning in the transport of food materials synthesized within the plant, e.g. sugars, proteins. Consists of thin-walled, elongated, living cells arranged in a longitudinal row and forming a connected series by means of perforations in their walls through which pass strands of cytoplasm. These perforations occur in groups known as *sieve-*

*plates* in the end or lateral walls. Remarkable in lacking nuclei in mature condition. Closely associated with parenchymatous *companion cells* with prominent nuclei.

SILICULA. See *Siliqua*.

SILIQUA. Special type of capsule (q.v.) found in cabbages and related plants (family Cruciferae). Dry, elongated fruit formed from an ovary of two united carpels and divided by a central false septum between the carpels into two compartments (locules). Dehiscing by separation of carpel walls from below upwards leaving septum bounded by persistent placentas (*replum*), with seeds adhering to it. The Silicula has a similar structure but is short and broad, e.g. honesty, shepherd's purse.

SILURIAN. Geological period (q.v.), lasted approximately from 440 till 395 million years ago.

SINANTHROPUS. Peking man. Lower Peistocene. Closely similar to (now put in same genus as) Pithecanthropus (q.v.).

SINUS. A space. (Bot.). Recess between two lobes of a leaf or other expanded organ. (Zool.). *Blood-sinus*, enormously expanded vein, found particularly in elasmobranchs. Applied also to haemocoel cavity of certain invertebrates. *Nasal sinus*, in mammals, air-filled space within certain bones of face, lined by mucous membrane, communicating with nasal cavity.

SINUSOIDS. Small blood-vessels which take the place of capillaries in some organs, notably liver and bone-marrow. Differ from capillaries in very various diameters (often much wider) and absence of regular lining composed of endothelial cells. Macrophages (q.v.) lie in walls.

SINUS VENOSUS. Chamber of vertebrate heart, lying between veins and auricle(s); thin-walled; absent in adult birds and mammals. See *Pacemaker*.

SIPHONACEOUS (SIPHONOUS). Term applied to coenocytic, sac-like or more or less tubular, filamentous algae.

SIPHONOPHORA. An order of coelenterates (class Hydrozoa) including the Portuguese man-of-war. Floating, colonial animal with extreme degree of specialization of members for, e.g. feeding, protection.

SIPHONOPODA. Cephalopoda (q.v.).

SIPHONOSTELE (SOLENOSTELE). Stele (q.v.) in which xylem and phloem form concentric cylinders around a central core of pith; *ectophloic*, with xylem cylinder surrounding pith and phloem surrounding xylem; *amphiphloic*, with phloem internal as well as external to xylem.

SIRENIA. Manatees, dugongs, seacows. An order of placental mammals. Aquatic (coastal) with transversely expanded tail, front legs as flippers, hind legs vestigial; vegetarian. Not closely related to whales (Cetacea) in spite of many similarities.

SKELETAL MUSCLE. Striped muscle (q.v.).

SKOTOPHILE. Literally 'dark loving'; dark receptive phase of circadian rhythm (q.v.), lasting about twelve hours. Cf. *Photophile*.

SLIDE. (1) Oblong of glass, usually 3 in. by 1 in. and 1–2 mm. thick, on which whole mounts, sections, etc., are placed for microscopical inspection. (2) The completed preparation made on such a piece of glass.

SLIME-FUNGI (SLIME-MOULDS). Myxomycophyta (q.v.).

SMOOTH (PLAIN, INVOLUNTARY) MUSCLE. Contractile tissue of vertebrates, consisting of numbers of individual elongated spindle-shaped cells, with no transverse striations (see *Striped Muscle*), bound together by connective tissue fibres. Found mainly in sheets surrounding hollow organs, e.g. blood-vessels, gut. Controlled by autonomic nervous system. Undergoes contraction rather slowly, and has marked power of maintaining certain degrees of contraction (tonus). Slow-contracting muscle of many invertebrates, e.g. molluscs, is rather similar.

SOCIETY. (Bot.). Minor climax community within a consociation (q.v.) arising as a result of local variation in conditions and dominated by species other than consociation dominant.

SOIL PROFILE. Series of recognizably distinct layers (horizons) visible in vertical section through soil down to parent material. Study of soil profiles yields valuable information on character of soils.

SOLENOSTELE. Siphonostele (q.v.).

SOMATIC CELLS (SOMA). The cells of an organism, other than the germ-cells; see *Germ-Plasm*. *Somatic tissues*. Tissues other than those of viscera or blood-vessels; or tissues which surround body cavity (q.v.). *S. motor nerves* supply striped muscle; *s. sensory nerves* supply receptors of somatic tissues.

SOMITIC MESODERM. Mesoderm on dorsal side of vertebrate embryo, flanking the notochord in two longitudinal strips, each of which as development proceeds becomes segmented (q.v.) into a series of blocks, the *somites*. (In front of the ears however there is usually no segmentation into somites). From each somite is derived a myotome (q.v.) innervated by one ventral nerve root (so that nerves are also segmentally arranged), and mesenchyme which forms connective tissue, and the vertebral column (latter also segmented). See *Lateral Plate; Pronephros*.

SOMATOTROPIC HORMONE. Growth hormone (q.v.).

SOREDIA. Organs of vegetative reproduction in lichens (q.v.). Minute clusters of algal cells surrounded by fungal hyphae. Formed in large numbers over lichen surface and dispersed by various agencies, wind, water, insects.

SORUS. (Bot.). Group, e.g. of fern sporangia.

SPADIX. Kind of inflorescence (q.v.).

SPATHE. Bract enclosing inflorescence of some monocotyledons, e.g. cuckoo pint.

SPECIALIZED. Having special adaptations to a particular habitat or mode of life which result in a wide divergence from presumed ancestral forms; and which tend to restrict the range of habitat which can be occupied and the variety of mode of life which can be followed and hence, it is assumed, to limit evolutionary flexibility. *Specialization*. (1) Acquisition of such special adaptations in the course of evolution. (2) Such a special adaptation.

SPECIATION. Origin of species.

SPECIES. The smallest unit of classification commonly used; i.e. the group whose members have the greatest mutual resemblance. The common names of familiar animals and plants often denote species e.g. man, fox, beech. For the great majority of animals and many plants, a species is roughly a group of individuals able to breed among themselves (if one disregards geographical separation) but not to breed with organisms of other groups. Consequently the members of a species form a reproductively isolated group, whose genes do not combine with those of outsiders, but are able to re-combine continually by sexual reproduction within the group. As a result no striking differences in genetic composition and in the characters controlled by genes occur within the species, though local differences, which are recognized in classification as a *sub-species*, may arise through reproductive isolation which is only partial or has recently occurred. Many of these sub-species are no doubt on the road to becoming full species, but are still capable of interbreeding within their species. Reproductive isolation however admits of degrees and so it is not easy to apply rigorously to the problem. Furthermore, it is usually unknown whether two kinds of organism are in fact able to breed together in natural conditions. Consequently species are in practice usually determined by experts in the particular group, on the basis of degree of difference, which is often, though not always, a close reflexion of reproductive isola-tion. Reproductive isolation, however, cannot be applied at all as a criterion to many organisms. Unless, for instance, sexual reproduc-tion with cross-fertilization freely occurs, the conception of species as a breeding unit breaks down; it does so therefore for some plants. Species must in such cases always be determined on the basis of difference, according to convenience; and while numerous species of such organisms are well-marked and undisputed, there can exist no general rule as to the minimum degree of difference separating any two species. A comprehensive definition of species applying to all kinds of organisms is in fact hardly possible. For naming of species see *Binomial Nomenclature*.

SPECIFIC. (1) Peculiar (to). (2) Characteristic of a species.

SPERM. Spermatozoon (q.v.).

SPERMATHECA (RECEPTACULUM SEMINIS). Organ in a female or hermaphrodite animal which receives and stores sperms from the mate.

SPERMATID. Animal cell resulting from the (second) meiotic division of a secondary spermatocyte (q.v.). At first a cell of normal
shape, it undergoes extensive cytoplasmic changes and condensation of nucleus which convert it into a spermatozoon.

SPERMATIUM. Non-motile male sex-cell; present in red algae,
and in fungi, in some members of the Ascomycetes and Basidiomycetes.

SPERMATOCYTE. (1) (Bot.). Cell which becomes converted into
spermatozooid (without intervention of cell division). Cf. *Spermatid.*
(2) (Zool.). Cell which undergoes meiosis, and thereby forms
spermatids (q.v.). *Primary spermatocyte* undergoes first of the two
meiotic divisions. As a result it gives rise to two *secondary spermatocytes.* The latter undergo the second meiotic division, each forming
two spermatids (q.v.). One primary spermatocyte thus produces
four spermatozoa (one primary oocyte producing only one ovum).
Cf. *Oocyte, Maturation of Germ-Cells.*

SPERMATOGENESIS. Formation of sperm. See *Maturation of Germ-
Cells, Spermatocyte.*

SPERMATOGONIUM. Cell of animal gonad which undergoes repeated
mitosis and eventually gives origin to spermatocytes (q.v.).

SPERMATOPHORE. Small packet of sperm, produced by some species
of animals having internal fertilization, e.g. newt, cephalopod.

SPERMATOPHYTA (SPERMAPHYTA). Seed plants (formerly
Phanerogamia). Division of plant kingdom providing dominant
flora of present day, including most trees, shrubs, herbaceous
plants, grasses, etc. Possessing a highly organized plant body of
stem, leaf and root, with a well developed vascular system. Heterosporous plants with dominant sporophyte and much reduced
gametophyte generations. The sporophyte generation is the plant
itself. The male gametophyte consists of the germinated pollen
grain with its pollen tube by which the non-motile gametes are
conveyed to the egg. The female gametophyte is retained on the
sporophyte, nourished and protected within the *ovule,* which after
fertilization of the egg within it becomes a *seed.* Within the seed,
protected by seed coat, is a young sporophyte plant, the *embryo.*
Including two groups, *Gymnospermae* (q.v.), with ovules lying unprotected on the megasporophylls, and *Angiospermae* (q.v.), in
which the megasporophylls, known here as *carpels,* enclose the
ovules in the *ovary.* After fertilization, ovary becomes a fruit containing one or more seeds. In gymnosperms, sporophylls are
usually arranged in cones; in angiosperms, sporophylls (stamens
and carpels) are borne in flowers. These groups are now frequently
classified as Classes of Subdivision Pteropsida in Division Tracheophyta.

SPERMATOZOID (ANTHEROZOID). (Bot.). Small motile male
gamete with flagella.

SPERMATOZOON. (Zool.). Small, motile, usually flagellated male gamete (not flagellated in Nematoda, decapod Crustacea, diplopod Myriapoda, mites).

SPERMOGONIUM (SPERMAGONIUM, SPERMAGONE, PYCNIUM). (Of fungi), flask-shaped or flattened, hollow structure in which spermatia are formed.

SPHENODON. The tuatara, a lizard-like New Zealand primitive reptile, sole living member of order Rhyncocephalia. Has a very well developed pineal eye (q.v.).

SPHENOPHYLLALES. Order of extinct Pteridophyta (q.v.) related to Equisetales (q.v.) which attained its maximum development in the Carboniferous and Permian periods (q.v.). Herbaceous or shrubby in habit, with grooved stem bearing whorls of leaves at nodes and terminating in a cone consisting of whorls of bracts bearing sporangiophores in their axils. Homosporous.

SPHENOPSIDA. Group (Subdivision) of Tracheophyta (q.v.) including horsetails (*Equisetum*) and related plants, living and extinct.

SPHINCTER. Ring of smooth muscle in wall of tubular organ or of an opening of a hollow organ, able by contraction to narrow or close lumen, e.g. pyloric sphincter (see *Pylorus*); anal sphincter.

SPIKE. Kind of inflorescence (q.v.).

SPINAL COLUMN. Vertebral column (q.v.).

SPINAL CORD. That part of the vertebrate central nervous system within the backbone. Consists of a hollow tube, but the hole is very small and the walls relatively and unevenly thick. Contains numerous nerve-cells and bundles of nerve fibres, particularly those connecting all levels of the spinal cord with the brain. Pairs of peripheral nerves, one nerve on each side per segment, leave the spinal cord to be distributed to the body. See *Nerve Root*. A great deal of simple co-ordination of movement of limbs, viscera, etc., is done in the spinal cord by reflexes (q.v.).

SPINAL NERVE. Peripheral nerve arising from spinal cord (q.v.) of vertebrate. One on each side in each segment. See *Nerve Root*. *Cranial Nerve*.

SPINDLE. Body formed within a cell at mitosis or meiosis, taking part in distribution of chromatids to the two daughter-nuclei. Commonly but not always ellipsoid. Appears at metaphase, and chromosomes become arranged at its equator. See *Spindle Attachment*. Spindle is relatively solid (a gel). It contains many microtubules (q.v.), some running from spindle-attachments (q.v.) to one spindle pole, others from pole to pole. The microtubules are evidently responsible for the movement apart of chromatids during anaphase. The microtubule protein is synthesized shortly before mitosis.

SPINDLE-ATTACHMENT (ATTACHMENT CONSTRICTION, CENTROMERE, KINETOCHORE, KINOMERE). Region of chromosome which attaches it to spindle (q.v.) at mitosis or meiosis. Under electron microscope appears as thin, dense, plate-like body to which a number of spindle fibres are attached. Unlike rest of chromosome, it is single during prophase of mitosis, and doubles only at metaphase. May be partly responsible for organizing the spindle. See Figs. 6A, 6B, pp. 180, 181.

SPINNERETS. Of spiders, four to six elevations at end of abdomen on to surface of which ducts of spinning glands open. Probably represent abdominal appendages.

SPIRACLE. (1) Dorsally situated reduced first (most anterior) gill-slit in many fish. Its small size results from the connection formed between mandibular and hyoid arches for firm attachment of jaws; between these arches the spiracle lies. See *Visceral Arch, Hyostylic Jaw Suspension*. In most living bony fish, spiracle is closed up. The gill-pouch of embryo tetrapods representing spiracle develops into cavity of middle ear (q.v.) and Eustachian tube. (2) Of insects, synonym of stigma; external opening of trachea.

SPIRAL CLEAVAGE. A type of cleavage (q.v.). First two divisions are longitudinal. Third is latitudinal and unequal, and forms four small cells at animal pole which by an obliquity of their spindles lie above the grooves between the large vegetal cells. These four small cells are usually extruded in a clockwise direction in relation to the large cells. At the next division, the large cells again form four large and four small cells, and the original small quartet divides; again the spindles lie obliquely, but this time the direction in all divisions is anticlockwise. Clockwise and anticlockwise alternate, and a highly characteristic and constant pattern of blastomeres is formed. This peculiar method of cleavage must be an indication of evolutionary relationship between groups possessing it: polyclad Turbellaria, Annelida, Mollusca (except cephalopods), perhaps rotifers.

SPIRAL THICKENING. Internal thickening of wall of a xylem vessel or tracheid in the form of a spiral band. Occurs in cells of protoxylem and, whilst providing mechanical support, permits longitudinal stretching as neighbouring cells grow.

SPIRAL VALVE. Spiral fold of mucous membrane projecting into intestine of certain fish, e.g. elasmobranchs, ganoids, and dipnoi, probably increasing absorptive surface.

SPIRILLUM. Corkscrew-shaped bacterium.

SPIROCHAETES. Elongated, spirally twisted unicellular bacteria with thin delicate wall; moving by flexions of the body which are caused by contraction of an *axial filament* wound spirally round the cell protoplast, within cell wall. Filament consists of two groups of flagella-like fibrils, one anchored in cytoplasm at each end, and overlapping in centre. Some free-living, some parasitic and cause disease, e.g. syphilis.

SPLANCHNOCRANIUM. Part of skull comprising jaws and their attachments. Cf. *Neurocranium*.

SPLEEN. Mass of lymphoid tissue in mesentery of stomach or intestine of gnathostomes; but unlike lymph nodes is interposed in blood, not lymph, circulation. An important source of lymphocytes, and an important part of reticulo-endothelial system (q.v.) defending the bloodstream against invading organisms, and removing red blood cells at the end of their life. Acts also as a store of red blood cells; in emergency contraction of smooth muscle in spleen squeezes them into blood stream.

SPONGE. See *Porifera*. *Bath sponge* is the cleaned skeleton of certain sponges, consisting of interlocking fibres of a collagen-like protein material, *spongin*.

SPONTANEOUS GENERATION (ABIOGENESIS). Present-day origin of organisms from non-living things, belief in which is now discredited. Until the rise of bacteriology, initiated by Pasteur, spontaneous generation was widely believed to be true for microorganisms, which were supposed normally to develop from non-living organic material. See *Biogenesis*.

SPORANGIOPHORE. (Of fungi), hypha bearing one or more sporangia; sometimes morphologically distinct from vegetative hyphae.

SPORANGIUM. (Bot.). Organ within which are produced asexual spores.

SPORE. Single-celled or several-celled reproductive body that becomes detached from the parent and gives rise either directly or indirectly to a new individual. Usually microscopic, of many different types and produced in a variety of ways. Thin or thick walled; often serving for very rapid increase in the population of the species, produced in enormous numbers and distributed far and wide by wind, water, animals; others are resting spores, the means of survival through an unfavourable period. Occurring in all groups of plants, particularly in fungi; in bacteria; and in Protozoa.

SPORE MOTHER CELL. (Bot.). Diploid cell giving rise by meiosis to four haploid spores.

SPOROGONIUM. Spore-producing structure of liverworts and mosses that develops after sexual reproduction; sporophyte generation of these plants.

SPOROPHORE. (Of fungi), general term for a structure producing and bearing spores, e.g. sporangiophore, conidiophore (simple sporophores), mushroom (complex sporophore).

SPOROPHYLL. Leaf that bears sporangia. In some plants indistinguishable from ordinary leaves except by presence of sporangia, e.g. bracken fern; in others, much modified and superficially quite unlike ordinary leaves, e.g. stamens and carpels of flowering plants.

SPOROPHYTE. Phase of life-cycle of plants which has diploid (q.v.) nuclei, and during which spores are produced. It arises by union of sex-cells produced by (haploid) gametophytes (q.v.). See *Alternation of Generations*.

STEGOCEPHALIA 273

**SPOROZOA.** Class of Protozoa, all parasitic. Includes malaria parasite and many others of great economic and medical importance.

**SPORT.** Somatic mutation, e.g. bud sport.

**SPRINGTAIL.** See *Collembola*.

**SQUAMATA.** Lizards and snakes. An order of Reptilia. Contains sub-orders Lacertilia (lizards) and Ophidia (snakes). Body covered with horny epidermal scales.

**SQUAMOSAL.** Membrane bone of skull, which in mammals takes over from quadrate the articulation with lower jaw. See *Ear Ossicle*.

**STAMEN.** Organ of flower which produces microspores (shed after development as pollen grains); a microsporophyll; comprising a stalk or *filament* bearing at its apex an *anther*. The anther consists of two lobes united by a prolongation of the filament (*connective*) and in each lobe there are two *pollen sacs*, containing pollen. See *Flower*.

**STAMINATE.** (Of flowers), possessing stamens but not carpels, i.e. male. Cf. *Pistillate*.

**STAMINODE.** Sterile stamen, one that does not produce pollen.

**STANDING CROP.** The amount of living material in a given population. May be measured as biomass (q.v.).

**STAPES.** One of the three mammalian ear ossicles (q.v.); stirrup-shaped because pierced by artery; representing columella auris of other tetrapods, hyomandibula of fish.

**STARCH.** One of principal reserve food materials of green plants; found in colourless plastids (*leucoplasts*) in storage tissues and, as product of photosynthesis, in stroma of chloroplasts in many plants. Formed in grains in which it is laid down in a series of concentric layers. Insoluble polysaccharide with two components, amylose and amylopectin. Stains blue with iodine.

**STARCH SHEATH.** Innermost layer of cells of cortex in young angiosperm stems, containing abundant and large starch grains; considered homologous with endodermis and may sometimes lose its starch and become thickened as an endodermis at a later stage.

**STATOBLAST.** Resistant reproductive body, vegetatively produced, which is capable of withstanding adverse conditions; formed by fresh-water Polyzoa.

**STATOCYST.** Organ of balance consisting of a vesicle, containing granules of lime, sand, etc. (*statoliths*) which stimulate sensory cells as the animal moves; present in some Crustacea, flatworms, etc. Sometimes known as otocyst and otoliths (q.v.).

**STATOCYTE.** Plant cell that contains statolith(s).

**STATOLITH.** (1) Solid inclusion of a plant cell, commonly a starch grain, free to move under influence of gravity; thought by some to provide stimulus by which plant perceives its position with respect to gravity. (2) See *Statocyst*.

**STEGOCEPHALIA.** Name (obsolete in classification) applied to fossil

Amphibia; have complete bony covering to head in contrast to modern Amphibia.

STELE (VASCULAR CYLINDER). Cylinder or core of vascular tissue in centre of roots and stems, consisting of xylem, phloem, pericycle, and, in some steles, pith and medullary rays; surrounded by endodermis. Structure of the stele differs in different groups of plants. See *Dictyostele, Protostele, Siphonostele, Vascular Bundle.*

STEM. Normally aerial part of axis of vascular plants, bearing leaves and buds at definite positions (nodes) and reproductive structures, e.g. flowers. Some stems are subterranean, e.g. rhizomes but these, like all stems, are distinguished externally from roots by the occurrence of leaves (scale-leaves on rhizomes) with buds in their axils, and internally by having vascular bundles arranged in a ring forming a hollow cylinder, or scattered throughout tissue of the stem, and with protoxylem most commonly endarch.

STENOHALINE. Unable to tolerate wide variation of osmotic pressure of environment. Cf. *Euryhaline.*

STENOTHERMOUS. Unable to tolerate wide variation of temperature of environment. Cf. *Eurythermous.*

STERIGMA. (Of fungi), minute stalk, bearing spore or chain of spores.

STERILE. (1) Unable to reproduce sexually. (2) Free from living micro-organisms.

STERNUM. (1) Breast bone. Bone of terrestrial vertebrates (tetrapods) in the middle of the ventral side of the chest, to which the ventral ends of most of the ribs are attached. At its anterior end attached to shoulder girdle (q.v.). (2) Of insects, cuticle on ventral side of each segment, often forming a thickened plate.

STEROIDS. Chemically similar but biologically diverse substances, e.g. bile acids; vitamin D; gonad and adrenal cortical hormones; some carcinogens; active parts of toad poisons and digitalis. Solubility similar to fats. Saturated hydrocarbons containing seventeen carbon atoms in a system of rings, three six-membered and one five-membered, condensed together (six atoms being shared between rings); usually excluding however the true sterols (q.v.).

STEROLS. Compounds with the general chemical ring-structure of a steroid, but with certain specific features of structure, including a long side-chain and an alcohol group. Sterols occur universally in plants and animals. E.g. cholesterol, ergosterol.

STH. Growth hormone (q.v.).

STIGMA. (1) (Bot.). Terminal expansion of style, surface of the carpel (q.v.) which receives pollen. (2) Eye-spot (q.v.) of algae or flagellata. (3) (Zool.). Spiracle (q.v.) of insect.

STIMULUS. Any change in the environment of an organism or of part of it, which is intense enough to produce a change in the activities of the living material, without itself providing energy for the new activities.

STIPE. Stalk. (1) Of fruit-bodies of certain higher fungi, e.g. mush-room. (2) Of thallus in sea weeds, e.g. bladder-wrack.

STIPULE. Small, usually leaf-like appendage, found one on either side of leaf-stalk in many plants, protecting axillary bud and often taking part in photosynthesis.

STOCK. Part of plant, usually consisting of the root system, together with a larger or smaller part of the stem, on to which is grafted a part of another plant (scion).

STOLON. (Bot.). Horizontally growing stem that roots at nodes, e.g. strawberry runner. (Zool.). Root-like part of colony of animals, e.g. hydroids, which fixes it to the substrate; in certain urochor-dates, outgrowth of body concerned with budding.

STOMA (plural STOMATA). (1) Pore in the epidermis of plants, present in large numbers, particularly in leaves, through which gaseous exchange takes place. Each stoma is surrounded by two special-ized, crescent-shaped epidermal cells known as *guard-cells*, whose movements, due to changes in turgidity, govern opening and closing of pore. (2) Includes both pore and guard-cells.

STOMACH. Enlargement of the anterior region of the gut. In verte-brates follows oesophagus, and usually has muscular walls which churn food, and lining cells which secrete pepsin and hydrochloric acid. Initial steps in digestion occur there, food being held by pylorus (q.v.) until reduced to a mush.

STOMIUM. Place in wall of fern sporangium where rupture occurs at maturity, releasing the spores.

STOMODOEUM. An intucking of ectoderm meeting endoderm of anterior part of gut, forming mouth.

STONE-CELL (SCLEREID). Element of sclerenchyma (q.v.).

STRATUM CORNEUM. Outer layer of epidermis of land-living verte-brates, cells of which have been converted to keratin (q.v.). Responsible for proofing the body against entry of bacteria and ultra-violet rays, and against loss of water.

STRIATED MUSCLE. Striped muscle (q.v.).

STRIDULATION. Production of sounds by rubbing together of certain modified surfaces; e.g. of part of hind leg against part of forewing by grasshoppers. In some insects important in bringing sexes together.

STRIPED (STRIATED, SKELETAL, VOLUNTARY) MUSCLE. Con-tractile tissue consisting (in vertebrates) of large elongated cells (muscle-fibres) with many nuclei, the cytoplasm of which bears conspicuous striations at right-angles to long axis. Cytoplasm contains numerous longitudinal fibrils (myofibrils), each having alternating bands of different composition; the cross-striations of the whole muscle fibre are the result of similar bands of the fibrils lying side by side. A muscle fibre, on stimulation by its nerve, or (artificially) by direct action of electrical or mechanical stimuli, contracts by shortening and thickening. See *Actin, Myosin*. Muscle fibres are bound together into muscular tissue by connective tissue fibres. Muscles made of striped fibres undergo very rapid contraction and are particularly concerned with locomotion, by moving skeletal parts to which they are usually attached, in vertebrates, insects and members of some other groups. Cf. *Cardiac Muscle, Smooth Muscle.*

STROBILA. The 'body' of a tapeworm, consisting of a string of pro-glottides.

STROBILUS. Cone (q.v.).

STROMA. (1) Tissue-like mass of fungal hyphae in or from which fruit-bodies are produced. (2) Colourless matrix of chloroplast (q.v.) in which grana are embedded. (3) Intercellular material or connective tissue component of an animal organ.

STRUCTURAL GENE. See *Operon.*

STRUCTURELESS LAMELLA. Mesogloea (q.v.).

STYLE. Prolongation of carpel supporting stigma. See *Carpel.*

SUBCUTANEOUS. Immediately below dermis of vertebrate skin. *S. tissue* is usually loose connective tissue, which may contain much fat (see *Blubber, Fascia*) and in many tetrapods a sheet of striped muscle (*panniculus carnosus,* conspicuous in some mammals) which can move the skin or its scales.

SUBERIN. Complex mixture of oxidation and condensation products of fatty acids; present in walls of cork cells rendering them im-pervious to water.

SUBERIZATION. Deposition of suberin (q.v.).

SUB-SPECIES. Subdivision of a species (q.v.) forming a group whose members resemble each other in certain characteristics, and differ from other members of the species, though there may be no sharp dividing line. Polymorphism (q.v.) is excluded. While breeding is possible and in many cases occurs between members of different sub-species of the same species, it does not occur as freely as within the confines of the sub-species. Because reproductive isolation is incomplete, sub-species nearly always grade into each other. The partial reproductive isolation is commonly due to the occupation of different geographical areas. Some sub-species are probably new species in the making. See *Binomial Classification.*

SUBSTRATE. (1) See *Enzyme.* (2) Ground or other solid object on which animals walk or to which they are attached. (3) Material on which a micro-organism is growing or is placed to grow, e.g. host organism, dead tissue, culture medium; solid surface to which cells in tissue culture are attached.

SUCCESSION. Progressive change in composition of a community of organisms towards a largely stable *climax*; e.g. from initial coloniz-ation of a bare area.

SUCCULENT. Type of xerophytic plant that stores up water within its tissues; having a fleshy appearance, e.g. cacti, houseleek.

SUCCUS ENTERICUS. Digestive juice secreted by walls of small intestine of vertebrates. Contains numerous enzymes, e.g. erepsin, sucrase, lactase, and enterokinase.

SUCRASE. See *Sucrose*.

SUCROSE. Cane sugar. A disaccharide (with twelve carbon atoms) widespread in plants, but not in animals. Not found in mammalian body, except in food in gut. It is a compound of glucose and fructose (into which it is split by enzyme *sucrase*, also called *invertase* or *saccharase*).

SUMMATION. Generally, additive effect of separate stimuli. In neurophysiology, additive effect of separate impulses arriving at a nerve-cell or effector-cell. As a very simplified example, suppose that nerve-cell A has synapses with the nerve-fibres of nerve-cells B and C. Impulses arriving in B alone or in C alone fail to stimulate the production of an impulse in A. But if impulses arrive, simultaneously or very shortly after each other in both B and C, their joint action produces an impulse in A. The separation of the summating impulses may be *spatial*, that is, the impulses arrive at different synapses on the same nerve-cell; or *temporal*, that is, they arrive successively at the same cell; or both. Many impulses may be involved in any one process of summation. Temporal summation at a single synapse probably does not occur in vertebrates owing to the short duration of effect of each impulse which fades before the refractory period (see *Impulse*) will allow the next impulse to arrive. Besides summation which produces impulses (i.e. is excitatory), summation of inhibition (q.v.) also occurs. In general, summation is one of the main ways in which impulses can interact, so that nerve-cells in co-operation can produce effects quite different from the sum of those due to the nerve-cells singly. The result is the exquisite gradation of behaviour corresponding to the immense variety of the stimulus situations to which an animal reacts.

SUPERIOR OVARY. See *Receptacle*.

SUPINATION. See *Pronation*.

SUPRARENAL GLAND. See *Adrenal Gland*.

SUPRAVITAL STAINING. See *Vital Staining*.

SURVIVAL VALUE. The nature or degree of the effectiveness of a given characteristic in promoting the organism's ability to contribute offspring to the future population. See *Natural Selection*.

SUSPENSOR. (1) In phycomycete fungi of the order Mucorales, cell supporting a gametangium. (2) In seed plants and in a few pteridophytes, structure developing from fertilized egg-cell, along with embryo, and bearing latter at its apex. By elongation of suspensor embryo is carried into nutritive endosperm or prothallus tissue.

SUTURE. Line of junction. (1) In flowering plants line of fusion of edges of a carpel is known as ventral suture. Mid-rib of carpel is known as dorsal suture, not implying any fusion of parts to form it but to distinguish it from the ventral (true) suture. (2) Junction between the irregular interlocking edges of certain contiguous skull bones in vertebrates; occupied by fibrous tissue. In man sutures slowly become obliterated during life by fusion of adjacent bones allowing age at death to be roughly judged. (3) In insects, junctions between plates of hardened cuticle of exoskeleton. (4) (Surgical), to sew a wound together.

SUTURE-LINE. On shell of ammonite (q.v.), line marking junction of edge of septum with side wall of shell; often very complex; its changes of form during evolution are known in great detail.

SWARM-SPORE. Zoospore (q.v.).

SWEAT GLANDS. Skin glands of mammal secreting a dilute (hypotonic) solution of the salts and other small molecules present in blood. Function, cooling the animal by evaporation. Usually under nervous control of sympathetic system. Formed from epidermis, but project deep into dermis. Present in very variable numbers in different mammals, e.g. dog has very few, and those mainly on pads of feet.

SWIM-BLADDER. Bladder containing gas, present in roof of the abdominal cavity in bony fish (Actinopterygii). Functions as a hydrostatic organ, varying the specific gravity of the fish to match the depth at which it is swimming, so that the fish can remain there effortlessly. Derived from the lungs of ancestral fish, which were partly air-breathers. See *Lung*.

SYMBIONT. Symbiotic organism.

SYMBIOSIS. (1) Association of dissimilar organisms whatever the relationship between the two partners. (2) Association of dissimilar organisms to their mutual advantage, e.g. association of nitrogen-fixing bacteria with leguminous plants (peas, beans, etc.). The bacteria, inhabiting nodules on roots, manufacture nitrogen compounds from nitrogen of the air, which become available to the plant. From the latter bacteria obtain carbohydrates and other food materials. Cf. *Commensal*.

SYMPATHETIC GANGLION. See *Autonomic Nervous System*.

SYMPATHETIC SYSTEM. (1) That part of autonomic nervous system (q.v.) sometimes called *orthosympathetic*. (2) Equivalent to autonomic nervous system.

SYMPATRIC. (Of geographical relationship of different species or sub-species) occurring together, i.e. with areas of distribution that coincide or overlap. Cf. *Allopatric*.

SYMPETALAE. Sub-class of Angiospermae in which the petals are united into a sympetalous (gamopetalous) corolla. Cf. *Archichlamydeae*.

SYMPETALOUS. Gamopetalous (q.v.).

SYMPHYSIS. Type of joint allowing only slight movement, in which the surfaces of the two articulating bones, both covered with a layer of smooth cartilage, are closely tied together by collagen fibres running between; e.g. pubic symphysis, joints between centra of vertebral column.

SYMPLASM. (Bot.). Protoplasmic continuum via plasmodesmata between cells e.g., from root hair cells to those of the stele. See *Syncytium*.

SYMPODIUM. Composite axis produced, and increasing in length, by successive development of lateral buds just behind the apex. Cf. *Monopodium*.

SYNANGIUM. Compound structure formed by lateral union of sporangia, present in certain ferns.

SYNAPSE. The nervous system of all animals contains immense numbers of distinct nerve-cells which touch each other only at certain places, synapses. There is no continuity between the nerve-cells at these places. Stimulation of one nerve-cell by another is probably confined to the synapses. A synapse is commonly formed by contact of the tip of a terminal banch of the axon belonging to one nerve-cell with the cell-body or with a dendrite of the other nerve-cell. Each axon (unless it is of a motor-fibre) usually has several synapses with each of several other nerve-cells; and each cell-body plus dendrites (unless it is a sensory-cell) has synapses with several nerve-fibres. The cell-body of a large vertebrate motor nerve-cell may bear several hundred or thousand synapses. An impulse, when it reaches a synapse, has to stimulate the next nerve-cell if it is to produce any further effect. This stimulation takes an appreciable time to occur (*synaptic delay*). Such stimulation may fail to occur if the impulse arrives from the wrong direction, since most synapses transmit only in one direction (from *pre-synaptic* side to *post-synaptic* side); thus sensory nerve-cells cannot usually be stimulated across synapses in the central nervous system. Furthermore the stimulation across a synapse may fail to produce an impulse in the nerve-cell receiving it, causing only a transitory rise in responsiveness. (See *Summatton, Facilitation*.) Through the operation of summation synapses are highly flexible interconnections. In those animals which have a C.N.S. most synapses are located there.

SYNAPSIS. *See Pairing*.

SYNAPTIC VESICLES. Organelles of nerve cells occurring at presynaptic side of synapse. Membrane-bounded sacs, 300-500 Angstroms in diameter. Supposed that they contain the neurohumoral substance, whose release at the nerve ending, when impulses arrive there, excites the post-synaptic nerve cell.

SYNCARPOUS. (Of the gynoecium of flowering plants), with united carpels, e.g. tulip. See *Flower*.

SYNCHRONOUS CULTURE. Culture (of micro-organisms or of tissue cells) in which, as a result of suitable treatment, all cells (often millions) are at any one time in approximately the same stage of development or of the mitotic cycle. Contrasts with untreated culture in which cells are in all stages. By vastly increasing amount of material available at any desired stage it provides opportunity to study changes, e.g. biochemical, that occur in development or in mitotic cycle that would be quite impossible using only a few cells.

SYNCYTIUM. (Zool.). Mass of cytoplasm, enclosed in a single continuous plasma membrane, containing many nuclei. The cytoplasm may be in the form of a sheet (forming an epithelium, e.g. trophoblast of many mammalian placentas); of a cylinder, e.g. striped muscle; of a network of almost discrete cells, each with a nucleus, but with cytoplasmic continuity through intercellular bridges, though it is difficult to establish this with certainty. The term is not used in botany; but where protoplasmic continuum exists via plasmodesmata between cells, the term symplasm is used. See *Cell*, *Plasmodium*, *Coenocyte*.

SYNECOLOGY. Ecology of communities as opposed to individual species (*autecology*).

SYNERGIDAE. See *Embryo sac*.

SYNERGISM. (1) Combined activity of agencies, e.g. drugs, hormones, which separately influence a certain process in the same direction, such that an effect is produced greater than sum of effects of each agency acting alone. (2) Sometimes used for combined activity such that effect is either sum of the separate effects (summation), or greater than the sum of the separate effects (potentiation), it does not matter which; i.e. the agencies are not antagonistic to each other. Cf. *Antagonism*.

SYNGAMY. Union of gametes in fertilization.

SYNGENEIC. Isogeneic (q.v.).

SYNGENESIOUS. (Of stamens), united by their anthers, e.g. dandelion and other members of family Compositae.

SYNOVIAL MEMBRANE. Membrane of connective tissue forming a bag (*synovial sac*) enclosing a freely movable joint, e.g. elbow joint, being attached to the bones at either side of the joint. The bag is filled with a viscous fluid (*synovial fluid*) containing mucoprotein, lubricating the smooth cartilage surfaces which make the contact between the two bones.

SYNTYPE. Each of several specimens cited in describing a new species, when a type specimen (q.v.) is not selected.

SYRINX. Sound-producing organ of birds, situated at point where trachea splits into bronchi (in quite a different region from larynx, q.v.).

SYSTEMATICS. Often used synonymously with taxonomy (q.v.); but sometimes interpreted more widely to include also identification, practice of classification, nomenclature.

SYSTEMIC. Generally distributed throughout an organism.

SYSTEMIC ARCH. Fourth aortic arch (q.v.) of tetrapod vertebrate embryo, becoming in adult main blood-supply for body other than head. In Amphibia and reptiles both right and left arches persist in the adult; in birds only the right, in mammals only the left (the aorta).

SYSTOLE. (1) Phase of heart-beat when heart muscle contracts, squeezing blood into arterial system. See *Pacemaker*. (2) Phase of contraction of contractile vacuole (q.v.). Cf. *Diastole*.

# T

**TACTILE.** (Adj.) Of touch. *T. corpuscle.* Receptor end-organ of touch.

**TAGMA** (plural **TAGMATA**). Division, each of several segments, into which body of arthropods is marked by differences in width, appendages, etc., e.g. head, thorax, abdomen.

**TANNINS.** Group of astringent substances of wide occurrence in plants, dissolved in cell-sap; particularly common in the bark of trees, unripe fruits, leaves, and galls. Complex organic compounds containing phenols, hydroxy acids, or glucosides. Function in plant not known with certainty. Used in production of ink and leather.

**TAPETUM.** (1) In vascular plants, layer of cells, rich in food material, surrounding a group of spore mother cells, e.g. in fern sporangium, pollen sacs of anther; gradually disintegrate and liberate their contents which are absorbed by the developing spores. (2) Of vertebrate eye, reflecting layer of retina or choroid.

**TAPEWORM.** Parasitic flat-worm (Cestoda). Adult lives in gut of vertebrates; body long and ribbon-like, consisting of a chain of proglottides, attached to host by scolex. Eggs develop into six-hooked embryos (onchosperes) which pass out with faeces of host, and if eaten by suitable animal, develop into larval stage (cysticercus, cysticercoid, or plerocercoid, q.v.). This becomes sexually mature only when eaten by the definitive host, which may not occur until after it has parasitized another intermediate host.

**TAP ROOT.** Root system with a prominent main root, directed vertically downwards and bearing smaller lateral roots, e.g. dandelion; sometimes becoming very swollen, containing stored food material, e.g. carrot, parsnip. Cf. *Fibrous root.*

**TARDIGRADA.** Bear-animalcules. Minute animals found in moss, etc. Probably specialized arthropods.

**TARSAL BONES (TARSALS).** Bones of the proximal part of the hind-foot (roughly the ankle) in tetrapod vertebrates. (Cf. *Carpal bones* of fore-foot). Primitively 10–12 bones in a compact group; in man there are 7, one of them (calcaneum) forming the heel. Articulate on proximal side with tibia and fibula, on distal side with metatarsals. See Fig. 7, p. 213.

**TARSIUS.** A primitive primate, in some ways intermediate between lemurs and anthropoids, found in East Indies.

**TARSUS.** (1) Region of hind-leg of tetrapod vertebrates containing tarsal bones (q.v.); roughly the ankle. (2) One of the segments (the fifth from the base) of an insect leg.

**TASTE-BUD.** Receptor end-organ for taste. See *Papillae of Tongue.* No structural differentiation of buds corresponding to the four tastes (sweet, bitter, sour, salty) is known.

TAXIS. Locomotory movement of an organism or cell, e.g. gamete, in response to a directional stimulus, the direction of movement being orientated in relation to the stimulus, e.g. to gradient of temperature or to direction of illumination. Chemotaxis, geotaxis, phototaxis, according to nature of stimulus. Cf. *Tropism, Kinesis.*

TAXON. General term for a taxonomic group whatever its rank.

TAXONOMY. Study of the classification of organisms according to their resemblances and differences. *Classical taxonomy* is concerned with description, naming and classification on the basis of morphology. Use is also made of biochemical and serological data. *Numerical taxonomy* applies mathematical procedures as an aid to objective and precise assessment of observable similarities and differences between taxonomic groups. *Cytotaxonomy* classifies on basis of characters of somatic chromosomes. *Experimental taxonomy* is concerned with analysing patterns of variation in order to discover how they evolved, with identification of evolutionary units, determining by experiment the genetical inter-relationships between them and the role of environment in their formation. See *Systematics.*

TELEOSTEI. A sub-class of Actinopterygii containing the great majority of existing fish (some 20,000 species).

TELEOSTOMI. A group of fish, now obsolete in classification, combining Actinopterygii and Crossopterygii, and excluding Dipnoi.

TELOPHASE. Terminal stage of mitosis (q.v.) or meiosis (q.v.) during which nuclei revert to resting-stage. See Figs. 6A, 6B, pp. 180, 181.

TELSON. The hindmost segment of the arthropod abdomen. In insects present only in the embryo.

TENDON. Cord or band of connective tissue attaching muscle, usually to a bone. Consists almost entirely of parallel collagen fibres.

TENDRIL. Stem, leaf, or part of leaf, modified as a slender, branched or unbranched, thread-like structure, used by many climbing plants for attachment to a support, either by twining round it, e.g. pea, grape; or sticking to it by means of an adhesive disc at the tip, e.g. virginia creeper.

TEPAL. Individual member of perianth (q.v.), particularly of perianths not clearly differentiated into corolla and calyx, e.g. tulip.

TERATOGENIC. Producing malformation in embryos.

TERGUM. Thickened plate of cuticle on dorsal side of a segment of an arthropod.

TERMINALIZATION. Process in late prophase of meiosis in which chiasmata between chromosomes move to ends of chromosomes, no longer coinciding with points where crossing-over has occurred, and their number decreases. Due to alteration in position of chromosomes relative to each other.

TERMITE. White ant. See *Isoptera.*

TERPENE. Unsaturated hydrocarbon occurring in plant oils and resins.

TERRITORY. (Zool.). An area or volume of the habitat occupied by an individual or group, trespassers on which, if they belong to the same species, are attacked. A common feature of vertebrate behaviour; has been found in fish, reptiles, birds, mammals. Particularly (though not exclusively) concerned with breeding behaviour, a male often holding a territory alone at first, being subsequently joined by female(s) who then share(s) in its defence throughout the breeding period.

TERTIARY. Geological period (q.v.); lasted approximately from 65 till 1½ million years ago.

TESTA. Seed coat. Protective covering of embryo of seed plants formed from integument(s); usually hard and dry.

TEST-CROSS. See *Double Recessive*.

TESTIS. Organ of animal which produces sperms. In vertebrates it also produces sex hormones. See *Androgen*.

TESTOSTERONE. An androgen (q.v.), probably the principal one produced within male vertebrates. A steroid.

TETRAD. (1) (Bot.). Group of four spores formed by meiosis within a spore mother-cell, e.g. formation of microspores within a microspore mother-cell. The process is often described as tetrad division. (2) Paired chromosomes of meiosis, after each chromosome has become visibly two-stranded.

TETRADYNAMOUS. (Of stamens) six in number, four longer than the other two, e.g. wallflower.

TETRAPLOID. Having four times the haploid number of chromosomes in a nucleus. A form of polyploidy. See *Allotetraploid*.

TETRAPODA. Four-footed animals. A grouping of vertebrate classes sometimes used in classification. Includes Amphibia, reptiles, birds, and mammals, i.e. all the essentially land-living vertebrate classes. All characterized by two pairs of pentadactyl limbs (q.v.).

TETRASPORE. First cell of gametophyte generation in many brown and red algae; formed in fours in a tetrasporangium following meiosis.

THALAMUS. (Bot.). Receptacle (q.v.) of flower. (Zool.). Part of the vertebrate fore-brain, a major sensory co-ordinating region.

THALLOPHYTA. Division of plant kingdom containing the most primitive forms of plant life. Characterized by a simple plant body (*thallus*) and varying from unicellular, microscopic forms, to multicellular forms such as large seaweeds, 60 to 70 metres in length. Although these latter show internal tissue differentiation, there is no differentiation of root, stem, and leaf as in higher plants. Asexual reproduction is by spores and (except in bacteria) sexual reproduction by fusion of gametes produced in sexual organs of various types but consisting essentially of single cells. Includes algae, bacteria, fungi, lichens, slime fungi. A very diverse group which in modern systems of classifications has been replaced by a number of divisions representing distinct evolutionary lines amongst organisms of simple structure.

THALLUS. Simple, vegetative, plant-body, showing no differentiation into root, stem and leaf. Unicellular or multicellular, consisting of branched or unbranched filaments or is more or less flattened and ribbon-shaped.

THERAPSIDA. Mammal-like reptiles. An extinct order of Reptilia. Lived from Permian to Triassic, the main reptile group until the appearance of the Dinosaurs. Important for being ancestral to mammals, the transition being well documented by fossils.

THERMOCLINE. Temperature stratification, e.g. of a lake.

THERMONASTY (Bot.). Response to a general, non-directional temperature stimulus, e.g. opening of crocus and tulip flowers with increase in temperature.

THERMOPHILIC. (Of a micro-organism), with optimum temperature for growth above 45°C.

THEROPHYTES. Class of Raunkiaer's Life Forms (q.v.).

THIAMIN (ANEURIN, VITAMIN B₁). Vitamin of B group. Its phosphate is a co-enzyme (cocarboxylase), very widely (universally?) distributed in living organisms, concerned in carbohydrate metabolism. Synthesized by some bacteria, moulds, and flagellates, and by green plants, but required as a vitamin by many living things, including man and all vertebrates and insects tested. Deficiency in man causes beri-beri.

THIGMOTROPISM. Haptotropism (q.v.).

THORACIC DUCT. Main lymph vessel of mammals receiving lymph from trunk (including lacteals) and hind-limbs, running up the thorax close to the vertebral column, and discharging into vena cava superior or an associated vein.

THORAX. (1) In terrestrial vertebrates region of the body containing heart and lungs (chest). Only in mammals is it clearly marked off from the abdomen by the diaphragm. (2) In insects, the group of three segments behind the head which bears the three pairs of legs and (when present) the wings.

THREAD CELL (CNIDOBLAST). Very specialized cell found only in coelenterates (of the phylum Cnidaria, i.e. hydroids, jelly-fish, sea-anemones, corals; not in Ctenophora) and in a few animals which prey upon them and 'adopt' their thread cells. Several kinds exist, having different functions, e.g. stinging, adhesion. A thread cell forms within itself an extraordinarily complicated body (nematocyst) consisting of a bladder within which a long hollow thread lies coiled until on stimulation, e.g. by touch of prey, the thread is shot out, and attaches to prey, or in case of stinging type, injects poison into it. Stinging of jelly-fish is due to thread cells present in enormous number on their tentacles.

THREADWORMS. Nematoda (q.v.).

THRESHOLD. That intensity of stimulus below which there is no response by a given irritable tissue.

THROMBIN. See *Blood-Clotting*.

THROMBOCYTE. See *Blood Platelet*.

THYLAKOID. In photosynthetic organisms, vesicle, wall of which bears photosynthetic pigments. Thylakoids vary in form and arrangement in different groups of organisms. See *Chloroplast*.

THYMONUCLEIC ACID. DNA (q.v.). First extracted from thymus, which is rich in nuclei.

THYMUS. Organ of vertebrates, usually in pharyngeal or neck region, formed embryologically from gill-pouches or gill-clefts. In mammals lies in chest (in mediastinum), and the cells from gill-pouches are mixed up with masses of lymphocytes; the organ reaches maximum size at puberty, and thereafter slowly diminishes. Exact functions still obscure, but concerned in the system producing antibodies.

THYROCALCITONIN. Calcitonin (q.v.).

THYROGLOBULIN. A protein containing thyroxin and tri-iodo-thyronine. The form in which these thyroid hormones are stored in the thyroid gland.

THYROID GLAND. An endocrine gland of vertebrates. Unpaired organ in neck region, formed embryonically from endodermal cells of floor of pharynx, homologous with endostyle of amphioxus and ammocoetes. Secretes iodine-containing hormones (see *Thyroxin, Thyroglobulin*), principal effect of which is to increase rate of oxidative processes. In amphibian tadpoles secretion of thyroid initiates metamorphosis. Thyroid gland is itself controlled by pituitary (thyrotrophic hormone). A trace of iodine in the diet is necessary to supply the thyroid, and deficiency of iodine produces enlargement (hyperplasia) of thyroid (one kind of goitre in man). Lack of the hormone from whatever cause, in human infants, produces mental and physical stunting (*cretinism*). Mammalian thyroid also secretes hormone calcitonin (q.v.).

THYROTROPIC (THYROTROPHIC) HORMONE (TSH). Hormone secreted by anterior lobe of pituitary, stimulating secretory activity and, in high doses, growth of thyroid gland. A protein.

THYROXIN. An iodine-containing amino-acid (tetra-iodo-thyronine). It and tri-iodo-thyronine are the hormones of the thyroid gland.

THYSANOPTERA. Thrips. An order of minute exopterygote insects most of which feed on sap of plants. Some are serious pests.

THYSANURA. See *Apterygota*.

TIBIA. (1) Shin-bone. The anterior of the two long bones (other is fibula) of the shank (below the knee) of the hind limb of tetrapod vertebrates. See Fig. 7, p. 213. (2) One of the segments (fourth from base) of an insect leg.

TICKS. Members of two families of the order Acarina. Blood suckers, some important carriers of disease, e.g. cattle fever tick.

TILLER. (Of grasses), side shoot arising at ground level.

TISSUE. Cellular fabric, of many varieties, of which organisms are made. Each consists mainly of cells of the same sort (performing the same function) associated in large numbers in characteristic arrangement, bound together by cell-walls (plants) or by intercellular material (animals); e.g. cells of plant cortex with their cellulose walls; or the numerous striped muscle fibres, bound together by collagen, with associated blood and lymph vessels, nerves and connective tissue cells, which make up muscle tissue.

TISSUE CULTURE (EXPLANTATION). A technique for maintaining fragments of animal or plant tissue or separated cells alive after their removal from the organism. The tissue fragments (*explants*) or cells are kept usually within some sort of glass vessel, in a medium of the right properties (isotonic, buffered to correct pH, with correct balance of metallic ions, see *Physiological Saline*, with suitable mechanical properties, at correct temperature, and containing the necessary oxygen and food material). Foreign organisms, especially bacteria and fungi, must usually be excluded. The medium may have to be frequently renewed to maintain food supply. The technique cannot be used for large pieces of tissue, because the cells in the middle of a large mass are not sufficiently close to the medium to receive food and dispose of excretions. See *Organ culture*.

TITRE. A relative measure of the amount of antibody in a fluid, usually in serum. The greatest dilution of the fluid capable of producing a particular antibody-antigen reaction to a detectable degree is the titre. It is expressed as the proportion to which the fluid has been diluted. The relative amounts of antibody present can thus be compared in different specimens of the fluid.

TOADSTOOL. Popular name for fruit-bodies of fungi other than mushrooms belonging to the family Agaricaceae of the Basidiomycetes; assumed generally, though often wrongly, to be poisonous.

TOLERANCE (IMMUNOLOGICAL). Failure to make an immune reaction when exposed to what should be an antigenic substance, the failure (tolerance) being induced by an exposure to this specific substance at a stage of life before the ability to make an immune reaction has fully developed.

TONOPLAST. (Bot.). Inner plasma-membrane, bordering vacuole.

TONSIL. Mass of lymphoid tissue in mouth or phraynx of tetrapods. Lies close underneath mucous membrane, deep crevices of which may communicate with interior of tonsil. Man has a pair of palatine tonsils (at junction of mouth and pharynx) and a single pharyngeal tonsil ('adenoids' at back of nose). Probably concerned in defence of mouth and pharynx against bacteria.

TONUS (TONE). Continuous but usually moderate, physiological activity of a tissue or organ; e.g. striped muscle, as a result of continuous nervous stimulation, is normally in a state of moderate contraction (tonus), by which the posture of the animal is maintained.

TORUS. (1) Receptacle (q.v.) of flower; (2) Thickened portion of
closing membrane of bordered pits (q.v.).

TRABECULAE. Bar-like structures. (Bot.). Slender rod-shaped supporting structures found in various plant organs (1) radially
elongated endodermal cells, each becoming a row of cells by
division, that supports stele in large air space in stems of lycopod
*Selaginella*, linking stele with cortex; (2) membranes, consisting
of rows of cells, traversing interior of sporangia in lycopod *Isoetes*;
(3) rod-like outgrowths of cell wall lying across lumen in tracheids.

TRACE ELEMENT. An element which must be available to an
organism for its normal health though it is necessary only in
minute amounts. E.g. higher plants need traces of at least the
elements zinc, boron, manganese, molybdenum, and copper; lack
of these may produce economically serious disease, such as 'heartrot' of sugar beet (boron deficiency). In animals such deficiency
disease is also known, e.g. 'coast disease' of cattle and sheep in
Australia from lack of cobalt. In man, thyroid deficiency (goitre,
cretinism) may be due to lack of semi-trace element, iodine. See
*Thyroid*. Trace elements are probably constituents of enzyme systems (cf. vitamins); and also, in animals, of hormones.

TRACER. The atoms of most chemical elements are not all alike, but
are of a few different kinds, called isotopes, differing in atomic
weight but not in chemical properties. Some isotopes are very rare
naturally, and these can be concentrated; and many radioactive
ones can be prepared artificially. These isotopes are used experimentally as 'tracers'; i.e. they can be incorporated into compounds
of biological importance, administered to an organism, and their
movements and changes of chemical combination determined by
analysis of the organism, or of its products. The radioactive isotopes are particularly easy to follow by their radiation; for instance
by autoradiographs (q.v.).

TRACHEA. (1) (Bot.). Conducting element of xylem. See *Vessel*. (2)
(Zool.). A tube which is part of the breathing apparatus of airbreathing animals. In land-living vertebrates the 'wind-pipe', a
single tube which leads from the throat, starting at the glottis,
through the neck to the point where it bifurcates into two bronchi.
In insects, tracheae ramify throughout the body and conduct air
from a few openings at the surface (spiracles) directly to the tissues;
made of epidermis and cuticle; finest branches are called tracheoles.

TRACHEAL GILL. Of aquatic insect larvae; organ whose thin-walled
surface in contact with water allows interchange of respiratory
gases between it and the tracheae it contains.

TRACHEID. Non-living element of xylem (q.v.) formed from a single
cell. Elongated, with tapering ends and with thick, lignified, and

pitted walls. It is a long, empty, firm-walled tube running parallel
with long axis of the organ in which it lies, overlapping and in
communication with adjacent tracheids by means of pits. Functioning in water conduction and in mechanical support. Primitive
compared with vessel (q.v.). Characteristic of vascular plants other
than flowering plants.

TRACHEOLE. Terminal branch of trachea (q.v.) of insects, pervad-
ing tissues in very large numbers. Interchange of oxygen and
carbon dioxide between tissues and gas in tracheoles takes place by
diffusion across their walls.

TRACHEOPHYTA. Group (Division) including all vascular plants
(includes Pteridophyta and Spermatophyta of older classifications); emphasizes physiological and phylogenetic importance of
the vascular system. Comprises sub-divisions Psilopsida, Lycopsida,
Sphenopsida, Pteropsida. Widely used in modern American texts.

TRACT. Spatially delimited bundle of nerve fibres, latter usually all
with similar connections, in the central nervous system. Tracts
connect nuclei with each other and with peripheral nervous
system.

TRANSCRIPTION. Synthesis of RNA, made up of a particular sequence of nucleotides, by matching with DNA, made up of a
corresponding sequence of nucleotides (see *Messenger RNA*).
Synthesis of DNA by matching with RNA is *reverse transcription*.
Cf. *Translation*.

TRANSDUCTION. Transfer of genetic material from one bacterium
to another through the agency of bacteriophage (q.v.). Gene or
genes of one (host) bacterial cell become incorporated in phage
particles which after release from dead host cell act as vectors in
the transport of this genetic material to other bacterial cells.

TRANSECT. Line of belt of vegetation selected for charting plants;
designed to study changes in composition of vegetation across a
particular area.

TRANSFER RNA. A relatively small molecule of RNA, whose function is to place the amino acids that will be linked into a polypeptide molecule in the specific sequence specified by a molecule of
*Messenger RNA* (q.v.). There is a different kind of transfer RNA
for each of the 20 fundamental amino acids. The amino acid
becomes attached to one end of the transfer RNA molecule
through the action of a specific activating enzyme, which links the
amino acid to ATP and then the resulting compound to its transfer
RNA. The other end of the transfer RNA molecule has a distinctive set of three nucleotides which attach (by base pairing, q.v.) to
a matching set of three nucleotides on the messenger RNA molecule. Each successive triplet of nucleotides on the messenger RNA
thus specifies a particular amino acid (see *Code, genetic*).

TRANSFER CELLS. Plant cells characterized by irregular wall ingrowth and unusually high surface to volume protoplast ratios.

Mitochondria numerous and endoplasmic reticulum conspicuous. Present in various locations in most major plant groups, e.g. gland cells of insectivorous plants; absorbing cells of dodder haustoria; minor veins of leaves, linking xylem vessels and phloem sieve tubes. Believed to be a specialization for intensive short distance transport of solutes as distinct from long distance conduction in vessels and sieve tubes.

TRANSFORMATION. (1) Phenomenon in which certain bacteria, when grown in the presence of killed cells, culture filtrates or extracts from other, related strains, acquire some of the genetic characters of these strains (i.e. they are transformed). Transforming principle is DNA. (2) Inherited change produced in cultured animal cells by infection with certain viruses, or by action of other agents, usually involving ability to form tumours.

TRANSFUSION TISSUE. Tissue of empty cells with pitted and, occasionally, internally thickened walls, and protein-containing, parenchymatous cells, accompanying vascular tissue in leaves of most gymnosperms, lying on either side of the vascular bundles of the single vein. Thought to represent an extension of the vascular system, taking the place of lateral veins.

TRANSLATION. Synthesis of a polypeptide made up of a particular sequence of amino acids by matching with an RNA made up of a corresponding sequence of nucleotides (see *Code, genetic*). It is the 'central dogma' of molecular biology that this operation never works in reverse, synthesizing nucleic acid by matching with polypeptide. Cf. *Transcription*.

TRANSLOCATION. (1) (Bot.). Transport of materials within plant. (a) Absorption of minerals from soil by roots and movement upwards in xylem to growing points, leaves. Absorption is under metabolic control, often taking place against a concentration gradient. In xylem minerals are carried upwards in transpiration stream but while rate of movement is influenced by rate of transpiration this relationship is not a consistent one. Some mineral ions are converted into organic substances and carried upwards in this form. (b) Movement of synthesized organic materials, sugars, nitrogenous compounds, and in addition, some inorganic ions, upwards and downwards in phloem, from leaves to regions of active growth and of storage, pattern of translocation changing during development, with changing needs in different parts of plant. Rate of movement of material in phloem is often very high, 100 cm. per hour or more, far faster than would be possible by simple diffusion; i.e. it is under metabolic control though precise mechanism of process is not yet resolved. (2) (Genetics). Transfer of part of a chromosome into a different part of a homologous, or into a non-homologous, chromosome. See *Mutation*.

TRANSMITTER. Neural transmitter (q.v.).

TRANSPIRATION. Loss of water-vapour by land plants. Occurs

mainly from leaves and differs from simple evaporation in that it takes place from living tissue and is therefore influenced by physiology of plant. Transpiration takes place chiefly through stomata (q.v.) and to a much less extent through the cuticle. Its significance is not completely understood. So long as stomata are open during interchange of gases between plant and atmosphere in photosynthesis and respiration, loss of water-vapour to the atmosphere must occur, i.e. for a healthy plant transpiration is inevitable. When it is excessive it is often harmful to the plant, causing wilting and even death. On the other hand there seems little doubt that it facilitates the upward movement of mineral salts in the xylem in the *transpiration stream*, though there is no consistent relationship between amount of water transpired and salt taken up; and it may also be of importance in preventing overheating in direct sunlight.

TRANSPIRATION STREAM. Flow of water through plant as a result of loss of water by transpiration. Diffusion pressure deficit (DPD) of cells of transpiring leaves causes osmotic withdrawal of water from xylem elements causing a tension (negative pressure) in water in xylem that exerts an upward pull (*transpiration pull*) through cohesion of water molecules. Tension is transmitted to roots from which water is withdrawn, aided by root pressure (q.v.). This then leads to increased DPD of root cells and increased water absorption by roots.

TRANSPLANTATION. (Zool.). Artificial removal of part of an organism from its normal position to an abnormal position in the same or another organism. Practically synonymous with grafting (see *Graft*) except that no close union with tissues of new position is necessarily implied.

TRANSVERSE PROCESS. Lateral projection, one on each side, of the neural arch of vertebra of tetrapod, with which head of rib articulates.

TREMATODA. (Flukes.) Class of Platyhelminthes. Parasites, with cuticle, two suckers, and forked gut. Usually complicated life-cycle. See *Fluke*.

TRIASSIC. Geological period (q.v.), lasted approximately from 225 till 190 million years ago.

TRIBE. Minor group used in classifying plants. Used in large families for groups of closely related genera within the family. Name of tribe ends in *-eae*.

TRICHOGYNE. In some green and red algae, Ascomycete fungi, and lichens; uni- or multicellular projection from female sex organ that receives male gamete or male nuclei before fertilization.

TRICHOME. Hair (q.v.). In blue-green algae (*Cyanophyta*), filament consisting of uniseriate or multiseriate chain of cells.

TRICHOPTERA. Caddis flies. Order of endopterygote insects with hairy bodies and wings; aquatic larvae live in cases which they make of wood, sand, leaves, etc.

TRICUSPID VALVE. Valve between right auricle and right ventricle of mammalian heart, consisting of three membranous flaps.

TRIGEMINAL NERVE. Fifth cranial nerve of vertebrates. In mammals mainly sensory, innervating teeth and skin of face. A dorsal root.

TRILOBITA. Class of Arthropoda. Now extinct but abundant from Cambrian to Silurian. Marine, superficially resembling woodlice; one pair of antennae, all other appendages biramous and similar to each other. Probably related to ancestors of Crustacea.

TRIPLOBLASTIC. Having the body made up of three layers (ectoderm, mesoderm, endoderm). As in all Metazoa except coelenterates, which are diploblastic (q.v.). See *Germ-Layers*.

TRIPLOID. Having three times the haploid number of chromosomes in a nucleus. A form of polyploidy.

TRISOMIC. Diploid except for one extra chromosome, homologous with one of the existing pairs; so that one kind of chromosome is represented three times. Type of aneuploidy.

TROCHANTER. (1) A prominence on the femur of vertebrates to which muscles are attached. There are three trochanters on each femur in mammals. The largest one in man is the conspicuous bony prominence at the hip joint. (2) One of the segments (second from base) of an insect leg.

TROCHLEAR NERVE. Fourth cranial nerve of vertebrates. Almost entirely motor, supplying eye-muscle (superior oblique). A ventral root.

TROCHOPHORE (TROCHOSPHERE). Larva of Polychaeta, Mollusca and Rotifera. Ciliated, usually planktonic. Develops by spiral cleavage. The main band of cilia encircles body in front of mouth. Coelom arises in blocks of mesoderm, i.e. not as pouches of gut. Two protonephridia sometimes present.

TROPHIC LEVEL. See Food-chain.

TROPHOBLAST. Embryonic epithelium which encloses all embryonic structures of placental mammal, forming outer layer of chorion (q.v.), and establishing close contact with maternal tissues. Forms embryonic side of placenta (q.v.); selectively permeable and hormone-secreting.

TROPISM. (1) Response to stimulus, e.g. gravity or light, in plants and sedentary animals by growth curvature, the direction of curvature being determined by the direction from which the stimulus originates. Cf. *Nastic Movement*. (2) (Zool.). Equivalent to taxis (q.v.) but this usage is becoming absolete.

TRUFFLE. Subterranean fruit-body of Ascomycete fungi belonging to order Tuberales; prized as a gastronomic delicacy.

TRYPANOSOMA. Genus of flagellate Protozoa, parasitic in the blood of vertebrates, and in the gut of tsetse flies and other insects, which transmit them to vertebrates. Trypanosomes cause important diseases in man (sleeping sickness) and horses and cattle in Africa.

TRYPSIN. Enzyme (peptidase, q.v.) splitting proteins and peptides at certain specific peptide links, in alkaline solution. Secreted by vertebrate pancreas. Trypsin-like enzymes occur in digestive juices of most animals.

TRYPSINOGEN. Almost inactive form in which trypsin is secreted by pancreas; a compound of trypsin and a polypeptide. Converted to trypsin by enterokinase (q.v.) and by trypsin already formed.

TSETSE FLY. Genus (*Glossina*) of dipteran insects. Blood-sucking flies which are responsible for carrying trypanosome diseases, e.g. sleeping sickness.

TSH. Thyrotropic hormone (q.v.).

TUBE FEET (PODIA). Of Echinodermata, hollow extensile append-ages connected to the water vascular system (q.v.). In some groups (starfish, sea-urchins) they end in suckers and are loco-motor, in others (brittle stars, crinoids) suckers are absent. Those around the mouth may be used for feeding (sea cucumbers, brittle stars). In crinoids they are ciliated and are part of food-collecting mechanism.

TUBER. Swollen end of underground stem bearing buds in axils of scale-like rudimentary leaves (stem tuber), e.g. potato, or swollen root (root tuber), e.g. dahlia. Tubers contain stored food material and are organs of vegetative propagation.

TUNICA CORPUS CONCEPT. See *Apical Meristem*.

TUNICATA. Urochordata (q.v.).

TURBELLARIA. Eddyworms, a class of Platyhelminthes. Mostly aquatic, free-living. Ciliated epidermis, gut a simple or branched sac.

TURGOR. State of cell in which the cell-wall is rigid, stretched by increase in volume of vacuole and protoplasm during absorption of water. The cell is described as turgid. Essential feature of mechani-cal support of plant tissues, loss of turgor (when water loss exceeds water absorption) being followed by wilting; and aids expansion of young cells in growth. Within a fully turgid plant cell osmotic pressure tending to force water into cell is balanced by hydrostatic pressure (turgor pressure) within the cell against its wall. When water is lost from cell, turgor pressure is reduced and more water enters by osmosis until turgidity is restored. Other illustrations of effects of alteration of turgidity include opening and closing of guard cells of stomata and sudden seismonastic (q.v.) drooping of leaves in the sensitive plant *Mimosa pudica*. Turgor pressure is also involved in mass flow hypothesis of transport in phloem.

TURION. Detached winter bud by means of which many water plants survive winter.

TURN-OVER. Continuous balanced generation and loss of cells or of their constituent molecules. *Turn-over time*, time taken to replace by turn-over a number of cells or molecules equal to that of the whole population.

TYLOSE (TYLOSIS). Balloon-like enlargement of the membrane of a pit in the wall between a xylem parenchyma cell and a vessel or tracheid, protruding into cavity of latter and blocking it; wall may remain thin or become thickened and lignified. Tyloses occur in wood of various plants, often abundantly in heartwood of trees, and may be induced to form by wounding. Often occur in xylem below developing abscission layer before leaf-fall.

TYMPANIC CAVITY. See *Ear, Middle.*

TYMPANIC MEMBRANE. Ear-drum. Double layer of epidermis with connective tissue between. See *Ear, Middle* and *Outer.*

TYPE SPECIMEN (HOLOTYPE). Original specimen(s) from which a description of a new species is made. When the exact specimen is not known or is lost, one has to be selected anew, and is called the *lectotype* (q.v.) or *neotype* (q.v.). See *Binomial Nomenclature.*

# U

ULNA. The posterior of the two bones (other is radius) of fore-arm of tetrapod vertebrate fore-limb. Articulates with side of hand (fore-foot) opposite to that on which thumb is. See Fig. 7, op. 213.

ULTRACENTRIFUGE. High speed centrifuge capable of sedimenting particles as small as a protein or nucleic acid molecule. Rate of sedimentation is used to estimate molecular weight or particle size. Since different kinds of protein or nucleic acid sediment at different rates, provides a means for determining whether a solution is a mixture or not.

ULTRASTRUCTURE. Structure, at the molecular or electron microscopical level.

UMBEL. Kind of inflorescence (q.v.).

UMBILICAL CORD. Stalk projecting from ventral surface of embryo of placental mammals, connecting it to placenta. Consists mainly of the mesoderm and blood-vessels of allantois, containing also part or all of the cavities of yolk-sac and allantois. Cord is surrounded by amniotic cavity. Usually breaks or is broken through at birth. See Fig. 8, p. 225.

UNDIFFERENTIATED. See *Differentiation*.

UNGULATE. Hoofed mammal; usually adapted for running on firm, open ground, herbivorous, living in herds. Since hooves have appeared independently in several groups of mammals, Ungulata is a term obsolete in classification. Most ungulates belong to orders Artiodactyla and Perissodactyla.

UNGULIGRADE. Walking on tips of digits, which have hooves, e.g. horse, cow. See *Artiodactyla*, *Perissodactyla*. Cf. *Digitigrade*, *Plantigrade*.

UNICELLULAR. Of organisms, consisting of one cell (q.v.) only, as distinct from multicellular; e.g. Protozoa. See *Acellular*.

UNIOVULAR TWINS. Monozygotic twins (q.v.).

UNISEXUAL. (1) (Of flowering plants or flowers) having stamens and carpels in separate flowers. Can be either monoecious or dioecious. Cf. *Hermaphrodite*. (2) (Of an individual animal) producing either male or female gametes, but not both. Cf. *Hermaphrodite*.

UNIT MEMBRANE. The common form, as seen in the electron microscope, of the membranes of cells: i.e. of the plasma membrane and of the membranes of organelles such as mitochondria, nucleus and endoplasmic reticulum. When suitably stained with heavy metals, the unit membrane appears in section as a pair of parallel dark lines (hence it is often called a 'double membrane'), the whole structure being about 75 Angstroms thick. Probably consists of a layer of lipid (two molecules thick) sandwiched between two layers of protein.

UNMYELINATED. Of a nerve fibre, lacking a myelin sheath (though nevertheless enclosed by Schwann cells). Such a nerve fibre is generally of very small diameter.

UREA. Main excreted product of protein break-down in ureotelic (q.v.) vertebrates. Occurs also in plants. A nitrogen-containing organic compound, $CO(NH_2)_2$, readily soluble in water.

UREASE. Enzyme which splits urea into ammonia and carbon dioxide. Present in many plants, but amongst animals only in a few invertebrates, e.g. Crustacea.

UREDINALES. Rust fungi. Order of Basidiomycetes comprising obligate parasites of higher plants with succession of several different spore forms in complicated life cycle that in some species involves two host species. Many rust fungi are of great importance as plant pathogens, most important being *Puccinia graminis*, cause of black stem rust of wheat and other cereals. See *Autoecious, Heteroecious, Physiologic Specialization.*

UREOTELIC. Excreting urea as main break-down product of amino-acids; ammonia from the latter (see *Deamination*) being converted to urea by ornithine cycle (q.v.). Characteristic of those vertebrates during whose embryonic development excretory products can freely diffuse away in this soluble form, i.e. those with aquatic or near-aquatic development (fish, Amphibia, Chelonia) and fully viviparous forms (mammals). Aquatic invertebrates excrete ammonia. Cf. *Uricotelic.*

URETER. Duct conveying urine away from kidney. In vertebrates term is usually restricted to duct leading from kidney (metanephros, q.v.) of amniote to urinary bladder; formed as outgrowth of Wolffian duct (q.v.).

URETHRA. Duct leading from urinary bladder (q.v.) of mammals to exterior. Joined by vas deferens (q.v.) in male.

URIC ACID. Complex nitrogen-containing organic compound, only slightly soluble in water. Main excreted product of breakdown of amino-acids and nucleic acids in uricotelic (q.v.) animals. Excreted by primates and Dalmatian dogs, but not by other mammals, as product of break-down of nucleic acids. Cf. *Ureotelic.*

URICOTELIC. Excreting uric acid as main break-down product of amino-acids. Characteristic of terrestrial animals which develop within a shell, unable to get rid of their excretory products, which they store in this insoluble form (squamata, birds, insects, and terrestrial gastropods). See *Cleidoic egg.* Cf. *Ureotelic.*

URINARY BLADDER. Sac storing urine; an expansion of the kidney duct in, e.g. Crustacea, teleosts. In tetrapods, a ventral diverticulum of hind end of gut (cloaca) which in embryo of amniotes leads into allantois (q.v.). Absent in adult birds and most reptiles.

URINIFEROUS TUBULE. Narrow coiled tube of vertebrate kidney leading from Bowman's capsule (q.v.) to the collecting ducts which convey the urine to the ureter or to the Wolffian duct. The fluid filtered into the Bowman's capsule is altered in composition as it travels along the tubule, valuable substances in it such as glucose, much of the salts, and in land vertebrates much of the water, being absorbed by the tubule walls; while some other substances are excreted into it. Blood supply to tubule is from renal portal system in anamniotes; from renal artery via glomerulus (q.v.) in amniotes.

UROCHORDATA (TUNICATA). Sea-squirts, etc. A group of marine chordate animals. See *Protochordata*. Adult sedentary (some secondarily free swimming), feeding by ciliary currents; gill slits; reduced nervous system; no notochord. Larva active, tadpole-like, with well-developed nervous system and notochord.

URODELA. Newts and salamanders; an order of the class Amphibia. Distinguished from the other orders, Anura and Apoda, by elongated body, with tail and normal limbs.

UROSTYLE. Unsegmented caudal region of vertebral column of Anura.

UTERINE TUBE. Fallopian tube (q.v.).

UTERUS. Womb. Muscular expansion of Müllerian duct (q.v.) of female mammals (excluding monotremes) in which the embryo develops. Usually paired, one connected with each Fallopian tube; but may, as in man, be single through fusion of lower part of Müllerian ducts in the embryo. Connected by vagina to exterior. Has glandular lining membrane (endometrium, q.v.; decidua, q.v.) which nourishes early embryo; and smooth muscle in its wall, which greatly increases in amount during pregnancy and whose contraction ultimately expels embryos and their placentae. Under control of sex hormones, it varies much in structure, enlarging at sexual maturity or in breeding season, diminishing during sexual inactivity; and in many mammals fluctuating in structure with oestrous cycle. See *Cervix, Placenta*.

UTRICLE (UTRICULUS). See *Ear, Inner*.

# V

**VACUOLE.** Fluid-filled space within the cytoplasm, bounded by a membrane. A single vacuole, taking up most of volume of cell, is present in many plant cells; contains solution (cell sap) isotonic with cytoplasm. Does not occur in cells of bacteria and blue-green algae. See *Contractile Vacuole*.

**VAGINA.** Duct of female mammal (excluding monotremes) connecting uteri with exterior via a short vestibule; receives penis of male during copulation. Embryologically derived either from terminal part of Müllerian duct or from cloaca. Usually single and median, owing to fusion of lower part of Müllerian ducts in the embryo, but paired in some marsupials. Lined with stratified non-glandular-epithelium. In many mammals undergoes cyclical changes with oestrous cycle (q.v.) and in mice recognition of these changes (from scrapings of vaginal wall known as *vaginal smear* technique) are of great importance in work on sex hormones. See *Oestrogen*.

**VAGUS NERVE.** Tenth cranial nerve of vertebrates. In mammals mainly parasympathetic (q.v.) supplying oesophagus, stomach, heart; and sensory, from, e.g. lungs and heart. A dorsal root.

**VALVE.** (Bot.). (1) One of several parts into which capsule (q.v.) separates after dehiscence by longitudinal splitting. (2) applied also to each half of wall of diatom cell (frustule, q.v.). (Zool.). (Heart) Flap or pocket of heart wall at entry and exit of each chamber of vertebrate heart, preventing back-flow. E.g. mitral valve (q.v.), tricuspid valve (q.v.). (Venous) Pocket-like flap within a vein, preventing back-flow, in birds and mammals. Similar structures occur in lymph vessels.

**VARIATIONS.** Differences between individuals of same species, apart from those referable to life cycle. May be due to differences in environment during development, and/or differences in the genes or cytoplasmic equipment with which the individual starts life.

**VARIEGATION.** Irregular variation of colour of plant organs, such as leaves and flowers, due to suppression of normal pigment development, e.g. chlorophyll, anthocyanin, in certain areas. An inherited character or a disease symptom, e.g. mosaic diseases due to virus infection.

**VARIETY.** (Bot.). The taxon (q.v.) below sub-species; a group which distinctly differs, for various reasons, from other varieties within the same sub-species. Often used loosely in Botany and Zoology to mean a variation of any kind within the species.

**VASCULAR.** Containing, or concerning, vessels which conduct fluid. In animals, the fluid is usually blood; in plants water, mineral salts, and synthesized food materials.

VASCULAR BUNDLE. Longitudinal strand of conducting (vascular) tissue consisting essentially of xylem and phloem; unit of stelar structure in stems of gymnosperms and angiosperms and occurring in appendages of stem, e.g. veins in leaves. In stems of gymnosperms and dicotyledons, arranged in a ring surrounding the pith, in monocotyledons, scattered throughout tissue of stem. May be (a) *collateral*, with phloem on same radius as xylem and external to it; typical condition in angiosperms and gymnosperms. (b) *Bicollateral*, with two phloem groups, external and internal to xylem, on same radius; uncommon, occurring in some dicotyledons, e.g. marrow. (c) *Concentric*, with one tissue surrounding the other. Concentric bundles are *amphicribral* when phloem surrounds xylem, e.g. in some ferns, and *amphivasal* when xylem surrounds phloem, e.g. in rhizomes of certain monocotyledons. Vascular bundles are further described as *open*, when cambium is present, e.g. in most dicotyledons, and *closed*, when cambium is absent, e.g. in monocotyledons.

VASCULAR CYLINDER. See *Stele*.

VASCULAR PLANT. Plant possessing vascular system (q.v.), member of Tracheophyta (Pteridophyta and Spermatophyta of older classifications).

VASCULAR SYSTEM. (1) (Bot.). Plant tissue consisting mainly of xylem and phloem which forms a continuous system throughout all parts of higher plants. It functions in conduction of water, mineral salts, and synthesized food materials and for mechanical support. Older stems and roots of perennial plants consist largely of vascular tissue. Its development in evolution was a primary feature underlying success of plants on land. (2) (Zool.). Blood system (q.v.) or Water Vascular System (q.v.).

VAS DEFERENS. Tube (one on each side) conveying sperm from testis to exterior. In male amniote vertebrate conducting sperm from epididymis (q.v.) to cloaca or urethra (q.v.). See *Wolffian Duct, Vas Efferens*.

VAS EFFERENS. Tube (of which there are many on each side) conveying sperm from testis of vertebrate to mesonephros or epididymis.

VASOCONSTRICTION. Narrowing of blood-vessels; usually refers to arterioles, occurring by contraction of smooth muscle in their walls, mainly controlled by sympathetic nervous system. Capillaries constrict apparently by change in shape of endothelial cells.

VASODILATATION. As vasoconstriction but *expansion* of blood-vessels, usually by *relaxation* of muscle.

VASOMOTOR. Concerned with constriction and dilatation of blood-vessels. *V. nerves*, sympathetic nerves of vertebrates controlling and maintaining tonus of smooth muscle of arterioles. There are separate constrictor and dilator nerves.

VECTOR. An organism (animal, fungus) which transmits parasites, e.g. mosquitoes are vectors of malaria parasite.

VEGETAL POLE (VEGETATIVE POLE). (Zool.). Point on surface of egg furthest from the egg nucleus, and usually at yolkiest end of the egg. See *Animal Pole*.

VEGETATIVE REPRODUCTION (V. PROPAGATION). (1) Asexual reproduction in plants by detachment of some part of the plant body distinct from spore, and its subsequent development into a complete plant, e.g. gemmae, rhizomes, bulbs, corms, tubers. (2) In plants and animals synonymous with asexual reproduction (q.v.).

VEIN. (1) (Bot.). Vascular bundle (q.v.) of a leaf. (2) (Zool.). Blood-vessel (of fairly small diameter to distinguish it from a venous *sinus*, q.v.) carrying blood from the minute vessels which supply tissues (the capillaries) to the heart. In vertebrates, veins have a smooth lining of flat cells (endothelium, q.v.) with muscular and fibrous tissue outside; compared with arteries their walls are thin and their internal diameter large; unlike arteries and capillaries they contain simple valves which permit blood-flow only towards the heart. The pressure of blood within them is low. (3) Of insect wings, fine tubes of toughened cuticle which make a supporting framework. Contain air-tubes (tracheae, q.v.) nerves and blood.

VELAMEN. Water-absorbing tissue occurring on the outside of aerial roots in certain plants, e.g. epiphytic orchids, consisting of several layers of dead cells often with spirally thickened and perforated walls, which act as a sponge, soaking up water that runs over it.

VELIGER. Larva of Mollusca, which develops from a trochophore. Ciliated bands have become larger; foot, mantle, shell, and other organs of adult are present.

VENA CAVA INFERIOR (POSTERIOR VENA CAVA, POSTCAVAL VEIN). Main vein of tetrapod vertebrates passing blood into the heart from veins of almost all body behind the fore-limbs. A single median vein, largest in the body. Has no homologue in fish, whose posterior cardinal veins (q.v.) serve same purpose.

VENA CAVA SUPERIOR (ANTERIOR VENA CAVA, PRECAVAL VEIN). Main vein of tetrapod vertebrates returning blood to the heart (to right auricle) from the fore-limbs and head. Usually a right and left pair, but in many mammals, including man, only the right one persists in adult. Homologous with ductus Cuvieri of fishes.

VENATION. (1) Arrangement of veins in a leaf. (2) System of veins (q.v.) in wing of insect. An important characteristic for classification.

VENTER. (Bot.). Swollen basal region of an archegonium, containing egg-cell.

VENTRAL. Situated at, or relatively nearer to, that side of the animal which (if not in the animal, at least in the group to which the animal belongs) is normally directed downwards with reference to gravity. In human beings, ventral side is directed forwards.

Opposite of dorsal. *V. aorta*. See *Aorta, Ventral*. (Bot.). Also used of leaves, synonymous with Adaxial (q.v.).

VENTRAL ROOT (ANTERIOR ROOT, MOTOR ROOT). Nerve-root (q.v.) of vertebrates, containing motor fibres.

VENTRICLE. (1) One of the chambers of the heart, the main pumping part, with thick muscular walls. Receives blood from the auricle(s) and passes it to the arteries. Occurs in molluscs and vertebrates. Fish and Amphibia have a single ventricle; reptiles have a partially divided ventricle, except crocodiles where division into two is complete; birds and mammals have two, right supplying blood to lung, left supplying rest of body. (2) Cavity within vertebrate brain filled with cerebrospinal fluid; lateral ventricles in cerebral hemispheres; third ventricle in rest of fore-brain; fourth in medulla oblongata.

VENULE. Small vein of vertebrates, differing from capillary by having more connective tissue, and in larger ones smooth muscle, in its wall. Collects blood from capillaries. Permeability of wall of small venule is similar to that of capillary (q.v.).

VERMES. Term formerly used for heterogeneous collection of animals, now recognized to be not closely related. Linnaeus used it to include all animals other than vertebrates and arthropods. Later it was restricted to more or less worm-like animals (Platyhelminthes, Nematoda, Nemertea, Annelida, Rotifera, Polyzoa.

VERNALIN. Hormone-like substance produced by vernalization (q.v.) that will pass across a graft union.

VERNALIZATION. Application of cold treatment to plants to effect flowering. Intimately related with day-length. See *Photoperiodism*. First studied in cereals some of which, if sown in spring, will not flower in the same year but continue to grow vegetatively. Such plants, known as winter varieties, need to be sown in the autumn of the year preceding that in which it is desired that they should flower, and they contrast with spring varieties which, planted in spring, flower in the same year. By vernalization winter cereals can be sown and brought to flower in one season. The seed is moistened sufficiently to allow germination to begin, but not so much as to encourage rapid growth, and when tips of radicles are just emerging, the seed is exposed to a temperature just above $0°C$. for a few weeks. Seed thus vernalized acquires properties of seed of spring varieties in that, sown in spring, it produces a crop in the summer of the same year. Vernalization as a practical technique has been developed particularly in Russia. Its significance in agriculture has been demonstrated in that country where it is used, e.g. to avoid killing of winter cereals in the severe winter months. Other possibilities arising from the treatment, e.g. introduction of a crop plant into a new area with a growing season shorter than that under which it normally grows, are being explored.

The cold stimulus is perceived by the apical meristem (in embryo;

or by apical bud of older plant). Factor that induces flowering has been shown capable of movement in some plants, e.g. grafting bud of a cold treated plant on to untreated plant induces response in buds of latter, i.e. factor acts like a hormone (q.v.). Mechanism of vernalization unknown; in some plants same response can be obtained by treatment with gibberellin (q.v.). Effect can be reversed in some plants by exposure to high temperature in anaerobic conditions.

VERNATION. Way in which leaves are arranged in relation to each other in the bud.

VERTEBRA. See *Vertebral Column*.

VERTEBRAL COLUMN (SPINAL COLUMN). Backbone. Longitudinally arranged chain of small bones or cartilages (*vertebrae*) near dorsal side, surrounding spinal cord, characteristic of vertebrates (q.v.). In most vertebrates (not cyclostomes) the vertebrae form a jointed hollow rod, attached to the skull in front, enclosing the spinal cord, and more or less replacing notochord during embryonic development. The mid-point of the length of each vertebra lies level with the interval between successive somites in the embryo. Each vertebra usually consists of a substantial mass (the centrum) where the notochord was, with an arch (neural arch) above enclosing the spinal cord and often a similar arch (haemal arch) below, or ventral projections, enclosing main axial blood-vessels. They are jointed to each other by their centra, and often by projections of the neural arch, though only restricted movement is possible between any two vertebrae. See *Symphysis*. In fish all vertebrae from skull to tail are very similar. But in tetrapods there are regional differences usually as follows: atlas and axis (q.v.); neck (cervical) with reduced ribs; thoracic, bearing ribs; lumbar, again without ribs; sacral, attached by rudimentary ribs to pelvic girdle; and tail (caudal).

VERTEBRATA (CRANIATA). Most important sub-phylum of the phylum Chordata. Contains the fish, amphibians, reptiles, birds, and mammals, i.e. classes Agnatha, Placodermi, Acanthodii, Choanichthyes, Actinopterygii, Chondrichthyes, Amphibia, Reptilia, Aves, Mammalia. Vertebrates differ from other chordates in having a skull, which surrounds a well-developed brain, and a skeleton of cartilage or bone. Not all the fossil ones have been shown to have a vertebral column (though most of them have), so that the term Craniata is perhaps preferable, though in much less common use. Vertebrata is occasionally used as synonym for Chordata.

VESICULA SEMINALIS. Seminal vesicle (q.v.).

VESSEL (TRACHEA). Non-living element of xylem (q.v.) consisting of a tube-like series of cells arranged end to end, running parallel with long axis of the organ in which it lies and in communication with adjacent elements by means of numerous pits in side walls.

Component cells of a vessel, known as vessel segments, cylindrical in shape, sometimes broader than long, with large perforations in end walls. Functioning in conduction of water and mineral salts, and for mechanical support. Have evolved from tracheids (q.v.), principal features of this evolution being elimination of multi-perforate end walls to form single large perforation, reduction or disappearance of taper of end walls and change from a long narrow element to one relatively short and wide. With few exceptions confined to flowering plants.

VESTIGIAL ORGAN. Organ, the size, structure, and function of which have diminished and simplified in the course of evolution until only a trace remains. Such vestiges may still have important function in organizing embryonic development, even if their former adult function has disappeared.

VIABLE. Able to live. Of seeds or spores, able to germinate.

VIBRISSAE. Whiskers. Stiff hairs projecting from face, and sometimes limbs, of most mammals, acting as touch receptors.

VICARIAD. One of a group of (vicarious) closely related species whose distribution is allopatric (q.v.).

VILLUS. Finger-like projection. *Intestinal villi* (about 1 mm. long in man), in enormous numbers, give lining of small intestine of many vertebrates velvet-like appearance. Each villus is covered by absorptive epithelium, contains blood-vessels and a lacteal, and moves continually by smooth muscle within it. Absorptive surface of intestine is thus immensely increased. *Chorionic villi*: projections of chorion (q.v.) in mammalian placenta (q.v.) which increase area of contact between embryonic and maternal tissues.

VIRION. A fully-formed, mature, virus (q.v.). Differs in shape in different kinds of virus: rod-shaped, almost spherical (polyhedral) or possessing a head and tail. Infection is initiated in a cell by a virion.

VIRUS. A member of a group of sub-microscopic agents that infect plants and animals, usually manifesting their presence by causing disease, and are unable to multiply outside the host tissues. Also attack bacteria (such a virus is a *Bacteriophage*). The fully formed, mature, virus (or *virion*) consists of nucleic acid within a protein or protein and lipid coat. Nucleic acid is either DNA or RNA in animal viruses, RNA in plant viruses and DNA (and occasionally RNA) in bacteriophages. Infectivity resides in nucleic acid component, which is released from the virion into the infected cell, where it initiates synthesis of more virions. A few kinds of virion contain enzyme(s) involved in penetration of host cell.

Of great agricultural and medical importance, causing, e.g. various diseases of potato, cereals; foot-and-mouth disease, common cold, influenza, poliomyelitis, small pox, measles, yellow fever. In plants mainly found in Angiosperms, but attack the cultivated mushroom, and have been isolated from a few other fungi; attack wild and domestic mammals, birds and insects, as well as man. Some virus infected plants are prized as ornamentals, e.g. certain tulips, variegated *Abutilon*. Some viruses, artificially introduced, are used as agents of biological control, e.g. polyhedral viruses attacking leaf eating insect larvae in forests; myxomatosis virus killing rabbits.

Viruses are transmitted from plant to plant mostly by insects, aphids being most common vectors. Some soil-borne viruses are transmitted by eelworms and a few by soil-borne phycomycete fungus root parasites, e.g. *Olpidium*. Other viruses are spread by plant to plant contact. Viruses that are systemic in plants are spread very effectively by vegetative propagation, in tubers, bulbs, runners, etc. Few viruses are seed-borne. Animal viruses are spread by insect vectors, by contact, or in droplets of mucus expelled from nose, throat and mouth of infected animal and inhaled by another. There has been much argument as to whether viruses are living or not. The fact is that they have some of the properties of obviously living things, and not others. Whether they are called living or non-living adds nothing to our understanding of their properties. Some viruses have been obtained in crystalline form. Different viruses are of varying grades of complexity; those that are roughly spherical are between 150 and 1300 Angstroms in diameter.

VISCERAL ARCHES. (1) The series of partitions on each side of pharynx between adjacent gill-slits, or between mouth and first gill-slit (spiracle) in fish; or between the corresponding gill-pouches or gill-slits of tetrapod embryos. (2) The skeletal bars (cartilage or bone) lying in these partitions in fish. The bars of each side meet the corresponding bars of the opposite side mid-ventrally, so that together they form a series of inverted arches beneath mouth and throat. The first ('mandibular') arch becomes the primitive jaw skeleton (palatoquadrate and Meckel's cartilage); the second ('hyoid') arch, behind the spiracle, is usually concerned in attachment of jaws to skull; and the remainder ('branchial arches') lie each behind a functional gill-slit.

VISCUS. Organ lying in abdominal cavity.

VISUAL PURPLE. Compound of a protein with a prosthetic group of which Vitamin A is an essential precursor. Occurs in rods (q.v.) of vertebrate retina. Chemically changed (and bleached) by light, the change being basis of function of rods as light-sensitive receptors. Increases in amount in dark, raising sensitivity of rods to faint light (dark adaptation).

VITAL STAINING. Staining of cells, or parts of them, while they are living. Several (basic) dyes stain cells placed in them (often called *supravital staining*): e.g. neutral red stains vacuoles and granules in many cells, Janus green stains mitochondria specifically, methylene blue stains axons. Used in determining morphogenetic movements in embryos. Other (acid) dyes, e.g. trypan blue when injected into an animal (often called *intra vitam staining*) are taken up by cells, especially by the macrophages of vertebrates.

VITAMIN. Organic substance which an organism must obtain from its environment, though it is necessary only in minute amounts. The essential amino-acids (q.v.), which are similarly needed, but in larger amounts, are not included amongst vitamins. A vitamin plays an essential role in metabolism, probably often as part of an enzyme system (hence the small amounts required), and in so doing is broken down, like many other substances in the organism, and lost. What distinguishes a vitamin from most other compounds essential in metabolism is that the organism cannot replace its loss by synthesizing it, and so must obtain it from outside. Occasionally an animal may be able to synthesize part of its requirement (e.g. D by man), and often symbiotic organisms provide part or all of the requirement (e.g. B vitamins synthesized by gut bacteria of insects and vertebrates). Vitamins are required only by heterotrophic organisms; autotrophic organisms, such as most of the green plants, are by definition independent of an external supply of organic compounds. What is a vitamin for one heterotrophic organism may be synthesized in adequate amounts by, and is therefore not a vitamin for, another; or it may even take no part at all in the metabolism of another. There is no such thing as a vitamin in general, but only for specified organisms. There may be mutant strains within one species, some requiring a substance as a vitamin, others synthesizing it. Some (like those of the B complex) which are perhaps universal *constituents* of existing organisms are however required by a very wide range of organisms; others (like C) by very few. Every vitamin necessary for a given organism is synthesized by other organisms, otherwise a continuous supply will not be available. The vitamin requirements of the vast majority of organisms are quite unknown. Sometimes several different compounds can substitute for each other in satisfying a given requirement (e.g. see *Vitamin D*); either because the organism requires, not a specific molecule, but a specific chemical grouping which is present in, and available from, each of the alternative compounds; or because conversion of a few closely related groupings into the one required is possible within the organism. Deficiency of the vitamin reduces the rate of the (often unknown) metabolic process in which it is concerned, with widespread effects (symptoms of deficiency disease). A general effect of deficiency of most vitamins, which was important in the early history of their discovery, is that growth of young animals is stunted.

VITAMIN A. Required by man and other vertebrates but not by other organisms. Fat soluble. Stored in liver. Deficiency in man causes night-blindness (the vitamin being a constituent of visual purple) and keratinization of cornea, and other effects involving epidermis and nervous tissue. Carotene (q.v.) which is synthesized by green plants, and some related pigments, can be converted by animals to Vitamin A, and the vertebrates obtain their supply of the vitamin ultimately from this source.

VITAMIN B COMPLEX. Several water-soluble vitamins, formerly thought to be a single vitamin. See *Thiamin* ($B_1$), *Riboflavin* ($B_2$), *Pyridoxine* ($B_6$), *Pantothenic Acid*, *Nicotinic Acid*, *Cobalamine* ($B_{12}$).

VITAMIN C. Ascorbic acid (q.v.).

VITAMIN D. Required as a vitamin by man, though some is synthesized; and by other vertebrates. Fat soluble. Stored in liver. Deficiency in childhood causes rickets; in adults, sometimes osteomalacia. Effect of the vitamin is on absorption and deposition of calcium and phosphate. Synthesis in man is by action of ultraviolet (in sunlight) on a precursor in skin. Several slightly different compounds have Vitamin D activity for man, though only one has for fowls. All are sterols.

VITAMIN E (TOCOPHEROL). Required as a vitamin by vertebrates. Fat soluble. Deficiency causes abortion, and sterility in male.

VITAMIN F. Linoleic acid (q.v.).

VITAMIN K. Required as a vitamin by man, other mammals, and birds. Fat soluble. Deficiency causes proneness to haemorrhage, since the vitamin takes part in synthesis of prothrombin in liver. Various slightly different compounds have Vitamin K activity. Has been synthesized in water soluble form. Part of human requirements probably come from bacteria living in gut.

VITELLINE MEMBRANE. Membrane which immediately surrounds ovum (q.v.) of animals. It is secreted by the ovum. E.g. membrane enclosing the yolk of a hen's egg.

VITREOUS HUMOUR. Jelly-like material which fills cavity of vertebrate eye behind the lens. See Fig. 3, p. 107.

VIVIPAROUS. Having embryos which develop within the maternal organism and derive nutriment by close contact with maternal tissues, frequently by a placenta, without interposition of any egg-membranes. Viviparity occurs in all placental mammals, and sporadically in other groups of animals. Cf. *Ovoviviparous, Oviparous.* (Bot.). Having seeds which germinate within the fruit, e.g. mangrove; or producing shoots for vegetative reproduction instead of an inflorescence, as in some grasses.

VOCAL CORD. See *Larynx*.

VOLUNTARY MUSCLE. Striped muscle (q.v.).

VOLUTIN. Reserve phosphate (inorganic metaphosphate polymer) occurring as highly refractive granules in many bacteria. Similar bodies found in many algae, and in some fungi and protozoa.

# W

**WALLERIAN DEGENERATION.** Break-up and autolysis of a nerve-fibre, and of the surrounding myelin sheath (if any), when cut off from the cell body, e.g. by injury.

**WALLACE'S LINE.** Boundary drawn across the Malay Archipelago, by A. R. Wallace, between the different faunas of the Oriental and Australian regions.

**WANDERING CELLS.** Cells of blood and connective tissue which actively migrate *in vivo*, e.g. macrophages, amoebocytes.

**WARNING (APOSEMATIC) COLORATION.** Conspicuous markings on an animal which is poisonous, distasteful, or similarly defended against predators. Coloration is presumed to facilitate learning, on the part of predators, to keep off. See *Mimicry*.

**WATER VASCULAR SYSTEM.** Of echinoderms, a system of canals containing fluid, open to either the sea or body-cavity, which supplies fluid to tube-feet (q.v.).

**WHALEBONE.** Baleen (q.v.).

**WHEEL ANIMALCULES.** Rotifera (q.v.).

**WHITE BLOOD CELL.** Cell of animal blood, containing no respiratory pigment. In vertebrates, may be polymorph, lymphocyte, or monocyte.

**WHITE MATTER.** Tissue of central nervous system of vertebrates, mainly formed of nerve fibres whose myelin gives it glistening white appearance. Glia and blood-vessels also present. Lies as a layer predominantly outside grey matter (q.v.), forming the tracts connecting different parts of the central nervous system together.

**WHOLE MOUNT.** An entire organism or part of an organism, prepared by fixation, staining, dehydration, and clearing (but not cut into sections by microtome), and placed on a slide, usually in Canada balsam under a coverslip, for microscopical examination.

**WILD TYPE.** Phenotype which is characteristic of the majority of individuals of a species in natural conditions. See *Dominance*.

**WILTING.** Condition of plants in which cells lose their turgidity, and leaves, young stems, etc., droop; resulting from excess of water loss (in transpiration) over water absorption.

**WOLFFIAN DUCT.** Vertebrate kidney duct, one on each side. Formed in embryo of all vertebrates from region of pronephros; and subsequently taken over by mesonephros, becoming its duct. In adult anamniotes is usually the kidney duct, and testis also discharges sperm through it. In adult amniotes, where functional kidney (metanephros) has separate duct, it persists only in male, for discharge of sperm, and forms epididymis and vas deferens.

**WOOD.** Xylem (q.v.).

# X

XANTHOPHYLL. Carotenoid (q.v.) plant pigment.

XANTHOPHYTA. Yellow green algae. Division of algae. Mostly unicellular, non-motile; others are colonial, filamentous, or tubular, coenocytic. Cell wall materials mainly cellulose and pectic substances, in some species impregnated with silica; often composed, in unicellular forms, of two halves but this is rarely obvious without chemical treatment. Possess chlorophyll a together with β-carotene and several xanthophylls. Reserve foods stored as oils and polysaccharide *chrysolaminarin*. A few colourless, heterotrophic forms are saprophytic or ingest food particles. Motile cells unequally biflagellate, rarely uniflagellate. Asexual reproduction by cell division, less commonly by zoospores or aplanospores. Sexual reproduction isogamous or anisogamous. Mainly in fresh water or terrestrial; few marine.

X-CHROMOSOME. A sex-chromosome found paired in the homogametic sex and single in the heterogametic sex. Unlike Y-chromosome (q.v.) contains numerous genes, which show sex-linkage (q.v.).

XENIA. Changes due to effect of foreign pollen in visible characters of endosperm. Result from influence of gene complement of male nucleus which fuses with primary endosperm nucleus as a prelude to endosperm formation. Classical examples afforded by maize, e.g. when variety with white endosperm is pollinated by one with deep yellow endosperm, endosperm of resulting seeds is pale yellow.

XENOPUS. African clawed toad. Used in pregnancy diagnosis, since produces eggs when injected with urine of pregnant woman.

XEROMORPHY. (Bot.). Possession of morphological characters associated with xerophytes.

XEROPHYTE. Plant of dry habitat able to endure conditions of prolonged drought, e.g. in areas of low rainfall such as deserts; due either to capacity during brief rainy seasons for internal storage of water that is used when none can be obtained from soil together with low daytime transpiration rate associated with closure of stomata, e.g. in succulents such as cacti; or to ability to recover from partial desiccation, e.g. desert shrubs such as creosote bush. As long as water is freely available there is evidence that non-succulent xerophytes transpire as, or more freely, than do mesophytes but unlike the latter they can endure periods of permanent wilting during which transpiration is reduced to very low levels. Features associated with this reduction, in different xerophytes, include dieback of leaves which cover and protect perennating buds at soil surface, shedding of leaves when water supply is exhausted, heavily cutinized or waxy leaves coupled with closure or plugging of stomata, sunken or protected stomata, orientation or folding of leaves to reduce insolation, microphyllous habit reducing possibility of drought necrosis of mesophyll. Cf. *Hydrophyte*, *Mesophyte*.

**XEROSERE.** A sere (q.v.) commencing on dry site.

**XYLEM.** Wood. Vascular tissue that conducts water and mineral salts, taken in by roots, throughout the plant and provides it with mechanical support. Of two kinds, *primary*, formed by differentiation from procambium and consisting of protoxylem (q.v.) and metaxylem (q.v.), and *secondary*, additional xylem produced by activity of cambium. Characterized by presence of tracheids and/or vessels, fibres, and parenchyma. In mature woody plants makes up bulk of vascular tissue itself and of entire structure of stems and roots, e.g. tree trunk.

# Y

**Y-CHROMOSOME.** The sex-chromosome (q.v.) found only in the heterogametic sex. Usually differs from the X-chromosome (q.v.) in size. Often only a short part of it with the X-chromosome at meiosis, and it usually contains few or no major genes.

**YEASTS.** Widely distributed unicellular fungi, belonging mainly to the Ascomycetes, which multiply typically by a budding process. Of great economic importance. The brewing and baking industries depend upon capacity of yeasts to secrete enzymes that convert sugars into alcohol and carbon dioxide. In the former industry alcohol is the important product; in the latter escaping carbon dioxide causes dough to rise. Yeasts are also used commercially as a source of proteins and vitamins.

**YOLK.** Store of food material, in form of protein and fat granules, in eggs, of majority of animals.

**YOLK-SAC.** Sac containing yolk which hangs from ventral surface of very yolky vertebrate embryos (elasmobranchs, teleosts, reptiles, birds). Has outer layer of ectoderm; inner layer, usually absorptive, of endoderm; with mesoderm containing coelom and blood-vessels between. The endoderm is in effect a diverticulum of the gut, the yolk- or fluid-filled space within it communicating with intestine of embryo (not in teleosts). In mammals the yolk-sac, quite empty of yolk, is only the endodermal sac, with its layer of mesoderm, homologous with that of the other vertebrates; the ectodermal layer with its mesoderm is called part of the chorion. The same terminology is often applied to the other amniotes. As absorption of yolk proceeds, yolk-sac is withdrawn until it merges into the embryo; but most of it is cut off from the embryo at birth in mammal. See Fig. 8, p. 225.

# Z

**ZEATIN.** A cytokinin (q.v.).

**ZONA PELLUCIDA.** Homogeneous (mucoprotein) membrane around the mammalian egg, which disappears before implantation in the uterus.

**ZOOGEOGRAPHY.** Study of the geographical distribution of animals.

**ZOOID.** Member of a colony of animals which are joined together, e.g. polyp, polypide.

**ZOOLOGY.** Study of animals.

**ZOOPLANKTON.** Animals of plankton (q.v.). Cf. *Phytoplankton*.

**ZOOSPORANGIUM.** (Bot.). Sporangium producing zoospores; present in certain fungi and algae.

**ZOOSPORE (SWARM-SPORE).** Naked spore produced within a sporangium (zoosporangium), motile by one, two, or many flagella; present in certain members of phycomycete fungi and green and brown algae.

**ZYGOMORPHIC.** See *Bilaterally Symmetrical*.

**ZYGOSPORE.** Thick-walled resting spore, product of sexual reproduction by fusion of contents of two similar gametangia; found in a group of phycomycete fungi, Zygomycetes, and in an order of green algae, Conjugales. Also used for product of fusion of motile isogametes, e.g. in *Chlamydomonas*.

**ZYGOTE.** The fertilized ovum, before it undergoes cleavage.

**ZYGOTENE.** Stage in prophase of first division of meiosis (q.v.), following leptotene, in which pairing (synapsis) of homologous chromosomes occurs with formation of bivalents.

**ZYMASE.** Enzyme system of yeast which breaks down (ferments) hexose sugars into alcohol and carbon dioxide. The first cell-free enzyme preparation (1897).

**ZYMOGENOUS.** Of soil micro-organisms, displaying a burst of metabolic activity, with conspicuous increase in number, after addition of organic matter using simple constituents as food substrates; with subsequent decline to original state as substrates are exhausted. Cf. *Autochthonous*. Probably, as the soil environment changes and the conditions become favourable for one group of organisms after another, all, in turn, display a zymogenous response.

# MORE ABOUT PENGUINS
## AND PELICANS

*Penguinews*, which appears every month, contains details of all the new books issued by Penguins as they are published. From time to time it is supplemented by *Penguins in Print*, which is a complete list of all titles available. (There are some five thousand of these.)

A specimen copy of *Penguinews* will be sent to you free on request. For a year's issues (including the complete lists) please send 50p if you live in the British Isles, or 75p if you live elsewhere. Just write to Dept EP, Penguin Books Ltd, Harmondsworth, Middlesex, enclosing a cheque or postal order, and your name will be added to the mailing list.

*In the U.S.A.*: For a complete list of books available from Penguins in the United States write to Dept CS, Penguin Books Inc., 7110 Ambassador Road, Baltimore, Maryland 21207.

*In Canada*: For a complete list of books available from Penguin in Canada write to Penguin Books Canada Ltd, 41 Steelcase Road West, Markham, Ontario.

# THE GROWTH OF PLANTS

## G. E. FOGG

*Second Edition Revised*

In a sense man and the animals are parasites on the vegetable world. Ultimately human survival depends and is likely always to depend on plant growth. This book, therefore, by a professor of botany, literally goes to the roots of human existence.

Traditional methods of agriculture may have served us in the past, but the sensational increase in the world population makes it certain that every resource of botanical science will soon have to be mobilized if we are to avoid disaster.

Outlining what we know today about the general behaviour of plants as they grow, the author explains photosynthesis – with its dependence on chlorophyll – and other processes; the organization of matter into protoplasm, cells, and tissues; the correlations of growth; the formation of roots, leaves, and flowers; the relations between plants and their surroundings, and the rhythms of growth and flowering.

'A large range of readers are going to benefit from this Pelican ... from all view-points in terms of value it rates as a "best-buy" and deserves to be a best-seller' – *Institute of Biology*

A PELICAN BOOK

# THE SECRET LIFE OF PLANTS

### PETER TOMPKINS AND CHRISTOPHER BIRD

If you are a rational person with faith in the orderly progress of established science, you will believe hardly a word in this book, which deals with unknown forces in the vegetable world, human communication with plants, psychic powers, radionic pesticides and such 'nonsense'.

If, on the other hand, you are irked by the strait-jacket of materialism, you may find this one of the most encouraging books you have ever read.

In one readable text the authors have assembled the bizarre conclusions of all the unorthodox experimenters who have ever prayed over plants, fed music to plants – they lean toward Bach but recoil from Rock – recorded their responses on instruments or influenced their growth, whether by mental or electric waves.

*The Secret Life of Plants* is an extraordinary and an exciting catalogue of discoveries – mostly inexplicable, often incredible, but fraught (if we credit some of the fantastic results) with the seeds of total scientific revolution.

# SOME PENGUIN REFERENCE BOOKS

'Penguin reference books are becoming indispensable; they are easy to travel with and, if they wear out, cheap to replace' – Cyril Connolly in the *Sunday Times*.

## A DICTIONARY OF GEOGRAPHY

### W. G. Moore

Because geography is largely a synthetic subject the items in this dictionary are derived from many sciences. The student will find in this revised and enlarged edition all the terms so frequently employed and seldom defined in geographical works.

## A DICTIONARY OF MODERN HISTORY 1789–1945

### A. W. Palmer

This book is intended as a reference-companion to personalities, events, and ideas. The prime emphasis is on British affairs and on political topics although the Dictionary aims to represent trends in the history of all the major regions of the world. There are entries on economic, social, religious and scientific developments, but not on the Arts.

## A DICTIONARY OF POLITICS

### Florence Elliott

Provides a comprehensive and informative background to current events and includes the life histories of the world's leading politicians and the political institutions, recent history and economy of almost every independent state in the world.

# SOME PENGUIN REFERENCE BOOKS

### A DICTIONARY OF ART AND ARTISTS

*Peter and Linda Murray*

This dictionary covers the last seven centuries and contains short and critical biographies of nearly 1,000 painters, sculptors and engravers as well as definitions of artistic movements, terms applied to periods and ideas, and technical expressions and processes. The art of eastern and primitive peoples is not covered.

### THE PENGUIN DICTIONARY OF ARCHITECTURE

*John Fleming   Hugh Honour   Nikolaus Pevsner*

Every facet of architectural design and the art of building is covered. The entries are supplemented by more than a hundred clear and detailed architectural drawings set into the text they illustrate.

### A NEW DICTIONARY OF MUSIC

*Arthur Jacobs*

A basic reference book for all who are interested in music, containing entries for composers (with biographies and details of compositions); musical works well known by their titles; orchestras, performers and conductors of importance today; musical instruments; and technical terms.

## SOME PENGUIN REFERENCE BOOKS

### A DICTIONARY OF SCIENCE

*E. B. Uvarov    D. R. Chapman    Alan Isaacs*

New material has been added to make this third edition more valuable to both student and layman, who can find in it reliable definitions and clear explanations of the numerous scientific and technical terms that are increasingly an important part of daily life.

### A DICTIONARY OF COMPUTERS

*Anthony Chandor with John Graham and Robin Williamson*

This is a glossary of some 3,000 words, phrases and acronyms used in connection with computers. It has been designed to assist both technical readers and those non-specialists whose work is affected by a computer.

### A DICTIONARY OF PSYCHOLOGY

*James Drever*

'It is commended with confidence as a document relevant not merely to the experimental psychology of former days, but to recent developments in psychometrics, social psychology, psychopathology, and industrial psychology' – *Higher Education Journal*.